"This book is an astonishingly rich exploration of the contours and textures of the overarching message of the whole Bible. Jim Hamilton painstakingly assembles a veritable mountain of evidence for the argument that the biblical writers, under God, knew exactly what they were doing, and that from the beginning, they were consciously paving the way for the Christ to come. Every page deserves careful study, for so much ground is covered in such stimulating (and sparkling) detail. Even where one disagrees with specific conclusions (and such is the scope of this book that this is almost inevitable), the depth of insight and nuance of the argument makes reading this book a delight."

GARY MILLAR, principal, Queensland Theological College

"Jim Hamilton has written a clear and theologically rich work on typology, demonstrating how the scriptural story of redemption is anchored in God's promises of the Messiah. *Typology: Understanding the Bible's Promise-Shaped Patterns* shows forth both the unity of Scripture and the beautiful layers of its truths, and best of all it provides fresh lenses for beholding the glories of our Savior. Here readers may feast on the Bible's teaching concerning the One who is the Last Adam, the Prophet like Moses, the Faithful High Priest whose work fulfills the Levitical Cult, the Royal Son of David, the Righteous Suffering Servant, and God With Us—read and rejoice!"

L. MICHAEL MORALES, professor of biblical studies,
Greenville Presbyterian Theological Seminary

"In his previous work, Jim Hamilton convinced me that we need biblical theology in order to help disciples learn to think and live, in terms of the Bible's symbolic universe. With *Typology*, Hamilton continues to help readers become biblically literate by sensitizing them to the micro-level clues as to the nature of what the Bible is all about. As God's declaratives ("let there be") shape the created order, so God's promises shape redemptive history. Discerning typological connections between these promises and their fulfillment in Christ, and the meaningful pattern they create, is part and parcel of coming to have a biblical worldview–seeing God, God's world, and God's people from the perspective of the biblical authors. If theology is faith seeking understanding, coming to grips with the unique scriptural imaginary that typology is and creates is an essential theological task."

KEVIN J. VANHOOZER, research professor of systematic theology,
Trinity Evangelical Divinity School

TYPOLOGY

UNDERSTANDING THE BIBLE'S
PROMISE-SHAPED PATTERNS

TYPOLOGY

UNDERSTANDING THE BIBLE'S
PROMISE-SHAPED PATTERNS

How Old Testament Expectations
Are Fulfilled in Christ

JAMES M. HAMILTON JR.

ZONDERVAN
ACADEMIC

ZONDERVAN ACADEMIC

Typology—Understanding the Bible's Promise-Shaped Patterns
Copyright © 2022 by James M. Hamilton Jr.

Requests for information should be addressed to:
Zondervan, *3900 Sparks Dr. SE, Grand Rapids, Michigan 49546*

Zondervan titles may be purchased in bulk for educational, business, fundraising, or sales promotional use. For information, please email SpecialMarkets@Zondervan.com.

ISBN 978-0-310-53440-2 (hardcover)

ISBN 978-0-310-53442-6 (ebook)

ISBN 978-0-310-13637-8 (audio)

Cover Design: Emily Weigel
Cover Image: art: © Heritage Images / Getty
Interior Design: Kait Lamphere

Printed in the United States of America

22 23 24 25 26 27 28 29 30 31 32 33 /TRM/ 16 15 14 13 12 11 10 9 8 7 6 5 4 3 2

For Isaiah John Hamilton
May you follow in the footsteps
of the men whose names you bear
growing to be mighty in the Scriptures
knowing Yahweh as the saving God
and giver of every good gift
in Christ by the Spirit

CONTENTS

PART 3: INSTITUTIONS

DETAILED TABLE OF CONTENTS

Typology—Understanding the Bible's Promise-Shaped Patterns

How Old Testament Expectations Are Fulfilled in Christ

PART 2: EVENTS

PART 3: INSTITUTIONS

ACKNOWLEDGMENTS

Writing a book is an exhilarating and frustrating endeavor (Eccl 1:18; 12:12). The truth is so beautiful and majestic, mere words so meager and frail. The Bible brims with life and power, but to seek to communicate that experience of searching the Scriptures and seeing their interconnectedness is to chase the wind (Eccl 2:11), which blows where it pleases (John 3:8). But what a blessed joy and privilege to try.

The limitations of this book vexed me until I landed on a way to structure the book's contents, a structure that serves as a vehicle for the book's message and is at the same time a key component of that message. What bothered me was the way that the topical nature of the discussion of typology—dealing first with people, then events, and finally institutions—kept me from being able to exposit everything all at once. My preference would have been to take readers on a leisurely stroll that went verse by verse, chapter by chapter, book by book through the whole Bible from Genesis to Revelation. That being impractical and impossible (imagine what it would have done to word limit and deadline!), I resigned myself to the topical arrangement. But then over Thanksgiving Break 2020, as I stared at the table of contents, a breakthrough solution came to me in the form of a simple question: why not structure my book according to the form the biblical authors so often use in theirs? You'll find more on that, which I found immensely satisfying, in the Introduction and Conclusion to this volume.

Readers who want to take that verse by verse, chapter by chapter stroll through the Bible with me can avail themselves of the BibleTalk podcast from 9Marks, where I join my friends Alex Duke and Sam Emadi in a conversational exposition of the Scriptures that gives a lot of attention to Typology and Biblical Theology. In addition, it is my privilege to pastor at Kenwood Baptist Church at Victory Memorial and to teach at the Southern Baptist Theological Seminary in Louisville, KY. The expositional sermons I have preached at Kenwood are freely available on our website and through the church's podcast, and the seminary accepts applications. The best way to explore the Scriptures together is through live, in-person, face-to-face interaction, so I would invite those who want more to move to Louisville, join us at Kenwood and/or enroll at Southern Seminary, that we might explore the Bible together at church and/or in class.

How could I thank the Lord for all his goodness to me? (cf. Ps 116:12). For the gospel, for my family, for my teachers, for the Scriptures, and for so much more that I could never enumerate (Ps 40:5).

I dedicate this book to my beloved youngest son, who bears the names of two of my favorite teachers, with the prayer that his eyes will see *the* Teacher, and that his ears will hear a word behind him saying, "This is the way, walk in it" (Isa 30:20–21).

May this book increase your love for God and neighbor as you grow in zeal for and understanding of the Scriptures.

Jim Hamilton
Louisville, KY
Easter, 2021

ABBREVIATIONS

When I cite from the Greek Translations of the Hebrew Bible, I will preface the verse reference with LXX as follows: LXX Mal 3:1.

When I refer to the superscriptions of the Psalms, which are verse 1 in the Masoretic Text (MT) but are not numbered in English translations, I will cite the number of the psalm with "ss" for "superscription," so the superscription of Psalm 18 would be presented as 18:ss.

In the book's footnotes I have spelled out the names of journals and monograph series rather than abbreviate them.

BHS	*Biblia Hebraica Stuttgartensia*
ET	English Translation
Gen. Rab.	Genesis Rabba
LXX	Septuagint
MT	Masoretic Text
NA[28]	*Novum Testamentum Graece*, Nestle-Aland, 28th ed.
NT	New Testament
OT	Old Testament

INTRODUCTION TO PROMISE-SHAPED TYPOLOGY

Micro-Level Indicators for Determining Authorial Intent

> Typology is the method of interpreting Scripture that is predominant in the NT and characteristic of it.
>
> **—LEONHARD GOPPELT**[1]

The aged father, the death of whose wife has just been narrated (Gen 23:1–20), commands his servant (עֶבֶד), "put your hand under my thigh" (24:2) and makes him "swear by Yahweh, the God of heaven and the God of earth" not to "take a wife for my son from the daughters of the Canaanites" (24:3), but to return to his kindred for a wife for his son, his only son, whom he loves, Isaac (24:4; cf. 22:2).[2] When the servant asks if he should take Isaac back

---

1. Leonhard Goppelt, *Typos: The Typological Interpretation of the Old Testament in the New* (Grand Rapids: Eerdmans, 1982), 198.
2. Unless otherwise noted, translations of the biblical text in this book will be my own. These will typically be as literal as possible in an attempt both to preserve the interconnectedness of the texts and communicate in English the way the biblical authors conceptualize and describe the world, even if this makes for awkward English. In these very literal renderings, I am not trying to produce smooth English (whose primary concern would be the target audience). My overarching concern in these excessively literal renderings is to allow contemporary speakers of English to glimpse the way the biblical authors put things. If everyone reading this book primarily accessed the Bible through original language texts, this would not be necessary. Since I hope people who have not yet studied Greek, Hebrew, and Aramaic will read this book, very literal translations will sometimes be presented.

1

to that land if the woman is not willing to follow him to the land of promise (24:5), father Abraham says he must certainly not take Isaac back there (24:6), and then Abraham references the way God called him to leave his country, his kindred, and his father's house and go to the land he would be shown (12:1), land God promised to give to the seed of Abraham (12:7), before promising the servant, "he will send his angel before you" (24:7, ESV).

Note the similarity between the phrases Moses used to tell the story:

Gen 12:1, "Go from your country and your kindred and your father's house to the land"

Gen 24:7, ". . . took me from my father's house and from the land of my kindred"

Gen 12:7, "To your offspring I will give this land."

Gen 24:7, "To your offspring I will give this land."

We fast-forward in the narrative to a time when the one whose years have no end (Ps 102:27) commands his servant, "Do not come near; take your sandals off your feet, for the place on which you are standing is holy ground" (Exod 3:5, ESV). He then identifies himself, "I am the God of your father, the God of Abraham, the God of Isaac, and the God of Jacob" (3:6), and he commissions Moses, his servant (עֶבֶד),[3] to return to Egypt. Abraham sent his servant to find a wife for Isaac, and Yahweh sends Moses to bring the one with whom he himself will enter into a marital covenant out of Egypt that they might inhabit the land promised to Abraham. Yahweh intends to be a husband to this people (Jer 31:32). Eventually he makes a statement to Moses reminiscent of the one Abraham made to his servant in Genesis 24:7 ("he will send his angel before you," ESV): in Exodus 23:20 the LORD tells Moses, "Behold, I send an angel before you" (ESV).

---

3. Stephen G. Dempster observes, "The precise expression ['servant of Yahweh'] is used mainly of Moses (eighteen times). It is also used to describe Moses's successor, Joshua (Jos. 24:29; Judges 2:8), David (Pss. 18:1; 36:1) and Israel (Is. 42:19)." Stephen G. Dempster, *Dominion and Dynasty: A Biblical Theology of the Hebrew Bible*, New Studies in Biblical Theology 15 (Downers Grove, IL: InterVarsity, 2003), 123 n. 25.

Gen 24:7, הוּא יִשְׁלַח מַלְאָכוֹ לְפָנֶיךָ

Exod 23:20, הִנֵּה אָנֹכִי שֹׁלֵחַ מַלְאָךְ לְפָנֶיךָ

By the reuse of this statement, it seems that Moses intends to prompt his audience to associate the mission on which Abraham sent his servant, to get a bride for Isaac, and the mission on which Yahweh sent Moses, his servant, to get a covenant partner for himself. This understanding of Moses's intention seems to be verified by the way the prophet Malachi employs the sentiment. In Malachi 3:1 the Lord promises another installment in the pattern, another occasion when the servant will be sent for a bride, and Malachi makes remarkable adjustments to the scenario:

Mal 3:1, הִנְנִי שֹׁלֵחַ מַלְאָכִי וּפִנָּה־דֶרֶךְ לְפָנָי
"Behold, I send my messenger, and he will prepare the way before me." (ESV)

The Lord again promises to send his "messenger," and the word rendered "messenger" is the same Hebrew term translated "angel" in Genesis 24:7 and Exodus 23:20 in the ESV, but this time the Lord promises to come himself: "he will prepare the way before me" (Mal 3:1, ESV). And then the sequence of events is repeated climactically: when the Father sends his servant on a mission to acquire a bride for the servant himself, who is also the beloved Son, and in preparation declares, "Behold, I send my messenger before your face, who will prepare your way" (Mark 1:2, ESV).

How are we to account for and understand these patterns of events, and what is the relationship between God's promises and such patterns? The rest of this introductory chapter will explore the relationship between God's promises and the patterns we find in the Scriptures, along with what I refer to in this chapter's title, "micro-level indicators for determining authorial intent." I have in view things like what we have just seen: the quotation of lines, the reuse of key terms, the repetitions in sequences of events, and the similarities in covenantal and salvation-historical import we find when we focus in on particular texts. These "micro-level" indicators stand in contrast with the "macro-level" indicators that will be discussed in the final chapter of this book, and by "macro-level" I refer to wide-angle literary structures. At the end of the

Conclusion to this book, in the final section of the final chapter, we return to Genesis 24, so that discussions of the central episode in the literary structure of Genesis form an inclusio around this treatise.[4]

The phrase "promise-shaped typology" attempts to capture what happens when God makes a promise that results in those who know him interpreting the world in the terms and categories either communicated in the promise or assumed by it. God's words shape the world in Genesis 1, and as the Bible unfolds, his promises shape the expectations and perceptions of his people. This is especially the case with biblical authors, who operate under the inspiration of the Holy Spirit.

I will be arguing in this book that God's promises shaped the way the biblical authors perceived, understood, and wrote. As this happens again and again across the Scriptures, from account to account, book to book, author to author, patterns begin to be discerned, patterns that have been shaped by promises: promise-shaped patterns.

To demonstrate understanding, we show that we have discerned what an author intended to communicate.[5] I am claiming that the biblical authors *intended* to communicate the types that will be discussed in this book. This stands in contrast with the approach of Richard B. Hays, who writes, "Figural reading of the Bible need not presume that the Old Testament authors—or the characters they narrate—were conscious of predicting or anticipating Christ."[6] Here I briefly attempt to set forth a step-by-step process whereby this seems to have worked, from creation to the composition of the biblical texts, acknowledging that for the biblical authors the logical progression of these steps could have been simultaneous, intuitive, and instinctive. That is, I am not claiming that the biblical authors themselves outline this process but that this process can explain what we find in their writings.[7]

---

4. Readers who turn to §5 of Chapter 11 at this point will not offend me. You have my permission to read the end from the beginning, that it might inform all in between.

5. See E. D. Hirsch, *Validity in Interpretation* (New Haven: Yale University Press, 1967); and Kevin J. Vanhoozer, *Is There a Meaning in This Text? The Bible, the Reader, and the Morality of Literary Knowledge* (Grand Rapids: Zondervan, 1998).

6. Richard B. Hays, *Echoes of Scripture in the Gospels* (Waco, TX: Baylor University Press, 2018), 2. For a strong critique of figural interpretation, see Aubrey Sequeira and Samuel C. Emadi, "Biblical-Theological Exegesis and the Nature of Typology," *Southern Baptist Journal of Theology* 21, no. 1 (2017): 25–28.

7. My goal is similar to what Emadi and Sequeira set out to achieve (I would include OT authors) when they write: "we are endeavoring to uncover the exegetical logic that undergirds the NT authors' interpretation and that leads them to interpret typology as a feature of divine revelation. Understanding

First, God made the world by his word, which shapes everything about human experience and perception, and then God spoke expectation and perception-shaping promises. My contention is that the creating and promising word of God resulted in earlier biblical authors (beginning with Moses) discerning certain patterns in their material. The promises and the patterns then began to work together, and later biblical authors had not only the promises but the patterns they produced influencing their perception. These later authors, then, having discerned the author-intended and promise-shaped patterns in earlier Scripture, saw similar patterns, which they then included in their own material.

When the biblical authors composed their writings, they intended to signal to their audiences the presence of the promise-shaped patterns. Thus, even if they did not fully understand the significance of the pattern and/or how the promise would be fulfilled (and see Eph 3:5 and 1 Pet 1:10–12), the Old Testament authors intended to draw attention to the recurring sequences of events, and they did so with a view to the future.[8] Because these sequences of events had themselves been shaped by the promises, the promises were reinforced by each new installation in the pattern of events, and a growing sense of the significance of both promise and pattern developed.

In the opening pages of the Bible, Moses establishes this feature of biblical literature. The biblical authors who follow Moses learn it from him and imitate his use of the convention: their worldview has been shaped by his words.[9] For Moses himself, the word of God—the promises—shaped his worldview (his assumptions and presuppositions, perceptions and interpretations), resulting in the promise-shaped patterns that he introduced into the accounts. Perhaps some of these patterns came to Moses in oral traditions he learned from his parents or from Aaron and Miriam. He then would have been carried along by the Holy Spirit (2 Pet 1:20–21) as he interpreted material passed down to

that logic will reveal a great deal about how the NT authors conceived of the nature of types. Put simply, we are attempting to describe how typology in the NT 'works.'" Sequeira and Emadi, "Nature of Typology," 11–12.

8. Cf. Basil of Caesarea's (AD 330–ca. 379) definition of typology: "Typology points out what is to be expected, indicating through imitation what is to happen before it happens." Saint Basil, *On the Holy Spirit*, trans. David Anderson (Crestwood, N.Y.: St Vladimir's Seminary Press, 1980), 53.

9. I have in mind the kind of thing Gibson describes when he writes concerning Malachi, "The core of the prophet's imagination is shaped by his reflection on an authoritative collection of texts." Jonathan Gibson, *Covenant Continuity and Fidelity: A Study of Inner-Biblical Allusion and Exegesis in Malachi*, Library of Hebrew Bible/Old Testament Studies 625 (Edinburgh: T&T Clark, 2019), xiii. See also his first chapter, which is subtitled, "The Core of Malachi's Imagination," 1–23.

him and made decisions about what to include and how to arrange what he presented in the Torah (the Torah, or Pentateuch, always and everywhere attributed in Scripture to Moses).[10]

The shaping of patterns by promise can be seen in the opening chapters of the book of Genesis, which is a profoundly self-referential book. To illustrate what I mean by the phrase "promise-shaped patterns," we begin by considering the influence of Genesis 3:15. The impact of what God says in Genesis 3:15 can be seen in the way Moses presents what happens between Cain and Abel, then later in the cursing of Canaan, and again in the blessing of Abraham. The three sections of this chapter will proceed as follows:

§1 Genesis 3:15, A Pattern-Shaping Promise
§2 Author-Intended Typology
§3 A Preview of What Follows

§1 GENESIS 3:15, A PATTERN-SHAPING PROMISE

As the Lord speaks words of judgment to the serpent in Genesis 3:14–15, we read,

And Yahweh God said to the serpent,

"Because you have done this,
cursed are you from all [i.e., more than all, comparative מִן]
the beasts
and from all [comparative מִן again] the living creatures
of the field.
On your belly you shall walk,
and dust you shall eat all the days of your life.

---

10. See Deut 31:9, 24; 33:4; Josh 8:31, 32; 22:5; 23:6; 1 Kgs 2:3; 2 Kgs 14:6; 21:8; 23:25; 2 Chr 23:18; 25:4; 30:16; 33:8; 34:14; Ezra 3:2; 7:6; Neh 8:1, 14; 10:29; Dan 9:11, 13; Mal 4:4. These references, and the fact that Jesus attributes the Torah to Moses (e.g., Mark 12:26; Luke 24:44; John 5:45–47), lead me to the position that Moses wrote the Torah. Those who hold different views on the authorship of the Pentateuch can attribute the correspondences to whoever was responsible for the text in its final canonical form. I am persuaded that the Torah of Moses is a literary masterpiece, a work of genius, and such literature is produced not by committee but by individuals, literary geniuses. This does not deny updating by those recognized as qualified to do so, but the evidence indicates this editorial updating was neither pervasive nor structural but minor and restrained.

And enmity I will put between you and the woman,
  and between your seed and her seed.
He will bruise you head,
  and you will bruise him heel."

The shaping character of the promise contained in these words of judgment becomes apparent when we consider the pervasive self-referentiality of Moses's presentation in Genesis. To explore the significance of Genesis 3:15, we will begin and end this sub-section with consideration of the nature of the book of Genesis, starting with its self-referentiality, ending with its foundational character. In the mirrored construction of this section, the outworking of Adam's sin in the life of his sons stands across from the outworking of Noah's sin in the lives of his sons and theirs. We then consider the way that Moses meant Genesis 4 to be read in light of Genesis 3, juxtaposing that with consideration of the way types impress themselves on our thinking. At the center of this discussion we will consider the cursed seed of the serpent. The mirroring panels of this subsection fall out as follows:

§1.1 The Self-Referential Nature of Genesis
  §1.1.1 Working and Keeping, Killed and Cursed
    §1.1.2 Genesis 4 in Light of Genesis 3
      §1.1.3 The Cursed Seed of the Serpent
    §1.1.4 The Impress of the Type
  §1.1.5 The Cursing of Canaan and Those Who Dishonor Abraham
§2.1 The Foundational Nature of Genesis

§1.1 The Self-Referential Nature of Genesis

In Genesis 3:14–15 Moses refers his readers back to material he introduced in the previous two chapters of Genesis: in 3:14 we read of "all the beasts" (כָּל־הַבְּהֵמָה) and "all the living creatures of the field" (כֹּל חַיַּת הַשָּׂדֶה). These are known to readers from both their introduction on the sixth day of creation in 1:24–25 ("beasts," בְּהֵמָה) and the expanded description of their origin in 2:18–20 ("all the living creatures of the field," כָּל־חַיַּת הַשָּׂדֶה, 2:19). Similarly, the statement that the serpent will eat dust in 3:14 refers back to the 1:30 grant of "every green herb for food," which the Lord takes from him in 3:14. An even nearer reference back can be seen in the way the serpent tempted the woman and the man to eat forbidden food (3:1–5), so the punishment inflicted upon him touches what he himself is permitted to eat (3:14)—his punishment fits his crime.[11]

Seeing typological patterns requires thinking about an account in light of those earlier and later, and as we read narratives we instinctively apply this kind of reflection to near contexts: statements from earlier in the narrative inform statements made later, and later statements clarify and build upon the earlier.[12] Seeking to understand types and patterns, then, extends to broader contexts something we intuitively do with immediate contexts. The study of typology amounts to active reflection on one passage in light of others.[13]

Continuing with the self-referentiality of Genesis, note that Yahweh God warned in 2:17 that eating from the tree would result in death. That warning produces the fear of death that prompts the man and woman to hide after their transgression in 3:8 and refuse to confess in 3:9–13. Once Yahweh has called them out and exposed their sin, the man and woman have no reason to think they will live—until God speaks to the serpent.

God promises to put enmity between the serpent and the woman in Genesis 3:15, and enmity entails ongoing conflict. Ongoing conflict requires ongoing life. In this ongoing life the woman will not side with the serpent against Yahweh but with Yahweh against the serpent. God's statements say it will be so. The woman has not yet joined battle with the serpent at this point, but God announces they will be at enmity. That God mentions the "seed of the woman" means the conflict will not be limited to the woman and the serpent—the man too will be involved, as he is necessary for any "seed" to be born of the woman. God's words to the serpent indicate that the man and woman will join his side against the serpent.

Does this imply that the man and woman have evaded the consequence

---

11. Gage sees this as the first instance in a pattern of punishments meting out retributive irony by matching the crime. See Warren Austin Gage, *The Gospel of Genesis: Studies in Protology and Eschatology* (Winona Lake, IN: Eisenbrauns, 1984), 46.

12. See the discussion of how information is encoded by authors and interpreted by readers in Elizabeth Robar, *The Verb and the Paragraph in Biblical Hebrew: A Cognitive-Linguistic Approach*, Studies in Semitic Languages and Linguistics (Boston: Brill, 2015), 1–18.

13. I agree with David L. Baker that this involves "theological reflection on relationships between events, persons and institutions [sic] recorded in biblical texts," but I disagree with his assertion that this means "typology is not exegesis." *Two Testaments, One Bible: The Theological Relationship Between the Old and New Testaments*, 3rd ed. (Downers Grove, IL: InterVarsity, 2010), 181.

articulated in Genesis 2:17? Not for a moment: when compared with their unashamed nakedness in 2:25, their hiding from one another in 3:7 and from God in 3:8 shows that their uninhibited purity is no more. The man and woman have experienced a ruinous spiritual calamity. They have sinned. As a result of their sin they are spiritually dead. Their spiritual unresponsiveness can be seen in their refusal to confess their sin and repent of it when God calls them out. A few lines later, in 3:19, God assures them that they will physically die.

The promise of seed in Genesis 3:15, however, means they will not die without hope (cf. Rom 8:20–21). The enmity between the serpent and the woman means that humanity has not altogether joined the serpent's cause. The woman and her seed (which, again, requires the man's participation) will resist the snake. Thus the enmity.

And that brings us to the last line of Genesis 3:15. I have rendered this tersely, "He will bruise you head, and you will bruise him heel," because in the original Hebrew the pronouns "you" and "him" do not modify the nouns "head" (as in, "your head") and "heel" ("his heel"). In each case the pronouns modify the repeated verb "bruise." The statements, thus, are "he will bruise you . . . and you will bruise him . . ." To bring across the Hebrew in smoother English, we might say, "he will bruise you *on* (or perhaps *with respect to*) the head, and you will bruise him *on* (or *with respect to*) the heel." Because a wound to the heel would not typically be life-threatening in the way a head wound might, Moses communicates to his audience that the man and woman have every reason to understand God's words to the serpent as a promise that their seed will triumph over him.

We should note that in Genesis 1 life began by the word of God, as God spoke the world into existence. Now in Genesis 3 life continues by the word of God. The Lord's word of judgment to the serpent declares ongoing life for mankind, as attested by the man's naming of the woman in 3:20, "And the man called the name of his wife 'Eve,' because she was the mother of all living."

The life and death struggle between the seed of the woman and the seed of the serpent is *the* plot conflict that informs the whole of the biblical narrative. The serpent has instigated sin and incurred a curse, and man has transgressed but heard words of God that indicate that the tempter will be defeated, suggesting that not only sin but also the consequences of sin (death and banishment from God's presence, which are different ways of saying the same thing) will be overcome.[14]

Supporting the idea that Moses intends his audience to understand the narrative as pointing to an ultimate resolution of the plot's conflict, the words of Lamech at the birth of Noah in Genesis 5:29 reflect hope for relief from the results of God's judgment. In the near context, Moses presents Eve articulating hope for the serpent-crushing seed at the births of Cain and Seth (4:1, 25). He then presents a carefully recorded line of descent from Adam in the Genesis 5 genealogy, tracing the progress of the seed of the woman with "and he died" as its refrain. The death-escaping account of how Enoch walked with God gives hope (5:21–24), and then in 5:29 we meet the reuse of the words of judgment from 3:17–19, as Lamech articulates hope that his child (cf. 3:15), Noah, will bring comfort.

As we consider the way that God's promises shape patterns in biblical narratives, we observe that in the words of judgment in Genesis 3:14–19 the serpent is cursed, and the land is cursed, but neither the man nor the woman hears the words "cursed are you." God blessed the man and woman in 1:28 (self-referentiality again), and that blessing will not be reversed. The man and the woman will be at enmity with the serpent and his seed, but they are not cursed. Who, or what, are the seed of the serpent? The observation that God curses the serpent but neither Adam nor Eve helps us address the question of how the seed of the serpent are to be understood. The self-referentiality of the narrative teaches Moses's audience to allow the narrative to interpret itself as it proceeds. We read the cross-referencing statements in light of each other so that they clarify one another. The Genesis 3:15 statement about the serpent's seed does not refer to literal snakes, as becomes clear when we keep reading into Genesis 4.

§1.1.1 Working and Keeping, Killed and Cursed

The narrative continues in its pervasively self-referential way. The man and woman were commanded to be fruitful and multiply in Genesis 1:28, and they begin to do so in 4:1–2. Eve's response to the birth of Cain in 4:1 indicates that she is looking for the seed promised in 3:15, and as Abel "became a shepherd of a flock while Cain was working [עבד] the ground" in 4:2, readers are reminded of Adam's responsibility to "work [עבד] and keep [שמר]" the

---

14. See Mitchell L. Chase, "The Genesis of Resurrection Hope: Exploring Its Early Presence and Deep Roots," *Journal of the Evangelical Theological Society* 57 (2014): 467–80.

garden (2:15). Adam's "working and keeping" of the garden in 2:15 was itself another way to describe his responsibility to "subdue" the earth and "have dominion" over the animals from 1:28.[15] In Genesis 4:2 Adam's "working" of the ground (subdue the earth, 1:28) is carried forward as Cain does the same, and Adam's "keeping" the garden (have dominion over, 1:28) is realized in Abel's shepherding of the flock (cf. 2:15).

TABLE 1.1 Working and Keeping

Work the Ground	Have Dominion over the Animals
1:28, subdue the earth כָּבַשׁ	1:28, rule over the animals רָדָה
2:15, work עָבַד	2:15, keep שָׁמַר (i.e., protect from the animals) the garden
4:2, Cain was working (עָבַד) the ground	4:2, Abel was shepherding (רָעָה) the flock

The two Hebrew terms from Genesis 2:15, work (עָבַד) and keep (שָׁמַר), appear in both Genesis 3 and Genesis 4. In Genesis 3:23, Yahweh sent Adam "from the garden of Eden to work the ground," while in 3:24 the cherubim and flaming sword "keep the way to the tree of life." Then in Genesis 4, we read of Cain's "working" (עָבַד) of the ground in 4:2, and after he murders Abel he asks if he is his brother's "keeper" (שָׁמַר) in 4:9.[16] The Lord then tells Cain

---

15. Gage observes, "in the divine command man is commissioned to reproduce God's own activity in creation, that is, to subdue and to fill the earth." Gage, *Gospel of Genesis*, 28.

16. R. W. L. Moberly opts for "recontextualization" and suggests, "it is arguable that what interpreters present as an author-hermeneutic is in fact generally a plausible text- and reader-hermeneutic that is articulated in a disciplined, historically oriented mode, however it is formally presented." He then states that he adopts a "rule of faith," stating that his "preference is to use the term loosely to refer to 'a sense of how things go'—that is, a set of interrelated moral and theological judgments as to the kind of sense that does, or does not, resonate within a biblical and Christian frame of reference." R. W. L. Moberly, *The God of the Old Testament: Encountering the Divine in Christian Scripture* (Grand Rapids: Baker, 2020), 8–9. By embracing recontextualization, "rule of faith" (which Moberly describes in a very subjective way—"a sense of how things go" and "the kind of sense that does, or does not, resonate"), and relativizing authorial intent (suggesting that it is merely a rigorous version of reader-response), Moberly makes moves that characterize some practitioners of "theological interpretation of Scripture." This stands in contrast with the kind of biblical theology pursued here, which seeks the intent of the human author and practices grammatical-historical interpretation in canonical context, and the differences have significant ramifications on interpretive conclusions, as can be seen from comparison of Moberly's account of Cain and Esau (ibid., 125–64) with mine in this book and in James M. Hamilton Jr., *Work and Our Labor in the Lord*, Short Studies in Biblical Theology (Wheaton, IL: Crossway, 2017), 45–48.

in 4:12 that when he "works" (עָבַד) the ground it will not yield its strength to him, and this reminds readers of the way that the words of judgment spoken to Adam included a curse on the ground (3:17), thorns and thistles (3:18), and banishment from the garden (3:23). The re-use of this "work" and "keep" terminology calls 2:15 to mind, reminding the audience of God's purpose for Adam in the garden and highlighting how far Cain has fallen from it.

The repetitions, again, instruct the audience to read the narrative so that its statements inform each other. Moses intends the different scenes of his broader narrative to be read in light of one another, and he presents the narrative such that what God says shapes not only the creation but the events that take place within it.

No narrative can comprehensively present everything that needs to be communicated. Authors must fill in gaps in audience understanding as they continue to provide new information. A promise was introduced into the narrative in Genesis 3:15, and this promise has decisively shaped Moses's understanding. Moses passes on to his audience his Genesis 3:15 promise-shaped understanding in his Genesis 4 narration of Cain's sin.

§1.1.2 Genesis 4 in Light of Genesis 3

The whole story of Cain murdering Abel in Genesis 4 makes constant reference back to Genesis 3. We see this from the pervasive repetitions of words and phrases from Genesis 3 in Genesis 4. Yahweh was not pleased with Cain's offering in 4:5, and in response to Cain's anger (4:6) he warns him that "sin is crouching at the door; and for you is its desire, but you must rule over it" (4:7). This statement recalls the words of judgment God spoke to the woman in 3:16, "and for your husband is your desire, but he will rule over you."

Gen 3:16, וְאֶל־אִישֵׁךְ תְּשׁוּקָתֵךְ וְהוּא יִמְשָׁל־בָּךְ

Gen 4:7, וְאֵלֶיךָ תְּשׁוּקָתוֹ וְאַתָּה תִּמְשָׁל־בּוֹ

The paralleling of these statements helps us understand the nature of the "desire" and the "ruling" described in both cases. The woman's desire for her husband is like sin's desire for Cain—a desire to influence, even control, behavior. The man's ruling over the woman will likewise parallel what Cain's response to sin *should* be. In addition to the way the re-use of terms helps us understand what they mean, the parallelism of the phrases suggests that we are to read Genesis 4 in light of Genesis 3.

Taking this interpretive hint from the text's author, we set Cain's murder of Abel (4:8) in parallel with the first couple's eating of the forbidden fruit (3:6). After Adam and Eve transgressed, Yahweh confronted Adam with a "where" question—"Where are you?" After Cain transgressed, Yahweh confronted Cain with a "where" question—"Where is Abel your brother?" The wording of the two questions is similar:

וַיִּקְרָא יְהוָה אֱלֹהִים אֶל־הָאָדָם וַיֹּאמֶר לוֹ אַיֶּכָּה ,Gen 3:9
"And Yahweh God called to the man, and he said, 'Where are you?'"

וַיֹּאמֶר יְהוָה אֶל־קַיִן אֵי הֶבֶל אָחִיךָ ,Gen 4:9
"And Yahweh said to Cain, 'Where is Abel your brother?'"

Adam's response to Yahweh's question in 3:10 revealed his guilt: he was afraid because he knew he had transgressed, and he knew he was naked because he had eaten of the tree. So also Cain's response to Yahweh's question in 4:9 reveals his guilt: the claim that he does not know Abel's location is a lie, and the indignant question about whether he is his brother's keeper reveals his lack of love for neighbor.

In Genesis 3:13, "Yahweh God said to the woman, what is this you have done?" And in Genesis 4:10 the Lord says to Cain, "What have you done?"

מַה־זֹּאת עָשִׂית . . . וַיֹּאמֶר ,Gen 3:13

וַיֹּאמֶר מֶה עָשִׂיתָ ,Gen 4:10

Having confronted the transgressors in Genesis 3:9–13, Yahweh curses the serpent in 3:14 with the words, "Because you have done this, cursed are you from . . ." Having confronted Cain with his transgression in 4:9–10, Yahweh curses him in 4:11 with the words, "And now, cursed are you from . . ."

כִּי עָשִׂיתָ זֹּאת אָרוּר אַתָּה מִכָּל־הַבְּהֵמָה ,Gen 3:14

וְעַתָּה אָרוּר אָתָּה מִן־הָאֲדָמָה ,Gen 4:11

The similarities between Genesis 3 and 4 indicate that the two chapters inform one another, and so we must compare *and* contrast them. The similarity between Genesis 3:14 and 4:11 shocks because of the connection it forges between Cain and *the serpent*. When God spoke words of judgment over Adam and Eve in 3:16–19, he did not say the words "cursed are you" to either of them. The only person to hear those words in Genesis 3 was the serpent in 3:14. When Moses presents God speaking those words to Cain, he provides a narrative answer to a question arising from 3:15—who are the seed of the serpent? Answer: people like Cain, whose actions incur God's curse in the same way the serpent's did.

§1.1.3 The Cursed Seed of the Serpent

How do these connections between Genesis 3 and 4 inform our understanding of the unfolding plot of Genesis, the Bible, and the world? The promise in Genesis 3:15 came in words of judgment to the serpent that there would be enmity between himself and the woman, between her seed and his. Eve's responses to the births of her sons in 4:1 and 4:25 indicate that she expects a male descendent to arise as the seed of the woman who will bruise the serpent's head. The cursing of Cain in 4:11 identifies him with his *figurative* father, the devil (Gen 3:14; cf. John 8:44–47; 1 John 3:8–15).

God's promise in Genesis 3:15 creates a set of expectations, which includes ideas along the following lines:

- those who rebel against Yahweh and his purposes will be identified with the serpent;
- those who embrace Yahweh and his purposes will be identified with the woman and her seed;
- there will be ongoing conflict between the seed of the woman and the seed of the serpent;
- and whereas the seed of the woman will inflict a head wound on the seed of the serpent, he will himself incur only a heel wound.

This set of expectations has been created by God's word of judgment to the serpent, which becomes a word of promise to the woman and her seed. That word of promise, further, shapes the expectations of those who believe it. In Genesis 4, Moses intends to present Cain's murder of Abel as an event to be understood in light of the sin and resulting words of judgment in Genesis 3, as attested by the repetition of so many phrases from Genesis 3 in Genesis 4. The words of God in Genesis 1–3 have shaped the way Moses perceives and narrates the events of Genesis 4 and following.[17]

§1.1.4 The Impress of the Type

On the basis of what we have seen so far, I would suggest a relationship between the literal and figurative meanings of the Greek word τύπος. We derive our English term "type" from the Greek term τύπος (see Rom 5:14; 1 Cor 10:6; and cf. τυπικῶς in 1 Cor 10:11). BDAG[18] seems to provide first the concrete meaning of τύπος, "a mark made as the result of a blow or pressure" (1019), and then metaphorical and figurative extensions of the concrete meaning, for example, "an archetype serving as a model" (1020).[19] It seems that the relationship between the concrete meaning and its metaphorical extensions is something along the following lines: a person sees something that *impresses* itself onto their consciousness, and other things are interpreted along the lines of that impression.[20]

I am suggesting that the word of God has been pressed into the consciousness of those who believe it, and that impress results in reality being

---

17. The shaping influence of Genesis 3 can also be seen in the way that God says to Adam in 3:17 (ESV), "Because you have listened to the voice of your wife . . ." Later when Sarai comes up with the faithless plan involving Hagar, "Abram listened to the voice of Sarai" (Gen 16:2, ESV). This pattern is broken, by contrast, when we read that Potiphar's wife "spoke to Joseph day after day, he would not listen to her" (39:10, ESV). The event in Genesis 16 is also connected to the sin in Genesis 3 by the wording in 3:6, ". . . she *took* of its fruit and ate, and she also *gave* some to her husband . . ." and 16:3, ". . . Sarai . . . *took* Hagar . . . and *gave* her to Abram . . ." (ESV). Moses intends the sin of Sarai and Abram in Genesis 16 to be understood along the lines of the sin of the man and woman in Genesis 3. The connection with Joseph refusing to listen to Potiphar's wife indicates that he overcame where Adam and Abram failed.

18. Walter Bauer, *A Greek-English Lexicon of the New Testament and Other Early Christian Literature*, ed. Frederick William Danker, trans. W. F. Arndt and F. W. Gingrich, 3rd ed. (Chicago: University of Chicago Press, 2001).

19. See also the entries in Franco Montanari, *The Brill Dictionary of Ancient Greek*, ed. Madeleine Goh and Chad Schroeder (Boston: Brill, 2015) that begin with the verb τυπάζω (pages 2166–67), active "to beat," passive "to be stamped." Related terms refer to things like drums (τυπάνον), woodpeckers (τυπάνος), and hammers (τυπάς); then terms like τυπίδιον, "model," seem to extend the idea to "what is beaten out" or the "impression stamped." For a full lexical analysis, see Richard M. Davidson, *Typology in Scripture: A Study of Hermeneutical Typos Structures* (Berrien Springs, MI: Andrews University Press, 1981), 115–90.

20. Leonhard Goppelt writes of the term τύπος, "It derives etym[ologically] from τύπτω "to strike," but retains the sense of "blow" only in the ancient saying in Hdt [Herodotus] I, 67, 4[1] . . . Elsewhere the ref. is always to the impress made by the blow, what is formed, what leaves its impress, the form-giving form, hence form gen. as outline. . . . In virtue of its expressiveness it has made its way as a loan word into almost all European languages" (τύπος κτλ., in *Theological Dictionary of the New Testament* 8:246–47).

interpreted in light of God's word. By this process the promises of God shape the interpretations that produce the patterns, and those patterns reflect the biblical authors' typological understanding of both what has happened and what it indicates about the future.

§1.1.5 The Cursing of Canaan and Those Who Dishonor Abraham

The shaping influence of Genesis 3:15 continues to be seen across the narrative of Genesis. After Ham sins against Noah, Noah curses his son's descendants in Genesis 9:25, אָרוּר כְּנָעַן ("cursed be Canaan"), with the same term God used to curse the serpent (Gen 3:14) and Cain (4:11). This identifies Ham's descendant Canaan with the serpent, marking him as seed of the serpent and laying groundwork for God's justice to be visited on the Canaanites when Israel, seed of the woman, conquers the land of Canaan, seed of the serpent, in Joshua (cf. Gen 15:16; 10:15–16).[21]

A few pages later Moses narrates that Yahweh promised Abraham, "I will bless those who bless you, and the one who makes light of you I will curse [אָאֹר]" (Gen 12:3). God declares that those who refuse to honor Abraham will be cursed the way he cursed the serpent, Cain, and Canaan. Moses hereby signals to his audience that, going forward, anyone opposed to Abraham is to be identified as the seed of the serpent, while anyone who aligns with Abraham will be identified as the seed of the woman.

When God promises at the end of 12:3 that all the families of the earth will be blessed in Abraham, the implication is that the serpent and his seed will be defeated through Abraham and his seed (cf. Gen 22:17–18), then all aligned with Abraham will experience the blessed peace that results from the triumph of the seed of Abraham, whose descent has been traced in Genesis 5 and 11 all the way back to Adam. The seed of the woman will bless the world through the defeat of the seed of the serpent (3:15; 12:1–3; 22:17–18).

§1.2 The Foundational Nature of Genesis

The beginning of Genesis sets the parameters and expectations for the rest of the book. And the story of God speaking the world into being, with all very good, of him making man in his image and placing him in the garden to work and keep it, with a prohibition on eating from the tree of life, of the making

---

21. This dynamic also explains why Abraham does not want Isaac to intermarry with Canaanites (Gen 24:3), and Isaac and Rebekah have the same concern for Jacob (28:1, 6–9; cf. 26:34–35).

of male and female and their cleaving to one another in marriage, and then of their transgression and God's word of hope-giving judgment—this story not only sets up the book of beginnings, Genesis, but the whole of the Torah of Moses (Genesis, Exodus, Leviticus, Numbers, and Deuteronomy). Every subsequent biblical author embraced the Torah of Moses and continued the story begun in the book of Genesis.

The content of Genesis is necessary for understanding the rest of the Torah, and in Genesis Moses teaches the biblical authors who follow him how to interpret, how to communicate, how to structure material, how to symbolize, how to typify. In this first chapter we are looking at how Moses does this at the micro-level with words, sentences, sequences, and matters of significance. In the final chapter of this book we will examine how Moses does this at the macro-level with literary structures that encompass the whole book of Genesis. All the biblical authors, I contend, embraced the teaching of Moses, learning from him how to understand the world and how to structure their own presentations.

§2 AUTHOR-INTENDED TYPOLOGY

The promise in Genesis 3:15 begins the shaping of the patterns the book you are reading seeks to exposit. Before we plunge into the patterns, significant questions about typology deserve some attention: How do we define "typology," what are its features, and what are the interpretive controls by which we can evaluate and establish that the biblical authors intended to communicate the typological patterns we might see in the text? I will work backward through these questions, beginning with the interpretive control of authorial intent, then moving to the features of typology, before suggesting a definition of this key term and concluding with reflections on the intent of the divine author of Scripture. This subsection has a concentric structure:

§2.1 The Intent of the Human Author
  §2.2 Features of Typology
    §2.2.1 Historical Correspondence
    §2.2.2 Escalation in Significance
  §2.3 Defining the Term "Typology"
§2.4 The Intent of the Divine Author

§2.1 The Intent of the Human Author

The most important criterion for determining what a text means is determining the intent of its human author.[22] As Elizabeth Robar has written, "To the extent that the reader construes the text as the author intended, successful communication has taken place."[23] We determine an author's intent by means of historical-grammatical interpretation of the text the author wrote.[24] We want to understand the grammatical meaning of the words and phrases the author has employed, and we want to understand that grammatical meaning in historical context. This study will employ grammatical-historical interpretation in pursuit of the intent of the human authors of the biblical texts.[25]

All texts have contexts, and all authors have ideological contexts in which they intend their writings to be understood. My working hypothesis is that the earliest biblical author, Moses, presents the whole of the Torah as relevant context for the isolated statements within his five books.[26] Continuing this line of thought, later biblical authors assume earlier Scripture as the wider

---

22. See the nuanced discussion advocating authorial intent in Dale C. Allison Jr., *The New Moses: A Matthean Typology* (Minneapolis: Fortress, 1994), 1–8. Ounsworth's replacement of authorial intent with "the concept of a plausible first audience" is unpersuasive. Richard Ounsworth, *Joshua Typology in the New Testament*, Wissenschaftliche Untersuchungen zum Neuen Testament 2/328 (Tübingen: Mohr Siebeck, 2012), 3, cf. 19–28. Audiences can so easily misunderstand or reject what authors/speakers intend to communicate (see, e.g., Deut 31:29; Matt 13:10; 16:22).

23. Robar, *The Verb and the Paragraph in Biblical Hebrew*, 41. Pace Moberly, *The God of the Old Testament*, 9.

24. In this study I will be interpreting the sixty-six books of the Protestant canon of Scripture, starting with the standard original language texts of the Old and New Testaments and moving from them into English translations. I will primarily work from the *BHS* text of the OT, the NA[28] for the NT, the Rahlfs text of the Greek translation of the OT (LXX), and the ESV, though as noted above I will also present my own translation.

25. E. D. Hirsch writes, "the intentional fallacy is properly applicable *only* to artistic success and to other normative criteria like profundity, consistency, and so on. . . . the intentional fallacy has no proper application whatever to verbal meaning." Hirsch, *Validity in Interpretation*, 12.

26. Moses seems to expect his audience to encounter his material repeatedly, so that after their first time through, they will know what he introduces early but only explains later. For instance, see the way that in Gen 13:10 Moses assumes the destruction of Sodom that will not be narrated until Gen 19 with the words, "This was before the Lᴏʀᴅ destroyed Sodom and Gomorrah" (Gen 13:10, ESV). Similarly, clean and unclean animals will not be delineated until Leviticus, but the classification is already assumed in the instructions for Noah in Genesis 7. The clean/unclean distinction seems to inform the release of the raven and the dove in Genesis 8:6–12, and the facts that doves will be used for sacrifice (e.g., Gen 15:9; Lev 12:6) and olive oil will be used for both the anointing of the tabernacle and the fueling of the menorah (Exod 27:20; 30:24–25) seem to cast light back on the dove returning with a freshly plucked olive leaf (Gen 8:11). The more confident we become that Moses means for the whole Pentateuch to be read together, the more significant becomes the fact that the serpent, which will later be declared unclean (Lev 11:42–44), got past the one charged to keep the clean realm of life (Adam), into the Garden, to tempt the woman to sin. For other examples along these lines, see footnote 4 on page 66.

context against which they intended their writings to be understood. As Beale has written,

> typology can be called contextual exegesis within the framework of the canon, since it primarily involves the interpretation and elucidation of the meaning of earlier parts of Scripture by latter parts. . . . Rather than exegeting a text only in light of its immediate literary context within a book, we are now merely exegeting the passage in view of the wider canonical context.[27]

The features of typology to which we now turn our attention will help us to establish the intent of the human authors.

§2.2 Features of Typology

The two essential features of typology are *historical correspondence* between events, persons, and institutions in the Bible's salvation-historical unfolding and the consequent *escalation in significance* that accrues to recurring patterns.[28] The kind of typological interpretation the biblical authors practice affirms the historicity of both the initial instance of the pattern and its recurrences.[29] As Melito of Sardis asserted in the second century, "the type happened."[30] That is to say, the biblical authors are not engaging in literary contrivance that creates these parallels and patterns.[31] Melito also affirmed escalation when he spoke of the type being surpassed by its fulfillment, which would be "taller in height,

---

27. G. K. Beale, "Did Jesus and His Followers Preach the Right Doctrine from the Wrong Texts? An Examination of the Presuppositions of Jesus' and the Apostles' Exegetical Method," in *The Right Doctrine from the Wrong Texts? Essays on the Use of the Old Testament in the New*, ed. G. K. Beale (Grand Rapids: Baker, 1994), 401.

28. E. Earle Ellis, "Foreword," in *Typos: The Typological Interpretation of the Old Testament in the New*, by Leonhard Goppelt, trans. Donald H. Madvig (Grand Rapids: Eerdmans, 1982), x.

29. Joshua Philpot persuasively applies this principle to demonstrate the historicity of Adam, otherwise the biblical authors would not have treated him as a type of the one to come, in "See the True and Better Adam: Typology and Human Origins," *Bulletin of Ecclesial Theology* 5, no. 2 (2018): 79–103. Bell's position that "Adam is a type of the one to come (5.14) but the passage has to be understood as mythical" eviscerates the connection of any saving import. Richard H. Bell, *The Irrevocable Call of God: An Inquiry into Paul's Theology of Israel*, Wissenschaftliche Untersuchungen zum Neuen Testament 184 (Tübingen: Mohr Siebeck, 2005), 186 n. 139.

30. My translation, in consultation with M. A. G. Haykin, of the Greek line, ὁ μὲν γὰρ τύπος [ἐγένετο]. Melito, *Peri Pascha* 4. Hall renders, "For the model indeed existed." See Stuart George Hall, ed., *Melito of Sardis on Pascha and Fragments: Texts and Translations* (Oxford: Clarendon Press, 1979), 4–5.

31. As Robert Alter, *The Art of Biblical Narrative*, 2nd ed. (New York: Basic, 2011), 55–78, seems to suggest.

and stronger in power, and beautiful in form, and rich in its construction."[32] Historical correspondence and escalation work together, as we will see when considering each in turn.

§2.2.1 Historical Correspondence

How do we establish historical correspondence?[33] We have evidence that later biblical authors seek to establish historical correspondence with earlier passages of Scripture when they re-use significant terms, quote whole phrases or entire sentences, repeat sequences of events, and establish parallels in covenantal or salvation-historical significance. Rarely-used terms or peculiar expressions naturally attract notice and establish connections in the minds of readers, as do quotations of earlier material. We must sometimes reflect to notice repeated event-sequences, but once noticed they cannot be un-seen. As for salvation-historical significance, another way to describe this would be to speak of a *covenantal* connection.

Consider the following examples:

Significant Terms. The word for "ark" (תֵּבָה) occurs in only two narratives in the Old Testament: in Genesis 6–9, where it describes Noah's ark, and Exodus 2:3 and 2:5, where it describes the "basket" (ESV) into which Moses's mother put him. This linguistic point of contact is regularly noted. I will argue in Chapter 4 that it is one of the features of historical correspondence between Noah and Moses. Here it is enough to observe that virtually all readers (of the Hebrew or of literal translations that preserve the connection) naturally think of Noah's ark when they read of the ark-basket carrying baby Moses in the bullrushes. Further, I would suggest that Moses employed this term to describe the basket into which his mother put him because he intended his audience to see a connection between himself and Noah.[34]

As another example of re-used terminology, note that in Exodus 15:5 Pharaoh's chariots and host sank in the sea "like a stone" (ESV). Just a few

---

32. Melito, *Peri Pascha*, 36. Hall, *Melito on Pascha and Fragments*, 18–19.

33. For a thorough discussion of "Evaluating the Evidence for Correspondence Between Texts: Established Criteria," with which I am in broad agreement, see Gibson, *Covenant Continuity and Fidelity*, 33–44.

34. Rightly Duane A. Garrett, *A Commentary on Exodus*, Kregel Exegetical Library (Grand Rapids: Kregel, 2014), 168: "Moses is a new Noah, who goes through water in his ark sealed with tar in order to save the people of God from a wicked generation."

verses later, in 15:16, the Song of the Sea sings that the inhabitants of Canaan will be still "as a stone" (ESV) as Israel passes over. Duane Garrett explains,

> The future conquest of Canaan, in this prayer, will see a repetition of God's actions. As the Egyptians sank to the bottom of the sea "like a stone" (15:5b), the prayer is that the Canaanites will be as immobile as a stone (15:16b) until Israel has "crossed over" into Canaan. The crossing over (עָבַר) into the Promised Land is a mirror of Israel's crossing of the *Yam Suph*; both are works of God (see also the description of Israel's crossing [עָבַר] of the Jordan in Josh. 3).[35]

On the basis of these kinds of uses and re-uses of language, I will argue in Chapter 8 that as Moses celebrates the crossing of the Red Sea in Exodus 15, he indicates that the conquest of Canaan will be a new exodus.

Quotations of Phrases or Lines. We have observed above the way the phrase "cursed are you" from Genesis 3:14 is quoted in 4:11, establishing a "kinship" between the serpent and his figurative seed, Cain. The biblical authors pervasively refer to and quote earlier Scripture. As another example, consider the way that Moses forges a connection between Abraham's experience and the exodus from Egypt by presenting the Lord saying the words, "I am Yahweh, the one who brought you out . . ." in both Genesis 15:7 and Exodus 20:2. Encountered in narrative sequence, Moses presents Yahweh quoting himself as he speaks the same words at the making of the Sinai covenant that he spoke when making covenant with Abraham:

Gen 15:7, אֲנִי יְהוָה אֲשֶׁר הוֹצֵאתִיךָ מֵאוּר כַּשְׂדִּים

Exod 20:2, אָנֹכִי יְהוָה אֱלֹהֶיךָ אֲשֶׁר הוֹצֵאתִיךָ מֵאֶרֶץ מִצְרָיִם

As argued elsewhere,[36] and to be presented again in Chapter 8 below, Abraham experiences a sequence of events that serves as a kind of preview of

---

35. Ibid., 405.
36. See, for instance, L. Michael Morales, *Exodus Old and New: A Biblical Theology of Redemption*, Essential Studies in Biblical Theology 2 (Downers Grove, IL: InterVarsity, 2020), 19–36; and James M. Hamilton Jr., *With the Clouds of Heaven: The Book of Daniel in Biblical Theology*, New Studies in Biblical Theology 32 (Downers Grove, IL: InterVarsity, 2014), 225–26.

the exodus from Egypt. The re-use of the quotation joins a parallel sequence of events, to which we turn our attention.

Repeated Sequences of Events. Often a number of features work together, as in this instance. Consider the parallels between the exoduses from Egypt of both Abraham and Israel:

1. Both Abraham and Jacob (and his offspring) descend into Egypt
2. because of a famine in the land of promise.
3. In both instances, the Hebrews are oppressed by the Egyptians, with Sarah taken into Pharaoh's harem and the children of Israel (eventually) enslaved.
4. In both cases the captives are liberated
5. when the Lord visits plagues on Pharaoh and Egypt,
6. and in both cases the Hebrews are enriched by the Egyptians,
7. before making their way out of Egypt and through the wilderness
8. to enter into a covenant ceremony with Yahweh,
9. who appears to Abraham as the smoking fire pot and flaming torch passing between the pieces, and to Israel in thick darkness and fire at Mount Sinai.
10. That Moses included these repetitions, and drew attention to them by means of the quotation of Genesis 15:7 in Exodus 20:2, suggests that Moses discerned an increasing significance in this repeated pattern and took pains to make sure his audience would see it as well.

As noted above with the "stone" language from the Exodus 15 Song of the Sea, it seems that Moses expected the pattern of events that took place in Abraham's life and at the exodus from Egypt to recur in Israel's future when they conquered Canaan.

Salvation-Historical Significance (i.e., Covenantal Import). I noted above that Moses uses the term תֵּבָה "ark" to describe both Noah's boat and the basket into which his own mother put him. Moses has obvious *covenantal significance*: he was the human mediator through whom Yahweh entered into covenant with Israel at Mount Sinai. Noah likewise has covenantal significance. When we considered *quotations* above we could have looked at the way Genesis 1:28 is quoted in Genesis 9:1, and in Chapter 2 below we will also see a repetition of the *sequence of events* that pertains to Adam's transgression in the episode of Noah's drunkenness. In the midst of the ways these features work together, having just considered the *covenantal import* of Moses, note that Yahweh declares himself to be *establishing his covenant* with Noah (Gen 9:9, 11, 12, 17). The (1) re-used term "ark" works with (2) quotations of phrases or whole lines, Genesis 1:28 in 9:1, and (3) repeated sequences of events (on which see in Chapter 2) all of which join with (4) similarity in salvation-historical and covenantal import to establish *historical correspondence* between Noah and Moses. As these elements of historical correspondence are established and then repeated, we begin to suspect that they point beyond themselves to the future, which sets us up for the discussion of the second essential feature of typology.

§2.2.2 Escalation in Significance

Against the idea that "prophecy is prospective whereas typology is retrospective,"[37] I would suggest that the patterns are noticed and recorded by the biblical authors for two reasons: first, they saw something significant in the patterns (repetitions of earlier patterns or similarities between events); and second, the significance they saw suggested to them that they should expect more of this kind of thing in the future. The repetitions of exodus-style deliverances portend future exodus-style deliverances, even if the patterns do not provide specific predictive details. The differences between, for instance, the preview of the exodus in Abraham's life, the exodus itself, and the conquest of Canaan, show us that while an Old Testament author could use exodus typology to point to the way God would save in the future, he was not necessarily detailing exactly what would take place.

The big ideas here are the following:

1. that the biblical authors themselves noticed these patterns;[38]
2. that they intend to signal the presence of the patterns to their audiences through the historical correspondences they build into their presentations;[39]

---

37. Baker, *Two Testaments, One Bible*, 181.

38. Against Walther Eichrodt's assertion, "a type possesses its significance, pointing into the future, independently of any human medium and purely through its objective factual reality." "Is Typological Exegesis an Appropriate Method," in *Essays on Old Testament Interpretation*, ed. Claus Westermann, trans. James Barr (London: SCM, 1963), 229.

39. Against Hays, *Echoes of Scripture in the Gospels*, 2. While I grant that the OT authors did not know specific details (cf. Eph 3:5; 1 Pet 1:10–12), I maintain that they were looking for the Genesis 3:15

3. and thus the repetitions were intended to cause a gathering
   expectation to increase with each new installment in the pattern
   of events.[40]

To summarize: the key features of typology are historical correspondence
and escalation, and historical correspondence is established by: (1) the re-use of
key terms, (2) the quotation of phrases or lines, (3) the repetition of sequences
of events, and (4) similarity in salvation-historical significance or covenantal
import. These means for establishing historical correspondence provide us
with *criteria* that can be used to determine when later biblical authors mean
to signal typological relationships with material in earlier passages of Scripture.
If we can establish that a later author *meant* to draw attention to a typological
pattern, we have warrant for regarding the historical correspondences, as well
as the escalations in significance and the resulting typological development,
as *intended by the human author of the passage*. These standards represent my
attempt to develop methodological rigor that can be applied in an attempt to
remedy a deficiency many perceive in earlier writing on typology. For instance,
S. Lewis Johnson wrote,

> the weaknesses of Fairbairn's work is largely the weakness of biblical studies
> done without the benefits of the knowledge derived from technical devel-
> opment in the study of the biblical languages, and without the benefits of
> knowledge derived from the biblical research of the last century or so.[41]

The fact that we arm ourselves with criteria, however, does not mean
that every question is answered. As Dale Allison concludes after a similar
discussion, "All uncertainty . . . is not thereby exorcised."[42] There is no substitute for long, slow, patient reading of the texts in their original languages,
supplemented by meditative reflection upon them. Thus Allison writes,

---

seed of the woman, whom they expected to bring about a climactic new-exodus style salvation that would
overcome sin and all its consequences, and further that their understanding of the patterns to which they
intentionally drew attention were shaped by the promises of God (e.g., John 5:39; 12:41, etc.).

40. *Pace* Baker, *Two Testaments, One Bible*, 183.

41. S. Lewis Johnson, "A Response to Patrick Fairbairn and Biblical Hermeneutics as Related to
the Quotations of the Old Testament in the New," in *Hermeneutics, Inerrancy, and the Bible: Papers from
ICBI Summit II*, ed. Earl D. Radmacher and Robert D. Preus (Grand Rapids: Zondervan, 1984), 796.
Referencing Patrick Fairbairn, *Typology of Scripture* (1845; repr., Grand Rapids: Kregel, 1989).

42. Allison, *The New Moses*, 21.

Only a delicate and mature judgment bred of familiarity with a tradition will be able to feel whether a suggested allusion or typology is solid or insubstantial: the truth must be divined, groped for by "taste, tact, and intuition rather than a controlling method."[43]

I would propose that the biblical authors instinctively understood that typological development functions as follows: when patterns of historical correspondences are repeated across narratives, expectations accumulate and cause escalation in the perceived significance of the repeated similarities and patterns. What they instinctively understood and communicated, we can validate by means of these criteria.

The Key Features of Typology

Historical Correspondence	Escalation in Significance
Established by 1. key terms 2. quotations 3. repetitions of sequences of events 4. similarity in salvation-historical or covenantal import	*When key terms, quotations of earlier material, and similarities in salvation-historical and covenantal import draw our attention to repeated installments in patterns of events, our sense of the importance of those patterns increases.*

The point being validated by these key features of typology is that the Old Testament authors *intended* to create the typological points of historical correspondence and escalation for which the New Testament authors claim fulfillment. That is to say, the interpretation of earlier Scripture by later biblical authors is *valid*. But I want to go one step further than saying that later biblical authors have correctly interpreted earlier Scripture and affirm that not only are their readings *valid* they are also *normative*. That is, through their interpretation of earlier Scripture, later biblical authors instruct their audiences regarding how to interpret the Bible.[44] The *normative* hermeneutic is the one that the biblical authors themselves have employed. If we are to read the Scriptures

---

43. Ibid. Citing M. H. Abrams, "Rationality and Imagination in Cultural History," in *Critical Understanding: The Powers and Limits of Pluralism*, by Wayne C. Booth (Chicago: University of Chicago Press, 1979), 176.

44. Against Richard N. Longenecker, *Biblical Exegesis in the Apostolic Period*, 2nd ed. (Grand Rapids: Eerdmans, 1999), xxxiv–ix.

such that our readings are *valid*, our readings must align with the *normative* interpretations provided by the biblical authors themselves.

With these ideas on the table, I am ready to hazard a definition of *typology*.

§2.3 Defining the Term "Typology"

Gathering together the features of typology discussed to this point, we can offer a working definition of the term:

> Typology is God-ordained, author-intended historical correspondence and escalation in significance between people, events, and institutions across the Bible's redemptive-historical story (i.e., in covenantal context).[45]

The only part of this definition not discussed above is the phrase "God-ordained." By this I refer to the way that the sovereign God of the Bible has orchestrated history such that the parallels noticed and highlighted by the biblical authors *actually happened*. As Earle Ellis has written, "Typological exegesis assumes a divine sovereignty over history."[46] Typology is not mere literary contrivance, nor is it a result of the imaginative creativity of either the biblical authors or those who interpret them. God ordained that the parallels would actually happen, and he also providentially ensured that the biblical authors would notice them. The Holy Spirit superintended the process so that the biblical authors rightly interpreted both the history they observed and the earlier Scripture to which they had access.

Having offered this working definition of typology, we can do the same for the phrase "typological interpretation."

---

45. Contra David Crump, who writes, "Typology in biblical interpretation involves the understanding of some characters and stories in the Old Testament as allegories foreshadowing events in the New Testament." David Crump, *Encountering Jesus, Encountering Scripture: Reading the Bible Critically in Faith* (Grand Rapids: Eerdmans, 2013), 26 n. 36. Typology and allegory are not to be equated. Mitchell Chase explains, "An allegory is a passage that says one thing in order to say something else." Mitchell L. Chase, *40 Questions About Typology and Allegory* (Grand Rapids: Kregel, 2020), 193. Chase gives the example of Isaiah 5, where the vineyard represents Israel, as an allegory. Peter J. Gentry and Stephen J. Wellum offer a similar definition of typology, distinguishing it from allegory, in *Kingdom through Covenant: A Biblical-Theological Understanding of the Covenants*, Second Ed. (Wheaton, IL: Crossway, 2018), 129–30.

46. Ellis, "Foreword," xv.

Typological Interpretation establishes historical correspondence on the basis of linguistic points of contact (i.e., the re-use of significant terms), quotations, repeated sequences of events, and similarities in salvation historical significance and covenantal context. As these features are discerned in the text, interpreters detect author-intended parallels between people, events, and institutions, and they have textual warrant to perceive a growing significance in the repeated patterns. The Holy Spirit's inspiration ensured that the biblical authors infallibly interpreted earlier Scripture and inerrantly presented it. Later interpreters, who are neither inspired by the Holy Spirit nor writing Scripture, are neither infallible nor inerrant, but they should neverthe-less seek to think and read and interpret in accordance with what the biblical authors intend to teach.

To clarify what I mean by this last statement (that we should seek to think and read and interpret in accordance with what the biblical authors intend to teach), as later biblical authors interpret earlier Scripture, they teach their audiences to do so. Those who embrace what the biblical authors teach will also seek to embrace the habits of mind, patterns of thought, and interpretive practices that the biblical authors model in their writings. The first sentence of the first chapter of Vernard Eller's book reads,

> It was, I think, Karl Barth who once said something to the effect that Christians have an obligation to become competent in 'the language of Canaan' (i.e., biblical ways of thinking and speaking) rather than simply demanding that everything be translated into *our* language (i.e., contemporary forms of thought).[47]

In my view this is the task of biblical theology—that of understanding and embracing the interpretive perspective of the biblical authors.[48] All this

---

47. Vernard Eller, *The Language of Canaan and the Grammar of Feminism* (Grand Rapids: Eerdmans, 1982), 1.

48. For a brief introduction, see James M. Hamilton Jr., *What Is Biblical Theology?* (Wheaton, IL: Crossway, 2014).

follows from the idea that the interpretive perspective of the biblical authors is both *valid* and *normative*.

§2.4 The Intent of the Divine Author

What about the intent of the divine author of Scripture? Believing that the Bible is inspired by the Holy Spirit (2 Tim 3:16), that its human authors "spoke from God as they were carried along by the Holy Spirit" (2 Pet 1:21, ESV), we can determine the intent of the divine author of Scripture by determining the intent of the human author of Scripture. In addition, we can see from later Spirit-inspired interpretation what the divine author meant to communicate in earlier Scripture. That is to say, where later biblical authors have interpreted earlier biblical texts, we can see what the divine author—whom I take to have been consistent with himself—meant to communicate in earlier texts. This principle goes in the other direction as well, as we should assume that what the divine author means to communicate through later biblical authors will be consistent with what he communicated through the earlier.[49]

§3 A PREVIEW OF WHAT FOLLOWS

As has been seen to this point in this chapter, typology deals in repetitions. The contents of this book have been adumbrated in this introductory chapter in the same way that an archetype and its ectypes[50] point forward to their anti-type. The biblical authors used literary structures to guide readers to see these repetitions, and as a result, understanding the literary structure of a passage is necessary for understanding what an author intended to communicate. In imitation of the method employed by the biblical authors, this book is struc-tured as a chiasm, and the chiasm helps me communicate the significance of what I am saying.

This Introduction has focused on what typology is and how we can verify whether an author intended to communicate it. We have looked at criteria for establishing author-intended typology at the micro-level: reuse of terms and phrases, quotation of earlier material, repetitions of event sequences, and

---

49. See the excellent reflections on this topic in Sequeira and Emadi, "Nature of Typology," 15–18.
50. Dictonary.com defines "ectype" as "a reproduction; copy (opposed to prototype)." I use the term to refer to an installment in a typological pattern between the archetype (or prototype), the initial instance, and the antitype, or final fulfillment to which the archetype and ectype(s) pointed.

similarities in significance. Another major authorial cue to typological patterning can be found at the macro-level, in the literary structure of the wider narrative, which I will discuss in the Conclusion, the final chapter of this book. The book thus opens and closes with discussions that seek to enable readers to validate and verify what the biblical authors meant to communicate. As with any chiasm found in the biblical writings, it is helpful to allow the corresponding units to interpret one another, as they were intended to do. Readers may be helped by reading the Introduction and then the Conclusion, as arguments throughout the book will deal with the kinds of literary structures discussed in the Conclusion.

The second and second-to-last chapters deal with the beginning and end of the Bible, where we see the weddings of the first and last Adam. The second chapter focuses on the way the biblical authors set us up to see Adam as the archetypal man, with his creation and marriage in Genesis 1–2 followed by the ectypal installments in the Adamic role across the pages of Scripture. The second to last chapter deals with the institution of marriage and the way it culminates in that of the last Adam with the wedding feast of the Lamb.

The chapters not only correspond to one another in chiastic structure, they also develop in linear fashion. Adam was a priestly, prophetic, royal figure, and chapters three, four, and five develop these typological realities. In the chiastic structure of this book, moreover, the chapter on Priests stands across from the chapter on the Levitical cult (a happy typo produced the form "Leviticult," which I have chosen to call into service). Naturally, the fulfillment of the priesthood and the cult are related concepts, but Christ brings to fulfillment both what the priests signified *as people* and what the cult served to achieve *as an institution.*

Similarly, chapter four deals with Prophets, and it was a prophet, Moses, who led Israel up from Egypt. Christ fulfills the role of Moses as he accomplishes the (*event of the*) new exodus and leads his people to the new and better land of promise. Thus the chapter on Prophets stands across from the chapter on the Exodus.

Chapter five on kings goes with chapter seven on Creation. God gave Adam dominion over the world that he made, and Christ will reign as king in the new creation.[51]

---

51. Christopher A. Beetham writes, "the theme of creation is inextricably interwoven with that of divine kingship and human vicegerency and . . . the divine program to renew creation is nothing less than

At the center of the chiastic structure of this book stands the Savior, the righteous sufferer, whose rejection and humiliation gave way to triumphant resurrection and enthronement, fulfilling typological patterns seen in the lives of (among others) Joseph, Moses, and David. God established his glory in the salvation through judgment accomplished through the death and resurrection of the Lord Jesus, in fulfillment of the Scriptures. That fact is not only the center of biblical theology, it is the central moment in human history, and the Lamb standing as though slain will be the centerpiece of praise for the redeemed in the age to come.

The chiastic structure of this book can be depicted as follows:[52]

1. Introduction to Promise-Shaped Patterns: Micro-Level Indicators for Determining Authorial Intent
  2. Adam
    3. Priests
      4. Prophets
        5. Kings
          6. The Righteous Sufferer
        7. Creation
      8. Exodus
    9. Leviticult
  10. Marriage
11. Conclusion to Promise-Shaped Patterns: Macro-Level Indicators for Determining Authorial Intent

Biblical theology is the attempt to understand and embrace the interpretive perspective of the biblical authors, and the attempt to understand *what* they communicate is facilitated by, and dependent upon, understanding *how* they communicate. Like many others, I have found the biblical authors to make

---

the reassertion of rightful divine rule through restored human vicegerency over the usurped kingdom of the world." "From Creation to New Creation: The Biblical Epic of King, Human Vicegerency, and Kingdom," in *From Creation to New Creation: Essays in Honor of G. K. Beale*, ed. Daniel M. Gurtner and Benjamin L. Gladd (Peabody, MA: Hendrickson, 2013), 235.

52. At the risk of belaboring the obvious, readers are encouraged to notice the matching character of the first and last chapters, and then that the only other chapter title that is not a single word is the central one. Similarly, the chapters of this book are headed by epitaphs, and the only epitaph from Scripture is reserved for that central chapter.

pervasive use of chiastic structures,[53] and here I seek to imitate their approach to communication. I will have more to say on how chiasms work and what they accomplish in the final chapter.

This book also falls into three parts that correspond to the ways typology is often described as dealing with people, events, and institutions who prefigure what God will do when he saves his people:

Introduction: Chapter 1
Part 1: People, Chapters 2–6
Part 2: Events, Chapters 7–8
Part 3: Institutions, Chapters 9–10
Conclusion: Chapter 11

When we look at People in Part 1 (Chapters 2–6), we will see several ways, some of them overlapping, in which key figures typify those who will come later. We will begin in Chapter 2 by considering the first man, the archetype, Adam, "who was a type of the one to come" (Rom 5:14, ESV), and we will trace the story through a number of ectypes, repetitions of the pattern, to culminate in the last Adam, Christ (1 Cor 15:45). The discussion of Priests, Prophets, and Kings in Chapters 3–5 will also begin with Adam, as he is the first to fill those roles. We will then move to the Righteous Sufferer in Chapter 6.

In Part 2 (Chapters 7–8), we turn our attention to events, beginning with creation in Chapter 7, before turning to the exodus in Chapter 8. This whole sequence will find fulfillment in the new exodus, the new wilderness sojourn, the new conquest of the land, in which is the new Jerusalem, which is the new holy of holies in the new cosmic temple of the new heaven and new earth.

Part 3 (Chapters 9–10) examines the Leviticult (Chapter 9) and Marriage (Chapter 10). Here again we will have fulfillment in the Melchizedekian high

---

53. Cf. John W. Welch and Daniel B. McKinlay, eds., *Chiasmus Bibliography* (Provo: Research Press, 1999). L. Michael Morales proposes a chiastic structure for the whole of the Pentateuch in L. Michael Morales, *Who Shall Ascend the Mountain of the Lord? A Biblical Theology of the Book of Leviticus*, New Studies in Biblical Theology 37 (Downers Grove, IL: InterVarsity, 2015), 23–38. For chiastic structures that I see in Revelation, Daniel, John, and Psalms, see James M. Hamilton Jr., *Revelation: The Spirit Speaks to the Churches*, Preaching the Word (Wheaton, IL: Crossway, 2012), 165; Hamilton, *With the Clouds of Heaven*, 83; James M. Hamilton Jr., "John," in *ESV Expository Commentary: John–Acts*, ed. Ian M. Duguid, James M. Hamilton Jr., and Jay Sklar (Wheaton, IL: Crossway, 2019), 28–29; and see the section on Literary Structure in the Psalms and the Context discussion of each psalm in James M. Hamilton Jr., *Psalms*, 2 vols., Evangelical Biblical Theology Commentary (Bellingham, WA: Lexham, 2021).

priesthood of Christ, whose death on the cross fulfills the sacrificial system and inaugurates the new marital covenant that will be celebrated at the wedding feast of the Lamb.

The book's Conclusion, Chapter 11, considers what chiasms are and do, and the way they function in Genesis. Literary structure facilitates typological patterning, and when authors build these into their work, they operate on readers even when not consciously recognized. People have a sense of development, climacteric, and closure, as well as an awareness of building expectation, even if they cannot put their finger on why.

PART 1
PERSONS

On what basis does Paul assert that Adam was "a type of the one to come" (Rom 5:14)? Applying the key hermeneutical question to this issue: did Moses intend for his audience to think of Adam as typifying one who would come after? If so, how does Moses establish that reality? A related set of questions has to do with how Moses presents Adam, and whether he develops his presentation of Adam in relationship to the nation of Israel. Is there anything more than a genealogical relationship between Adam and the nation of Israel? If so, how is that developed? We can ask similar questions about the relationship between Adam and David. Is there more to the presentation of the relationship between Adam and David than the line of descent traced through the genealogies? Do the biblical authors mean to indicate that if the future king promised to David will be a son to God, he will be a new Adam?

The next five chapters of this book (Chs. 2–6) deal with "Persons," and the first four (Chs. 2–5) are closely related. Chapter 2 seeks to tease out the way that Moses intended his audience to understand Adam, and then Chapters 3–5 consider Priests, Prophets, and Kings. Because of the way Adam is granted dominion (Gen 1:26, 28), he is a royal figure, so kingship could easily be discussed in Chapter 2. The amount of material to be covered, however, results in discrete treatment of these topics, which in turn affords the structural possibilities pursued here (see §3 of Chapter 1). Priests, prophets, and kings will be discussed in different chapters, but they are related to one another, not least for the fact that Adam embodied these offices in his prototypical person.

We now apply the discussion in Chapter 1 to Moses's presentation of Adam and the way that develops across the Torah into the Prophets and Writings to find fulfillment in the New Adam of the New Testament.

ADAM

The NT's understanding and exposition of the OT lies at the
heart of its theology, and it is primarily expressed within the
framework of a typological interpretation.

—E. EARLE ELLIS[1]

D id Moses intend to present Adam as a type, and if so, how does he establish
and develop that reality? I will argue in this chapter that Moses presents
Adam not only as a type of the one to come but of key figures who come after
him, and that he does this by means of quoted lines, repeated phrases, repetitions
in sequences of events, and key covenantal and salvation-historical similarities.[2]

Having shown how Moses ties later characters in his writings back to
Adam, we will move to consider the ways that later biblical authors discerned
Moses's intentions: they correctly interpreted him and developed his ideas in
accordance with his expectations. I do not mean to suggest that Moses knew
precisely *how* the expectations would be fulfilled, but expect fulfillment he did.

This chapter begins by looking at Noah as a new-Adam and ends with
Christ as the new-Adam who succeeded where archetypal Adam and all his
ectypes failed. The second and fourth sections of the chapter deal with the
patriarchs Abraham, Isaac, and Jacob on the one hand and David on the other.
The central third section of the chapter deals with the nation of Israel as a
new-Adam. The chapter's paneled structure can be depicted as follows:

---

1. Ellis, "Foreword," xx.
2. For a discussion of "Adam and Christ in St Irenaeus," see Jean Daniélou, *From Shadows to
Reality: Studies in the Biblical Typology of the Fathers*, trans. Wulstan Hibberd (London: Burns and Oates,
1960), 30–47.

§1 New-Adam Noah

   §2 New-Adams Abraham, Isaac, and Jacob

      §3 New-Adam Israel

   §4 New-Adam David

§5 New-Adam Christ

This chapter begins by exploring the ways that Moses ties first the patriarchs then the nation back to Adam. From there we turn to the way that the narrative of Samuel links David with Israel, Abraham, and Adam, an understanding also reflected in Psalm 8. We will then consider expectations for the "one like a son of man" in Daniel 7, who comes as a new Adam, king from the line of David, to exercise dominion over the beasts in an everlasting kingdom.[3] The chapter concludes with the way that both Luke and Paul compare and contrast Jesus and Adam.

To be clear: I am claiming that by tying later figures in the Pentateuch back to Adam, Moses intends to teach his audience that Adam is the prototypical man, with successive figures presented as ectypal installments in the Adamic pattern, in expectation of the antitypical fulfillment when *the* seed of the woman arises to conquer and redeem where Adam was defeated and subjected. From their presentation of David and the expected one like a son of man, later Old Testament authors can be seen to have learned this perspective from Moses, which we in turn find in the New Testament writings of Luke and Paul.

§1 NEW-ADAM NOAH

I sought to show in Chapter 1 that God's promises prompted the biblical authors to notice patterns. The Genesis 3:15 promise that there would be enmity between the seed of the woman and the seed of the serpent shaped the interpreted presentation of Cain as seed of the serpent after his killing of Abel. Moses has interpreted the material, and his interpretation was guided by what God said. In this instance, according to Genesis 3:14 and 4:11, God spoke

---

3. The fact that God granted Adam dominion, effectively making him king of creation, reveals that both kingship and land are equally significant in God's program. Bell is therefore mistaken to assert, "The promise of land was, for example, more fundamental than say that of Israel having a king." Bell, *The Irrevocable Call of God*, 377 n. 3.

the words that identified Cain with the serpent. For Moses to identify them with one another, then, was for him to take his interpretive cues from the Lord—as the word of God came to Moses, God's own word taught Moses the perspective reflected in what he wrote. In his presentation of Noah, Moses gives his readers a new Adam in a new creation with a new covenant, who then experiences a new fall into sin.

The promise of the seed of the woman in Genesis 3:15 also provides the rationale for both the genealogy in Genesis 5 and the words of hope at Noah's birth in 5:29. That first promise prompts the genealogy because the genealogy reflects attention to the line of descent of the seed of the woman. It provides the rationale for Genesis 5:29 because the hopes of Noah's father Lamech are based on God's promise in Genesis 3:15. Note the similarity in wording from Genesis 3:17 to Genesis 5:29:

Gen 3:17, אֲרוּרָה הָאֲדָמָה בַּעֲבוּרֶךָ בְּעִצָּבוֹן תֹּאכֲלֶנָּה

"cursed is the ground because of you; in painful toil you will eat of it"

Gen 5:29, וּמֵעִצְּבוֹן יָדֵינוּ מִן־הָאֲדָמָה אֲשֶׁר אֵרְרָהּ יְהוָה

"'. . . and the painful toil of our hands from the ground which Yahweh cursed.'"[4]

When Moses recounts Lamech's words at Noah's birth, he depicts hope informed by God's word: Lamech desires a relief he has discerned in the words God spoke. Not only that, but the difficulties he hopes to see overcome were introduced by God's word of judgment. The word of God has shaped the world.

The ten-member genealogy in Genesis 5 traces the line of descent from Adam to Noah. Why trace such a line of descent so carefully? My own family history does not extend beyond living memory. Not having done genealogical research, my knowledge of my ancestry does not extend beyond the name of my father's father's father. Why then was this line of descent so assiduously preserved and passed down to Moses, who saw fit to include it in the first of his five books? The answer, it would seem, is that the promise regarding the seed of the woman prompted attention to the line of descent. If Genesis 5:29 shows that God's promise has shaped the *hopes and beliefs* of his people,

---

4. Note that עצבון "painful toil" also occurs in Gen 3:16, and ארור "cursed" in 3:14.

the genealogy shows that it also shaped the *action* they took in keeping record of the line of descent.

But is there more to it than the genealogical line of descent? Is there evidence that Moses intended to present Noah as a new Adam, as an ectype of the archetype?

Consider the similar description of the creation in which readers encounter both Adam and Noah. In Genesis 1:2 the Spirit of God (רוּחַ אֱלֹהִים) was hovering over the face of the waters, and then in 1:9 the waters are gathered together so that the dry land can appear. When God brings the flood, the waters are let loose to re-cover the dry land in 7:10–12. And then as in 1:2, God (אֱלֹהִים) made a wind (רוּחַ) pass over (עָבַר) the land in 8:1, and the waters abated. When the waters subside after the flood, just as the dry land had appeared in 1:9, so it does again in 8:5. By forging these connections between the setting in which his readers encounter the two men, Moses indicates that Noah should be understood as a new Adam. Beetham writes, "Just as the destruction by flood is depicted as de-creation, so the postdiluvian renewal is depicted as re-creation, as new creation."[5]

Even more significant than the placement of Adam and Noah in similar settings where similar things happen, Moses presents God *saying the same thing* to Noah that he had earlier said to Adam. Genesis 9:1 presents a restatement of Genesis 1:28, providing us with another feature of author-intended historical correspondence—the quotation of earlier material:

וַיְבָרֶךְ אֹתָם אֱלֹהִים וַיֹּאמֶר לָהֶם אֱלֹהִים פְּרוּ וּרְבוּ וּמִלְאוּ אֶת־הָאָרֶץ ,Gen 1:28
"And God blessed them, and God said to them, 'Be fruitful and multiply and fill the earth.'"

וַיְבָרֶךְ אֱלֹהִים אֶת־נֹחַ וְאֶת־בָּנָיו וַיֹּאמֶר לָהֶם פְּרוּ וּרְבוּ וּמִלְאוּ אֶת־הָאָרֶץ ,Gen 9:1
"And God blessed Noah and his sons and said to them, 'Be fruitful and multiply and fill the earth.'" (ESV)

The "be fruitful and multiply" language will be significant across Genesis, and Moses presents the Lord speaking to Noah in these terms again in 9:7. Along with the quotation of earlier material pertaining to Adam (1:28 in 9:1),

---

5. Beetham, "From Creation to New Creation," 242.

Genesis 6:18 (וַהֲקִמֹתִי אֶת־בְּרִיתִי) and 9:9 (מֵקִים אֶת־בְּרִיתִי) arguably present Yahweh *establishing* with Noah the covenant he implicitly *cut* (כָּרַת) with Adam. On the basis of his exhaustive analysis of the term "covenant" in the Old Testament (בְּרִית), my colleague Peter Gentry maintains that the normal pattern is for a covenant to be "cut" (כָּרַת) when it is made, and then when that existing covenant is referred back to its terms are upheld or "established" (הֵקִים).[6] If this is correct, then when God says he will *establish* his covenant with Noah, the statement implies a covenant that has already been *cut*—presumably with Adam. If God establishes the Adamic covenant with Noah, then Noah stands in the same *covenantal relationship* with Yahweh that Adam had previously enjoyed. Even if this understanding of the relationship between the *cutting* and *establishing* of the same covenant is rejected, however, in narrative terms the focus moves from Adam standing as the main human agent to Noah doing so. The Bible's storyline moves forward from Adam to Noah.

Genesis has moved from Adam as a main character in the narrative, from his creation until his death is recorded in Genesis 5, to Noah taking center stage in Genesis 6–9. From a salvation-historical perspective, what God charged Adam to do in Genesis 1:28, he charges Noah to do in 9:1. With 1:28 quoted in 9:1, God's blessing of Adam in 1:28 has been communicated to Noah in 9:1. Adam and Noah's situations are not exactly the same (Adam in the garden prior to sin; Noah in the post-sin, post-flood world), but whether we call the relationship between God and Adam a covenant or not, God established a relationship with both Adam and Noah, blessed them both, and charged both to be fruitful and multiply and fill the earth. The hope for the seed of the woman who would defeat the serpent and his seed begins with a child whom Adam fathered (Seth) and continues through one Noah fathered (Shem). Along with the quotation of earlier material, then, we have the similar salvation-historical and covenantal significance of Adam and Noah.

We also see significant terms re-used from the description of Adam in the description of Noah. Several Hebrew terms for "man/male" are used to describe Adam in Genesis 1–2. He is referred to as "man/adam" (אָדָם) in 1:26, "male" (זָכָר) in 1:27, and as "man" (אִישׁ) in 2:23. In Genesis 2:7 Yahweh forms the "adam" (אָדָם) from the dust of the ground (אֲדָמָה). The connection

---

6. Gentry and Wellum, *Kingdom through Covenant*, 187–95. See the full annotated lexical analysis of *berit* (בְּרִית) in pages 841–904. I find Gentry compelling on this point, but my argument about Moses presenting Noah as an ectype in the Adamic pattern does not stand or fall with it.

between the "ground" (אֲדָמָה) and the "man" (אָדָם) might be reflected in English if we rendered "ground" with a form that included "man," perhaps something like "manland," or if instead of "man" we called him a "groundling" or some other expression that included "ground" or "earth" (earthling? grounder?). The point is that in Genesis 2 the man seems to be named by what he is made from, just as the woman will be (אִשָּׁה, "woman," made from the rib of the אִישׁ, "man" in 2:23). Not only does the man come from the ground, he is made to work the ground. Genesis 2:5 speaks of the time "when there was no man [אָדָם] to work the ground [אֲדָמָה]" (ESV). These realities make it so that Adam is again called to mind when we read in 9:20 that "Noah began to be a man of the ground [אִישׁ הָאֲדָמָה]," and that brings us to a parallel sequence of events between Adam and Noah.

Yahweh God planted (וַיִּטַּע) a garden in Eden in the east in 2:8, and in 9:20 Noah planted (וַיִּטַּע) a vineyard. Adam ate forbidden fruit (Gen 3:6), at which point his nakedness was exposed (3:7), and words of judgment followed (3:14–19). Just as Adam ate of the fruit of the forbidden tree in the garden, Noah drank himself drunk by the wine of his vineyard (9:21a). As Adam's nakedness was exposed, Noah lay uncovered, naked, in his tent (9:21b). As God cursed the serpent after Adam's sin, so Noah cursed Canaan (9:25), descendant of Ham, identifying both the Egyptians (Ham) and the Canaanites as seed of the serpent (3:15; cf. 10:6).

By means of the reuse of key terms, the quotation of whole lines, the repeated event-sequences, and the similar role in the covenantal outworking of redemptive-history, Moses presents Noah after the pattern of Adam. Adam is the archetypal man, and Noah is an ectypal installment in the Adamic pattern.[7]

§2 NEW-ADAMS ABRAHAM, ISAAC, AND JACOB

The covenantal and salvation-historical relationship established between Abraham, Isaac, and Jacob show them to be ectypal installments in the Adamic typological pattern. The genealogies of Genesis 5 and 11 trace a direct line of descent from Adam to Abraham, and just as God had blessed Adam in Genesis 1:28, he blesses Abraham in Genesis 12:1–3. The narrative reiterates

---

7. So also Kenneth A. Mathews, *Genesis 1–11:26*, New American Commentary (Nashville: Broadman & Holman, 1996), 351.

the blessing of Abraham throughout the account of his life (Gen 12:7; 13:15–18; 14:19–20; 15:5, 18–20; 17:4–8; 18:18–19; 22:16–18; 24:1, 7, 35), and then the Lord passes the blessing of Abraham directly to Isaac (26:2–4, 24). Isaac in turn pronounces the blessing of Abraham over Jacob (28:3–4), before the Lord himself does the same (28:13–15).

§2.1 The Covenantal Significance of Abraham, Isaac, and Jacob

The blessing of Abraham not only extends and elaborates upon God's blessing on Adam (Gen 1:28) and Noah (9:1), it also answers the judgment spoken after sin in 3:14–19 point for point. There are three categories of difficulties introduced in Genesis 3:14–19: first, the enmity between the seed of the woman and the seed of the serpent; second, the reproductive pain and conflict between male and female; and third, the curse on the ground. God's promise to Abraham directly addresses these difficulties: first, the enmity between the cursed seed of the serpent and the seed of the woman (3:14–15) will be overcome as God curses all who dishonor Abraham and blesses all who bless him—thus all the families of the earth will be blessed in Abraham and in his seed (12:3; 18:18; 22:18; 26:4; 28:14). Second, though Sarah's barrenness (11:30) is an outworking of the pain in childbearing (3:16a), and though her plan to have seed by Hagar (16:2) is an example of her seeking to take the initiative in the relationship (3:16b), God promises to make a great nation of Abraham (12:2), a promise of seed fulfilled with the birth of Isaac (21:1–3). And third, even in the midst of famines that result from the 3:17–19 curse on the ground (e.g., 12:10), God's promise of the land to Abraham indicates that the curse on the land will be overcome through the gift of the land (implicit in 12:1–2, explicit in 12:7), pointing as it does to God's promise to bless his people in his place. Dempster is on the mark: "God's programme with and through Abram is to restore the original conditions of creation described in Genesis 1–2 (Gen. 14:19–20)."[8]

Within the book of Genesis, Joseph represents an initial fulfillment of these promises when all the earth comes to him to buy grain (41:57), being blessed by his wise and discerning management (41:33, 39). Joseph also typifies the seed of Abraham who will overcome the enmity with the seed of the serpent: though he is thought to be dead (37:33–35), he lives and reigns over gentiles (45:8) and overcomes enmity by forgiving those who sought his life (45:3–15; 50:15–21).

---

8. Dempster, *Dominion and Dynasty*, 79.

In covenantal and salvation-historical terms, what God set out to achieve with Adam and carried forward with Noah is continued through Abraham, Isaac, and Jacob. In addition to the significance of the roles these key figures play, we have abundant re-use of key terms, quotations of whole phrases and lines, and significant repetitions of sequences of events.

§2.2 Key Terms and Quotations
§2.2.1 And I Will Establish My Covenant

God blessed Adam (1:28) and then established his covenant with Noah (6:18; 9:9). Similarly, God blesses Abraham (12:1–3) and then cuts a covenant with him (15:7–20, esp. 15:18, כָּרַת יְהוָה אֶת־אַבְרָם בְּרִית, "Yahweh cut a covenant with Abram"). The very words spoken to Noah in 6:18 and 9:11 ("and I will establish my covenant") are spoken to Abraham in 17:7 and regarding Isaac in 17:19.

Gen 6:18, וַהֲקִמֹתִי אֶת־בְּרִיתִי

Gen 9:11, וַהֲקִמֹתִי אֶת־בְּרִיתִי

Gen 17:7, וַהֲקִמֹתִי אֶת־בְּרִיתִי

Gen 17:19, וַהֲקִמֹתִי אֶת־בְּרִיתִי

"and I will establish my covenant"

This is not to suggest that the covenants God makes with Abraham and Noah are coterminous, but through both these covenants God preserves life, continues the purposes he set out to achieve when he placed Adam in the garden, and mercifully blesses his people in a way that delivers them from his own just wrath.

Not only does Moses connect these figures by showing God *blessing* and *entering into covenant* with Adam, Noah, and Abraham, he also uses and reuses the language first seen in Genesis 1:28 when God commanded the first man and woman to "be fruitful and multiply." Like Adam, Noah was blessed and told to be fruitful and multiply and fill the earth (9:1, 7). In all these instances (1:28; 9:1, 7) as well as in 1:22, the phrase is פְּרוּ וּרְבוּ (cf. also 8:17).

Excursus: Is Ishmael an Installment in a Typological Pattern?

As we consider the "be fruitful and multiply" language, we have reuse of significant language that does not alone, in itself, establish a typological relationship with Adam and the line of promise. The angel of the Lord tells Hagar, "multiplying I will multiply your seed, so that they cannot be counted for multitude [הַרְבָּה אַרְבֶּה אֶת־זַרְעֵךְ]" (16:10), and God even says to Abraham, "And as for Ishmael, I have heard you. Behold, I have blessed him, and I will make him fruitful and multiply him exceedingly . . ." (17:20). Yahweh, however, does not enter into a covenantal relationship with Ishmael. In fact, in the verses that precede and follow the 17:20 statement of the *blessing* and the *making fruitful and multiplying* of Ishmael, the Lord asserts that he will establish his covenant with Isaac not Ishmael (17:19, 21). Along with other features of the narrative, these realities indicate that Ishmael *is* an installment in a typological pattern but *not the one* that traces the seed of promise.

In the case of Ishmael, we have repeated language and phrases, but we do not have either covenantal/salvation-historical significance or repeated sequences of events with Adam and the seed of the woman. It seems that Ishmael was blessed and multiplied simply because he physically descended from Abraham. God blessed Ishmael because of his connection to Abraham, but God entered into covenant with Isaac not Ishmael (Gen 17:20–21). Ishmael does not participate in the typological patterns seen in the development from Adam through Noah to Abraham, Isaac, and Jacob.

There are, however, other patterns in which the story of Ishmael does make installments: the passing over of the firstborn son; the problems stemming from polygamy; and the enmity between the seed of the woman and the seed of the serpent. Adam's firstborn Cain was passed over: God was pleased with Abel's offering (Gen 4:4–5), and then Seth called on the name of Yahweh (4:26). Abraham's firstborn Ishmael was passed over in favor of the child of promise born to Sarah, Isaac (17:15–21). Isaac's firstborn Esau was passed over in favor of Jacob, as Rebekah was told that the older would serve the younger (25:23). This happens again as Jacob's firstborn Reuben does not receive the blessing because the much younger Joseph is the favorite of his father (37:3), and the last instance of this in Genesis comes when Jacob crosses his hands to place his right hand on the head of the younger Ephraim rather than the firstborn son of Joseph, Manasseh (48:13–20). Again and again in Genesis the older son is passed over, and the younger receives the blessing. That Moses includes this pattern in his narrative reveals that he understands Yahweh to be one who chooses not according to worldly and cultural expectations but according to his own secret counsels.

In contrast to those whom Yahweh chooses in his unexpected way, Moses presents a series of proud, strong characters who are boastful and impressive by worldly standards. The Lamech of Cain's line brags of his murders and promises extreme vengeance (Gen 4:23–24). Nimrod seed of Ham was a mighty hunter (10:8–11). And similarly, Ishmael will "be a wild donkey of a man, his hand against everyone and everyone's hand against him" (16:12, ESV). Later we read, "He lived in the wilderness and became an expert with the bow" (21:20, ESV), which is not unlike Esau: "a skillful hunter, a man of the field" (25:27, ESV). When Isaac commissions Esau to prepare the feast at which he means to bless him, the blessing Jacob steals, Isaac sends Esau out with Ishmael's weapon, the bow (27:3). Hagar acquired for Ishmael a wife from Egypt (21:21), and Esau first marries daughters of Heth, Hittites (26:34), then a daughter of Ishmael (28:9). These women all descend from Ham, whose son Canaan Noah cursed (9:25; 10:6–15).[9]

The story of Ishmael also makes a contribution to a pattern of events showing that problems stem from polygamy. Sarai thinks it will be a good idea for Abram to go into Hagar, but she failed to anticipate how Hagar would respond when she conceived (Gen 16:1–6). Jacob marries both Leah and Rachel and gets no shortage of domestic strife (see Gen 29–35). Later, in a story remarkably similar to that of Abram, Sarai, and Hagar, a man named Elkanah is married to Hannah and Peninnah.[10] Like Sarai, Hannah had no children (1 Sam 1:2). Like Sarai, however, God grants her a son (1:19–20). Surprisingly, Hannah gives her son a name that carries the same meaning as Ishmael's, "God hears." The names Samuel (שְׁמוּאֵל) and Ishmael (יִשְׁמָעֵאל) are both built from the words "hear" (שָׁמַע) and "God" (אֵל). The author of Samuel accomplishes several things by telling his story the way he does: he reinforces the idea that polygamy produces problems; he links the conception of formerly-barren Hannah to that of formerly-barren Sarah (meanwhile fertile Hagar is identified with fertile Peninnah); and

---

9. Moberly's failure to understand what Moses intended to communicate is reflected in his comment, "It is a pity that in the history of interpretation, Esau has generally received a bad press." R. W. L. Moberly, *The Theology of the Book of Genesis*, Old Testament Theology (New York: Cambridge University Press, 2009), 98 n. 13. Esau has received bad press because he has generally been recognized as seed of the serpent, because though he sought blessing he found no place for repentance (Heb 12:17).

10. We will return to the births of Samuel and Ishmael in §4.2 of Chapter 4 below.

thereby he links the miraculous births of Samuel and Isaac. These instances become installments in a pattern of barren women giving birth (Sarah, Rebekah, Rachel, Samson's mother, Hannah, the Shunammite, Elizabeth).

What we learn from Ishmael shows that understanding the Bible's typology is not like understanding a basic mathematical formula. If the application of these criteria were a simple numerical equation,[11] on the basis of Genesis 16:10 and 17:20 we might expect Ishmael to be one of the good guys. Like Adam, Abraham, Isaac, and Jacob, the Lord promises to multiply Ishmael's offspring (Gen 16:10), blessing him and making him fruitful and multiplying him (17:20). The Lord even makes him father of twelve tribe-like princes (17:20; 25:12–17; cf. Nahor's twelve descendants in 22:20–24 and Jacob's twelve sons), and we later read of Ishmael, "God was with the boy" (21:20, ESV). Biblical interpretation, however, is more than merely following rules and applying criteria. We are dealing with literature, and we have to *read* it—preferably in its original language, in big chunks, repeatedly, sympathetically—as we seek to understand the intentions of its authors.

Ishmael's part of the story connects him with the seed of the serpent as he opposes the seed of the woman: Cain kills Abel; Ishmael mocks Isaac; Esau seeks to kill Jacob; and Joseph's brothers sell him into slavery. There is enmity between the seed of the woman and the seed of the serpent (Gen 3:15), and Ishmael, the "wild donkey of a man," lives out that enmity with "his hand against everyone" and as he dwells "over against all his kinsmen" (16:12; 25:18).

To return to evidence that Moses means to make installments in the Adamic-seed-of-the-woman typological pattern, we continue to consider the use of the language first seen in Genesis 1:28 when, having blessed the man and woman, God commanded them to "be fruitful and multiply."

§2.2.2 Be Fruitful and Multiply

The Lord promised to make Abraham's offspring as innumerable as the dust of the earth (Gen 13:16) and the stars of the sky (15:5) before telling him that he would give him his covenant and multiply (רָבָה) him "to exceeding excess (בִּמְאֹד מְאֹד)" (17:2). Just a few verses later the Lord promised to make Abraham "fruitful (פָּרָה) . . . to exceeding excess (בִּמְאֹד מְאֹד)" (17:6). The Lord next tells Abraham, "blessing I will bless you, and multiplying I will multiply

---

11. I am thankful for my brother-in-law, mathematics professor Clint Armani, who brought mathematical paradoxes to my attention.

your seed" (22:17). Every time he re-uses the *be fruitful and multiply* language Moses reminds his audience of what God set out to achieve when he blessed the first man and woman and commanded them to do just that (1:28).

As those made in God's image and likeness, the first man and woman were the visible representatives of the invisible God in the cosmic temple the Lord made.[12] When God commanded them to be fruitful and multiply and fill the earth, he indicated that he wanted the world to be filled with those who represent him, those responsible to bring his character, his authority, his presence, and his reign to bear on all creation. In short, God wanted the man and woman to be fruitful and multiply because he wanted the world filled with his glory. This aspect of God's creation-purpose is reinforced when we encounter references to God's people *multiplying* and *being fruitful*.

When Abraham's servant found Rebekah and she agreed to become Isaac's wife, Moses recounts how as Rebekah's family said goodbye to her, "they blessed Rebekah and said to her, 'Our sister, may you be thousands of multitudes [רְבָבָה], and may your seed possess the gate of those who hate him'" (Gen 24:60). The Lord then tells Isaac, "... I will bless you ... and I will establish the oath that I swore to Abraham your father; and I will multiply [רְבָה] your seed as the stars of the heavens ... and they shall be blessed in your seed—all the nations of the earth" (26:3–4). Upon his arrival in Rehoboth, Isaac states his confidence that he and his people will "be fruitful (פָּרָה)" in the land (26:22), and just a few lines later Yahweh appears to him and assures him that he will "bless" him and "multiply (רְבָה)" his "seed" (26:24).

As he blesses Jacob Isaac says, "El Shaddai bless you and make you fruitful and multiply you ..." (Gen 28:3). Later God appeared to Jacob and said to him, "I am El Shaddai, be fruitful and multiply ..." (35:11; cf. 48:4). When Joseph's second son is born in Egypt, he gives him a name etymologically related to the idea of "fruitfulness," Ephraim (אֶפְרַיִם), with the explanation, "God has made me fruitful (פָּרָה)" (41:52, ESV; cf. 49:22).

To this point we have looked at the covenantal significance of Abraham, Isaac, and Jacob, and we have seen how the "be fruitful and multiply" language also connects them to Adam. The covenantal significance and the re-use of key phrases and quotations of earlier material, moreover, were intended by Moses

---

12. See further Chapters 3 and 7 on priests and creation below, and cf. John H. Walton, "Creation," in *Dictionary of the Old Testament: Pentateuch*, ed. T. Desmond Alexander and David W. Baker (Downers Grove, IL: InterVarsity, 2003), 164–65.

to draw the attention of his audience to repeated installments in patterns of events. As Beetham puts it,

> The intentional use of the language of the original Gn 1 vicegerency mandate and its application to the patriarchal family further demonstrates that God's original creation intentions have been concentrated in and are being accomplished through the seed of Abraham.[13]

§2.3 Event Sequences

§2.3.1 A Promise of Life Overturning Expected Death

The God who consistently chooses the younger son over the firstborn is also the God who chooses to respond to death with a promise of seed—offspring. God had warned Adam in Genesis 2:17 that he would surely die in the day he ate forbidden fruit. The man and woman ate, and they fled from God expecting death. As God cursed the serpent, he declared that the man and woman would have seed, a child, who would bruise the head of the serpent (Gen 3:15). God threw the promise of seed right into death's face.

Abraham's case is similar: once the narrative has worked down to him through the genealogies of Genesis 5 and 11, we read that his wife is barren (11:30). A barren wife is like the death of the family line. As Jon Levenson notes, "infertility and the loss of children serve as the functional equivalent of death."[14] Into that death, however, God spoke life, promising to make Abraham into a great nation (12:2), to multiply his seed (e.g., 13:16), and specifying that the child would come through barren Sarah (17:16). In both cases the expectation of death (3:8; 18:11) is overturned when God promises seed (3:15; 17:21; 18:10, 14).

The overturning of expected death through birth by a previously barren woman happens not only in Sarah's case (21:1–7) but also with Isaac's wife Rebekah (25:21) and Jacob's wife Rachel (29:31). The expectation of death being overturned by God giving life ties the Genesis 3:15 promised seed of the woman to the births by barren women in the line of descent, linking the pattern of events to the covenantal significance, the quotations, and the re-use of key terms. We considered above the "be fruitful and multiply" language across Genesis, which is obviously connected to the event sequence under consideration here.

---

13. Beetham, "From Creation to New Creation," 246.

14. Jon D. Levenson, *Resurrection and the Restoration of Israel: The Ultimate Victory of the God of Life* (New Haven: Yale University Press, 2008), 119.

These three interlinked features of the narrative (the command/promise that God would make fruitful and multiply, barren women giving birth, and the overthrow of expected death) show that in all these cases God brought new birth and new life where no one had a right to expect anything but death.

§2.3.2 A Deep Sleep in a Covenantal Context

In some cases the key term draws our attention to the event sequence, as happens when we notice that Moses uses the term rendered "deep sleep" (תַּרְדֵּמָה) only twice in all his writings, at Genesis 2:21 and 15:12. God caused a "deep sleep" to fall upon Adam when he took the rib from his side, made the woman, and brought her to the man for the two of them to enter into a covenantal union. When we encounter this rare[15] term for "deep sleep" again in Genesis 15:12, once again we have a covenantal context, as the Lord has caused a "deep sleep" to fall upon Abraham before prophesying to him of the exodus and conquest (15:13–16) and cutting the covenant by causing the smoking fire pot and flaming torch to pass between the pieces of the halved animals (15:17–18).[16]

While the Genesis 2 marital covenant between the man and woman is obviously distinct from the Genesis 15 covenant, the use of the rare term for "deep sleep" (תַּרְדֵּמָה) naturally forges an association between Genesis 2 and Genesis 15. Encountering this rare word in Genesis 15 causes readers to think back to the only other place they have seen it, in Genesis 2. The use of this term in only these places in the whole Pentateuch prompts readers to associate the covenants with which the Lord blessed Adam and Abraham. For both men, the Lord caused a "deep sleep" to fall upon them, as a result of which they were passive participants while the Lord prepared covenantal blessings for them. The same term is not used to describe Jacob's sleep in Genesis 28:11–12, but Sailhamer notes that in the cases of Adam, Abraham, and Jacob, "the recipient of God's provision sleeps while God acts. . . . the man's sleep in the face of the divine activity appears to be intended to portray a sense of passivity and acceptance of the divine provision (cf. Ps 127:2)."[17] The linkage of Genesis 2 and 15 also connects marriage, the covenant, the exodus, and the overturning of

---

15. The term is used only in these two places in all of Genesis, nowhere else in the Pentateuch, and only five more times in the rest of the Old Testament at 1 Sam 26:12; Isa 29:10; Job 4:13; 33:15; and Prov 19:15.

16. The exegetical connection I am highlighting here between Genesis 2:21 and 15:12 may explain the interest in Adam's sleep in patristic commentary, on which see Daniélou, *From Shadows to Reality*, 48–56.

17. John H. Sailhamer, "Genesis," in *The Expositor's Bible Commentary*, ed. Frank E. Gaebelein, vol. 2 (Grand Rapids: Zondervan, 1990), 46.

death by the seed, related concepts each pregnant with meaning as the gospel gestates in the pages of Scripture.

§2.3.3 A Failure to Protect

Adam cannot accomplish what God has charged him to do—be fruitful and multiply (Gen 1:28)—apart from his wife.[18] Adam has further been charged to "guard" the garden, "guard" being another connotation of "keep" in the phrase "work and keep" (2:15). In a sense, then, Adam must protect the woman in order to do what God has charged him to do. Snakes are not designated as unclean until the book of Leviticus (Lev 11:42–44), but Moses probably intends that information to influence his audience's consideration of the presence of the snake in the garden in Genesis 3:1.[19]

Rather than confront the snake, though he was present the whole time the snake tempted the woman (Gen 3:6b), Adam stood idly by and allowed the snake to question God (3:1), contradict God (3:4), and call into question the character of God (3:5). The man whose responsibility it was to "keep" the garden should long ago have interrupted the father of lies, politely asked him to leave, and, if the snake refused to depart, informed him that he could only continue to poison the mind of the woman over his own dead body. That is to say, Adam should have protected the woman, and if necessary, he should have fought the snake to the death.[20] This, alas, he did not do.

We have seen how the narrative moves from Adam to Abraham by means of the genealogies, the covenants, the quotations, and the key terms, and Adam was not the only one to fail to protect a wife vital to God's purposes. Immediately after God promised Abraham land, seed, and blessing (Gen 12:1–3), Abraham put Sarah in position to be seized by Pharaoh and taken into his harem (12:10–16). Sarah is as necessary to God's purposes as Eve was. Through Sarah and Sarah alone God intended to give seed to Abraham, and as her husband, Abraham's responsibility was to lead her, provide for her, and protect her. He led her right into jeopardy and then not only did not protect her but used her for his own protection (12:12–13).

---

18. See further James M. Hamilton Jr., "A Biblical Theology of Motherhood," *Journal of Discipleship and Family Ministry* 2, no. 2 (2012): 6–13.

19. See footnote 26 on page 18 above, along with footnote 4 on page 66 below discussing the way Moses assume his audience will know material he presents later in his writings.

20. See Michael Barber, *Singing in the Reign: The Psalms and the Liturgy of God's Kingdom* (Steubenville, OH: Emmaus Road, 2001), 43–46.

The narrative does not explore Abraham's other options (go somewhere else, find some other way to protect his own life, etc.), but surely the course of action he took was not the only one open to him. Even if it were, he should have trusted Yahweh to preserve his life and protected Sarah come what may. Instead, he placed his own safety above hers and treated her as expendable. And he did this not once but twice! The second time (Gen 20:1–7) is arguably worse because by then God has explicitly promised to raise up Isaac through Sarah (17:16–21), and at that point (Gen 20) Sarah might even have been pregnant with Isaac (cf. 18:10, 14; 21:1–7).

Like Adam, Abraham failed to protect the wife God had given him, the wife necessary for the fulfillment of God's promises. When Isaac sins in the same way with Rebekah (Gen 26:6–11), we have a confirmed pattern of male abdication of the responsibility to protect as an expression of self-sacrificial love. Men will keep right on taking and using and lying and abdicating until one comes who will say: "If then you seek me, permit these to go" (John 18:8). This is not to imply that no men until Jesus protected the women under their care, but even the good examples, such as Boaz in the book of Ruth, point forward to the one who would do this perfectly. Jesus gave himself to protect those under his care the way Adam, Abraham, Isaac, David, and many others,[21] failed to do.

In spite of the fact that Adam would show himself unable to protect his wife (Gen 3:1–6), God blessed him (1:28) and, having put him into a deep sleep in a covenant making context (2:21), God promised that the seed of the woman would arise from his line to conquer (3:15). Surprisingly, the line of destiny descends not through the firstborn but through a younger son (4:25–26), as the Lord shapes the plot in which the hope of the world will be realized in an unexpected way.

In spite of the fact that Abraham would show himself repeatedly unable to protect his wife (Gen 12:10–16; 20:1–7), God blessed him (12:1–3) and, having put him into a deep sleep in a covenant making context (15:12), God promised that his barren wife would give birth to the seed of promise (17:16). Surprisingly, the line of destiny descends not through Ishmael, Abraham's firstborn, but through the younger Isaac (17:18–21), as the Lord creates patterns in his plotline, in which the hope of the world will be realized in an unexpected way.

---

21. Lot, for instance, despicably offered to use his daughters to protect his visitors (Gen 19:8; cf. Judg 19:24–25).

§2.4 Adamic Ectypes: Noah, Abraham, Isaac, and Jacob

Why does Moses include the episodes he does, and why does he word them the way that he does? In Genesis Moses intends to present Noah, Abraham, Isaac, and Jacob as installments in an Adamic pattern. This thesis accounts for the event sequences that are repeated across the book, sequences established or highlighted by the re-use of key terms, the quotation of earlier material, and the similar roles these men play as God covenants with them to keep his promises. The key terms are re-used and the quotations repeated because the author intends to draw his audience's attention to repeated patterns of events. As we continue to make our way through the Bible, tracing the salvation-historical narrative across the covenants, which do comprise "the backbone" of the biblical story,[22] we will see that the developing patterns begin to function as both *interpretive schemas* and *predictive paradigms*.

§3 NEW-ADAM ISRAEL

Already in the earliest mention of "man" in Genesis 1:26–27 there is a sense in which to refer to Adam is to refer to humanity: "Let us make *man* [אָדָם] . . . and let *them* rule [וְיִרְדּוּ] . . . And God created *the man* [הָאָדָם] . . . male and female he created *them* . . ." What I am pointing to here is a dynamic between the singular and the plural, the one and the many. The first man is the representative human, and the descriptions of him move easily between describing him as an individual, on the one hand, and as a kind of representative "everyman" on the other.

The same dynamic can be detected in the Genesis 3:15 reference to the "seed" of the woman, the word "seed" being a collective singular that can refer to one individual descendant or to descendants as numerous as the stars of the heavens. The singular pronouns and verbs in Genesis 3:15 indicate that one particular seed is in view,[23] but on the other hand when the Lord tells Abraham that his "seed" will be like the dust of the earth (Gen 13:16) the collective seed is in view.

I draw attention to this reality here because of the way that it relates to

---

22. Gentry and Wellum, *Kingdom through Covenant*, 31. On this the opening page of the first chapter of their book, the authors assert, *"the progression of the covenants* forms the backbone of Scripture's metanarrative" (emphasis theirs).

23. Jack Collins, "A Syntactical Note (Genesis 3:15): Is the Woman's Seed Singular or Plural?," *Tyndale Bulletin* 48 (1997): 139–48.

the fact that as we make our way through Genesis, the name "Israel" comes to refer to either the patriarch Jacob or the nation that descends from him. Jacob's name had been changed to Israel in Genesis 32:28 (MT 32:29), but by 34:7 the humiliation of Dinah is referred to as a disgraceful thing "in Israel." The move to referring to *the people* by the name of the *patriarch* is like the one by which *humanity* is referred to by the term that designates the first *man*.

§3.1 Corporate Personality

The dynamic relationship between first *man* and *mankind* and then between *Jacob-Israel* and *nation-Israel* can be captured by the phrase "corporate personality," and it is related to the way that across the Old Testament nations will be identified with their kings and/or personified as an individual human, whether male or female. This concept of "corporate personality" informs a text like Genesis 47:27, which reads, "And *Israel* dwelled in the land of Egypt, in the land of Goshen, and *they* took possession of it; and *they* were fruitful and multiplied exceedingly." Most references to "Israel" in Genesis continue to point to Jacob, as does the one that immediately precedes 47:27, when Israel, that is Jacob, speaks to Joseph in 46:30. We expect the Israel in 47:27, then, to be Jacob, until the plural forms later in the verse force us to recognize that the reference is to the *collective* Israel not the *individual* Israel.

§3.2 Be Fruitful and Multiply

That the people have been fruitful and multiplied in Genesis 47:27 ties them to Adam and what he was charged to do in Genesis 1:28. This connection between Adam and the *collective* Israel is reinforced in Exodus 1:7, "and the sons of Israel were fruitful and swarmed and multiplied and grew strong in excessive excess, and the earth was filled with them" (cf. Exod 1:12). The reference to the "earth" being "filled" with the sons of Israel adds to the "swarming" and the *fruitful* and *multiply* language to point back to Genesis 1:28. The story of Adam is carried forward by the collective Israel, or to put it another way, the nation of Israel is a new Adam.

§3.3 Israel Is My Firstborn Son

The genealogy of Genesis 5 implicitly presents Adam as God's son, an implication rightly recognized in Luke's genealogy of Jesus, when, working back from Jesus to the first man, Luke arrives at Adam and refers to him as "the son of God" (Luke 3:38). The idea is communicated in Genesis 5 as Moses begins, "On the day that God created man [Adam], in the image of God he made him . . . and he called the name of them Man [Adam] in the day he created them" (Gen 5:1–2). The genealogy continues in verse 3: "And it came about, man [Adam] was 130 years, and he fathered in his likeness, according to his image, and he called his name Seth." To bring out the point, let me set the phrases of the verses in visual parallel:

5:1–2	5:3
"On the day that God created man [Adam],	"And it came about, man [Adam] was 130 years,
in the image of God he made him . . .	and he fathered in his likeness, according to his image,
and he called the name of them Man [Adam] in the day he created them."	and he called his name Seth."

If Seth, fathered according to Adam's image and likeness, is *Adam's son*, then it would seem that Adam, created in the image and likeness of God, is *God's son*. The text does not overtly state this, but it seems to be implied.[24] The implication, again, is reflected in the reference to Adam as God's son in Luke 3:38.

The idea that Adam is God's son factors into this discussion because of the way that Yahweh instructed Moses to speak of Israel in Exodus 4:22–23,

And you shall say to Pharaoh, "Thus says Yahweh: my son, my firstborn, is Israel. And I say to you: send my son that he may serve me. And if you refuse to send him, behold, I am going to kill your son, your firstborn."

Exodus 4:22–23 indicates that Israel, which has been fruitful and multiplied and filled the earth (Exod 1:7), is a new Adam. Adam, God's son, has his role carried forward by Israel, God's son. The identification of Israel with Adam also suggests that we should identify the land of promise with the garden of Eden, and Adam's banishment from the garden with Israel's exile

---

24. So also Beetham, who writes, "As Seth is the son of Adam, so Adam is the son of God." "From Creation to New Creation," 239.

from the land.[25] But Adam and Israel are not the only figures to be identified as God's son in the Old Testament.

§4 NEW-ADAM DAVID

Both Adamic sonship and corporate personality inform the promises God makes to David in 2 Samuel 7. These promises pertain to kingship, which will occupy our attention in Chapter 5 below. Here we are concerned with the way that what God says to David through the prophet Nathan connects David and the future king from his line to Adam.

The context of the passage includes a number of pointers back to Adam and Abraham. The "rest" in 2 Samuel 7:1 recalls God's rest in Genesis 2:2–3.[26] David's desire to build God a house also recalls the Lord's work at creation building his own cosmic temple (see Chapter 7). The Lord's promise to make David "a great name" in 2 Samuel 7:9 recalls his promise to make Abraham's name great in Genesis 12:2. When the Lord tells David he will raise up his "seed" in 2 Samuel 7:12, notes sound from the seed theme that stems from Genesis 3:15 and continues through God's promise to Abraham and his seed (e.g., Gen 22:17–18). The associations with Abraham are strengthened by the next phrase from 2 Samuel 7:12, "who will come from your body," the whole of which occurs in only one other place in the Old Testament, at Genesis 15:4.

Gen 15:4, אֲשֶׁר יֵצֵא מִמֵּעֶיךָ

2 Sam 7:12, אֲשֶׁר יֵצֵא מִמֵּעֶיךָ

"who will come from your body"

The seed God promised to raise up from David, then, is firmly linked to the seed God promised to raise up from Abraham, and thereby, to the promised seed of the woman. The Lord then promises in 2 Samuel 7:14, "I will be to him a father, and he will be to me a son." The *sonship* of the king from David's line means that this king will reign as God himself would, and this brings out the

---

25. Ibid., 246–47.
26. Genesis 2:2–3 use שָׁבַת to describe God's rest, but Exodus 20:11 employs the same verb in 2 Samuel 7:1, נוּחַ, when it says that God rested on the seventh day.

sonship of the Adamic vice-regency the Lord communicates about the seed of David. Not only will the king from David's line be a new Adam, he will also be the representative of the corporate son of God in the Old Testament, Israel.

As the king of Israel, the seed of David will be the representative Israelite and the new Adam. In his person he will stand for the people, as David did when he fought Israel's battle for her against Goliath (1 Sam 17).

Understanding the Davidic king as the representative Israelite and new-Adam son of God would make sense of what David says in Psalm 8.[27] He begins and ends by affirming that God achieved what he set out to accomplish in creating the world—making his name majestic in all the earth (Ps 8:1, 9). David then asserts that Yahweh has established his strength from the mouths of babies and infants, and that he has done this because of his foes, "to still the enemy and the avenger" (8:2, ESV). The reference to the singular "enemy" and "avenger" here seems to point to the archenemy behind all enemies, and the establishing of strength from babies would seem to point to the way that God promised that the seed of the woman would bruise the serpent's head (Gen 3:15) and then preserved the seed's line of descent though repeatedly mothers in the line were barren.

Psalm 8:3, with its references to creation, would add to the interaction between Psalm 8 and the early chapters of Genesis. This interaction seems to continue, subtly, in 8:4. I have noted above that the first man's name, Adam, also became a way of referring to humanity, so that when the Hebrew term (אָדָם) is encountered we rely on context to tell us whether we are reading of Adam or mankind. Something similar seems to have happened with Adam's son's son's name: Adam had Seth, and Seth had Enosh (אֱנוֹשׁ). We can see Enosh's name in the plural form of another Hebrew term: singular אִישׁ, man; plural אֲנָשִׁים, men. When we consider Psalm 8:4 in Hebrew, we see a subtle reference to Adam's genealogy:

Ps 8:5 in Hebrew: . . . מָה־אֱנוֹשׁ . . . וּבֶן־אָדָם

Ps 8:4 in English (ESV): "What is man . . . and the son of man . . ."

---

27. See further the discussion in Hamilton, *Psalms* ad loc. and James M. Hamilton Jr., "David's Biblical Theology and Typology in the Psalms: Authorial Intent and Patterns of the Seed of Promise," in *The Psalms: Exploring Theological Themes*, ed. David M. Howard and Andrew J. Schmutzer (Bellingham, WA: Lexham, forthcoming).

English translations cannot preserve the connection between these terms for "man" and the names of "Adam" and "Enosh." We can, however, present a rendering that transliterates the names rather than translating them as terms for "man" as follows:

Ps 8:4/5 (to preserve the names): "What is Enosh . . . the son of Adam . . ."

To draw out the import of what the names connote: the verse begins from the third generation, Enosh, then implicitly mentions Seth, "son of," before mentioning Adam. Heard in concert with the reference to the babies and infants of verse 2, these questions can be understood to allude to the line of descent from which the seed of the woman comes.[28]

The next verse speaks of how man was made a bit lower than heavenly beings and crowned with glory and honor (Ps 8:5), before the terms of Genesis 1:26 and 1:28 are trumpeted in Psalm 8:6–8. God gave man dominion over the animals in Genesis 1:26 and 1:28, the same dominion over the same animals named in Psalm 8:6–8.[29]

I would suggest that Psalm 8 attests to David's understanding of himself as a new Adam, king of Israel, vice-regent of Yahweh. Going forward, we see that the line of descent from Adam through Abraham, Judah, and David will culminate in *the* Son of God, the last Adam, the true Israel, the one who is the image of the invisible God.

§5 NEW-ADAM CHRIST

The first man, Adam, was granted dominion over the animals (Gen 1:28). That first man was further charged to work and keep the garden (2:15)—he

---

28. In his book *Eschatology in the Greek Psalter*, Joachim Schaper has argued that the Greek translation of the Psalms is messianic and eschatological. The approach to Psalm 8 proposed here understands the original Hebrew text of the Psalm to be messianic and eschatological, which could indicate that the connections Schaper argues the Greek translator made with Numbers 24:7, 17 were in keeping with the intentions of Moses and David. Cf. Joachim Schaper, *Eschatology in the Greek Psalter*, Wissenschaftliche Untersuchungen zum Neuen Testament 2/76 (Tübingen: J.C.B. Mohr [Paul Siebeck], 1995), 76–78.

29. Note the citation of Psalm 8:6 (MT 8:7) in reference to all things being put under Christ's feet in 1 Cor 15:27 and Hebrews 2:8. Jamieson observes, "Paul concludes that death is numbered among 'all things' subjected to the risen Christ, and that God, the one who subjected all things to Christ, is not himself subject to Christ (15.27)." R. B. Jamieson, "1 Corinthians 15.28 and the Grammar of Paul's Christology," *New Testament Studies* 66 (2020): 189.

was to protect it. An animal later Scripture designates as unclean, the serpent, infiltrated the garden, tempted the woman, and led the man into sin.

§5.1 The Son of Man in Daniel 7

In the apocalyptic symbolism of Daniel 7, the worldly kingdoms that successively exercise dominion in the land of promise are identified as beasts (Dan 7:1–8). This imagery links these kingdoms not with God but with the serpent. It is as though these idolatrous powers are identified with their father the devil. The kingdom of God, by contrast, comes when the last beast is killed, the others have their dominion taken away, and everlasting dominion is granted to "one like a son of man" (7:11–14).[30]

Daniel 7 was composed in Aramaic rather than Hebrew, and the expression for "son of man" therefore lacks explicit reference to Adam (but not to Enosh!). The Aramaic expression for "son of man" employs the term that appears to derive from Enosh, name of the son of Seth, son of Adam: כְּבַר אֱנָשׁ. The "one like a son of man" who comes with the clouds of heaven and is presented before the Ancient of Days in Daniel 7:13 receives everlasting dominion and a kingdom never to be destroyed in 7:14.[31] There is only one kingdom in the Old Testament that lasts forever—the one God promised to David in 2 Samuel 7. As Andrew Chester notes, "There are also clear affinities in the Hebrew Bible between Ps. 110.1 and Dan. 7.9–14 . . ."[32]

This one like a son of man, then, should be identified as the future king from the line of David. Some interpreters of Daniel 7 have questioned that conclusion because of what, on their reading, seems to be left out of the rest of the chapter. Daniel's vision is recounted in 7:1–14, and then in 7:15–28 he relates the interpretation of the vision provided by a member of the heavenly host (7:16; cf. 7:10).[33]

---

30. Cf. Beetham, "From Creation to New Creation," 240.

31. Commenting on the way that on the Day of Atonement the high priest "entered the holy of holies, the cultic counterpart to the heavenly throne room of God," where he put incense on the fire "that the cloud of the incense may cover the mercy seat that is over the testimony, so that he does not die" (Lev 16:12–13), Morales writes, "the high priest indeed entered 'heaven' with the clouds. This being the case, when during the exile the prophet Daniel envisions an Adam-like figure approaching God's throne with the clouds of heaven we are probably to understand this as a priestly image." Morales, *Who Shall Ascend the Mountain of the Lord?*, 172.

32. Andrew Chester, *Messiah and Exaltation: Jewish Messianic and Visionary Traditions and New Testament Christology*, Wissenschaftliche Untersuchungen zum Neuen Testament 207 (Tübingen: Mohr Siebeck, 2007), 37.

33. On the date and authorship of Daniel, see Hamilton, *With the Clouds of Heaven*, 30–40.

Whereas in the vision, the "one like a son of man" receives the kingdom in Daniel 7:13–14, in the interpretation of the vision the phrase "one like a son of man" does not recur and "the saints of the Most High" receive the kingdom (7:18, 22, 25, 27). This has led to a "collective interpretation of 7:13," as Ernest Lucas explains,

> The collective interpretation was very much a minority one until the nineteenth century. By the mid-twentieth century it had become the common view. Basic to it is the equation of the 'one like a son of man' with 'the holy ones of the Most High' (18, 22, 25) and 'the people of the holy ones of the Most High' (27), both of which are assumed to be the Jewish people.[34]

The collective interpretation, however, has not accounted for the use of two different terms that mean "Most High" in Daniel 7.[35] Throughout the Aramaic section of Daniel (Dan 2:4–7:28), the normal Aramaic term for "Most High" (עֶלְיָא) is used with reference to Israel's God (3:26, 32; 4:17, 24, 25, 32, 34 [MT 4:14, 21, 22, 29, 31]; 5:18, 21; 7:25), the Ancient of Days who takes his seat in 7:9. Every time the phrase "saints of the Most High" appears, however, another term for "Most High" is used (7:18, 22, 25, 27): the Hebrew plural עֶלְיוֹן, made doubly plural (so BDB and HALOT) by the addition of the Aramaic plural ending, resulting in the form עֶלְיוֹנִין (cf. BDB ad loc., 1106). The NASB recognizes the two different terms and renders the Aramaic term (עֶלְיָא) "Most High" and the Aramaicized Hebrew term (עֶלְיוֹנִין) "the Highest One."

These two terms for "Most High" occur together in the same verse in Daniel 7:25, "And words against the Most High (עֶלְיָא) he shall speak, and the saints of the Most High (עֶלְיוֹנִין) he shall wear out . . ." Why would Daniel distinguish between the Ancient of Days, to whom he refers with the Aramaic

---

34. Ernest C. Lucas, *Daniel*, Apollos Old Testament Commentary 20 (Downers Grove, IL: InterVarsity, 2002), 186.

35. Commentators do not typically attempt to explain the two different terms for "Most High" in Daniel 7. See John J. Collins, *Daniel: A Commentary on the Book of Daniel*, Hermeneia (Minneapolis: Fortress, 1993); Lucas, *Daniel*; and Andrew E. Steinmann, *Daniel*, Concordia Commentary (Saint Louis: Concordia, 2008). For interpretations similar to the one offered here, see Chrys Caragounis, *The Son of Man: Vision and Interpretation*, Wissenschaftliche Untersuchungen zum Neuen Testament 38 (Tübingen: Mohr Siebeck, 1986), 66–67, 75–81; Peter J. Gentry, "The Son of Man in Daniel 7: Individual or Corporate?," in *Acorns to Oaks: The Primacy and Practice of Biblical Theology*, ed. Michael A. G. Haykin (Toronto: Joshua Press, 2003), 59–75; and Hamilton, *With the Clouds of Heaven*, 147–53.

term, and this other figure with whom the saints are identified, to whom he refers with the Aramaicized Hebrew term?

We can make progress toward answering this question by comparing Daniel 7:14 and 7:27 (the **bold font**, *italics*, SMALL CAPS, and ALL CAPS denote matching phrases):

7:14	7:27
And to him *will be given* **dominion** and honor and a **kingdom**, and all the peoples, tribes and tongues to him WILL PAY REVERENCE.	And the **kingdom** and the **dominion** and the greatness of the kingdoms under all the heavens *will be given* to the people of the saints of the Most High (עֶלְיוֹנִין).
His dominion is a dominion OF THE AGE, which will not pass away, and **his kingdom** one that will not be destroyed.	**His kingdom** is a kingdom OF THE AGE, and all the dominions to him WILL PAY REVERENCE and be obedient.

Daniel 7:27 makes the same statements about the kingdom that will be received by "the saints of the Most High" that were made about the kingdom of the one like a son of man in 7:13–14. This suggests that Daniel refers to the *one like a son of man* as the Most High with the Aramaicized Hebrew term עֶלְיוֹנִין, to distinguish him from the Ancient of Days, to whom he refers as Most High with the Aramaic term עֶלְיָא. On this understanding, the "saints" would be understood as the citizens of the kingdom over which the Most High (עֶלְיוֹנִין) Son of Man will reign. It is worth pointing out here, too, that Daniel presents the angelic interpreter (7:16) as introducing this phrase in 7:18, then Daniel himself repeats it in 7:22, before again the angelic interpreter employs it in 7:25 and 7:27. It would seem that the angelic interpreter begins to refer to the one like a son of man as "Most High" (עֶלְיוֹנִין), and from him Daniel learned to do likewise.

To summarize Daniel's vision: he sees the kingdoms of the world as beastly, like their father the devil, overthrown, and then dominion is granted to one like a son of man, who is already present in the heavenly court at the time of Daniel's vision. This figure, moreover, travels on the clouds, as God does elsewhere in the Old Testament, and then like God this figure is referred to as Most High, but with an Aramaicized form of the Hebrew term rather than the Aramaic term that has been used to refer to the Ancient of Days. It is as though the one like a son of man is granted equal status with the Ancient of Days, even as he is distinguished from him, with both being referred to by different terms that mean "Most High."

The son of man in Daniel is the son of Enosh, son of Adam, image and likeness of God, who will exercise Adamic dominion as the Davidic king over all the earth, including the beasts and their kingdoms.[36]

§5.2 The Son of Adam in Luke and Romans

For the purposes of this discussion I want to draw attention to two passages in the New Testament that seem to compare and contrast Adam and Jesus, presenting Jesus as the one who succeeded where Adam failed.[37] We will look first at Luke's account of Jesus being tempted by Satan, then at Paul's comparison and contrast of Adam and Jesus in Romans 5. Paul and Luke traveled and ministered together to make disciples and plant churches (Col 4:14; 2 Tim 4:11; Phlm. 24; and the "we" passages in Acts), and these passages reveal their fundamental agreement on the typological relationship between Adam and Christ.[38]

§5.2.1 Son of Adam, Son of God

Whereas Matthew's genealogy works down from Abraham to Jesus, Luke's genealogy works back from Jesus to Adam. The last verse of Luke 3 reads, "the son of Enos, the son of Seth, the son of Adam, the son of God" (Luke 3:38, ESV), and then Luke 4 goes immediately into the temptation narrative, in which the devil repeatedly says to Jesus, "If you are the Son of God" (4:3, 9, ESV).

Luke juxtaposes the genealogy that concludes, "Adam, son of God" (Luke 3:38), with the temptation narrative in which the devil challenges Jesus with the words, "If you are the son of God" (Luke 4:3, 9). By setting the

---

36. Several "son of man" statements in the New Testament present Jesus as the fulfillment of the figure from Daniel 7:13–14 (see, e.g., Matt 26:64; Mark 10:45; John 3:13–14).

37. For discussion of both where Adam is directly named in the New Testament (Luke 3:38; Rom 5:14; 1 Cor 15:22, 45; 1 Tim 2:13–14; Jude 14) and where he is implied, see Robert W. Yarbrough, "Adam in the New Testament," in *Adam, the Fall, and Original Sin: Theological, Biblical, and Scientific Perspectives*, ed. Hans Madueme and Michael Reeves (Grand Rapids: Baker, 2014), 33–52.

38. Kavin Rowe writes, "in light of this reading of Luke's Christology, it becomes possible to situate Luke in closer proximity to Paul and John than is usual in modern NT scholarship." C. Kavin Rowe, *Early Narrative Christology: The Lord in the Gospel of Luke* (Grand Rapids: Baker, 2009), 28.

genealogy next to the temptation, Luke invites readers to compare and contrast Jesus and Adam.[39]

- Adam was in the lush garden of Eden. Jesus was in the wilderness.
- Adam was not alone but with his suitable help-meet. Jesus was alone.
- In the garden, Adam had been granted the right to eat freely from all trees save one (Gen 2:16). Jesus had eaten nothing for forty days.
- Adam was tempted and sinned. The devil challenged Jesus, and Jesus answered him with Scripture, remaining faithful to God's commandments.

Earle Ellis notes regarding Satan's offer to give Jesus the kingdoms of the world: "To accept the offer would not be to displace Satan's lordship but, like Adam, to fall into bondage to it."[40]

§5.2.2 A Type of the One to Come

In Romans 5 Paul asserts that Adam was "a type of the one to come" (5:14). He compares the way sin came into the world, spreading death to all men, through the one man, Adam (5:12), with the way that the free gift of righteousness came through the obedience of the one man, Jesus Christ (5:15). Whereas many died because of Adam's sin, many experienced abounding grace because of Jesus. The trespass of Adam resulted in condemnation and judgment for many, but after all the many sins that had been committed, the free gift of Jesus brings justification (5:16). Adam's sin made it so death reigned (5:17a, 14). The obedience of Jesus, however, made it so that those who receive abounding grace and the free gift of righteousness reign in life through him (5:17b). Through Adam came condemnation and death. Through Jesus comes justification and life (5:18), extending to the making righteous of those justified (5:19).[41]

In this instance Adam and Jesus function as representative heads of humanity. All people are affected by what Adam did (5:12), and in the same way what Christ did affects all who receive the abundant grace and the free gift of righteousness (5:17). Salvation hinges on the connection: because of the

---

39. E. Earle Ellis, *The Gospel of Luke*, New Century Bible Commentary (Grand Rapids: Eerdmans, 1981), 93–94.

40. Ibid., 95.

41. See the interpretation in Thomas R. Schreiner, "Original Sin and Original Death: Romans 5:12–19," in *Adam, the Fall, and Original Sin*, 271–88.

typological fulfillment of Adam's role in Christ, those who receive grace and the gift of righteousness can be saved from the condemnation that results from what Adam did.

Paul puts this relationship more succinctly in 1 Corinthians 15:21–22, "For as by a man came death, by a man has come also the resurrection of the dead. For as in Adam all die, so also in Christ shall all be made alive" (ESV). In 1 Corinthians 15:45 Paul even compares the moment when God made Adam alive in Genesis 2:7 to the way that Christ gives life: "Thus it is written, 'The first man Adam became a living being'; the last Adam became a life-giving spirit" (ESV).

The goal of this chapter has been to show that the biblical authors who followed him grasped what Moses intended from the beginning. In Genesis Moses forges connections between Adam, the prototypical man, and the ectypal installments in the Adamic pattern who come after him: Noah, Abraham, Isaac, Jacob, and then in Exodus, the nation of Israel. This Mosaic presentation of Adam influenced later biblical authors, as can be seen from the promise to David in Samuel, David's words in Psalm 8, and the Daniel 7 one like a son of man. Jean Daniélou has it right:

> It is particularly noticeable that the Son of Man of Daniel is represented as triumphant over the animals, which represent the idolatrous nations. This would certainly recall the first Adam and his dominion over the animal world. Psalm 8 is apparently the link between Genesis and Daniel, showing as it does, a son of man who should reign over creation and particularly the animal world.[42]

Luke and Paul, then, have learned from Moses himself, from later Old Testament authors, and from "those who heard" Jesus (Heb 2:3) how to interpret Moses, and their Spirit-inspired presentation of Jesus as the new and better Adam fits with broader claims that Christ is the fulfillment of everything written of him in the Law, the Prophets, and the Writings (e.g., Luke 24:44; John 5:39, 46; 2 Cor 1:20; Eph 1:10).

---

42. Daniélou, *From Shadows to Reality*, 15.

PRIESTS

One of the happier results of twentieth-century scholarship has been the rediscovery of the importance of typology for the understanding of the Bible.

—S. L. JOHNSON[1]

For this discussion of priests, we begin with the priestly character of Adam's role in the garden and what it implies about the priestly character of humanity. From there we will consider Melchizedek and the ways that he corresponds to Adam, before turning our attention to the way God made Israel a kingdom of priests. Next comes examination of the Old Testament critique of the Aaronic priesthood, along with key promises the Lord makes about how he will provide a priest for his people, before concluding the chapter by looking at patterns shaped by those promises. This discussion is mainly concerned with promise-shaped patterns regarding priests when they are considered as *persons*; the *institution* of the Leviticult will be considered in Chapter 9 below. The outline of this chapter falls out like this:

§1 Adam the (King) Priest
§2 Melchizedek the (King) Priest
§3 Israel the (King) Priest Nation
§4 Aaron and the Priests
§5 Promises of a Faithful Priest

---

1. Johnson, "A Response to Patrick Fairbairn," 794.

Hebrews 7 argues that Christ is a priest according to the order of Melchizedek. Melchizedek typified the way that Jesus would fulfill his role as priest-king. Melchizedek's priesthood preceded the old covenant and the giving of the law at Sinai, and the author of Hebrews understands Psalm 110:4 to indicate that God's people will likewise have a non-Levitical priest whose ministry comes with a new covenant in distinction to the old (see Heb 7–8, esp. 7:12). This chapter will look at other Old Testament evidence that points in the same direction, from the indications that the Aaronic priesthood would fail in the Torah, to the declaration in the Former Prophets that the Aaronic house would be removed, to prophecies in the Latter Prophets that point to a new kind of priesthood, one not authorized by the Mosaic law and the Sinai covenant.

In conjunction with the promise-prompted expectation of a faithful priest, those who served as priests became installments in typological patterns. Because several of these figures also had royal roles, in the subtitles below I reference their kingly status in parentheses. The ways kings typified the one to come will be discussed in Chapter 5.

§1 ADAM THE (KING) PRIEST

When we consider creation in Chapter 7 we will outline the evidence for the view, which I hold, that Moses intends his audience to forge mental connections between the creation in Genesis 1–2 and the tabernacle in Exodus 25–40.[2] I mention this here because if the creation is intended to be understood as a cosmic temple, that fact supports the notion that Adam is a prototypical priest. Referring readers to that later discussion, I will proceed in this chapter under the assumption that creation is understood as a cosmic temple with the garden of Eden analogous to the holy of holies. This will have obvious implications for Adam: if the garden corresponds to the later holy of holies, and if only the high priest of Israel can enter the holy of holies, what does this imply about the status of the one charged to work and keep the garden?

---

2. See also R. E. Averbeck, "Tabernacle," in *Dictionary of the Old Testament: Pentateuch*, 816–18.

§1.1 Prior to Sin

The idea that God created the world as a cosmic temple also informs the very concept of humanity being made in the image and likeness of God (Gen 1:26–28). Whereas worshipers of other gods built temples that were meant to symbolize the cosmos, into which they put a statue of rock or wood or molten metal meant to represent the presence, character, and authority of their god, the Bible tells the true story. Yahweh built *creation* as a cosmic temple, and into that cosmic temple he placed a living, breathing, worshiping representation of himself and his own authority, character, presence, and rule.

For us to conceptualize Adam as the high priest in the garden holy of holies in the cosmic temple is for us to understand his role. God blessed the first man and woman and commanded them to be fruitful and multiply and fill the earth, subduing it by working and keeping it, exercising dominion over all creation in accordance with Yahweh's own character (Gen 1:26–28; 2:15).

To be fruitful and multiply and fill and reign (Gen 1:28) means that in all places those who bear the image and likeness of God are to increase life and thereby make God's image present. To subdue seems to suggest that they are to make things better for all living things, and with the multiplication of people, this means expanding the borders of the inhabited land, making what is outside the garden more like the garden, with the creation subdued to man's needs and the animals subjected to his reign. Adam's responsibility is to mediate the knowledge of the creator God to all creation, and to bring the creator's character to bear in and on all creation. As he is fruitful and multiplies, there will be more image-bearers, who as they join in the tasks of filling and subduing and exercising dominion, will cover the dry lands with the glory of Yahweh as the waters cover the seas, so that from the rising of the sun to the place of its setting the name of Yahweh will be praised.

God puts Adam in the garden "to work it and keep it" (Gen 2:15). The connotations of these two terms deserve comment since they are translated different ways in different passages. The term rendered "work" (עָבַד) can also be translated "serve" or "minister," and the term rendered "keep" (שָׁמַר) is sometimes translated "guard." Elsewhere in the Pentateuch these terms are used together to describe the duties of the Levites at the tabernacle (Num 3:8), reflecting the way the cosmos as the dwelling place of God, with the garden as the holy of holies, has its appointed "guard" and "minister," just as the later tabernacle has the Levites and the priests from that tribe (Num 1:53; 3:38).[3]

Gen 2:15, "The Lord God took the man and put him in the garden of Eden to *work* it and *keep* it." (ESV, italics added)

Num 3:8, "They shall *guard [keep]* all the furnishings of the tent of meeting, and keep guard over the people of Israel as they *minister [work]* at the tabernacle." (ESV, italics added)

Adam's priestly role, then, is to fill the world with image-bearers of Yahweh, those who will live out Yahweh's character in Yahweh's world. He is to work, serve, and minister, interceding between the creator and his creation, so that all creation knows the reigning hand of the maker. Adam's responsibilities—and those of his offspring—carry a strong priestly component. We will consider Adam as king (having "dominion," Gen 1:26, 28) below, but here we observe that man was made to be a *priest*-king, reigning over God's world, interceding between the world and God, making the creator known throughout the creation.

From the way Genesis assumes instructions that will only be given later,[4] it seems that Moses intended the whole Pentateuch to be read together, which would mean that in early narratives he assumes information that will only be supplied later. The entrance of an unclean serpent into the garden holy of holies suggests that the man has failed to *keep* the garden (Gen 3:1, cf. 2:15). Adam failing in his priestly task by not keeping the garden against the intrusion of the unclean serpent in turn explains why even though the woman ate first, God called the man to account for his failure and sin (Gen 3:9; Rom 5:12).

---

3. Gordon J. Wenham, "Sanctuary Symbolism in the Garden of Eden Story," in *I Studied Inscriptions from Before the Flood: Ancient Near Eastern, Literary, and Linguistic Approaches to Genesis 1–11*, ed. Richard Hess and David Toshio Tsumara (Winona Lake, IN: Eisenbrauns, 1994), 399–404.

4. For instance, the command not to intermarry with the peoples of the land (Deut 7:3–5) informs Ishmael's marriage to an Egyptian (Gen 21:21), Abraham's insistence that Isaac not marry a Canaanite (24:3), Esau's marriages that trouble his parents (26:34–35; 28:6–9), and the desire for Jacob not to marry a Hittite (27:46). Similarly, the instruction in Leviticus 18:7–8 informs Reuben sinning with his father's concubine in Genesis 35:22, and the instructions for Levirate marriage in Deuteronomy 25:5–10 are assumed in the story of Judah's sons and Tamar in Genesis 38:6–14. For other examples, see footnote 26 on page 18 above.

§1.2 After Sin

After the man and woman sin (Gen 3:1–7), are called to account (3:8–13), and have heard words of judgment and promise (3:14–19), the man names his wife as an act of faith. Though he deserves to die, he believes that God will give life (3:20). In Genesis 3:21 (ESV), "the LORD God made for Adam and for his wife garments (כְּתֹנֶת) of skins and clothed (לָבַשׁ) them."

I have taught this passage many times in classes and in churches, and people regularly ask about whether the skins were acquired from animals slain as sacrifices. As far as I can tell, the text does not overtly indicate that was the case. What I mean is that I do not see direct connections between Genesis 3:21 and later texts from the same author (Moses) that deal with sacrifice.[5] Were we to find such connections, we could be confident that Moses meant for us to connect the skins with which Yahweh clothed Adam and Eve to the sacrificial deaths of animals described later in Leviticus. While I do not know of overt *sacrificial* connections, however, there are suggestive *priestly* connections.

God *clothed* the man and woman with *garments* of *skin*. While in some cases the skin (עוֹר) of the sacrificial animal was to be consumed by fire (Lev 4:11–12; 8:17), Leviticus 7:8 states, "And the priest who offers any man's burnt offering shall have for himself the skin of the burnt offering that he has offered." The terms in Genesis 3:21 rendered "garments" (כְּתֹנֶת) and "clothed" (לָבַשׁ) are predominantly used in the rest of the Pentateuch for the "garments" worn by the priests and the way they were "clothed" when they took up their duties.[6] In the Pentateuch, the term rendered "garments" (כְּתֹנֶת) is used only in the following instances: for those provided by the Lord for the man and woman in Genesis 3:21; for the special coat Joseph's father made for him (Gen 37:3, 23, 31, 32, 33); and for the priests' clothing (Exod 28:4, 39, 40; 29:5, 8; 39:27; 40:14; Lev 8:7, 13; 10:5; 16:4). The usage of this term in the Pentateuch forges important connections between Adam (and Joseph) and the priests. Similarly, while not used exclusively of priests being clothed, the verb rendered "clothed" in Genesis 3:21 (לָבַשׁ) is overwhelmingly used with reference to the clothing of

---

5. Here again, if Moses intends the Pentateuch to be read as a whole, thinking of the sacrifices in Leviticus provides a logical connection between the skins and the presumably slain animal from which they were taken.

6. My attention was first drawn to this by Mathews, *Genesis 1–11:26*, 254–55.

priests (Exod 28:41; 29:5, 8, 30; 40:13, 14; Lev 6:10, 11 [MT 6:3, 4]; 8:7, 13; 16:4, 23, 24, 32; 21:10; Num 20:26, 28).[7]

Adam is not overtly called a priest, but (1) there are strong connections between the cosmos and the temple, the garden and the holy of holies, suggesting that in the garden he is like the high priest in the holy of holies; (2) his role is to mediate the knowledge and presence of God to God's creation; (3) his "job description" of working and keeping the garden (Gen 2:15) employs the same terms used to speak of the Levites working and keeping (guarding and ministering at) the tabernacle (Num 3:8); and (4) the terms used to describe his garments and his being clothed with them are the same used with reference to the priests. These features indicate that Adam is a prototypical (king) priest.

§2 MELCHIZEDEK THE (KING) PRIEST

The accounts of Noah and Abraham have priestly features (e.g., Noah distinguishes between clean and unclean animals, and both he and Abram build altars where they worship), but the first figure to be called a "priest" in the narrative is Melchizedek (Gen 14:18). The author of Hebrews finds the name significant. A compound word formed from Hebrew terms for "king" (מֶלֶךְ) and "righteousness" (צֶדֶק), Melchizedek's name (מַלְכִּי־צֶדֶק) means "king of righteousness" (Gen 14:18; Heb 7:2). He is further designated as "king of Salem" (Gen 14:18), and "Salem" is identified with Jerusalem. Hebrews points out that because of the connection between "Salem" (שָׁלֵם) and "peace" (שָׁלוֹם), Melchizedek is not only "king of righteousness" but also "king of peace" (Heb 7:2; cf. 2 Sam 12:24; Isa 9:6 [MT 9:5]).

Moses did not overtly identify Adam, Noah, or Abram as priest-kings, but he includes a king-priest, Melchizedek, in his narrative, and he will later announce to Israel that they are to be to Yahweh a "kingdom of priests" (מַמְלֶכֶת כֹּהֲנִים, Exod 19:6). David came to reign in Jerusalem long after the time of Moses, so while Moses may not have expected that point of contact between Melchizedek and Israel's future king, from what we see in his writings, we can say that Moses would have affirmed: (1) that Israel would have a king from Abraham's line (Gen 17:6, 16); (2) that God had promised the land of

---

7. This verb "clothed" is also used in Genesis with reference to Jacob (Gen 27:15, 16; 28:20), Tamar (38:19), and Joseph, and it appears in Deuteronomy to forbid both cross dressing (Deut 22:5) and the mixing of wool and linen (22:11).

Canaan to Abraham (12:7); and (3) that as a king-priest Melchizedek embodied roles given to Adam (see §2.1 above) that would be fulfilled in Israel's
future king, the one who represented the "kingdom of priests" (Exod 19:6),
the "son of God" (Exod 4:22–23) that was national Israel (cf. 2 Sam 7:14, and
see the discussion of Kings in Chapter 5 below). The fact that Melchizedek
reigned in Salem likely influenced David as he composed Psalm 110. The key
takeaways from this paragraph are that Adam was a prototypical priest-king,
Melchizedek was an ectype of one who embodied those roles, and then the
nation of Israel becomes a kingdom of priests.

Abram defeats the kings who abducted Lot, taking captivity captive (see
further Chapter 5 §1.2 below), and then in Genesis 14:18 Melchizedek brings
out bread and wine. This sequence of events matches the way that Yahweh's
defeat of the gods of Egypt (Exod 12:12) comes on the night of the Passover
Feast, which includes unleavened bread (12:8) and probably also wine.[8] That
Passover Feast is to be celebrated yearly to commemorate what Yahweh did
for his people (12:1–27) and is fulfilled in the Lord's Supper, instituted on
the night Jesus was betrayed.[9] We seem to have a pattern, then, of the heroic
defeat of enemies whereby captives are liberated, followed by a priestly celebration of victory with bread and wine. Moses may have included the detail
that Melchizedek brought out bread and wine in Genesis 14:18 because he saw
a parallel with the eating and drinking of not only the Passover but also the
covenant meal in Exodus 24:11.

Melchizedek is identified as "priest of God Most High" in Genesis 14:18,
then when he blesses Abram in 14:19 Melchizedek speaks of "God Most High,
Possessor of heaven and earth." Just a few verses later, when Abram refers to
"God Most High, Possessor of heaven and earth" in 14:22, the reader sees
that Abram has identified God with the same terms Melchizedek used, indicating that Abram and Melchizedek worship the same God. This naturally
invites reflection on the fact that whereas Yahweh enters into covenant with
Abram (Gen 15, 17), we are told nothing about the covenant under which

8. Wine is not specifically included in the instructions for the Passover, but reading Deut 14:24–26
with 16:1–8 may indicate that it was assumed. By the time Jesus celebrates the Passover with his disciples,
a cup of wine seems to have become firmly ensconced in the celebration of the feast (Matt 26:27–29; Mark
14:23–25; Luke 22:20; 1 Cor 11:25–26).

9. For a typological understanding of Paul's treatment of the fulfillment of Passover in Christ, see
James M. Hamilton Jr., "The Lord's Supper in Paul: An Identity-Forming Proclamation of the Gospel,"
in *The Lord's Supper: Remembering and Proclaiming Christ Until He Comes*, ed. Thomas R. Schreiner and
Matthew R. Crawford (Nashville: Broadman & Holman, 2010), 68–102.

Melchizedek serves as priest. The only covenant overtly mentioned to this point in Genesis has been the Noahic (see 6:18; 9:8–17). Perhaps speculation on the Noahic covenant and Melchizedek's priesthood contributed to attempts to identify Melchizedek with Shem, son of Noah,[10] but the text of Genesis does not specify either that Melchizedek is Shem or that Melchizedek serves under the Noahic covenant. The Aaronic priesthood will later be established as part of the covenant Yahweh makes with Israel at Sinai (cf. Exod 4:14–16; 28:1, etc.).

Drawing attention to the way that Genesis often provides both the genealogical descent of its main characters and a notice when they die, the author of Hebrews picks up on the fact that Moses does not include such information for Melchizedek, which makes him like the son of God, "without father or mother or genealogy, having neither beginning of days nor end of life" (Heb 7:3, ESV). Hebrews also highlights the fact that Abraham gave a tithe to Melchizedek (Gen 14:20; Heb 7:4–10) and was blessed by him (Gen 14:19; Heb 7:6).

By including Melchizedek in his narrative, Moses presents in Genesis a figure like Adam: a reigning king who also mediates between people and God as a priest. After Melchizedek, we next encounter a royal priest when the nation of Israel, having been designated the "son of God," is told that God's purpose for them is to be a kingdom of priests.

§3 ISRAEL THE (KING) PRIEST NATION

What is the rationale for the Lord's assertion, "And you shall be to me a kingdom of priests and a holy nation," in Exodus 19:6? In §3 of Chapter 2 above we saw that Adam was the son of God who was to be fruitful and multiply, which means he was a prototype of the nation of Israel, the son of God (Exod 4:22–23) who was fruitful and multiplied greatly (1:7). If the nation of Israel was a new Adam, and if Adam was a king-priest, it follows that the nation would be a kingdom of priests. If Adam's role was to mediate the knowledge of God to all creation, Israel's role was to mediate the knowledge of God to all nations.

The nation of Israel was to accomplish as a priest what Adam failed to do: fill the earth, subdue it, and reign over it for Yahweh's glory. Like Adam,

---

10. Scott W. Hahn notes that "in ancient Jewish and Christian traditions" Shem "is typically identified as Melchizedek," and Hahn contends this is correct. Scott W. Hahn, *Kinship by Covenant: A Canonical Approach to the Fulfillment of God's Saving Promises* (New Haven: Yale University Press, 2009), 97–100, 390–92. The identification, however, lacks explicit exegetical warrant in either the narrative of Genesis or the Epistle to the Hebrews.

who was placed in the garden, Israel was placed in the holy land, and just as Adam was to expand the borders of the garden (subduing the land, Gen 1:28) so that God's dwelling place might encompass all the land, so Israel was to expand her borders, that the nations might be her inheritance, the ends of the earth her possession (cf. Ps 2:8). As Adam transgressed the stipulations of the covenant and was driven from the garden, so Israel broke the Sinai covenant and was exiled from the land. In their history, the nation of Israel repeats the pattern of Adam's failure as a priest.

The Lord's worldwide intention for the priestly role of the nation of Israel seems to be reflected in Isaiah 49:6 (ESV), "It is too light a thing that you should be my servant to raise up the tribes of Jacob and to bring back the preserved of Israel; I will make you as a light for the nations, that my salvation may reach to the ends of the earth." The Lord means to save not merely the remnant from Israel but all nations, and the salvation will come from the work of his servant. Adam was the first of the Lord's servants given this task, then Israel took it up, and once they failed, Jesus accomplished it. As he proclaims what Jesus accomplished, the apostle Paul quotes Isaiah 49:6 with reference to his own mediatorial, priestly ministry of the gospel to the gentiles in Acts 13:47. Paul's quotation of Isaiah 49:6, with its priestly overtones, fits perfectly with the way that he speaks of his ministry to the gentiles in priestly terms in the book of Romans (Rom 1:9; 15:16).

> Romans 1:9, "... whom I serve [λατρεύω] with my spirit in the gospel of his Son" (ESV)

> Romans 15:16, "to be a minister [λειτουργὸν] of Christ Jesus to the Gentiles in the priestly service of the gospel of God [ἱερουργοῦντα τὸ εὐαγγέλιον], so that the offering [προσφορὰ] of the Gentiles may be acceptable [εὐπρόσδεκτος], sanctified by the Holy Spirit" (ESV).

Christ's fulfillment of the priestly mediatorial role not only enables Paul to follow him in serving the Lord that way, mediating the knowledge of God to the world, it constitutes his people as a kingdom of priests (1 Pet 2:9; Rev 1:5–6; 5:10). Adam was put in the garden as a royal priest and failed. Israel was put in the land as a royal priest and failed. Christ came as a royal priest and succeeded, then commissioned Paul his apostle to be a light to the nations, that the church might be a royal priesthood making disciples of Jesus, the royal priest.

§4 AARON AND THE PRIESTS

In addition to the wide-angle priesthood trajectory that runs from Adam through Melchizedek to Israel to Christ to the church, we also find ways that the law of Moses indicates the Aaronic priesthood will fail. These indications are developed through the Former and Latter Prophets, and the direction in which they point is crystallized in the Writings, specifically in Psalm 110, which points forward to a new priesthood, based on what Melchizedek typified, not associated with the Sinai covenant. Still, the Aaronic priesthood typifies the priesthood Christ would fulfill in role, responsibility, and action.

According to the presentation in the Pentateuch, Israel had no king when Aaron and his sons were made priests, and nothing in the Pentateuch indicates that the priests were to function as kings. Moses is never called a king, but he functions as later kings will: interacting with the king of Egypt (e.g., Exod 7:1; 9:1, 13; 10:28–29) and judging the people of Israel (18:13; cf. 1 Kgs 3:16–28). Together, Moses and Aaron almost form a king-priest tandem.

In the instructions that come with the Sinai covenant in the Pentateuch, the only *persons* to be anointed are the priests (Exod 28:41; 29:7; 30:30; 40:13, 15; Lev 8:30, etc.; the tabernacle itself and implements of worship are also to be anointed). Since the law never gives instruction for the anointing of kings, when the Lord instructs Samuel to do just that—anoint Saul as king (1 Sam 9:16; cf. Judg 9:8)—the anointing naturally associates the kingship with the priesthood. Similar things could be said about the instruction God later gave to Elijah to anoint Jehu as king and Elisha as a prophet (1 Kgs 19:16).

The installation of Aaron and his sons as priests comes with the giving of the law and the making of the covenant at Sinai. That body of revelation carries not only indications that the Sinai covenant will be broken (e.g., Lev 26:15; Deut 31:20) but also that Yahweh will show mercy to his people on the basis of the covenant he made with Abraham (e.g., Lev 26:42; Deut 4:31; 7:8; 10:15; 30:5). Before the nation ever set out from Sinai, both Aaron (Exod 32) and his sons (Lev 10) had failed in devastating, covenant-breaking ways (Exod 32:19; Lev 10:2). Within the Pentateuch, then, there are indications that both the Sinai covenant and the priesthood associated with it will fail.

As we continue through the Old Testament, we find promises in both Former and Latter Prophets that the Lord will replace the Aaronic priesthood with one that will be faithful and effective.

§5 PROMISES OF A FAITHFUL PRIEST

David Steinmetz has compared reading the Old Testament to the reading of a mystery novel.[11] Authors who master this craft provide their readers with all necessary information, but they do so in a way that makes it very difficult to solve the crime as the story is being read.[12] Once a reader has finished the story and experienced the reveal, however, on re-readings, it is as though the author has hidden all the clues in plain sight.

The author of the mystery novel knows where the story is going. The Old Testament authors, likewise, seem to have known to a certain degree where the story was going. They did not know the person or time (1 Pet 1:11), and certain things were not made known to them (Eph 3:5), but the rest of this chapter chases clues hidden in plain sight about the promise of a faithful priest. We begin with 1 Samuel 2.

§5.1 The Faithful Priest in 1 Samuel 2:35

Eli the priest's sons Hophni and Phinehas were "sons of Belial" (בְּנֵי בְלִיָּעַל, 1 Sam 2:12), and because of their grievous sin (2:13–17, 22–23), "it was the will of the LORD to put them to death" (2:25, ESV). Accordingly, a man of God came to Eli with the prophecy that his two sons would die on the same day (2:34), and the narrative relates how this came to pass (4:11).

The man of God's denunciation, however, goes beyond merely the house of Eli. His opening words recall the time when Aaron was made priest at the time of the exodus:

Thus says the LORD, "Did I indeed reveal myself to the house of your father when they were in Egypt subject to the house of Pharaoh? Did I choose him

---

11. David C. Steinmetz, "Uncovering a Second Narrative: Detective Fiction and the Construction of a Historical Method," in *The Art of Reading Scripture*, ed. Ellen F. Davis and Richard B. Hays (Grand Rapids: Eerdmans, 2003), 54–65.

12. For instance, the famous "Detection Club," consisting of Agatha Christie, Dorothy Sayers, G. K. Chesterton, and others, had agreed upon rules designed to keep them from cheating their readers.

out of all the tribes of Israel to be my priest, to go up to my altar, to burn
incense, to wear an ephod before me? I gave to the house of your father all
my offerings by fire from the people of Israel." (1 Sam 2:27–28, ESV)

In these statements to Eli, the references to "the house of your father"
cannot be exhausted by reference to one of Aaron's sons. Aaron was the head
of the household chosen to serve as priests (1 Sam 2:28; Exod 28:1) "when
they were in Egypt subject to the house of Pharaoh" (1 Sam 2:27). Aaron
had four sons, but Nadab and Abihu died, leaving only Eleazar and Ithamar
(Exod 6:23; Lev 10; 1 Chr 24:2). The line of Eli, the priest being addressed in
1 Samuel 2:27–35, descends from Ithamar (1 Sam 14:3; 22:20; 23:6; 1 Chr 24:3),
whereas that of Zadok descends from Eleazar (1 Chr 6:1–15, 50–53; 24:3).

The reference in 1 Samuel 2:27 to God revealing himself to the house
of Eli's father "when they were in Egypt subject to the house of Pharaoh"
demands that the "house of your father" mean more than merely Ithamar,
son of Aaron, as opposed to Eleazar, son of Aaron, for Aaron is the priestly
figure active in Egypt prior to the exodus. It was not merely Eli's ancestor
Ithamar, son of Aaron, who was chosen to serve as priest (1 Sam 2:28). Rather,
Aaron and his sons were chosen.

Having addressed both the sins of Eli's sons and Eli's failure to discipline
them in 1 Samuel 2:29 (though Eli spoke reprovingly in 1 Sam 2:23–25), the
man of God announces not only the end of Eli's line but also that *the house of
his father will be cut off*:

Therefore the LORD, the God of Israel declares: "I promised that your house
and the house of your father should go in and out before me forever,"[13] but
now the LORD declares: "Far be it from me, for those who honor me I will
honor, and those who despise me shall be lightly esteemed. Behold, the
days are coming when I will cut off your strength and the strength of your
father's house, so that there will not be an old man in your house. . . ."
(2:30–31 ESV)

---

13. This statement points back to promises made in passages such as Exod 27:21, where "Aaron and
his sons shall tend [the tent of meeting] from evening to morning before the LORD. It shall be a statute
forever to be observed throughout their generations by the people of Israel" (ESV). See also Exod 29:9,
"you shall gird Aaron and his sons with sashes and bind caps on them. And the priesthood shall be theirs
by a statute forever. Thus you shall ordain Aaron and his sons" (ESV).

The cutting off of Eli's strength is detailed in 1 Samuel 2:32–34, where Eli is told that his two sons will die (2:34), that there will not be an old man in his house (2:32), and that his only surviving descendant will weep over the death by sword of the rest of Eli's house (2:33, ESV). These statements in 1 Samuel 2:33 would seem to be fulfilled when Doeg, at Saul's command, slaughters the priests of Nob, and only Abiathar escapes to David (1 Sam 22:11–23).

We have seen that the references to the house of Eli's father (1 Sam 2:27, 28, 30, 31) must refer to the house of Aaron (see esp. 2:27 "the house of your father when they were in Egypt subject to the house of Pharaoh"). Note again the words of 1 Samuel 2:31, "I will cut off your strength and the strength of your father's house." This would seem to indicate not only that Eli's line will be cut off but also Aaron's, and that reality appears to be addressed in 1 Samuel 2:35, "And I will raise up for myself a faithful priest, who shall do according to what is in my heart and in my mind. And I will build him a sure house, and he shall go in and out before my anointed forever."

Before we look more closely at 1 Samuel 2:35, we should consider 1 Kings 2:27, "So Solomon expelled Abiathar from being priest to the LORD, thus fulfilling the word of the LORD that he had spoken concerning the house of Eli in Shiloh" (ESV). The fulfillment spoken of in 1 Kings 2:27 pertains specifically to "the house of Eli," and it is accomplished as Eli's descendant Abiathar is displaced by Zadok. Abiathar descends from Aaron's son Ithamar, and Zadok descends from Aaron's son Eleazar, but both lines descend from Aaron. If it is correct, therefore, that the references to the house of Eli's father in 1 Samuel 2:27–35 pertain to the Aaronic house (and see again "when they were in Egypt" in 1 Sam 2:27), then while 1 Kings 2:27 brings to fulfillment the prophecy against the house of Eli, the parts of the prophecy that pertain to the whole house of Aaron await fulfillment, for the Zadokite line is part of the Aaronic house.

Phrase by phrase 1 Samuel 2:35 resonates with other significant statements. The first English phrase, "And I will raise up for myself," employs the same verbal form (וַהֲקִימֹתִי) seen in 2 Samuel 7:12, "I will raise up your seed after you" (וַהֲקִימֹתִי). What the Lord asserts he will raise up for himself in 1 Samuel 2:35, "a faithful priest" (כֹּהֵן נֶאֱמָן), stands in contrast to Eli and his sons (1 Sam 2:12–25), who die as prophesied (4:11, 18; 22:11–19). Eli's line is later removed from priestly service (1 Kgs 2:26–27, 35). The promised "faithful priest" of

1 Samuel 2:35 also stands in contrast with the sons of Samuel (1 Sam 8:1–5), and looking backward, the promised one stands in contrast with Aaron (Exod 32) and his sons (Lev 10). If the Lord is going to "cut off . . . the strength of [Eli's] father's house" (1 Sam 2:31), that is, Aaron's house (2:27), whence comes this "faithful priest" (2:35)?

The description of this priest in 1 Samuel 2:35 continues with the words, "who shall do according to what is in my heart and in my mind" (ESV, כַּאֲשֶׁר בִּלְבָבִי וּבְנַפְשִׁי יַעֲשֶׂה). A similar expression appears when Samuel tells Saul, "But now your kingdom shall not continue. The Lord has sought out a man after his own heart . . ." (1 Sam 13:14, ESV, כִּלְבָבוֹ). The near context of that 1 Samuel 13 statement forges an association between David and Jonathan, whose armor bearer says to him, "Do all that is in your heart [בִּלְבָבֶךָ] . . . I am with you heart and soul [כִּלְבָבֶךָ]" (14:7, ESV). After the Lord makes his 2 Samuel 7:1–17 revelation to David, David says to Yahweh, "Because of your promise, and according to your own heart [וּכְלִבְּךָ], you have brought about all this greatness, to make your servant know it" (2 Sam 7:21, ESV). The similarity between these heart-statements indicates that Yahweh wants a "faithful priest" in the same way that he wants an obedient king—the 1 Samuel 13:14 statement to Saul comes in Samuel's rebuke of Saul's disobedient sacrifice (1 Sam 13:8–15).

The Lord's next 1 Samuel 2:35 assertion could make readers think they are reading 2 Samuel 7: "And I will build him a sure house" (וּבָנִיתִי לוֹ בַּיִת נֶאֱמָן, 1 Sam 2:35, ESV). In response to David's desire to build (בָּנָה) a house (בַּיִת) for Yahweh (esp. 2 Sam 7:5), in 2 Samuel 7:11 Nathan tells David, "the Lord declares to you that the Lord will make you a house" (בַּיִת, ESV). The Lord tells David that his seed "shall build a house for my name" (הוּא יִבְנֶה־בַּיִת לִשְׁמִי, 2 Sam 7:13, ESV), and the Lord promises David, "your house and your kingdom shall be made sure forever before me" (וְנֶאֱמַן בֵּיתְךָ, 7:16, ESV). It is not insignificant that in both 1 Samuel 2:35 and 2 Samuel 7:16 the Lord promises a "sure" (נֶאֱמַן/נֶאֱמָן) "house" (בַּיִת).

The final phrase describing the "faithful priest" for whom Yahweh will build a "sure house" in 1 Samuel 2:35 reads, "and he shall go in and out before my anointed forever" (ESV). This rendering follows the pointing of the Masoretic Text, and the Greek translation reads the text this way as well (καὶ διελεύσεται ἐνώπιον χριστοῦ). On the basis of grammatical and contextual considerations, however, Karl Deenick has proposed a slight emendation that would result in the translation: "my anointed shall go in and out before me forever."[14]

The question turns on whether the preposition "before" (לִפְנֵי) is suffixed by a *patach-yod* (לְפָנַי, "before me"), for which Deenick argues, or by a *sere-yod* (לִפְנֵי, "before my anointed") as the Masoretes pointed the text, and as the Greek translator rendered it:

1 Sam 2:35, וְהִתְהַלֵּךְ לִפְנֵי־מְשִׁיחִי כָּל־הַיָּמִים

If Deenick's contention is correct, "my anointed" (מְשִׁיחִי) becomes the subject of the verb "go in and out" (as in, "my anointed shall go in and out") rather than the object of the preposition ("he [the priest, who is to be distinguished from the anointed king mentioned later] shall go in and out before my anointed"). Deenick's proposal is attractive, but without textual evidence that the preposition "before" (לִפְנֵי) was taken as pointed with a *patach-yod* rather than a *sere-yod*, it seems unwise to rest too much on his reading.[15]

Still, from 1 Samuel 2:27–35 we have a prophecy that the house of Eli's father, which on the basis of 2:27 looks like the house of Aaron, will be cut off from the priesthood and replaced. The fulfillment seen in 1 Kings 2:27 pertains to the house of Eli, but it does not fulfill the removal of the house of Eli's father, that is, Aaron's house. As later Old Testament texts point forward to alterations in the Levitical priesthood, they seem to indicate that a fundamental change will have taken place in the nature of the law and the priesthood, specifically, in the legal requirement regarding who can serve in these roles. Also relevant is the way that what was typified in Adam and Melchizedek, in conjunction perhaps with the Moses-Aaron tandem, would find fulfillment in the reign of a king-priest.

§5.2 Isaiah on Future Priests and Levites

In Isaiah 61:6, speaking to God's people, the prophet points to a day when the restriction of the priesthood to the line of Aaron will be removed: "you shall be called the priests of the LORD; they shall speak of you as the ministers [מְשָׁרְתֵי,

---

14. Karl Deenick, "Priest and King or Priest-King in 1 Samuel 2:35," *Westminster Theological Journal* 73 (2011): 325–39.

15. There is no discussion of 1 Samuel 2:35 in Dominique Barthélemy, *Critique Textuelle de L'Ancien Testament* (Göttingen: Vandenhoeck and Ruprecht, 1982), 150.

λειτουργοὶ] of our God." In these statements Isaiah asserts that the Lord's purpose for the nation asserted in Exodus 19:6, for it to be a kingdom of priests, will be realized. This assertion has the same implications about the Mosaic law and the Levitical priesthood as Psalm 110:4, which is exposited in Hebrews 7:11–21.

But Isaiah does not stop with the declaration that all Israelites will be priests: he includes gentiles as well. Having listed a series of gentile nations to whom survivors will be sent—Tarshish, Pul, Lud, Tubal, and Javan (Isa 66:19)—Isaiah asserts, "And they shall bring all your brothers from all the nations as an offering to the LORD . . . And some of them also I will take for priests and for Levites, says the LORD" (66:20–21). Here again, there is nothing in the Torah of Moses about non-Israelites serving as priests or Levites. By definition, men from the tribe of Levi serve as Levites. Aaron and Moses descended from Levi, and only men who descend from Aaron could serve as priests. Just as the assertion in Isaiah 61:6 overrides the law concerning priests by saying all Israel will be priests, even more flagrantly the Isaiah 66:21 prophecy that gentiles will serve as priests points beyond the genealogical requirement of the law (cf. Num 3:5–13).

As Isaiah heralds a day when all God's people will know and keep the covenant—"All your children shall be taught by the LORD" (Isa 54:13)—he announces a day when the terms of the covenant will be changed, when the Lord will raise up for himself faithful priests from all Israel and Levites from the nations. Jeremiah likewise makes an important statement about the Levitical priests in 33:14–26.

§5.3 Jeremiah on Future Levitical Priests

The prophets teach that when God does the new exodus salvation (e.g., Jer 16:14–15; 23:7–8), he will make a new covenant with his people that will not be like the one he made with them after the exodus (31:31–34). Isaiah indicates that this will result in not only Israelites but also gentiles serving as priests and Levites. Does this hold for Jeremiah as well? Or does Jeremiah teach that in the same way that God will cause a Davidic king to reign forever, he will cause the Levitical priests to minister forever? If the Levitical priests were to continue forever, would that not mean that the covenant under which they minister, the Sinai covenant, would also continue to be in force forever (cf. Heb 7:12)?

The ESV's rendering of Jeremiah 33:17–18 could lend itself to the impression that the two verses are parallel statements:

Jeremiah 33:17	Jeremiah 33:18
For thus says the LORD:	and
David shall never lack a man	the Levitical priests shall never lack a man in my presence
to sit on the throne of the house of Israel,	to offer burnt offerings, to burn grain offerings, and to make sacrifices forever.

Read this way, verses 17 and 18 seem to indicate (1) that a descendant of David will always sit on the throne of Israel, and (2) that a descendant of Aaron from the tribe of Levi will always serve as priest.[16] The CSB and NASB have similar readings, but the renderings in the KJV and NET are more open a different understanding. Consider my own very literal translation of these two verses (italics denote matching phrases):

Jeremiah 33:17	Jeremiah 33:18
For thus says Yahweh:	and for the priests, the Levites,
He shall not be cut off for David,	*he shall not be cut off,*
a man sitting on the throne of the house of Israel,	*a man* from before me offering up burnt offerings and making tributes smoke and making sacrifices all the days.

The word order and phrasing of these two verses leaves open the possibility that the man who "shall not be cut off for David" in verse 17 is the same who "shall not be cut off" for the priests, the Levites, in verse 18. Note that in verses 17 and 18 the same expression is used for "he shall not be cut off . . . , a man" (לֹא־יִכָּרֵת . . . אִישׁ).

As reflected in my literal translation above, verse 17 has the "for David"

---

16. Apparently taking the text this way, J. A. Thompson writes, "The Levitical priesthood, as well as the Davidic dynasty, is seen as sharing the same promise." J. A. Thompson, *The Book of Jeremiah*, New International Commentary on the Old Testament (Grand Rapids: Eerdmans, 1980), 602. The tension I highlight here can be seen in F. B. Huey's commentary, where he states, "These verses contain a promise that the Davidic and Levitical lines in Israel would be permanent," but then writes on the next page, "it is not unreasonable to conclude that Christ in his priestly role fulfills the Levitical priestly role." F. B. Huey, *Jeremiah, Lamentations*, New American Commentary (Nashville: Broadman & Holman, 1993), 301–2. In my view, to understand Jeremiah 33:18 as a promise of ongoing Levitical priesthood is to misread Jeremiah. The author of Hebrews teaches that for one from the tribe of Judah to become a priest, a new covenant is required in which the priesthood is not limited to the tribe of Levi (Heb 7:12–22).

clause immediately following the verbal phrase, "He shall not be cut off." In verse 18, by contrast, the phrase "and for the priests, the Levites," precedes the verbal clause, indicating that rather than presenting parallel statements in which neither the man from David nor the man from the Levitical priesthood will be cut off, there could be one man who will not be cut off "for David . . . and for the priests, the Levites" (33:17–18a). On this reading, the repetition of the phrase "he shall not be cut off" in verse 18 serves to reiterate that *the same man* from verse 17, who "shall not be cut off for David," will also stand for the priests.

Five lines of evidence support the idea that Jeremiah 33:17–18 speaks of one figure (the future Davidic king) who will not be cut off, not two (a Davidic king and a Levitical priest): first, the literary structure of Jeremiah 33:14–26; second, lexical points of contact with 1 Samuel 2:27–35; third, points of contact with 1 Kings 8:25; fourth, the usage of the terms "Levites" and "priests" in Jeremiah (and Isaiah); and fifth, the typological interpretation of these matters in Zechariah 6:9–15.

§5.3.1 The Literary Structure of Jeremiah 33:14–26

Jeremiah 33:14 opens with the phrase, "Behold, the days are coming, declares the Lord." This three-part statement (1, "Behold"; 2, "the days are coming"; 3, "declares the Lord") occurs thirteen times in Jeremiah (Jer 7:32; 9:25 [MT 9:24]; 16:14; 19:6; 23:5, 7; 30:3; 31:27, 31; 33:14; 48:12; 49:2; 51:52; cf. also 31:38) and only once elsewhere (Amos 9:13). Jeremiah 30–33 is widely recognized as a unit pointing to Israel's eschatological salvation, and the phrase appears to have been strategically placed within these chapters. Jeremiah uses it at the beginning of this section of his prophecy in 30:3, and he employs the phrase again as the opening statement of the final unit of these chapters in 33:14–26. The phrase occurs two (or three) times near the center of this unit at 31:27 and 31:31, passages that carry obvious significance (cf. also 31:38, where there is a textual problem). This heading marks 33:14–26 off as a unified statement, and the unity of the passage is reinforced by the focus throughout on David (33:15, 17, 21, 22, 26), the fulfillment of God's promises to Abraham and Israel/Jacob (33:14, 17, 22, 24–26), and the mention of "the Levitical priests" (ESV, 33:18, 21, 22, see further below).

Jeremiah 33:14–26 falls into two units, 33:14–18 and 33:19–26. The first of these, 33:14–18, follows the "Behold, the days are coming" statement in 33:14 with two "In those days" statements in 33:15 and 33:16. These two "In those days" statements are then grounded in the "For thus says the Lord" statement in 33:17–18.

The second unit, 33:19–26, consists of two sections, each of which opens with "The word of the Lord came to Jeremiah" (33:19, 23, ESV). Both sections (33:19–22 and 33:23–26) consist of an "if/then" statement introduced by "Thus says the Lord" (33:20–21; 33:25–26, ESV).

The predominant theme through this clearly structured passage is that God will fulfill his promises by raising up the saving king from the line of David: he is the promised one in verse 14; the righteous branch who will spring up in verse 15; the one who brings salvation and bears the name Yahweh our Righteousness in verse 16; the ever-reigning Davidic king in verse 17; and I contend that he is the one who will not be cut off for the new Levites, the priests, in verse 18.

The two if/then statements in verses 19–26 promise first that God's covenant with David (which will benefit the transformed Levitical priests) is as certain as day and night (Jer 33:19–21), and second that the fixed order of day and night verify that God has not rejected "the two clans he chose" (33:24), and those two clans are identified as "Jacob and David" (33:26). God chose the house of Israel, designated here by the patriarch's name prior to its change to Israel, "Jacob," and God chose the house of David within Israel.

It appears, then, that Jeremiah 33:14–26 points to the fulfillment of God's promises concerning Israel and David, promises that do not include the continuation of the Mosaic covenant under which the Levites serve the tabernacle and men from Aaron's line serve as priests (see Jer 31:31–34). Though "the Levitical priests" are mentioned in this passage, we have reason to think that phrase should not be taken to refer here to a tribal line of descent. For now we observe that whereas Jeremiah 31:31–34 proclaims a new covenant that will not be like the old one made at Sinai, in 33:22 Jeremiah alludes to passages such as Genesis 15:5 and 22:17 to assert that the seed of David will bring about the fulfillment of the covenant with Abraham as those who worship Yahweh are multiplied.

§5.3.2 Lexical Points of Contact with 1 Samuel 2:27–35

We saw above that the three part phrase—(1) "Behold," (2) "the days are coming," (3) "declares the Lord"—occurs regularly in Jeremiah but only once outside the book. The first two parts of this phrase—(1) "Behold," (2) "the days are coming"—occur fourteen times in Jeremiah and only six times elsewhere (in addition to the thirteen instances of the three part phrase noted above, see Jer 51:47). Of the phrase's six appearances outside Jeremiah, three are in Amos (Amos 4:2; 8:11; and 9:13), two appear in a parallel passage found in both Isaiah and Kings (2 Kgs 20:17; Isa 39:6), which leaves the phrase's first occurrence in the Bible in 1 Samuel 2:31.

1 Sam 2:31, "Behold, the days are coming"

הִנֵּה יָמִים בָּאִים

Jer 33:14, "Behold, the days are coming"

הִנֵּה יָמִים בָּאִים

As we have seen in the preceding discussion, in 1 Samuel 2:27–35 a man of God prophesies to Eli both that the strength of his house and the house of his father will be cut off and that the Lord will raise up for himself a faithful priest. In Jeremiah 33:14–26, Jeremiah declares that the Lord will fulfill the new covenant promises to Abraham and David, adding that this will include the Levitical priests not lacking someone to stand for them. Jeremiah begins with a phrase first used in the midst of the oracle against Eli and his father's house in 1 Samuel 2:31.

In 1 Samuel 2:33 the man of God says to Eli, "The only one of you whom I shall not cut off from my altar shall be spared to weep his eyes out to grieve his heart, and all the descendants of your house shall die by the sword of men" (ESV). As noted above, this prophecy would appear to be fulfilled when Saul orders Doeg to slaughter the priests, with only Abiathar escaping (1 Sam 22:11–23). Note the similarity between the references to these who will not be cut off:

1 Sam 2:33, "and a man I will not cut off for you"

וְאִישׁ לֹא־אַכְרִית לְךָ

Jer 33:17, "a man will not be cut off for David"

לֹא־יִכָּרֵת לְדָוִד אִישׁ

Jer 33:18, "a man will not be cut off before me"

לֹא־יִכָּרֵת אִישׁ מִלְּפָנָי

In each of these statements we see the negative particle לֹא ("not"), the verb for "cut off" (כָּרַת), and the term "man" (אִישׁ). The author of Kings presents

David using this terminology as he speaks to Solomon in 1 Kings 2:4, "a man will not be cut off for you from upon the throne of Israel," and Solomon using it as he prays in 1 Kings 8:25 (see §5.3.3. below and the parallel in 2 Chr 6:16). In 1 Kings 9:5 the author presents the Lord reiterating the promise to Solomon with the same language: "a man shall not be cut off for you" (see parallel in 2 Chr 7:18). Isaiah speaks this way with reference to the offspring of Jacob (Isa 48:19; cf. 48:12), to the enduring nature of God's future glory (55:13), and to the name God will give to the eunuchs who choose what pleases him (56:4–5). Jeremiah makes this kind of promise to the Rechabites (Jer 35:19), and Zechariah to those who will survive the end (Zech 14:2). The phrase לֹא־יִכָּרֵת ("he will not be cut off") occurs twelve times in the Old Testament, with at least six of these referring to the future Davidic king, seven if Jeremiah 33:18 refers to the same figure as 33:17.

Jeremiah's phrases "Behold, the days are coming" and "a man shall not be cut off" match the same in 1 Samuel 2:31 and 2:33, and the phrase rendered "forever" in Jeremiah 33:18 appears in 1 Samuel 2:32 and 2:35.

1 Sam 2:32, "all the days" (i.e., "forever")

כָּל־הַיָּמִים

1 Sam 2:35, "all the days" (i.e., "forever")

כָּל־הַיָּמִים

Jer 33:18, "all the days" (i.e., "forever")

כָּל־הַיָּמִים

This phrase occurs forty-six times in the Old Testament, but it is not the only way to say forever in Hebrew (cf., e.g., לְעֹלָם literally, to the age; עַד־עוֹלָם, unto the age; לָנֶצַח, to the extremity; and לָעַד, to perpetuity, etc.). The ESV uses the term "forever" to render one of Jeremiah's various expressions sixteen times, but Jeremiah only employs this phrase, "all the days," four times (Jer 31:36; 32:39; 33:18; 35:19). In this passage in which he speaks of a man not being cut off for the Levitical priests, he chooses a phrase that occurs twice in 1 Samuel 2:27–35, and he chooses that phrase in conjunction with at least two other phrases that match that same passage.

In view of the three phrases discussed to this point, other lexical points of contact between 1 Samuel 2:27–35 and Jeremiah 33:14–26 seem to confirm that Jeremiah intends to evoke 1 Samuel 2:27–35. For instance, though the phrase "thus says Yahweh" occurs 291 times in the Old Testament, it appears prominently in our two passages:

1 Sam 2:27, "Thus says Yahweh"

כֹּה אָמַר יְהוָה

Jer 33:17, "Thus says Yahweh"

כִּי־כֹה אָמַר יְהוָה

Jer 33:20, "Thus says Yahweh"

כֹּה אָמַר יְהוָה

Jer 33:25, "Thus says Yahweh"

כֹּה אָמַר יְהוָה

Both passages also deal with God's choice:

1 Sam 2:28, "Did I choose (בָּחַר) him?"

Jer 33:24, ". . . the two clans he chose (בָּחַר)?"

And both passages rehearse sacrificial terminology:

1 Sam 2:28–29 (ESV)	Jer 33:18 (ESV)
". . . to go up to my altar (לַעֲלוֹת עַל־מִזְבְּחִי),	". . . to offer burnt offerings (מַעֲלֶה עוֹלָה),
to burn incense (לְהַקְטִיר) . . .	to burn (וּמַקְטִיר)
my sacrifices (בְּזִבְחִי)	grain offerings (מִנְחָה),
and my offerings (וּבְמִנְחָתִי) . . ."	and to make sacrifices (וְעֹשֶׂה־זֶּבַח) . . ."

In view of this evidence, it seems likely that in 33:14–26 Jeremiah means to remind his audience of 1 Samuel 2:27–35, and further, Jeremiah appears to prophesy of the fulfillment of what was prophesied there.

§5.3.3 Points of Contact with 1 Kings 8:25

First Kings 8:25 presents Solomon praying at the dedication of the temple, and what he prays has significant points of contact with 1 Samuel 2:27–35 and Jeremiah 33:17–18. Since Solomon petitions the Lord about the fulfillment of God's promise to David, the use of similar phraseology in 1 Samuel 2:35 and Jeremiah 33:18 confirms the Davidic coloring of those passages:

> Now therefore, O Lᴏʀᴅ, God of Israel, keep for your servant David my father what you have promised him, saying, "You shall not lack a man to sit before me on the throne of Israel, if only your sons pay close attention to their way, to walk before me as you have walked before me." (1 Kgs 8:25 ESV)

The ESV's rendering, "You shall not lack a man," translates the phrase we have seen in 1 Samuel 2:33 and Jeremiah 33:17–18, "a man will not be cut off for you" (לֹא־יִכָּרֵת לְךָ אִישׁ, 1 Kgs 8:25). This man will not be cut off for Solomon "before me," the Lord speaking, and the phrase in 1 Kings 8:25 matches the phrase in Jeremiah 33:18,

1 Kgs 8:25, "a man will not be cut off for you from before me"

לֹא־יִכָּרֵת לְךָ אִישׁ מִלְּפָנָי

Jer 33:18, "a man will not be cut off from before me"

לֹא־יִכָּרֵת אִישׁ מִלְּפָנָי

The next phrase of 1 Kings 8:25 asserts that this not-cut-off-before-Yahweh man will be "sitting upon the throne of Israel." In Jeremiah 33:17, the man who will not be cut off for David will likewise be "sitting upon the throne of the house of Israel."

1 Kgs 8:25, "sitting upon the throne of Israel"

יֹשֵׁב עַל־כִּסֵּא יִשְׂרָאֵל

Jer 33:17, "sitting upon the throne of the house of Israel"

יֹשֵׁב עַל־כִּסֵּא בֵית־יִשְׂרָאֵל

Jeremiah 33:17–18, then, simply restates 1 Kings 8:25, as can be seen on the following table:

1 Kings 8:25	Jeremiah 33:17	Jeremiah 33:18
"a man will not be cut off for you from before me sitting upon the throne of Israel . . . to walk before me as you have walked before me."	"a man will not be cut off for David sitting upon the throne of the house of Israel"	"a man will not be cut off from before me"

In the final phrase of 1 Kings 8:25, Solomon is presented quoting the Lord's promise about the need for David's sons to "pay close attention to their way, to walk before me as you have walked before me." These statements are very similar to both 1 Samuel 2:30 (the Lord's gift of the priesthood to the house of Aaron and the house of Eli) and 1 Samuel 2:35 (the faithful priest).

1 Kgs 8:25, "to walk before me as you walked before me"

לָלֶכֶת לְפָנַי כַּאֲשֶׁר הָלַכְתָּ לְפָנָי

1 Sam 2:30, "they would walk before me"

יִתְהַלְּכוּ לְפָנָי

1 Sam 2:35, "and he will walk before my Messiah"

וְהִתְהַלֵּךְ לִפְנֵי־מְשִׁיחִי

As discussed above, if the ending on the preposition takes a *patach* rather than a *tsere*, 1 Sam 2:35 would read, "and my Messiah will walk before me." If the identity of the figure in 1 Samuel 2:35 is uncertain, in 1 Kings 8:25, with whom those other texts (1 Sam 2:35; Jer 33:17–18) share so much, he is indisputably the king from the line of David.

§5.3.4 Levites and Priests in Jeremiah (and Isaiah)

Jeremiah regularly points to the eschatological future, and this is especially so in chapters 30–33. In these prophecies of what will be, the priests and Levites play almost no role at all. In fact, the only verses in all of Jeremiah that mention the Levites are 33:18, 21, and 22.[17] Most of Jeremiah's references to priests pertain to historical priests in Jeremiah's own day. Aside from the references to priests in Jeremiah 33:18 and 33:21, the only other reference to eschatological priests is found in 31:14, "I will feast the soul of the priests with abundance, and my people shall be satisfied with my goodness, declares the LORD." The point here is that whereas Jeremiah regularly points to a future king from David's line, in only a few places does he say anything about the place of Levites and priests in the eschatological future. If the Levites and priests from the line of Aaron were to factor in the new covenant Jeremiah prophesies in 31:31–34, we might expect Jeremiah to prophesy of them as future priests as he does of the future king from David's line. As it is, he has relatively little to say about either priests or Levites, and there is no reason to think he would disagree with what Isaiah prophesied about the identity of the future Levites.

Isaiah uses the term "priest" only four times in his prophecy, and each refers to historical priests of his own time (Isa 8:2; 24:2; 28:7; 37:2). Isaiah refers to "Levites" only once (66:21), and in that passage he says that gentiles will serve as Levites. Isaiah, then, seems to anticipate a transformed set of qualifications for Levites.

Does Jeremiah 33:18 indicate that the tribe of Levi and priests from Aaron's line will never be cut off, or does that verse indicate that the king from David's line, who will not be cut off in 33:17, will stand for the Levites, the priests, in verse 18? Perhaps the interpretation offered by a prophet who came after Jeremiah, Zechariah, can help us to answer that question.

§5.3.5 Zechariah 6:9–15

The strongest indication that in Zechariah 6:9–15 the prophet interprets Jeremiah comes in the reference to "the man whose name is the branch" in 6:12 (ESV). Jeremiah had prophesied that the Lord would "raise up for David a righteous Branch" in 23:5 (ESV), and again in 33:15, "I will cause a righteous Branch to spring up for David" (ESV, cf. Isa 4:2).

---

17. Thompson writes: "this is the only reference in the book where the revival of the priesthood is mentioned." *Jeremiah*, 602.

Like Jeremiah, Zechariah refers to this figure twice. In the first instance the Lord declares to Joshua the high priest that he will bring his servant the Branch: "Hear now, O Joshua the high priest, you and your friends who sit before you, for they are men of portent, for behold, I will bring my servant the Branch" (Zech 3:8). Because of what we will see in Zechariah 6, we note here that Joshua is not identified as the branch, though he and the men with him are "men of portent [מוֹפֵת]," indicating that they "portend" or "prefigure" what is to be.[18] We see this "portending" enacted in the second "branch" passage in Zechariah 6:12.

Zechariah calls for a parabolic performance of what will take place in the future. The word of Yahweh instructs that Joshua the high priest himself is to be crowned as king and identified as "the Branch." Joshua was not the branch in 3:8, but he portends, that is typifies, the branch in 6:12. Aside from this symbolically enacted prophetic sign-act, Joshua the high priest was never crowned king, so the prophecy was not fulfilled in that way. Yet Zechariah stakes his authenticity as a prophet on fulfillment: when what he has prophesied in 6:9–15a comes to pass, Zechariah declares, "you shall know that Yahweh of hosts has sent me to you" (Zech 6:15b). It would seem, then, that Zechariah points to a day when the high priest of the people of God will also be their king.

Do we have reason to think that Zechariah's typological prophecy was shaped by earlier promises? In what follows we examine points of contact between Zechariah 6 and the passages considered in this discussion.

Zechariah instructs returned exiles to make a crown and place it on the head of Joshua the high priest (Zech 6:9–10), and he opens his declaration about "the man whose name is the Branch" in 6:12 (ESV) with the same formula seen in 1 Samuel 2:27, Jeremiah 33:17, 20, and 25, "Thus says the Lord" (כֹּה אָמַר יְהוָה, Zech 6:12, ESV). Though a common formula, with other features of the passage it joins to point to Jeremiah 33:14–26.

When the high priest Joshua is crowned in this symbolic action, Zechariah announces in 6:12, "Behold the man, Branch is his name." This statement shares with Jeremiah 23:5–6 and 33:15 the focus on the king from David's line being *named* as the *Branch*:

---

18. Rose observes, "The same word מופת is used for the prophet Isaiah and his children (Isaiah 8.18 . . .)." Wolter Rose, *Zemah and Zerubbabel: Messianic Expectations in the Early Postexilic Period*, Library of Hebrew Bible/Old Testament Studies 304 (Sheffield: Sheffield Academic Press, 2000), 44.

Zech 6:12, "Behold the man, Branch is his name"	הִנֵּה־אִישׁ צֶמַח שְׁמוֹ
Jer 33:15, "I will cause a righteous Branch to branch for David"	אַצְמִיחַ לְדָוִד צֶמַח צְדָקָה
Jer 23:5–6, "And I will raise up for David a righteous Branch, and he shall reign as king and act wisely, . . . and this is his name by which he will call him, 'Yahweh our righteousness.'"	וַהֲקִמֹתִי לְדָוִד צֶמַח צַדִּיק וּמָלַךְ מֶלֶךְ וְהִשְׂכִּיל . . . וְזֶה־שְּׁמוֹ אֲשֶׁר־יִקְרְאוֹ יְהוָה צִדְקֵנוּ

Note that in Jeremiah 23:5 the "I will raise up" (וַהֲקִמֹתִי) statement employs the same form we saw in 1 Samuel 2:35 and 2 Samuel 7:12. Further, Jeremiah here directly states that this figure will "reign as king [וּמָלַךְ מֶלֶךְ] and act wisely [וְהִשְׂכִּיל]."

Zechariah directly engages the 2 Samuel 7 promises further when he asserts in 6:12, "and he will build the temple of Yahweh" (וּבָנָה אֶת־הֵיכַל יְהוָה). Zechariah restates this point in the very next verse, 6:13, "and he will build the temple of Yahweh" (וְהוּא יִבְנֶה אֶת־הֵיכַל יְהוָה). These statements recall 2 Samuel 7:13, which Zechariah 6:13 comes close to quoting, where Yahweh says of the seed of David, "he will build a house for my name" (הוּא יִבְנֶה־בַּיִת לִשְׁמִי, 2 Sam 7:13).

We saw references to the future king from David's line "sitting upon the throne" in 1 Kings 8:25 and Jeremiah 33:17, and now Zechariah declares that the branch, the high priest who will be crowned king and build the temple, "shall sit and rule on his throne" (וְיָשַׁב וּמָשַׁל עַל־כִּסְאוֹ, Zech 6:13). Zechariah makes the situation explicit in the next phrases of 6:13 when he asserts, "And a priest will be on his throne, and the counsel of peace will be between the two of them" (וְהָיָה כֹהֵן עַל־כִּסְאוֹ וַעֲצַת שָׁלוֹם תִּהְיֶה בֵּין שְׁנֵיהֶם).

To review what we saw above in 1 Samuel 2 and Jeremiah 33: the Masoretic pointing of 1 Samuel 2:35 would indicate that a faithful priest will walk before the Lord's Messiah. An unpointed Hebrew text could be interpreted to say that the Messiah will be the faithful priest who will walk before the Lord. And while some translations lend themselves to the interpretation that Jeremiah 33:17–18 indicates that the Lord will never allow two figures, a king from David's line or a Levitical priest, to be cut off, the text's context, syntax, and grammar indicate that the king from David's line will never be cut off, and he will never be cut off for the benefit of the Levitical priests.

These observations suggest that Zechariah 6:9–15 engages and sheds further light on 1 Samuel 2:35 and Jeremiah 33:17–18. Depending on the identity of the author(s) of Samuel, David might have composed Psalm 110 by the time that 1–2 Samuel were written. Jeremiah lived well after David and would have had access to Psalm 110, with its assertion that David's Lord would be a priest forever according to the order of Melchizedek (Ps 110:4), and so also with Zechariah. We have seen strong points of contact between 1 Samuel 2, Jeremiah 33, and Zechariah 6 (and related passages such as 1 Kgs 8:25). If we are uncertain after 1 Samuel 2:35, the meaning of Jeremiah 33:17–18 in context brings clarity, and Zechariah 6:9–15 depicts a typological crowning of the high priest as king, pointing forward to a day when the offices of king and priest will be united in one person, both held by the temple-building Davidic king.[19]

The promise of a faithful priest prompts the pattern in Zechariah, a pattern in which the high priest is crowned king. The pattern in turn reinforces the promise.

§5.4 Patterns of the Coming Priest (King)

In addition to the patterns seen in the lives of Adam, Melchizedek, Israel, and Aaron, and the promises of a faithful priest in the future, the narratives dealing with David include a number of interesting priestly overtones. As we saw in §4 above, the only people to be anointed in the Pentateuch were the priests. The anointing of the king (Judg 9:8; 1 Sam 9:16; 16:1–3), therefore, smears the king with oil that calls priests to mind. In addition to being anointed, when David brought the ark into Jerusalem he wore a linen ephod in 2 Samuel 6:14. The phrasing of David wearing the ephod in 2 Samuel 6:14 exactly matches the description of Samuel (who was a Levite, 1 Chr 6:1, 28 [MT 5:27; 6:13], ministering in the temple, 1 Sam 3:1, 3) wearing the same in 1 Samuel 2:18 and closely corresponds to the description of the priests slain by Doeg in 1 Samuel 22:18.

2 Sam 6:14, David, חָגוּר אֵפוֹד בָּד
"girded with an ephod of linen"

1 Sam 2:18, Samuel, חָגוּר אֵפוֹד בָּד
"girded with an ephod of linen"

---

19. Similarly Anthony R. Petterson, "Zechariah," in *ESV Expository Commentary: Daniel–Malachi*, ed. Iain M. Duguid, James M. Hamilton Jr., and Jay Sklar (Wheaton, IL: Crossway, 2018), 677.

1 Sam 22:18, priests, נֹשֵׂא אֵפוֹד בָּד

"bearing an ephod of linen"

David was anointed as priests were anointed, clothed as priests were clothed when the ark was brought into Jerusalem, and once he brought the ark into Jerusalem he organized the service of song at the house of Yahweh (1 Chr 6:31). When David declares Yahweh to be his tribal inheritance in Psalm 16:5–6, he chooses for himself the one given to Aaron (Num 18:20). In addition, the last phrase of 2 Samuel 8:18 reads, "and David's sons were priests" (ESV). Some translations take the plural for "priests" (כֹּהֲנִים) in this verse to refer to "chief ministers" (NASB) or "chief officials" (CSB), but the use of this term is intriguing.

Perhaps David understood that Adam was a priest-king in the garden and that the designation of Melchizedek as that kind of figure in Genesis 14 had implications for the future new-Adam king from his line. Such an understanding of Adam and Melchizedek would likely color one's understanding of Abraham, who built altars like a priest (Gen 12:7–8; 13:18) and won battles and negotiated with rulers like a king (Gen 14).

In Psalm 110 David prophesies of how his Lord will be seated at Yahweh's right hand (Ps 110:1) and made "a priest forever after the order of Melchizedek" (110:4, ESV).[20] As we consider the way the Old Testament builds to the New Testament explanation of the Melchizedekian High Priesthood of Jesus (see esp. Heb 5–7), the Old Testament types provide the building blocks for the New Testament conclusion. These include the Adamic archetype, the failure of the Aaronic priests at Sinai and afterward (Exod 32; Lev 10), and the prophecies of a faithful priest (1 Sam 2:35). To these are added the Melchizedekian pattern of a priest-king and the patterns from David's own life, complemented by the prophecies of Jeremiah and Zechariah. The prophecies and the patterns work together to prefigure the one who would fulfill what Joshua the high priest portended (Zech 3:8), one who would indeed "build the temple of Yahweh" and be "a priest on his throne" (6:13).[21]

---

20. See further Matthew Emadi, "You Are Priest Forever: Psalm 110 and the Melchizedekian Priesthood of Christ," *Southern Baptist Journal of Theology* 23 (2019): 57–84.

21. If this is correct, it would agree with Hensley's argument pertaining to covenant relationships in the Psalter: "the Psalter's editors viewed the Abrahamic, Mosaic, and Davidic covenants as a theological unity and anticipated their common fulfillment through a future Davidic successor. The Psalter attributes the traditionally Mosaic role of mediator of the covenant renewal (cf. Exod 33–34) to this 'new David,' who fulfills traditionally Abrahamic covenantal promises, supersedes Moses as intercessor for the people in the face of their covenant unfaithfulness, and is faithful to Mosaic covenantal obligations." Adam D. Hensley, *Covenant Relationships and the Editing of the Hebrew Psalter*, Library of Hebrew Bible/Old Testament Studies 666 (New York: T&T Clark, 2018), 9.

PROPHETS

You find that whatever is written in regard to our father, Abraham,
is written also with regard to his children.

—GEN. RAB. 40.6[1]

O ne approach to exploring the Bible's types would be to move exegetically
lectio continua (continuous reading in sequence) through every passage
of the Bible. Pursuing that method, we could look at different layers of typological significance before moving to the next passage. Dealing with Adam
in this way, we could discuss all at once the way he typifies later figures—his
prophetic, priestly, and royal significance, his marriage, his sin, and his exile—
until the patterns culminate in Christ, the new Adam. Such an approach would
make for *very* long chapters, to say nothing of the whole project.

As an organizational strategy for this book, I have chosen to move through
the widely used typological categories of Persons (Part 1), Events (Part 2), and
Institutions (Part 3). Within these Parts of the discussion, moreover, we will
consider different, related aspects of the Bible's typological development. This
will result in overlapping, layered explorations of the way typological expectation builds from the Old Testament to the New.

As this relates to Adam, in the previous two chapters we considered two
typological layers: how Moses forges a series of patterns that build from first
Adam to last, so that Adam typifies the Messiah, and how Adam serves as an
archetypal priest, pointing forward to the eternal Melchizedekian priesthood
of the second Adam. Now a third layer adds yet more texture to the Bible's

---

1. I owe this reference to Mathews, *Genesis 1–11:26*, 53.

fabric: how Adam is a prototypical instance of a prophetic figure, and how the prophets stand in relationship to one another across the Old Testament, the patterns of their experiences merging with the promises of God to provoke anticipation of the one who fulfills all they typify.

This chapter will begin with the first Adam and end with the last, with the whole centering on Moses, having moved through the likes of Noah and Isaiah, Abraham and Elijah/Elisha, as well as Isaac and Joshua. The chapter has a chiastic structure:

§1 Adam
  §2 Noah
    §3 Abraham
      §4 Isaac
        §5 Moses
      §6 Joshua
    §7 Elijah and Elisha
  §8 Isaiah
§9 Jesus

We begin with key figures in Genesis seeking to show (1) that they were prophets, and (2) that Moses intended his audience to connect them to one another. A fulsome description of how the Lord reveals himself to prophets is provided in Numbers 12:6–8,[2]

> If there is a prophet [נָבִיא] among you, I the LORD make myself known [יָדַע] to him in a vision [מַרְאָה]; I speak [דָּבַר] with him in a dream [חֲלוֹם]. Not so with my servant Moses. He is faithful in all my house. With him I speak [דָּבַר] mouth to mouth [פֶּה אֶל־פֶּה], clearly [מַרְאָה], and not in riddles [חִידָה], and he beholds [נָבַט] the form [תְּמוּנָה] of the LORD. (ESV)

The content that Yahweh reveals is here described as *making himself known* (Num 12:6). The Lord articulates several ways in which he *speaks*, including *visions* and *dreams* and *riddles*, but with Moses the Lord speaks *face to face* as he *beholds* the *form* of Yahweh. Moses hereby presents Yahweh outlining

---

2. Cf. the discussion of the seminal nature of Numbers 12 and Deuteronomy 18 in O. Palmer Robertson, *The Christ of the Prophets* (Phillipsburg, NJ: P & R, 2004), 33–39.

how he reveals himself to prophets, and so this passage helps us consider the relationships between the prophets to whom Yahweh revealed himself.

§1 ADAM

As the first man and the first human character to be encountered in the Bible's narrative, it would be difficult for Adam not to be prototypical. The text never refers to Adam as a prophet, but when Yahweh God tells the man he can eat freely of every tree in the garden (Gen 2:16) except the tree of the knowledge of good and evil, warning that in the day he eats of that tree he will die (2:17), the woman has not yet been created. That the woman knows of the warning in 3:2–3 indicates that the man communicated it to her. We will discuss a lexical point of contact between Genesis 2:17 and Genesis 20:7, where Abraham is called a prophet, in the discussion of Abraham below (§3). A prophet is one who receives God's revelation and communicates it to others, and the implication of the narrative of Genesis 2–3 is that Adam has carried out this prophetic role.

§2 NOAH

We saw significant points of contact between Adam and Noah in Chapter 2. Though the text does not identify Noah as a prophet, we do find suggestive points of contact between Noah and Moses. So that we can set them next to our consideration of Moses, we will consider the similarities between Noah and Moses in the discussion of Moses below. Here I merely note that the connections between Adam and Noah and Noah and Moses likely provide the basis for the identification of Noah as a "preacher of righteousness" in 2 Peter 2:5.

§3 ABRAHAM

The Genesis narrative begins with Adam, and the genealogies of Genesis 5 and 11 trace the line of descent to Abraham, who like Adam carries prototypical significance because of his early appearance and obvious import for everything that follows. The covenant promises God gives to Abraham are those that will be fulfilled when God brings about the final salvation of his people (see Gen 12, 15, 17; *passim* below, and, e.g., Luke 1:54–55, 72–73; Rom 4; Gal 3:14).

In §2 of Chapter 2 above we saw connections between Adam and Abraham that fulfill criteria for establishing historical correspondence: linguistic points of contact, similar patterns of events, and comparable salvation-historical/ covenantal significance.

In Genesis 20:7 Moses presents Yahweh saying of Abraham, "he is a prophet [נָבִיא]." Even with this direct statement that Abraham is a prophet, it is easy to overlook the features of the narrative in which Yahweh reveals himself to Abraham and, on several occasions, gives him information about what will happen in the future.

The Lord speaks (אָמַר) to Abraham in Genesis 12:1–3, then "appears" (רָאָה in the *niphal*) and speaks to him in 12:7. Yahweh's revelation of himself to Abraham in Genesis 15:1 employs language that, though not used in Numbers 12:6–8, is synonymous with terms found there: "the word of Yahweh came to Abram in a vision." The phrase "the word of Yahweh came to . . ." (הָיָה דְבַר־יְהוָה אֶל) appears frequently as the Lord reveals himself to prophets (Jer 14:1; 46:1; 47:1; 49:34; Ezek 1:3; Hag 2:10; Zech 1:1, 7; 7:1; Dan 9:2; 2 Chr 12:7).[3] The way the word of Yahweh came to Abram here, "in a vision," employs a different term (מַחֲזֶה) from the one used in Numbers 12:6 (מַרְאָה), but the synonymous nature of the two terms can be seen from the fact that English translations routinely render both Hebrew terms "vision" (CSB, ESV, JPS, KJV, NASB, NIV). Yahweh revealed himself so that the human recipient of revelation saw things.

In view of the "night visions" of Zechariah (e.g., Zech 1:8) and Daniel (e.g., Dan 7:13), it is interesting to observe that as Yahweh makes a covenant with Abram in Genesis 15, he gives him a "night vision." The word "vision" appears in Genesis 15:1, then Abram is instructed to number the stars in 15:5, setting the scene at night, before the "deep sleep" and "great darkness" fall on Abram in 15:12, as Yahweh speaks to him of the future in 15:13–16.

Throughout the Genesis narratives Yahweh reveals himself and speaks with Abraham, and he again reveals the future to him in Genesis 17. Yahweh tells Abraham that kings will come from his body and from Sarah (Gen 17:6, 16). The Lord even specifies that barren Sarah will have a son "at this time next year" (17:21; cf. 18:10, 14), revealing the immediate future directly to Abraham.

---

3. The references listed have the exact phrase as it appears in Gen 15:1. If we alter our search by taking out the "to be" verb (הָיָה, the inflection of which varies), we find many more instances of the phrase "word of Yahweh to" (דְבַר־יְהוָה אֶל). See, e.g., Gen 15:4.

Once again, before the Lord destroys Sodom, he asks himself the rhetorical question in Genesis 18:17, "Shall I hide from Abraham what I am about to do?" The Genesis 18 revelation of what Yahweh is about to do to Sodom results in Abraham interceding on behalf of Lot and any other righteous people who might be found in the city (18:22–33). We might instinctively associate the mediatorial act of intercession with what priests do, but on reflection, the prophet Moses was Israel's intercessor *par excellence* (see esp. Exod 32:10–15 and Num 14:12–23). Similarly, the Lord identifies Abraham as a prophet in Genesis 20, when he says to Abimelech, who has taken Sarah from Abraham:

> Now then, return the man's wife, for he is a prophet, so that he will pray for you, and you shall live. But if you do not return her, know that you shall surely die [מוֹת תָּמוּת], you and all who are yours. (20:7)

Yahweh identifies Abraham as a prophet, and then he tells Abimelech that Abraham will intercede for him in prayer. Prophets communicate with people on Yahweh's behalf, and they also communicate with Yahweh on behalf of people.

The richly self-referential character of Genesis has manifested itself yet again in Genesis 20:7. Adam engaged in prophetic activity when he communicated the Genesis 2:17 prohibition to the woman: "in the day that you eat of it you shall surely die [מוֹת תָּמוּת]." The only two instances of the phrase "you shall surely die" in Genesis are at 2:17 and 20:7. There is a third closely related assertion that employs third-person statements ("he") in place of the second persons ("you") in Genesis 26:11 (מוֹת יוּמָת, "he shall surely die"). We will have more to say on the inter-connectedness of these "sister-fib" episodes in Genesis 12, 20, and 26 below. Here we observe this point of contact between them because the connections between Adam, Abraham, and Isaac point to all three being understood in prophetic terms. In the first Adam acts as a prophet; in the second Abraham is identified as one; and in the third Isaac is presented as an installment in the pattern of Abraham, his father. The distinctive character of the phrase, "you shall surely die," naturally prompts readers to think of its first instance when they encounter the second and third. Here again we have strong indication that Moses intended his audience to make mental associations between Adam and Abraham. And as for Isaac, another feature of the Genesis 26 narrative that links him back to Adam is the fact that once Abimelech knows Rebekah is his wife, he warns his people with the words,

"Whoever touches [יִגַּע] this man or his wife shall surely be put to death" (Gen 26:11). This reminds us of Eve's answer to the serpent in Genesis 3:3, "neither shall you touch [תִגְּעוּ] it, lest you die," and of God's word to Abimelech in 20:6, "I did not let you touch [לִנְגֹּעַ] her."

As the first figure in the book to be called a prophet, Abraham shapes the expectations of the audience of Genesis. That is to say, the impress of the pattern of Abraham's prophetic role forms the way that students of the Torah of Moses will interpret future prophets. Though Isaac is not called a prophet, the many narrative similarities and the way Yahweh directly reveals himself to Isaac suggest that he is an installment in the prophetic pattern.

§4 ISAAC

Why does Genesis 26 read the way it does? If we fail to see the connections that Moses makes with what he has already narrated and what he will narrate in coming chapters, we will speculate with the higher critics or remain mystified by the seemingly random details.[4] The details, however, are not random, and Moses accomplishes a remarkable amount in the relatively small space he devotes to Isaac's adult life. Abraham's death is narrated in Genesis 25, and Jacob steals Esau's blessing in Genesis 27. Isaac is center stage only in Genesis 26.

The first five verses of Genesis 26 are like a patchwork quilt constructed almost entirely of phrases readers of Genesis have already encountered, and then the rest of the chapter tells a series of stories so remarkably similar to events from the life of Abraham as to have been regarded as unremarkable by many interpreters. To make that judgment is to fail to see what Moses seeks to accomplish in Genesis 26.

§4.1 Isaac as a Prophet

I will seek to show here that by repeating the *promises* to Isaac and presenting him as an installment in a *pattern* of events, Moses establishes Isaac as an installment in the pattern of Abraham. What is the significance of this pattern? A later biblical author, the psalmist who wrote Psalm 105, has correctly interpreted what Moses intended to communicate. The psalmist speaks of "the covenant that he [Yahweh] made with Abraham, his sworn promise to Isaac"

---

4. For the literary structure of the book of Genesis, see Chapter 11 below.

in 105:9. Then apparently describing the sister-fib events (Genesis 12:10–20 when Yahweh delivered Abram and Sarai from Pharaoh, Genesis 20:1–18 when the same kind of thing happens with Abimelech, and Genesis 26:6–11 when Isaac does what his father did) the psalmist writes in 105:12–15 (ESV),

> When they were few in number, of little account and sojourners in it [the land], wandering from nation to nation, from one kingdom to another people, he allowed no one to oppress them; he rebuked kings on their account, saying, "Touch not my anointed ones, do my prophets no harm!"

Because of the mention of Abraham and Isaac in Psalm 105:9, and the reference to the rebuke of kings in 105:14, it seems the psalmist has the sister-fib incidents in view. There is a similar event in Jacob's life when the Lord rebukes Laban (Gen 31:29), but unlike Abimelech Laban is not directly called a king, so we think primarily of Abraham and Isaac. Jacob eventually sojourned in Egypt (Ps 105:23), but Abraham and Isaac fit the description of "few in number, of little account and sojourners in" the land of Canaan (105:11–12).

When Pharaoh seized Sarai, Yahweh rebuked him (Gen 12:17). When Abimelech seized Sarah, God rebuked him (20:3–7). And when Abimelech seized Rebekah, God providentially delivered her (26:6–11). Though the Lord reveals himself to Isaac just as he had to Abraham (e.g., Gen 26:2), Moses never calls him a prophet in the book of Genesis. Nor, however, does Moses present an account when either Abraham or Isaac were anointed with oil, and yet Abraham and Isaac seem to be referred to as both "anointed ones" and "prophets" in Psalm 105:15.

The psalmist, then, forges a connection between Abraham and Isaac and those who were anointed with oil later in the Scriptural narrative. Priests were anointed (Exod 28:41; 30:30), kings were anointed (1 Sam 10:1; 16:13; 1 Kgs 1:39), and Elijah is told to anoint Elisha as prophet (1 Kgs 19:16). Calling Abraham and Isaac "anointed ones" identifies them with later prophets, priests, and kings of Israel.

The psalmist seems to have applied the Lord's statement that Abraham "is a prophet" from one of the sister-fib episodes (Gen 20:7), to both Abraham and Isaac, and my argument here is that the psalmist has rightly discerned what Moses intended to communicate. I will seek to show this by demonstrating: the linguistic points of contact between narratives dealing with Abraham and

Isaac, the quotation of earlier material, the parallel sequences of events, and the similarity in redemptive historical and covenantal significance. To put it plainly, these points demonstrate that Moses intended to present Isaac after the pattern of Abraham, and the psalmist has recognized that interpretive point and reflected it in Psalm 105:15.

Genesis 26:1 describes a "famine (רָעָב) in the land, besides the first famine that took place in the days of Abraham." This statement ties the sister-fib context of Genesis 26 (see Gen 26:6–11) to the famine that drove Abram and Sarai to Egypt in 12:10, occasioning that first sister-fib incident in Genesis (12:10–13). Moses uses the same phrase to open both narratives:

Gen 12:10, וַיְהִי רָעָב בָּאָרֶץ

Gen 26:1, וַיְהִי רָעָב בָּאָרֶץ

"And it came about that there was a famine in the land"

The mention of the famine in 26:1, and its reference back to the first one in 12:10, also anticipates the famine that Joseph will predict to Pharaoh (see 41:27), which will in turn take Jacob and his sons to Egypt. The famines in Genesis 12 and 41, then, resulted in Abraham and Jacob "sojourning" in Egypt (12:10; 47:4), and that informs Yahweh telling Isaac not to go to Egypt in Genesis 26:2.[5]

Isaac goes "to Gerar to Abimelech king of the Philistines" at the end of Genesis 26:1, recalling the way that in the sister-fib incident in Genesis 20, "Abraham journeyed . . . and he sojourned in Gerar. . . . And Abimelech king of Gerar sent and took Sarah" (Gen 20:1–2). Moses presents Isaac experiencing the same events in the same place and interacting with people with the same name: the pattern of Abraham's life is the pattern of Isaac's. Isaac is an installment in the Abrahamic typological pattern.

The significance of Abraham in Genesis 26 can be seen from the literary structure of the chapter's first five verses. These verses form a chiasm in which Abraham is named at beginning, middle, and end, and the promises of land, seed, and blessing made to Abraham are stated in the first half and again in the second, with mention of the oath Yahweh swore to Abraham at the center:

---

5. Cf. Gen 46:2, where God appears to Jacob and tells him not to fear going down to Egypt.

26:1, Abraham
   26:2, Land
      26:3a, Blessing
         26:3b, Seed
            26:3c, Oath to Abraham
         26:4a, Seed
      26:4b, Land
   26:4c, Blessing all Nations
26:5, Abraham

We read of the Lord appearing to Isaac in Genesis 26:2, "And Yahweh appeared to him" (וַיֵּרָא אֵלָיו יְהֹוָה), and this exact phrase occurs only three times in all the Hebrew Bible: at Genesis 18:1, 26:2, and 26:24. First used in Genesis 18:1 with reference to the Lord appearing to Abraham, Moses describes the Lord appearing to Isaac the same way.

What the Lord says to Isaac in Genesis 26:2 is reminiscent of what he said to Abram in 12:1 and 22:2.

Gen 12:1, "go . . . to the land that I will show you"
אֶל־הָאָרֶץ אֲשֶׁר אַרְאֶךָּ

Gen 22:2, "one of the mountains of which I shall tell you"
הֶהָרִים אֲשֶׁר אֹמַר אֵלֶיךָ

Gen 26:2, "dwell in the land of which I shall tell you"
בָּאָרֶץ אֲשֶׁר אֹמַר אֵלֶיךָ

These will not be the only quotations of Genesis 12 and 22 in chapter 26, and to see the significance of these quotations we must consider the literary structure of the life of Abraham. Moses has constructed his account of Abraham's life as a chiasm that spans from Genesis 11:27–22:24.[6] At beginning and end we find genealogies of Abraham's father Terah (Gen 11:27–32) and brother Nahor (22:20–24). The second and second to last units focus on

6. I have adapted the chiasm presented by Kenneth A. Mathews, *Genesis 11:27–50:26: An Exegetical and Theological Exposition of Holy Scripture*, New American Commentary (Nashville: Broadman & Holman, 2005), 90.

God's promises to Abraham and their realization, also paralleling God's call to Abraham to leave country, kindred, and father's house with God's call for him to take his son, his only son, whom he loves to Mount Moriah to sacrifice him (12:1–9; 21–22). In the third and third to last episodes Abraham employs the sister-fib about Sarah, first to Pharaoh (12:10–20) and then to Abimelech (20:1–18). The fourth and fourth-to-last units consist on each side of two chapters dealing with Lot—Abraham gives him the choice of the best land in chapter 13 then rescues him in chapter 14, and then Abraham intercedes for him in chapter 18 before God rescues him from Sodom in chapter 19. At the center of this chiastic structure stands God's covenant-prophecy in chapter 15, followed by Abraham's sin with Hagar in chapter 16, and the covenant sign of circumcision in chapter 17:

> 11:27–32, Genealogy of Terah
>   12:1–9, Blessing of Abraham: Land, Seed, Blessing
>   12:10–20, SISTER-FIB 1 (Exodus Preview)
>   13–14, Lot
>   15 Eliezer, Faith, Covenant, Exodus,
>   16 Hagar, Ishmael,
>   17, Circumcision, Covenant with Isaac
>   18–19, Lot
>   20:1–18, SISTER-FIB 2
>   21–22, Birth of Isaac, Offering of Isaac, Reiteration of Blessing
> 22:20–24, Genealogy of Nahor

The parallels between Genesis 12 and 21–22 (seed promised and born, Abraham called to leave and called to sacrifice) and the literary structure of the narrative make it so that quoting from chapters 12 and 22 evokes the whole of Abraham's life. Genesis 26 is not the first place Moses does this. The sending of the servant to the family of Nahor to find a wife for Isaac in Genesis 24 also employs this strategy, quoting the Genesis 12:7 promise of land to Abraham's seed early (in 24:7), and then quoting the Genesis 22:17 promise that the seed of Abraham will possess the gate of his enemies near the end (in 24:60). The long chapter (Gen 24) on the servant's journey to get Rebekah as Isaac's wife, ensuring the ongoing line of descent, is sandwiched between the deaths of Sarah and Abraham:

Yahweh says to Isaac in 26:3, "I will be with you and bless you," and the exact form for "and I will bless you" only occurs at Genesis 12:2 and 26:3 (וַאֲבָרְכֶךָ).[7] Similarly, the exact phrase used here when the Lord says, "I will be with you," (וְאֶהְיֶה עִמָּךְ) only occurs four times in all the Old Testament: with reference to Isaac in Genesis 26:3, Jacob in 31:3, David in 2 Samuel 7:9, and in the parallel in 1 Chronicles 17:8. This distinct, notable expression naturally connects Isaac, Jacob, and David to one another.

The Lord then declares to Isaac in Genesis 26:3, "to you and to your offspring I will give all these lands," a phrase that reiterates God's promise to Abram in Genesis 12:7, "To your offspring I will give this land."

Gen 12:7, "To your offspring I will give this land."

לְזַרְעֲךָ אֶתֵּן אֶת־הָאָרֶץ הַזֹּאת

Gen 26:3, "To your offspring I will give all these lands."

וּלְזַרְעֲךָ אֶתֵּן אֶת־כָּל־הָאֲרָצֹת הָאֵל

Cf. also Gen 24:7, "To your offspring I will give this land."

לְזַרְעֲךָ אֶתֵּן אֶת־הָאָרֶץ הַזֹּאת

The next phrase in Genesis 26:3 confirms that the repetitions of these phrases are establishing covenantal significance: "and I will establish [וַהֲקִמֹתִי] the oath [הַשְּׁבֻעָה] that I swore [נִשְׁבַּעְתִּי] to Abraham your father." For God to "establish" the "oath" that he "swore" is for him to keep the terms of the covenant he cut. In the making of the covenant, God made promises, and for God to make promises is for him to take "oaths," promissory statements, the failure of which to keep will bring down the curses of the covenant (cf. Gen 15:7–11, 17–18; Jer 33:18). God will never suffer the curses of the covenant

---

7. The Hebrew form for "I will bless you" is pointed slightly differently in Gen 12:2 as compared with 26:3 because at 26:3 the form is in pause (note the *athnach*). In both cases we have *piel* imperfects with 2ms suffixes.

because he will never break any of his oaths. He keeps his promises. God made these promises to Abraham in Genesis 12, 15, 17, and 22.

There were overtones of God's Genesis 1:28 blessing of the first man and woman when God said he would bless Isaac in 26:3, and 26:4 sounds the "be fruitful and multiply" note from Genesis 1:28 when God promises Isaac, "I will *multiply* your offspring." The next words recall the Lord telling Abraham to "look toward heaven, and number the stars" in Genesis 15:5, as the Lord says Isaac's seed will be multiplied "as the stars of heaven" (Gen 26:4), before reiterating the land promise and then reprising the 12:3 promise that "in you all the families of the earth shall be blessed" with the words, "And in your offspring all the nations of the earth shall be blessed" (26:4; cf. 18:18; 22:18; 28:14). These promises to Isaac in Genesis 26:4 are word-for-word quotations of the promise to Abraham in 22:17–18.

> Gen 22:17, "and multiplying I will multiply your seed as the stars of the heavens"
>
> וְהַרְבָּה אַרְבֶּה אֶת־זַרְעֲךָ כְּכוֹכְבֵי הַשָּׁמַיִם
>
> Gen 26:4, "and I will multiply your seed as the stars of the heavens"
>
> וְהִרְבֵּיתִי אֶת־זַרְעֲךָ כְּכוֹכְבֵי הַשָּׁמַיִם
>
> Gen 22:18, "they will be blessed in your seed—all the nations of the earth"
>
> וְהִתְבָּרֲכוּ בְזַרְעֲךָ כֹּל גּוֹיֵי הָאָרֶץ
>
> Gen 26:4, "they will be blessed in your seed—all the nations of the earth"
>
> וְהִתְבָּרֲכוּ בְזַרְעֲךָ כֹּל גּוֹיֵי הָאָרֶץ

In the final phrase of Genesis 22:18 the Lord explains to Abraham why all the nations of the earth will be blessed in his seed: "because you have obeyed my voice." The very same explanation is offered to Isaac after Genesis 22:18 is quoted in 26:4, "because Abraham obeyed my voice . . ." (Gen 26:5; cf. 26:24). Because of the quotations from Genesis 12 and 22, the obedience in view would seem to include everything from Abraham's faith-based departure from Ur of the Chaldees (11:31) to his act of faith in offering up Isaac (Gen 22). This obedience is like Noah's, when in response to the word of God Noah prepared the ark. These believing responses to God's commands result in Abram having his faith counted as righteousness (15:6) and Noah being "seen" as righteous (7:1). This is what it means to "find grace in Yahweh's eyes" (6:8), to be righteous, blameless, and to walk with God (6:9): to hear the word of God, believe it, and act in accordance with it.

In Genesis 26:1–5, then, we have the reuse of key terms, the quotation of whole phrases, repeated sequences of events, and similarity in covenantal and salvation historical significance. God pursues the fulfillment of the promises to Abraham through Isaac. Then in 26:6–11 Isaac sins in the same way his father had, repeating the sister-fib that puts his wife—through whom the promised seed will come—in jeopardy.

Moses has connected the sister-fib episodes in Genesis 12, 20, and 26 by means of the criteria we have been discussing. In all the Old Testament, the phrase "my sister is she" (אֲחֹתִי הִוא) occurs only at 12:19, 20:2, 5, and 26:7, 9. The concern of the patriarch that he will be killed is articulated in 12:12, 20:11, and 26:7. Abram and Isaac are both concerned about being killed because of their "beautiful" wives (12:11; 26:7). Both Abram and Isaac are told by the foreign king, "she is your wife!" (אִשְׁתְּךָ הִוא, 12:18; 26:9). Moses signals the sinfulness of what Abram and Isaac have done when he has the foreign king ask both of them, "What is this you have done . . . ?" (12:18; 26:10). The same question built of the same words in the same order was asked of the woman in Genesis 3:13, "What is this you have done?" (In all three instances, the Hebrew reads מַה־זֹּאת עָשִׂיתָ, the only variation being the feminine form when the question is posed to the woman in 3:13.)[8]

By showing Abraham doing this twice, once in Genesis 12 and again in Genesis 20, Moses has established the pattern. When Isaac repeats this course of action, we see that he is walking in the footsteps of his father Abraham, footsteps not only of faith but also of failure. The recipients of the promise believe what God has said, but they are flawed and foolish men capable of valuing their own temporary safety over their wives and the fulfillment of God's long-term promise.

As with Abraham so with Isaac: in spite of the patriarch's sinful folly, the Lord delivers his wife and blesses him (Gen 26:11–12). There is enmity between seed of the woman and seed of the serpent (26:14–16, 20), but Yahweh

---

8. Later in Genesis 29:25, Jacob poses this question to Laban when he realizes that he has married Leah rather than Rachel. A similar question worded slightly differently is posed to Cain in 4:10, "What have you done?" (מֶה עָשִׂיתָ).

enables the seed of the woman to be fruitful and multiply (26:22, 24). When Isaac builds an altar and calls upon the name of Yahweh in Genesis 26:25, we are reminded of the way that Seth, Noah, and Abraham did the same (4:26; 8:20; 12:7, 8; 13:4, 18; 21:33).

Abraham and Isaac are tied together by means of the sister-fib episodes in Genesis 12, 20, and 26, and Abraham is called a prophet in the one in Genesis 20 (Gen 20:7). The psalmist's reference to Isaac also being a prophet in Psalm 105:15 can be understood from two prominent features in the narrative of Genesis: first, the Lord did reveal himself to Isaac and grant him revelation that he communicated to others (esp. Gen 26:2, 24).[9] Second, the many linkages between Abraham and Isaac strongly suggest that what the Lord said about Abraham in Genesis 20:7 can also be said of Isaac.

§4.2 Isaac's Remarkable Birth

Moses links Isaac to several other figures in Genesis by noting that they have "barren" (עקרה) mothers. Several women in Genesis are said to be barren but then give birth: this is true of Isaac's mother Sarai (Gen 11:30), of Jacob and Esau's mother Rebekah (Isaac's wife, 25:21), and of Joseph and Benjamin's mother Rachel (Jacob's wife, 29:31).

The author of Judges connects Samson to Abraham, Isaac, and Jacob by noting that his mother too is barren (עֲקָרָה, Judg 13:2, 3), and the author of Samuel tells the story of how Hannah, Samuel's mother, had no children until the Lord remembered her (see 1 Sam 1, cf. 2:5). Though the word "barren" is not used in 2 Kings 4, the author of Kings recounts a story from Elisha's ministry with connections to the story of Isaac (2 Kgs 4:11–17).

A barren wife means the death of the family line.[10] No offspring, no *seed*, will continue the line of descent of the man whose wife has a dead womb. For a barren woman to have a child is akin, therefore, to the resurrection of a corpse from the dead. This way of thinking seems to explain the juxtaposition of a barren woman giving birth and resurrection from the dead seen in 1 Samuel 2:5b–6 (ESV),

---

9. Ken Mathews suggests that when Rebekah "went to inquire of the Lord" in Gen 25:22, she did so through her husband. Mathews, *Genesis 11:27–50:26*, 387.

10. Levenson points out "the functional equivalence of infertility with death and, correlatively, of miraculous conception or the restoration of the lost child with resurrection." *Resurrection and the Restoration of Israel*, xi.

The barren has borne seven,
> but she who has many children is forlorn.

The LORD kills and brings to life;
> he brings down to Sheol and raises up.

The context of this statement in Hannah's prayer is linked to Isaac's story in a number of ways. The nature of these links is surprising because the birth of Samuel is tied not directly to the birth of Isaac, even though both men had barren mothers, but to a birth that takes place in the context of the birth of Isaac, that of Ishmael.[11] Consider these parallels:

- Both Hagar and Hannah are in (unhappy) polygamous marriages (Gen 16:1–6; 1 Sam 1:1–2).
- Both Hagar and Hannah are mistreated by their rival wives, and both suffer "affliction" (עֳנִי, Gen 16:11; 1 Sam 1:11; cf. Gen 16:6; 1 Sam 1:6).
- Hagar knows that God has "seen" and "looked after" her (four forms of רָאָה in Gen 16:13–14), and Hannah calls on the Lord to "look on" her affliction (רָאָה in 1 Sam 1:11).
- Perhaps the most prominent parallel between the births of Ishmael and Samuel is the fact that both are given a name that means "God hears." The names Ishmael (יִשְׁמָעֵאל) and Samuel (Shmuel, שְׁמוּאֵל) are both built from the word for "hear" (שָׁמַע) and the word "God" (אֵל).

These parallels prompt readers of Samuel to recall the birth of Ishmael. The contrasts between Hagar and Hannah put Hannah in a positive light, and the contrasts between Ishmael and Samuel do the same for Samuel. Meanwhile, the barrenness of Hannah links her to Sarah, and Samuel the prophet's remarkable birth points back to Isaac and forward to others who will come after.

One figure between Isaac and Samuel should be noted before we move on because of the parallels between himself and Samuel. We read of the barren mother of Samson in Judges 13:2–3, and when the angel of the LORD announces Samson's birth to her in 13:5, he says, "No razor shall come upon his head, for the child shall be a Nazirite to God from the womb, and he shall

---

11. We considered some of these parallels and their implications in the Excursus on Ishmael in Chapter 2 above.

begin to save Israel from the hand of the Philistines" (ESV). Samson's mother fills in more detail when she reports on the incident in 13:7 to her husband, saying, "he said to me, 'Behold, you shall conceive and bear a son. So then drink no wine or strong drink, and eat nothing unclean, for the child shall be a Nazirite to God from the womb to the day of his death'" (ESV).

Perhaps informed by the story of Samson, the author of Samuel presents Hannah praying in 1 Samuel 1:11 (ESV), "O Lord of hosts, if you will indeed look on the affliction of your servant and remember me and forget not your servant, but will give to your servant a son, then I will give him to the Lord all the days of his life, and no razor shall touch his head." Like Samson, it appears that Samuel will be a Nazirite from birth.

Both Samson and Samuel were born to barren mothers and designated as Nazirites from birth, and the barrenness of their mothers (with other points of contact discussed above) connects them to Isaac. One part of this typological pattern is fulfilled when the angel of the Lord appears to Zechariah, aged husband of an aged wife, to announce that barren Elizabeth will give birth to a prophet like Samson and Samuel who will be a Nazirite from birth (Luke 1:5–15). The pattern in some ways repeats, but in all ways is transcended, when the angel announces to the virgin Mary that she will give birth to Jesus, who will bring to fulfillment the pattern of devoted prophets whose births are unexpected, indeed impossible (1:26–33).

§4.3 The Offering of Isaac and His Resurrection

Isaac was the beloved son of his father (Gen 22:2), and Luke presented Jesus using the Greek translation of the phrase in question in his parable of the wicked tenants:

LXX Gen 22:2, τὸν υἱόν σου τὸν ἀγαπητόν
"your son, the beloved" (i.e., "your beloved son")

Luke 20:13, τὸν υἱόν μου τὸν ἀγαπητόν
"my son, the beloved" (i.e., "my beloved son")

In addition, to being the beloved son, Isaac's birth was a miracle (Gen 11:30). And Yahweh repeatedly revealed himself to Isaac (26:2, 24), declaring the future to him. This beloved son of his father, born a miracle, prophet who received revelatory appearances of Yahweh, moreover, was offered up by his father as a sacrificial burnt offering and came back alive from the experience. The quotation of the material in the New Testament, the similarity in event sequence, and the covenantal significance establish that what happens in Jesus fulfills what Isaac typified. The more thoroughly we understand the Bible, the more interconnected we see it to be.

Still, there are questions. For instance, why might the author of Hebrews conclude that Abraham was expecting God to raise Isaac from the dead (Heb 11:17–19)? We have seen above that the birth of a child to a barren woman is conceptually like resurrection from the dead, a perspective reflected by the apostle Paul when he describes Abraham believing in God "who gives life to the dead," and then speaks of how Abraham "did not weaken in faith when he considered his own body, which was as good as dead . . . or when he considered the barrenness of Sarah's womb" (Rom 4:17, 19, ESV).

In addition to the birth of Isaac in Genesis 21 being like resurrection from the dead, there is also the concern to bury Sarah in the land of promise in Genesis 23, likewise with Abraham (Gen 25:1–11), Jacob (49:29–33), and Joseph (50:25; cf. Heb 11:22). The concern for burial in the land, even though they have not received the land as promised, indicates that they hope to be raised from the dead to receive the land as promised.[12]

Within the narrative of Genesis 22 itself, Abraham clearly means to obey Yahweh and offer Isaac up as a sacrifice. When he uses first-person plurals in 22:5 to say, "*we* will go over there and *we* will worship and *we* will come again to you," he indicates that though he will offer Isaac up as a sacrifice, he also believes that Isaac will return with him alive. The overtones of resurrection from the surrounding context indicate that Moses intended his audience to understand that Abraham thought Isaac would be raised from the dead, just as the author of Hebrews says (Heb 11:19). This conclusion is substantiated by the way the author of Kings connects the story of Isaac to the story of Elisha raising a child from the dead.

The author of Kings, I contend, reinforces what Moses taught in Genesis by linking a resurrection account in 2 Kings 4 to the Isaac narrative in Genesis.[13]

---

12. See esp. Chase, "Genesis of Resurrection Hope," esp. 477–80.

13. For a similar, independent, analysis, see Levenson, who writes of these narratives, "specific points of diction suggest that we may be dealing not merely with a similar theme, deeply rooted in Israelite culture, but with actual literary dependence as well." Levenson, *Resurrection and the Restoration of Israel*, 123–26, quote on p. 124.

This later biblical author has himself rightly discerned what Moses intended to communicate, and to further that Mosaic agenda, he tied a narrative where Elisha raises a boy from the dead to the story of Isaac, to bolster faith in the God who brings good out of evil and life out of death.

The author of Kings relates how a Shunammite woman began to provide for the physical needs of Elisha the prophet (2 Kgs 4:8–11; cf. Luke 8:2–3). On one of his stops to rest, Elisha inquires as to how he might bless the Shunammite woman for her kindness to him (2 Kgs 4:11–13). In 2 Kings 4:14 we read of how Elisha "said, 'What then is to be done for her?' Gehazi answered, 'Well, she has no son, and her husband is old'" (ESV). To anyone familiar with the story of Abraham and Sarah, reference to an old husband and a childless wife will call them to mind. When Elisha has the woman summoned in 2 Kings 4:15 we read that "she stood in the doorway" (ESV), and the term rendered "doorway" here (פֶּתַח) is the same one used to speak of Sarah "listening at the tent door (מִפֶּתַח הָאֹהֶל) behind" (ESV) Abraham when one of the three men (Gen 18:2) who speaks for Yahweh announced to him the birth of Isaac (Gen 18:10).

With the same kinds of characters (spokesperson for Yahweh, aged husband, barren wife) in the same location (at the door), Elisha makes the same promise to the Shunammite woman that was made to Abraham and Sarah: "At this season, about this time next year, you shall embrace a son" (2 Kgs 4:16, ESV). In the next verse we read that "she bore a son about that time the following spring, as Elisha had said to her" (4:17, ESV). What Elisha says to the Shunammite closely corresponds to what Sarah heard spoken to Abraham when she was standing at the door: "I will surely return to you about this time next year, and Sarah your wife shall have a son" (Gen 18:10, ESV). In response to Sarah's laughter, Yahweh says to Abraham in Genesis 18:14 (ESV), "Is anything too hard for the LORD? At the appointed time I will return to you, about this time next year, and Sarah shall have a son." In the previous chapter of Genesis, God had promised Abraham, "I will establish my covenant with Isaac, whom Sarah shall bear to you at this time next year" (17:21, ESV). These statements recur in 2 Kings 4:16 and 4:17.

Gen 17:21, אֲשֶׁר תֵּלֵד לְךָ שָׂרָה לַמּוֹעֵד הַזֶּה בַּשָּׁנָה הָאַחֶרֶת

"whom Sarah will bear to you **at this appointed time**, in the following year"

שׁוֹב אָשׁוּב אֵלֶיךָ כָּעֵת חַיָּה וְהִנֵּה־בֵן לְשָׂרָה אִשְׁתֶּךָ ,Gen 18:10

"returning I will return to you **according to the time of life** [i.e., spring], and behold, a son to Sarah your wife"

לְמוֹעֵד אָשׁוּב אֵלֶיךָ כָּעֵת חַיָּה וּלְשָׂרָה בֵן ,Gen 18:14

"**at the appointed time** I will return to you, **according to the time of life**, and to Sarah a son"

לְמוֹעֵד הַזֶּה כָּעֵת חַיָּה אַתְּ חֹבֶקֶת בֵּן ,2 Kgs 4:16

"**at this appointed time, according to the time of life,** you will embrace a son"

וַתֵּלֶד בֵּן לַמּוֹעֵד הַזֶּה כָּעֵת חַיָּה ,2 Kgs 4:17

"and she bore a son **at this appointed time, according to the time of life**"

By his repetition of the famous phrases from the announcement of Isaac's birth in Genesis, the author of Kings indicates that he means for his audience to think of the promise of the birth of Isaac when he presents Elisha promising that the Shunammite woman will have a son. The phrase "at this appointed time" (לְמוֹעֵד הַזֶּה) occurs only three times in all of the Old Testament: at Genesis 17:21, 2 Kings 4:16, and 4:17. Similarly, the phrase "according to the time of life" (כָּעֵת חַיָּה) occurs only four times in all of the Old Testament: at Genesis 18:10, 18:14, 2 Kings 4:16, and 4:17.

Another interesting point of contact between the two passages is that Sarah denies having laughed, and her attempt at deception is rejected (Gen 18:15). When Elisha tells the Shunammite woman she will have a son, she tells him not to lie to her (2 Kgs 4:16, cf. 4:28). He is of course not lying.

So the narrative of the birth of the Shunammite's son is linked back to the narrative of the birth of Isaac. What is the significance of that? Consider the parallels: after the birth of Isaac in Genesis 21, the next event in which he is directly involved is when he is taken to Mount Moriah to be sacrificed in Genesis 22. In the 2 Kings narrative, after the boy is born in 2 Kings 4:17, he dies when he is with his father among the reapers in 4:18–21, and after his mother goes to Elisha in 4:22–31, Elisha raises the boy from the dead in 4:32–37. By noting the similarity between the announcement of the birth of the Shunammite's son to the announcement of the birth of Isaac, the author of

Kings puts the raising of the Shunammite's son from the dead in the same narrative "slot" occupied by the sacrifice of Isaac in Genesis. Later in this chapter we will return to Elisha's prophetic ministry. At this point my purpose has been to indicate that the author of Kings connected Elisha's promise of a child to a barren woman, and then his raising of that child from the dead, to the birth and sacrifice of Isaac, confirming and extending the overtones of resurrection already present in the Genesis narrative. As Levenson puts it concerning the narratives of Genesis and Kings, "the former averts a death, the latter reverses a death, but each acts to guarantee that the couple's line survives and that they have descendants, which is to say, continuation after their individual deaths."[14]

Abraham did not spare his beloved son—born of miracle, recipient of prophetic revelation—but offered him up as a sacrifice. And nor did the Father, who brought to fulfilment all that Isaac typified in his beloved Son, whom he did not spare but gave him up for us all (Rom 8:32).

More could be said about prophets in Genesis, not least with respect to Jacob and Joseph. We go forward, however, to Moses, which will allow us to return to Noah.

§5 MOSES

Moses is the paradigmatic Old Testament prophet.[15] From the threat to his life at his birth (Exod 2:1–10), to the promise of a prophet like him (Deut 18:15–19), which joins up with the statement that none like him has yet arisen (Deut 34:10–12), everything about Moses is like a soundboard, reverberating with the past, resonating into the future before it comes to pass. We begin by considering ways that connections are established between Moses and Noah by means of lexical points of contact, event sequences, and covenantal significance, before briefly summarizing salient features of the narratives concerning Moses to sow the seeds that will be watered when we consider prophets like Moses.

§5.1 Noah and Moses

The linguistic points of contact between the narratives concerning Noah and Moses draw our attention to similarities in sequences of events between

---

14. Levenson, *Resurrection and the Restoration of Israel*, 126.

15. Having written this sentence, I later came across Rendtorff's discussion entitled, "The paradigmatic prophet," in Rolf Rendtorff, *The Canonical Hebrew Bible: A Theology of the Old Testament* (Leiden: Deo, 2005), 550–52.

the two, and these features join with the covenantal and salvation historical significance of both Noah and Moses to produce a typological dynamic. Noah is an installment in an Adamic pattern, and the historical correspondence between Noah and Moses makes Moses an installment in the pattern of Noah. Both Noah and Moses point forward to *the* prophet through whom God will make covenant with his people.

The narratives dealing with Noah and Moses employ the same language: Genesis 7:2 recounts how the Lord instructed Noah to take seven pairs of clean (טָהוֹר) animals and one pair of unclean (לֹא טְהֹרָה) animals. For readers of the Pentateuch, the clean/unclean distinction forges a connection between the instructions given to Noah and the instructions given to Moses (see Lev 11, esp., 11:47, טָמֵא, "unclean," טָהוֹר, "clean"). Similarly, anticipating the altar building of Abraham and his seed and the instructions in the Mosaic covenant (Exod 20:24–26), Noah "built an altar" and "offered burnt offerings on the altar," and "the LORD smelled the pleasing aroma" (Gen 8:20–21, ESV; see Exod 29:18, 25, 41; Lev 1:9, 13, 17, etc.).

Note the way the same phrases appear in Genesis 8:20 and Exodus 17:15,

Gen 8:20, וַיִּבֶן נֹחַ מִזְבֵּחַ
"And Noah built an altar."

Exod 17:15, וַיִּבֶן מֹשֶׁה מִזְבֵּחַ
"And Moses built an altar."

At many points the people of Israel offer burnt offerings under Moses's leadership (e.g., Exod 24:5), and of course under the Mosaic law only clean animals are to be offered up to Yahweh (e.g., Lev 14:4). The phrase "pleasing aroma" appears regularly with reference to how Yahweh will perceive the sacrifices prescribed in the Mosaic law. In Genesis 9:4 the post-flood Noahic covenant prohibition on eating "flesh with its life, that is, its blood" anticipates the fuller explanation of the principle behind the prohibition, with its restatement, in Leviticus 17:10–11. With both Noah and Moses we read of significant seven and forty day periods of time (Gen 7:4, 10, 12, 17; 8:6, 10, 12; Exod 7:25; 12:15; 20:9–11; 24:18; 34:28), and both Noah and Moses are given "signs" (אוֹת, Gen 9:12–17; e.g., Exod 3:12).

We could continue this way with lexical points of contact, but the more significant question is whether the reuse of language occurs to establish parallel event sequences. The answer is yes, they do. Consider these parallels:

- Noah "found grace in the eyes of Yahweh" (Gen 6:8), and the Lord saw him as righteous (7:1). In Exodus 33:17 Yahweh says to Moses, "you have found grace in my eyes" (cf. Exod 33:12). What Moses's mother perceived about him being "a fine child" (Exod 2:2) seems to have indicated to her that he would be significant in God's purposes (cf. Acts 7:20, "beautiful in God's sight;" see also Heb 11:23). The point here is that in the accounts of both Noah and Moses we have textual indication that they were "seen" to be significant before the deliverance took place.
- God revealed himself to Noah and gave him instructions that he had to believe in order to be delivered (Gen 6:13–21). God revealed himself to Moses and gave him instructions that he had to believe in order for Israel to be delivered (Exod 3–4).
- God instructed Noah to build an "ark" (תֵּבָה) and "cover it . . . with pitch" (Gen 6:14, term for "pitch" here כֹּפֶר), and in this ark Noah was saved through waters of judgment in which all his contemporaries died. Moses's mother put him in an "ark" (תֵּבָה) "and daubed it with pitch" (Exod 2:3, term for "pitch" here זֶפֶת), and in this "basket" (ESV) Moses was saved through waters of death in which all the male Hebrew children his age were to die (Exod 1:22).
- Both Noah and Moses did all that Yahweh commanded. Consider the clearly parallel utterances in Genesis 6:22 and Exodus 40:16.

> Gen 6:22, "And Noah did according to all that God commanded him, thus he did."
>
> וַיַּעַשׂ נֹחַ כְּכֹל אֲשֶׁר צִוָּה אֹתוֹ אֱלֹהִים כֵּן עָשָׂה
>
> Exod 40:16, "And Moses did according to all that Yahweh commanded him, thus he did."
>
> וַיַּעַשׂ מֹשֶׁה כְּכֹל אֲשֶׁר צִוָּה יְהוָה אֹתוֹ כֵּן עָשָׂה

This comment on Noah comes in the midst of his preparation for the flood, before the deliverance happens. The comment on Moses, by contrast, comes after he himself was delivered by the ark in the Nile, after the exodus from Egypt, and after the construction of the tabernacle at Mount Sinai. Still, the parallel seems to indicate that the biblical author intended his audience to connect the obedience of Noah with that of Moses. The fact that the parallel statements are not placed at the same points in the sequence indicates that the parallels actually happened this way in history and are not mere literary contrivances of the author—a point that stands for this parallel and many others. Typology is concerned with things that actually took place in history.

- After they each experience deliverance in the ark through the waters of judgment, both Noah and Moses stand at the beginning of new eras in the progress of redemptive history, and in both cases Yahweh enters into covenant with his people (Gen 9:8–11; Exod 24:3–8), Noah and Moses representing them before Yahweh.
- Shortly after the ark-deliverances and the making of the covenants, in both cases there is significant sin: Noah's drunkenness and Ham's dishonoring of his father (Gen 9:20–29), and the people's sin with the golden calf (Exod 32).

The linguistic points of contact, the similarities in event-sequences, and the parallel covenantal significance of Noah and Moses validate the idea that Moses is an installment in a typological pattern seen in Noah. As Kenneth Mathews has written,

> There are remarkable similarities between Noah's deliverance and that of Moses as recounted in Exodus 1–2 . . . [evidence and observations] . . . Moses, then, is another Noah whose career inaugurates a new epoch.[16]

At this point the following can be observed: after the baptism of the world in the floodwaters of God's wrath, God makes a covenant with Noah. After the baptism of the army of Pharaoh in waters of judgment at the Red Sea, God makes a covenant with Moses. After the baptism that Jesus undergoes, experiencing the fulfillment of the outpouring of God's wrath, God makes the new covenant with him. Morales writes,

---

16. Mathews, *Genesis 1–11:26*, 363, see also p. 351.

Israel was not merely delivered from the waters of death, but through them, dying to the old life-in-Egypt in the process and in preparation for life-with-God in the land of Canaan, even as Noah was delivered through the waters of death, dying to the old creation so as to live in the present one.[17]

We could paraphrase this by saying they experienced salvation through judgment for the glory of God, or, to put it Paul's way: "We were buried therefore with him by baptism into death, in order that, just as Christ was raised from the dead by the glory of the Father, we too might walk in newness of life" (Rom 6:4, ESV; cf. 1 Pet 3:20–21).

The flood baptism is followed by a covenant with Noah.

The Red Sea baptism by a covenant with Moses.

And the baptism Christ undergoes on the cross inaugurates the new covenant with Jesus.

§5.2 Moses as a Prophet

There was a time when I wrote blog posts, and I would occasionally get notifications from the blogging platform with references to "pingbacks." These pingbacks happened when another website linked to a blog I had posted. Though everything we know about Moses and his ministry from Exodus, Leviticus, Numbers, and Deuteronomy is relevant to his prophetic ministry, to sharpen our discussion here I want to focus on just a few examples where what happens in Moses's life has created a pingback to an earlier passage and where later passages create pingbacks to Moses. I will take these in the order they appear in the Pentateuch. These connections forge typological identifications between people who served as prophets, suggesting that they are installations in prophetic patterns.

After Moses was delivered alive through waters of death in his ark-basket, we read in Exodus 2:10, "When the child grew older, she brought him to Pharaoh's daughter, and he became her son. She named him Moses [מֹשֶׁה], 'Because,' she said, 'I drew him out of the water [מִן־הַמַּיִם מְשִׁיתִהוּ]'" (ESV). In Psalm 18:16 (MT 18:17), David writes, "He sent from on high, he took me; he drew me out of many waters [יַמְשֵׁנִי מִמַּיִם רַבִּים]." With the 2 Samuel passage parallel to Psalm 18 (2 Sam 22:17), these are the only places this verb

---

17. Morales, *Who Shall Ascend the Mountain of the Lord?*, 129.

("drew . . . out," מָשָׁה) appears in all the Old Testament. This comes after
Sinai imagery in Psalm 18:7–14 (MT 18:8–15) and a quotation of Exodus 15:8
in Psalm 18:15 (MT 18:16), "Then the channels of the sea were seen . . . at the
blast of the breath of your nostrils [מִנִּשְׁמַת רוּחַ אַפֶּךָ]." Exodus 15:8 speaks
of the parting of the Red Sea with the words, "At the blast of your nostrils
[וּבְרוּחַ אַפֶּיךָ] the waters piled up . . ." David seems to be describing the Lord
delivering him in terms drawn from the way the Lord delivered Israel at the
exodus and at the parting of the Red Sea, and in the reference to Exodus 2:10 in
Psalm 18:16 (MT 18:17) David speaks of himself in Mosaic terms.[18] As the Lord
made the covenant at Sinai through Moses, so the Lord made a covenant with
David regarding the future king from his line. David is elsewhere presented
as a prophet (see esp. 2 Sam 23:1–2; Acts 2:30).

Immediately after the daughter of Pharaoh names Moses, having drawn
him from the waters in Exodus 2:10, we read in 2:11–15 of how Moses's Hebrew
kinsmen answered him with the words, "Who made you a prince and a judge
over us?" (Exod 2:14). Then Pharaoh seeks to kill Moses (2:15). This rejection
of Moses by his kinsmen is not unlike the way Joseph's brothers rejected him
(Gen 37:18–28). Just as Joseph and Moses were rejected by kinsmen, David will
be answered harshly by his brothers and then hunted ferociously by his Israelite
kinsman Saul (1 Sam 17–31; see further Chapter 6 on the Righteous Sufferer).[19]

Having fled from Egypt, Moses meets his wife by a well in Exodus
2:15–22. Abraham's servant met Rebekah, who would be Isaac's wife, at a
well (Gen 24:11–15), and Jacob met Rachel at a well (29:8–9). Jesus interacts
with the Samaritan woman, in a passage laden with symbolic significance, at
a well in John 4.

When the Lord appeared to Moses in the burning bush, the ensuing conversation involved a number of exchanges between Yahweh and Moses. Moses
protests that he is "not eloquent" (ESV, lit. "not a man of words" לֹא אִישׁ דְּבָרִים,
Exod 4:10), and the Lord tells him, "I will be with your mouth and teach you
what you shall speak" (4:12). Moses, the prophet who is to speak for God, says
there is a problem with his ability to speak, and the Lord resolves the problem
by saying he will be with Moses. Later "prophets like Moses" include Isaiah
and Jeremiah. Both Isaiah and Jeremiah assert some problem with their ability

---

18. See the discussion of Psalm 18 in Hamilton, *Psalms* ad loc.
19. Chapter 8 of Hensley's excellent study is entitled, "David as a New Moses," Hensley, *Covenant and the Editing of the Psalter*, 157–82.

to speak (Isa 6:5; Jer 1:6; cf. also Exod 6:30), and in both cases the Lord brings resolution to the problem (Isa 6:6–7; Jer 1:7–9; cf. also Exod 7:1–2).

The genealogical line from Adam to Abram is traced in Genesis 5 and 11. A similar genealogical concern for the ancestry of Moses appears in Exodus 6:14–27.

In a significant incident in the life of Moses, the Lord took some of the Spirit upon him and gave it to the seventy elders (Num 11:16–25). When Moses was asked if he wanted two of the elders who had remained in the camp and were prophesying there to be stopped, he exclaimed his wish that all God's people had the Spirit, that all of them were prophets (11:26–29). If they all had the Spirit and were prophets, they would all instinctively know what God would want them to do. This episode seems to be engaged when Elisha asks for a double portion of Elijah's spirit (2 Kgs 2:9–15), and Joel seems to point to a day when what Moses wished for would become reality: all God's people would have the Spirit and be prophets (Joel 2:28–29, MT 3:1–2; cf. Acts 2:16–21).

Moses not only faced rejection from his kinsmen in Exodus 2, he was betrayed by those closest to him when Miriam and Aaron spoke against him in Numbers 12:1–9. The betrayal of Moses by his brother is reminiscent of Cain's treatment of Abel and Joseph's brothers' treatment of him. It also anticipates the betrayal of David by Ahithophel and then Absalom. All these contribute to the theme of the righteous sufferer (see Chapter 6 below).

The rebellion against Moses continues in Numbers 14 when, in response to the bad report of the spies (Num 13), the people grumble against Moses and Aaron and want to choose a leader to return to Egypt (Num 14:1–4). As he did at the golden calf episode (Exod 32:10), Yahweh threatens to destroy and disinherit the people and make a greater nation from Moses (Num 14:12). As on that earlier occasion (Exod 32:11–14), Moses intercedes and Yahweh relents (Num 14:13–20). The pattern of Mosaic intercession informs the experiences of prophets-like-Moses such as Eli (1 Sam 3:10–18), Elijah (see 1 Kgs 19:9–18), and Jeremiah, whom the Lord tells not to pray for Israel (Jer 7:16; 11:14; 14:11).

It might not be an overstatement to say that any one of the details from the narratives of the way Moses led Israel out of Egypt, through the wilderness, to the plains of Moab could serve to evoke Yahweh's mighty acts on his people's behalf. The whole complex of events from the exodus to the conquest serves as a paradigm for the way that Yahweh would save his people in the future, and Moses can be referenced in any number of ways, as we will see as we continue.

§5.3 Prophets like Moses

In Deuteronomy 18:9–14 Moses warns Israel not to imitate the way the people of Canaan seek supernatural information. They burn their children as offerings (Deut 18:10), apparently to solicit the help of wicked deities who would receive such horrific acts as something good, and they practice divination, tell fortunes, interpret omens, and make use of sorcerers, charmers, mediums, and necromancers, but all this is abominable to Yahweh and not to be practiced by Israel (18:10–14). How, then, is Israel to get supernatural guidance? Moses answers that question in Deuteronomy 18:15–22. Yahweh promises to raise up a prophet like Moses for Israel (Deut 18:15), and the prophet's ministry is compared to the way that Moses interceded for Israel by getting the revelation from Yahweh for them at Sinai in 18:16–17. Yahweh reiterates his promise to raise up a prophet like Moses in 18:18, then cautions that he will deal with those who do not listen in 18:19, before warning of those who claim to be prophets but whom he did not send in 18:20–22.

Because of the way the ministry of the prophet like Moses in 18:15–19 follows the abominable Canaanite attempts to get revelation in 18:9–14, it seems we should understand that Yahweh has promised to raise up a prophet like Moses in an ongoing, regular way. When we combine the immediate context (the prophet contrasted with ongoing Canaanite practice) with the fact that later prophets are compared with Moses and presented in terms that recall his ministry, it seems that Moses intended to indicate that Israel could expect a series of prophets like Moses raised up as Yahweh saw fit. Later biblical authors, beginning with Joshua, seem to have presented the prophets who followed Moses as prophets like Moses. Arguably, this begins within the Pentateuch with the way that Joshua is appointed as Moses's successor in Numbers 27:12–23.

In addition, however, to the way that the context of Deuteronomy 18 and the presentation of later prophets point to a succession of prophets like Moses, Deuteronomy 34:10 also attests to an expectation for a prophet *uniquely* like Moses: "And there has not arisen a prophet since in Israel like Moses, whom the LORD knew face to face" (ESV). At the end of the Torah, then, Deuteronomy engenders expectation for the Lord to raise up for Israel a succession of prophets like Moses (Deut 18:15–19) *and* a prophet uniquely like Moses (34:10).

The Torah's narratives of the prophetic leadership of Moses set down an archetypal pattern, and that pattern intertwines with the promise of prophets like Moses to shape expectation and guide interpretation. Moses himself presents Joshua as the first prophet like Moses, as we will see in the next section, by his treatment of Joshua in the book of Numbers. For later biblical authors, the pattern of the ministry of Moses and the promise of others like him guides the way they see and interpret what happens, and the Spirit inspires them to write up their accounts of later prophets in accordance with the teaching of earlier Scripture. These later prophets, then, become installments in the typological pattern seen in Moses.

§6 JOSHUA

The appointment of Joshua as successor to Moses in Numbers 27 points back to earlier prophetic figures, including Moses, and forward to those who will lead Israel after Joshua. Because of the order in which key phrases occur in the text, we will first consider the way Numbers 27 points forward, then how it points backward.

§6.1 Pointing Forward

Numbers 27:12–23 recounts how the Lord instructed Moses to appoint Joshua as his successor. Moses was not a king, and Joshua is not a king. Yet both lead the people in royal ways, doing so as prophets of God whom the Lord has designated to lead his people and through whom the Lord gives guidance and revelation to his people. The archetypal quality of the leadership of Moses and Joshua can be seen from the way that later narratives about kings will employ phrases first used with reference to Joshua in Numbers 27. Joshua is not a king, but kings are interpreted in light of what he did and presented in terms that recall the way he led Israel. Allison comments,

> if, as appears, Joshua himself is intended to be "the prototype of the ideal king of Israel," . . . , it follows that Moses is, so to speak, the model for the model of the king. That is, Moses, as Joshua's type, is implicitly the prototype of Israel's (or Judah's) ruler. The author of Joshua made his hero the standard of kingship by, among other things, indelibly stamping Moses' shape upon him.[20]

---

20. Allison, *The New Moses*, 27.

The Lord tells Moses that he will be allowed to see but not enter the promised land in Numbers 27:12–14, in response to which Moses calls on Yahweh in Numbers 27:16 to "appoint (פָּקַד) a man over the congregation," describing the nation's need in 27:17 for a man "who shall go out before them and come in before them, who shall lead them out and bring them in, that the congregation of the Lord may not be as sheep that have no shepherd" (ESV).

The paradigmatic nature of Joshua's prophetic leadership can be seen from the way later biblical authors include language from Numbers 27:17, chiefly the reference to the need for one "who shall go out before them and come in before them" (ESV), in accounts dealing with kings (following the ESV in the bullet points below):

- 1 Samuel 8:20, "that our king may judge us and go out before us and fight our battles."
- 1 Samuel 18:13, "So Saul removed him from his presence and made him a commander of a thousand. And he went out and came in before the people."
- 1 Kings 3:7, "And now, O Lord my God, you have made your servant king in place of David my father, although I am but a little child. I do not know how to go out or come in."
- 2 Chronicles 1:10, "Give me now wisdom and knowledge to go out and come in before this people, for who can govern this people of yours, which is so great?"

Also related is what Joshua 14:11 presents Caleb saying, "I am still as strong today as I was in the day that Moses sent me; my strength now is as my strength was then, for war and for going and coming" (ESV).

The "sheep without a shepherd" statement in Numbers 27:17 also reverberates through the Old Testament into the New (here too the texts in the following bullet points follow the ESV):

- 1 Kings 22:17, "I saw all Israel scattered on the mountains, as sheep that have no shepherd. And the Lord said, 'These have no master; let each return to his home in peace.'"
- Ezekiel 34:5, "So they were scattered, because there was no shepherd, and they became food for all the wild beasts."

- Zechariah 10:2, "For the household gods utter nonsense, and the diviners see lies; they tell false dreams and give empty consolation. Therefore the people wander like sheep; they are afflicted for lack of a shepherd."
- Matthew 9:36, "When he saw the crowds, he had compassion for them, because they were harassed and helpless, like sheep without a shepherd" (similarly Mark 6:34).

The whole-canon resonance of this reference to the people needing Joshua to lead them that they might not be like sheep without a shepherd attests to the prototypical nature of the whole-nation leadership of Moses, followed by the ectypal installments of Joshua and other prophets like Moses, culminating in Jesus, the antitype. The way the prophetic conqueror Joshua's leadership shaped the references to Israel's kings highlights the intersecting and overlapping significance of the offices of prophet and king.

§6.2 Pointing Backward

As later texts will pick up the language of Numbers 27:17, so Numbers 27:18 picks up language from an earlier text: "So the Lord said to Moses, 'Take Joshua the son of Nun, a man in whom is the Spirit [אִישׁ אֲשֶׁר־רוּחַ בּוֹ], and lay your hand on him." In Genesis 41:38 Pharaoh says of Joseph, "Can we find a man like this, in whom is the Spirit of God [אִישׁ אֲשֶׁר רוּחַ אֱלֹהִים בּוֹ]?"[21] Moses appears to have noticed the similarity of what Yahweh said about Joshua to what Pharaoh said about Joseph, and because Moses wanted his audience to connect Joseph and Joshua, he made sure to include both statements in his narrative.

Many features of the narrative of Joshua will be discussed when we consider the conquest as a new-exodus in Chapter 8 below. Here I want to survey parallels between Joshua and Moses that show him to be a prophet like Moses, an installment in a typological pattern that will be fulfilled when *the* prophet like Moses arises. Joshua is presented as Moses's direct successor (Josh 1:1–2), and Yahweh promises to be with Joshua *as he was with Moses* (1:5; 3:7; cf. 1:17).

The conquest of the land is presented as a new exodus, and this extends to Joshua having an experience remarkably like that of Moses at the burning bush (Exod 3:1–6), where like Moses Joshua is told to remove his sandals for

---

21. Compare similar statements in Daniel 4:8, 18; 5:11, 14. For discussion, see Joshua M. Philpot, "Was Joseph a Type of Daniel? Typological Correspondence in Genesis 37–50 and Daniel 1–6," *Journal of the Evangelical Theological Society* 61 (2018): 681–96.

the ground is holy (Josh 5:13–15). Joshua intercedes for Israel as Moses did (Josh 7:6–15; cf. Exod 32; Num 14), and he executes justice as Moses did (Josh 7:16–26; cf. Num 15:32–36).

At the end of Deuteronomy, near the end of Moses's life, Moses charged Israel to avoid idolatry and warned of their inability to keep the law without Yahweh's enabling power (Deut 28–33; see esp. 29:4 [MT 29:3]). Similarly, at the end of the book of Joshua, near the end of Joshua's life, Joshua charged Israel to avoid idolatry and warned of their inability to keep the law without Yahweh's enabling power (Josh 23–24; see esp. 24:19). The description of Moses writing in Deuteronomy 31:24–26 seems to serve as the template for Joshua 24:26–27. These passages are parallel in at least four ways, and the four points of correspondence come in the same order in both passages:

TABLE 4.1: Correspondences between Deuteronomy 31:24–26 and Joshua 24:26–27 (Scripture on this Table ESV)

Point of Correspondence	Deuteronomy 31:24–26	Joshua 24:26–27
1. The Prophet Wrote	"When Moses had finished writing	"And Joshua wrote these words
2. In the Torah Scroll	the words of this law in a book to the very end, Moses commanded the Levites who carried the ark of the covenant of the LORD, 'Take this Book of the Law	in the Book of the Law of God.
3. At the Holy Place	and put it by the side of the ark of the covenant of the LORD your God,	And he took a large stone and set it up there under the terebinth that was by the sanctuary of the LORD.
4. As a Witness	that it may be there for a witness against you . . .'"	And Joshua said to all the people, 'Behold, this stone shall be a witness against us, for it has heard all the words of the LORD that he spoke to us. Therefore it shall be a witness against you, lest you deal falsely with your God.'"

The end of the books of Deuteronomy and Joshua are concerned with "witnesses" (Deut 31:26; Josh 24:22), and whereas the end of Deuteronomy describes the death of Moses (Deut 34:1–8), the end of Joshua narrates his death (Josh 24:29–30).

We will consider the way that Joshua's crossing of the Jordan River re-enacts Moses leading Israel through the Red Sea in Chapter 8 below. In view of what we will see about Elijah and Elisha in the next section, however, we must note the way that the crossing of the Jordan in Joshua re-enacts and is directly compared with the crossing of the Red Sea: "For the LORD your God dried up the waters of the Jordan for you until you passed over, as the LORD your God did to the Red Sea, which he dried up for us until we passed over . . ." (Josh 4:23, ESV).

The clear succession from Moses to Joshua is marked by the repetition of the Red Sea crossing in the Jordan River crossing. The prophets-like-Moses Elijah and Elisha join together to repeat patterns seen in Moses and Joshua, and the repetitions cause expectation to increase, generating anticipation for another pair of prophets to come later.

§7 ELIJAH AND ELISHA

As mentioned in Chapter 1, the reuse of key terms, the quotation of lines, repetitions of event sequences, and similarities in significance can be considered indicators that biblical authors are forging historical correspondence on the micro-level. These features are also used to forge repetitions and parallels in broader narratives to create macro-level correspondences by means of wide-angle literary structures. This section provides a foretaste of the discussion of literary structures that concludes this study in Chapter 11.

§7.1 The Literary Structure of Kings

The narrative of 1–2 Kings has been carefully structured and appears to have a concentric arrangement. At the beginning of the narrative the nation is united under the Davidic king (1 Kgs 1–11), and at the end only Judah remains, Israel having been exiled (2 Kgs 18–25). The second and second to last sections narrate the division of the kingdom into Israel and Judah (1 Kgs 12) and the downfall of Israel (2 Kgs 17). The third and third to last sections of the book alternate between accounts of the kings of Israel and Judah

(1 Kgs 13–16; 2 Kgs 8–16). The central section of the book describes the ministries of Elijah and Elisha (1 Kgs 17–2 Kgs 7). The chiastic structure can be depicted as follows:[22]

> 1 Kings 1–11, United Davidic Kingdom
>> 1 Kings 12, Divided into Israel and Judah
>>> 1 Kings 13–16, Kings of Israel and Judah
>>>> 1 Kings 17–2 Kings 7, Elijah and Elisha
>>> 2 Kings 8–16, Kings of Israel and Judah
>> 2 Kings 17, Fall of Israel
> 2 Kings 18–25, Judah until Exile

The central section on Elijah and Elisha also appears to have a concentric structure as follows:

> 1 Kings 17:8–24, Widow's Oil and Resurrection
>> 1 Kings 17–19, No Rain, Baal, Jezebel, Sinai-Moses
>>> (1 Kings 20–21, Syria, Ben Hadad, Naboth's Vineyard)[23]
>>>> 1 Kings 22, Ahab and Jehoshaphat Inquire of Micaiah
>>>>> 2 Kings 1, Fire Falls from Heaven
>>>>> 2 Kings 2, Elijah to Heaven by Whirlwind
>>>>> 2 Kings 3, Jehoram and Jehoshaphat Inquire of Elisha
>>>> 2 Kings 3, No Water, Water to Blood (Moses), Human Sacrifice
>> 2 Kings 4, Widow's Oil and Resurrection
> 2 Kings 5–7, Elisha's Double Portion of Mighty Works

§7.2 Historical Correspondence between Elijah and Elisha

The striking parallels between the ministries of Elijah and Elisha suggest that they are to be understood in relationship to one another. At the center of

---

22. Adapted from Bruce K. Waltke, *An Old Testament Theology: An Exegetical, Canonical, and Thematic Approach* (Grand Rapids: Zondervan, 2007), 693.

23. First Kings 20–21 does not fit neatly into the chiastic structure proposed here, and Elijah is noticeably absent between his call of Elisha at the end of 1 Kings 19 through 21:17. In this section we read of "a prophet" (1 Kgs 20:13), "the prophet" (20:22), "a man of God" (20:28), "a certain man of the sons of the prophets" (20:35), and "one of the prophets" (20:41) but find no reference to Elijah. Cf. Leithart's observation on literary artistry: "texts are as structurally complex as a musical composition, which can be organized by many structures (melodic, harmonic, rhythmic) simultaneously." Peter J. Leithart, *1 & 2 Kings*, Brazos Theological Commentary on the Bible (Grand Rapids: Brazos, 2006), 154 n. 2.

the chiastic structure of the account of the ministries of Elijah and Elisha, a transition from the ministry of Elijah to Elisha takes place at the Jordan River, with Elisha requesting a double portion of the spirit of Elijah, and the spirit of Elijah coming to rest upon Elisha. The author of Kings narrates some ten mighty works performed by (or marking the ministry of) Elijah, and this number is more than doubled by the twenty-two mighty works performed by Elisha.[24] This seems to set up a pattern of events where a more prolific prophet succeeds his predecessor at the Jordan River with the involvement of the s/Spirit.[25] The mighty works of Elijah and Elisha are enumerated on Table 4.2, and here we will discuss the paralleling of their ministry, moving from the outer rings to the central episodes, to set up a discussion of the expectation that this pattern would be fulfilled in later Scripture, and the presentation of its fulfillment in the New Testament.

TABLE 4.2 The Mighty Works of Elijah and Elisha

Elijah	Elisha
1. Drought (1 Kgs 17:1)	1. Jordan parted (2 Kgs 2:14)
2. Fed by ravens (17:6)	2. Water healed (2:19–22)
3. Provision for widow involving jar of oil (17:14–16)	3. Bears tear boys (2:23–25)
4. Resurrected boy (17:17–24)	4. Flash flood water provision (3:16–17, 20)
5. Fire consumes offering on Mount Carmel (18:38)	5. Provision for widow involving jar of oil (4:1–7)
6. Rain (18:41–46)	6. Barren wife conceives (4:16–17)
7. Forty Day/Forty Night journey to Horeb (19:8)	7. Resurrected boy (4:18–37)
8. Fire from heaven consumes enemies twice (2 Kgs 1:9–12)	8. Death in the pot removed (4:38–41)

(continued)

24. The ways the mighty works are enumerated varies, and there are different estimations of what counts as a mighty work. For my assessment, see Table 4.2, "The Mighty Works of Elijah and Elisha."

25. Rightly Leithart: "Elijah is a type of John the Baptist . . . , and the transition from Elijah to Elisha foreshadows the succession from John to Jesus." Leithart, *1 & 2 Kings*, 171.

Elijah	Elisha
9. Jordan parted (2:8)	9. One hundred men fed by twenty loaves (4:42–44)
10. Taken by whirlwind to heaven (2:11)	10. Naaman the leper healed (5:1–15)
	11. Knowing what Gehazi did and making Naaman's leprosy cling to him (5:26–27)
	12. Axe head floats (6:6)
	13. Knowing the plans of the Syrian King (6:9–10, 12)
	14. His servant's eyes opened to see horses and chariots of fire (6:17)
	15. Syrians struck blind (6:18)
	16. Syrians' eyes opened (6:20)
	17. Provision of food by abandoned and plundered Syrian camp (7:1, 16)
	18. Captain sees but does not eat (7:2, 19)
	19. Warning of seven-year famine (8:1–6; cf. Joseph in Gen 41:25–32; Elijah in 1 Kgs 17:1)
	20. Prediction that Hazael will kill King of Syria (8:7–15)
	21. Prediction of Victory over Syria (13:14–19)
	22. Dead man resurrected by Elisha's bones (13:20–21)

§7.2.1 Provision for a Widow and Resurrection of a Son (1 Kings 17 and 2 Kings 4)

My attention was initially drawn to the parallels between Elijah and Elisha by the similarity of 1 Kings 17 to 2 Kings 4. Elijah provides for a widow in a way that involves a jar of oil and then raises a boy from the dead in 1 Kings 17, and Elisha does the same mighty works in the same order in 2 Kings 4.

- Both provisions involve widows (1 Kgs 17:9; 2 Kgs 4:1) who have nothing left but jars of oil (1 Kgs 17:12, 14; 2 Kgs 4:2) that the prophet announces will not to be spent until sufficient provision is made (1 Kgs 17:14; 2 Kgs 4:3–6).
- In both chapters the provision for the widow is immediately followed by the resurrection of a boy.
- In 1 Kings 17 the widow's son dies, but in 2 Kings 4 Elisha first announces to a barren woman that she will conceive, and then when that boy dies, Elisha raises him from the dead.
- The annunciation of the child's birth makes the account of what Elisha did in 2 Kings 4 even more impressive than 1 Kings 17 (escalation).
- In both narratives the dead child is taken into the prophet's own upper room and laid on the prophet's own bed (1 Kgs 17:19; 2 Kgs 4:10, 21), and in both cases the prophet "stretched himself upon" the child (1 Kgs 17:21; 2 Kgs 4:34, ESV).
- Both narratives conclude with the prophet returning the child to the mother alive (1 Kgs 17:23; 2 Kgs 4:36), and the mother honoring the Lord's work through the prophet (1 Kgs 17:24; 2 Kgs 4:37).

These stupendous parallels are more than a re-run of Elijah's ministry in Elisha's. They signal *author-intended historical correspondence* between Elijah and Elisha, and with the addition of the annunciation that the barren wife with the old husband will have a child, the significance *escalates* as we move from Elijah to Elisha.

§7.2.2 Water, Idolaters, Moses (1 Kings 17–19 and 2 Kings 3)

The complex of events in 1 Kings 17–19 has features that match up with elements in 2 Kings 3, as both passages deal with the lack of water and then the provision of it, both include points of contact with Moses,[26] and both have conflict with idolaters. Elijah announces that there will be no rain or dew in

---

26. On the evidence for Elijah as a new Moses, see Allison, *The New Moses*, 39–45. See also the fascination discussion in Duane A. Garrett, *The Problem of the Old Testament: Hermeneutical, Schematic, and Theological Approaches* (Downers Grove, IL: InterVarsity, 2020), 272–90.

1 Kings 17:1, and at points through the narrative the drought is referenced (17:14; 18:1) until rain finally comes (18:41–45).[27] Elisha confronts a similar circumstance in 2 Kings 3:9, as "there was no water for the army or for the animals that followed them" (ESV). Elisha announces that the Lord will provide water that comes not by wind or rain but that nevertheless fills the streambed in 3:17.

A significant point of contact between these two narratives is the phrase, "As Yahweh of hosts lives, before whom I stand" (חַי יְהוָה צְבָאוֹת אֲשֶׁר עָמַדְתִּי לְפָנָיו), which occurs only at 1 Kings 18:15 and 2 Kings 3:14.[28] In the first, Yahweh tells Elijah to show himself to Ahab and he will send rain (18:1). Elijah presents himself to Obadiah, who fears that Elijah will not follow through on appearing before Ahab (18:7–14), in response to which Elijah utters this statement to assert that he will indeed show himself to Ahab. There follows the contest with the prophets of Baal, and then the rain comes. Similarly, Elisha makes this statement as he sets out to resolve the problem of the lack of water in 2 Kings 3. The use of the same words in the same order in similar contexts functions to link the two passages, creating historical correspondence between Elijah and Elisha.

Another point of contact between these narratives has to do with the way that both deal with idolaters. In the case of Elijah, he has the epic contest with the prophets of Baal on Mount Carmel (1 Kgs 18:20–40). In 2 Kings 3:27, by contrast, the king of Moab sacrifices his oldest son and wrath comes on Israel.

More significantly, both narratives contain details that are reminiscent of

---

27. First Kings 17:1 says, "there shall be neither dew nor rain these years," and then 18:1 relates that "the word of the LORD came to Elijah, in the third year . . ." Luke 4:25 presents Jesus specifying that "the heavens were shut up three years and six months, and a great famine came over all the land," and James 5:17 says that when Elijah prayed "for three years and six months it did not rain on the earth." By noting the three-and-a-half-year time period, Luke and James tie Elijah's drought to the halving of Daniel's seventieth week (Dan 9:27), otherwise referred to as "a time, times, and half a time" (7:25; 12:7) and by day counts of "1,290 days" (12:11), "1,335 days" (12:12), and "2300 evenings and mornings" (8:14). The three and a half year period also factors significantly in Revelation: "forty-two months" (Rev 11:2; 13:5, 12 × 3=36, 3yrs, 36+6=42, 3 ½ yrs); "1,260 days" (11:3, days of a month, 30, multiplied by 3 ½ years of months, 42, 42 × 30=1,260); and "a time, and times, and half a time" (12:14, cf. 1,260 days in 12:6). Elijah's three and a half year drought provides the archetypal visitation of God's judgment. The Daniel 8:14 three and a half year period under the third kingdom (Antiochus Epiphanes) provides an ectypal installment in the pattern. And the antitypical fulfillment arrives with the depiction of the three and a half year persecution visited by the Antichrist in Daniel 7:25 and Revelation 13:5. See further discussion of these passages in Hamilton, *Revelation*; Hamilton, *With the Clouds of Heaven*; and James M. Hamilton Jr., "Suffering in Revelation: The Fulfillment of the Messianic Woes," *Southern Baptist Journal of Theology* 17, no. 4 (2014): 34–47.

28. Cf. similar statements at 1 Kings 17:1, 12; 18:10; 22:14; 2 Kings 2:2, 4, 6; 4:30; 5:16, 20. None of these are worded exactly the same as 1 Kings 18:15 and 2 Kings 3:14.

Moses. Elijah travels "forty days and forty nights to Horeb, the mount of God" (1 Kgs 19:8). On that very mountain Moses famously fasted forty days and forty nights as he met with Yahweh—twice! (Exod 24:18; 34:28). When 1 Kings 19:9 notes that Elijah "came to the cave," the cave in view is most likely the cleft of the rock where Yahweh put Moses as he passed by (Exod 33:22). Yahweh then passes by Elijah and reveals himself to him (1 Kgs 19:9–18), recalling the way that Yahweh passed by Moses (Exod 34:6–7).[29] The points of contact between Elisha and Moses are less detailed, more subtle, but as Moses brought water from the rock in the wilderness in Exodus 17 and Numbers 20, Elisha brings water that does not come by rain in 2 Kings 3:17–20. Also, as Moses turned the water in Egypt to blood (Exod 7:14–25), we read in 2 Kings 3:22, "And when they rose early in the morning and the sun shone on the water, the Moabites saw the water opposite them as red as blood." Just as the water turned to blood led to the defeat of Egypt, the water appearing as blood led to the defeat of Moab. As the people received manna from heaven in the wilderness under Moses (Exod 16), and pointing to another prophet who would multiply loaves of bread, Elisha fed one hundred men with a mere twenty loaves in 2 Kings 4:42–44.

§7.2.3 Is There Not a Prophet of Yahweh? (1 Kings 22 and 2 Kings 3)

The points of contact between 1 Kings 22 and 2 Kings 3 are particularly strong. In 1 Kings 22:4 Ahab asks Jehoshaphat, "Will you go with me to battle . . . ?" In 2 Kings 3:7 Ahab's son Jehoram asks Jehoshaphat the same question:

1 Kgs 22:4, "Will you go with me to battle at Ramoth-gilead?"

הֲתֵלֵךְ אִתִּי לַמִּלְחָמָה רָמֹת גִּלְעָד

2 Kgs 3:7, "Will you go with me to Moab to battle?"

הֲתֵלֵךְ אִתִּי אֶל־מוֹאָב לַמִּלְחָמָה

When Jehoshaphat wants to inquire for the word of Yahweh in 1 Kings 22:5, Ahab brings out the prophets who tell him what he wants to hear in 22:6, prompting Jehoshaphat to ask in 22:7, "Is there not here a prophet of Yahweh of whom we may inquire?" Similarly, when there is no water in 2 Kings 3:9

---

29. See further Allison, *The New Moses*, 39–45.

and Jehoram despairs in 3:10, Jehoshaphat asks the same question in 2 Kings 3:11 he had asked in 1 Kings 22:7.

1 Kgs 22:7, "Is there not still here a prophet of Yahweh, that we may inquire from him?"

הַאֵין פֹּה נָבִיא לַיהוָה עוֹד וְנִדְרְשָׁה מֵאוֹתוֹ

2 Kgs 3:11, "Is there not here a prophet of Yahweh, that we may inquire of Yahweh from him?"

הַאֵין פֹּה נָבִיא לַיהוָה וְנִדְרְשָׁה אֶת־יְהוָה מֵאוֹתוֹ

In 1 Kings 22 Ahab produces Micaiah, of whom he says, "I hate him, for he never prophesies good concerning me but evil" (1 Kgs 22:8, ESV). Once summoned, Micaiah has a confrontational interaction with Ahab's false prophets as he reveals what will come to pass (22:9–28). Similarly, in 2 Kings 3 Elisha is produced, and when he comes on the scene he says to Ahab's son Jehoram, "What have I to do with you? Go to the prophets of your father and to the prophets of your mother" (2 Kgs 3:13). Like Micaiah, Elisha reveals what will take place (3:15–19).

We saw above how the phrase "As Yahweh of hosts lives, before whom I stand" occurs only twice (1 Kgs 18:15; 2 Kgs 3:14), linking Elisha and Elijah. Another phrase that occurs only twice in Kings is the "hand of Yahweh," which comes on Elijah in 1 Kings 18:46 and Elisha in 2 Kings 3:15.

§7.2.4 Two Prophets at the Jordan (2 Kings 1–2)

At the center of the chiastic structure at the heart of the book of Kings stand the first two chapters of 2 Kings. In the first of these there are many references to "going up" and "coming down" (2 Kgs 1:2, 3, 4, 6, 9, 10, 11, 13, 14, 15, 16).[30] Elijah's apparel is described in 2 Kings 1:8, "He wore a garment of hair, with a belt of leather about his waist." And twice he calls down fire from heaven to consume those sent to summon him and vindicate his status as "a man of God" (1:10, 12). Driving the chapter is the fact that Ahaziah king of Israel has sent to "inquire of Baal-zebub, the god of Ekron" (1:2), in response to

---

30. A point brought to my attention by J. Gary Millar, "1–2 Kings," in *ESV Expository Commentary: 1 Samuel–2 Chronicles*, ed. Iain M. Duguid, James M. Hamilton Jr., and Jay Sklar, vol. 3 (Wheaton, IL: Crossway, 2019), 726.

which Elijah asks, "Is it because there is no God in Israel that you are going to inquire of Baal-zebub, the God of Ekron" (1:3, 6, 16). Ahaziah inquires of Baal-zebub to know if he will recover from his fall (1:2), and Elijah announces that he will not (1:16). The veracity of the prophetic word punctuates the narrative: "So he died according to the word of Yahweh that Elijah had spoken" (1:17).

In 2 Kings 1 captains of fifty twice came for Elijah and twice he called down fire from heaven upon them, until the third captain humbly pled for his life and Elijah went down with him to the king (2 Kgs 1:9–15). In 2 Kings 2 Elijah twice asks Elisha to stop following him, Elisha twice tells Elijah that as the LORD lives and as he lives he will not leave him, the sons of the prophets twice tell Elisha that his master will be taken, and twice Elisha silences them (2:2–5). The third time through this same sequence Elijah and Elisha arrive at the Jordan River, which Elijah parts, and he and Elisha cross it as Moses led the people across the Red Sea and Joshua across the same river, "on dry ground" (2:8). The term rendered "dry ground" (חָרָבָה) occurs in Exodus 14:21 to describe the crossing of the Red Sea and in both Joshua 3:17 and 2 Kings 2:8 to describe the crossing of the Jordan River. It seems the author of Kings intended his audience to think of the transition from the ministry of Moses to that of Joshua as he told the story of the translation of Elijah and the carrying forward of his ministry by Elisha.

At that point Elisha requests a double portion of Elijah's spirit (2 Kgs 2:9), and Elijah promises that if he sees him as he is taken "it shall be so" (2:10). The chariots and horses of fire appear, Elijah is taken to heaven by whirlwind, Elisha utters his exclamation, tears his own clothes, and takes up the mantle of Elijah (2:11–13). "Then he took the cloak of Elijah that had fallen from him and struck the water [of the Jordan River], saying, 'Where is Yahweh, the God of Elijah?' And when he had struck the water, the water was parted to the one side and to the other, and Elisha went over" (2:14). The sons of the prophets then recognize that "The spirit of Elijah rests on Elisha" (2:15).

§7.3 Moses–Joshua and Elijah–Elisha

The transition from the ministry of Elijah to that of Elisha at the Jordan River with the gift of the spirit of Elijah has a number of points of contact with the transition from the leadership of Moses to that of Joshua, and these help us to interpret the historical correspondence between the ministries of the two prophets:

- Elisha's request to Elijah for "a double portion of your spirit on me" in 2 Kings 2:9 almost certainly reflects the LORD saying to Moses, "And I will take some of the Spirit that is on you and put it on [the seventy elders]" in Numbers 11:17. Though it is not clear that Joshua is one of the seventy elders, he does appear in that passage (Num 11:28). Still, the Lord clearly continues the ministry of Moses through Joshua (see next).

- The ministry of the first prophet (Elijah/Moses) is obviously continued in the ministry of the second (Elisha/Joshua). This is attested by clear statements in Torah (see discussion of Numbers 27 above in §6.1 and passages such as Deut 31:3, 7–8) and in Joshua 1 (esp. Josh 1:1–2, 5, 17, etc.). The narrative of Kings, meanwhile, clearly states, "The spirit of Elijah rests on Elisha" (2 Kgs 2:15).

- This carrying forward of Elijah's ministry can be seen in the way that Elisha takes up Elijah's mantle (2 Kgs 2:13), which indicates that he continues Elijah's ministry. Along these lines, Joshua was charged not to let the Torah depart from his mouth, for he was to continue the ministry of Moses (Josh 1:8).

- Elijah exits the land by parting the Jordan to cross "on dry ground" (2 Kgs 2:8), and then Elisha reenters the land by parting the Jordan (2:14). This matches the Red Sea crossing of Moses followed by the Jordan River crossing of Joshua, and whereas Moses and Elijah were going east when they crossed the water, Joshua and Elisha were going west.

These points of historical correspondence suggest that the transition from Elijah to Elisha is an installment in the pattern of the transition from Moses to Joshua. The doubling of the mighty works of Elijah in Elisha's ministry adds escalation in significance to the historical correspondence, signaling a typological pattern of events that generates expectation for more of the same in the future.

After Elijah's ascent into heaven "by a whirlwind" in 2 Kings 2:11, the sons of the prophets at Jericho look for his body but cannot find it (2 Kgs 2:15–18). The nearest parallels to this in earlier Scripture are Enoch being taken by God in Genesis 5:24 and Moses being buried by God in an undisclosed location in Deuteronomy 34:5–6.

It seems, too, that as Elisha continues the ministry of Elijah, he becomes something of a new Moses himself, or to put it another way, a prophet like Moses. This can be seen in the parallel event sequences in Exodus 14–15 and 2 Kings 2. In Exodus 14 Moses leads the people across the Red Sea on dry ground, celebrated in the Song of the Sea, and after a three-day time period and a failure to find water, the very next thing Moses does is sweeten the waters in Exodus 15:22–27. Similarly, having crossed the Jordan (2 Kgs 2:14), once the sons of the prophets have searched for three days in vain for Elijah, Elisha heals the waters in 2 Kings 2:19–22.

Both contexts mention three-day time periods, and in both contexts there is a group that fails to find what they seek:

Exod 15:22, "They went three days in the wilderness and found no water"

וַיֵּלְכוּ שְׁלֹשֶׁת־יָמִים בַּמִּדְבָּר וְלֹא־מָצְאוּ מָיִם

2 Kgs 2:17, "for three days they sought him [Elijah] but did not find him"

וַיְבַקְשׁוּ שְׁלֹשָׁה־יָמִים וְלֹא מְצָאֻהוּ

In Exodus 15:25, the prophet Moses threw (וַיַּשְׁלֵךְ) a log into the bitter water, "and the water became sweet." In 2 Kings 2:21 the prophet Elisha threw (וַיַּשְׁלֶךְ) salt into the bad water with the words, "Thus says Yahweh, I have healed (רִפִּאתִי) this water . . ." Similarly, in Exodus 15:26 Yahweh declares, "for I am Yahweh, your healer (רֹפְאֶךָ)."[31]

This event sequence—water-crossing, followed by three-day time period and fruitless search, followed by the healing/sweetening of drinking water by throwing something into it—indicates that the author of Kings means for Elisha to be understood as a prophet like Moses, an installment in the Mosaic typological pattern. At the same time, Elijah is a prophet like Moses, and the transition from his ministry to Elisha's reinforces the way that the ministry of Moses was continued by Joshua. These patterns seem to inform what Malachi prophesies.

---

31. There is no account of Jesus healing or sweetening waters in the Gospels, but he does turn water to wine on the third day (John 2:1–11), which transcends what Elisha and Moses accomplished, and he offers living water (4:10–14; cf. 7:37–39). In various other ways Jesus fulfills what both Elisha and Moses typified, on which see further below.

§7.4 Elijah and the Day of the Lord in Malachi

Perhaps engaging the way that Elijah's ministry prepared for and was continued by Elisha, Malachi asserts,

"Behold, I will send you Elijah the prophet before the great and awesome day of Yahweh comes. And he will turn the hearts of the fathers to their sons and the hearts of sons to their fathers, lest I come and strike the land with a ban." (Mal 4:5–6)

The turning of the hearts of fathers and sons to one another recalls Elijah's prayer in the contest with the prophets of Baal, "Answer me, O Yahweh, answer me, that this people may know that you, O Yahweh, are God, and that you have turned their hearts back" (1 Kgs 18:37). Malachi, then, seems to expect the new Elijah to have a ministry like that of the historical Elijah.

The mention of Elijah in Malachi 4:5 seems to develop what Malachi said in 3:1, "Behold, I send my messenger, and he will prepare the way before me. And the Lord whom you seek will suddenly come to his temple; and the messenger of the covenant in whom you delight, behold, he is coming, says the Lord of hosts" (ESV). Malachi 3:1 in turn picks up the language of Exodus 23:20, indicating that the "messenger" whom Yahweh sends to "prepare the way" will be a new Elijah who will be a prophetic forerunner to the coming of the Lord for the fulfillment of the climactic new-exodus salvation (cf. the discussion of Gen 24:7, Exod 23:20, Isa 40:3, Mal 3:1, and Mark 1:2 in the opening and closing pages of this book).

§7.5 Elijah and Elisha in the New Testament

The New Testament authors present fulfillment of Elijah and Elisha at a number of points. There are important correspondences between Elijah and the Baptist, and just as there was a transition from Elijah to Elisha at the Jordan, the Baptist and the Christ meet at the Jordan. The New Testament presents Jesus as the expected prophet like Moses (Luke 9:35; Acts 3:22; 7:37), and it also presents the Baptist as the Elijah who was to come (Matt 11:14). In view of Elisha asking for a double portion of Elijah's spirit at the Jordan, the descent of the Spirit as John baptizes Jesus at the Jordan takes place in fulfillment of the prophetic pattern.

§7.5.1 Elijah and the Baptist

All four of the Gospels present John the Baptist preparing the way for the coming of Jesus. In various ways they present John typologically fulfilling the role that Elijah played with relationship to Elisha, of which Malachi prophesied. Matthew and Mark note that the Baptist was clothed like Elijah:[32]

Matt 3:4 (cf. Mark 1:6), "Now John wore a garment of camel's hair and a leather belt around his waist." (ESV)

2 Kgs 1:8, "He [Elijah] wore a garment of hair, with a belt of leather about his waist." (ESV)

Matthew, Mark, Luke, and John all quote Isaiah 40:3 as being fulfilled in the Baptist's ministry of preparing the way for Jesus, "A voice cries: 'In the wilderness prepare the way of the Lord . . .'" (Isa 40:3; Matt 3:3; Mark 1:2–4; Luke 3:4–6; John 1:23). Mark adds Malachi 3:1 (with its quotation of Exodus 23:20) to the beginning of his quotation of Isaiah 40:3, "Behold, I send my messenger before your face" (Mark 1:2; Mal 3:1). Jonathan Gibson points out the possibility of an allusion to Isaiah 40:3 in Malachi 3:1,[33] and there is a remarkable similarity between the two texts:

Isa 40:3, פַּנּוּ דֶּרֶךְ יְהוָה
"prepare the way of Yahweh"

Mal 3:1, וּפִנָּה־דֶרֶךְ לְפָנָי
"and he will prepare the way before me"

The New Testament quotes Isaiah 40:3 to establish that the Baptist's role is to prepare the way for Jesus. The quotation of Malachi 3:1 in Mark 1:2 joins with the fact that Jesus himself identifies the Baptist as "Elijah who is to come" (Matt 11:14, ESV) to assert that the Baptist typologically fulfills the role

---

32. Allison comments on this similarity, "The text might just as well say: John was like Elijah." Allison, *The New Moses*, 19.

33. Gibson, *Covenant Continuity and Fidelity*, 174–77. Gibson notes, "The syntactical sequence of piel פנה + direct object דרך is shared by Mal. 3.1b and Isa. 40.3 only, which suggests an intended allusion" (176).

of Elijah in preceding the prophet who comes after him, one who will have an even greater experience of the Spirit (John 3:34) and do even more mighty works than himself (21:25).

Elijah's translation to heaven and Malachi's declaration that the Lord would send him could have led to the idea that the literal, historical Elijah would return one day. This seems to be what the Baptist denies in John 1:21, "They asked him, 'What then? Are you Elijah?' He said, 'I am not'" (ESV). The exchange fits the pattern of the Johannine misunderstandings, where those who listen to Jesus think he is speaking of literal birth (3:4), physical water (4:15), or actual bread (6:34), when Jesus speaks of the new birth and the spiritual food and drink that he gives to those who abide in him. Similarly here in John 1:21, the Baptist denies that he is the literal, historical Elijah returned to earth, but he is clothed as he is, located where he is, and doing what he does to bring about the typological fulfillment of the pattern of Elijah's ministry seen in 1–2 Kings and prophesied in Malachi 3:1 and 4:5.

§7.5.2 Two Prophets at the Jordan (John 1)

We saw above how Elijah and Elisha crossed the Jordan, Elisha requested a double portion of the Spirit on Elijah, after which he was taken to heaven by a whirlwind, and Elisha recrossed the Jordan (2 Kgs 2:1–15). This sequence of events finds typological fulfillment when the "Elijah who is to come" (Matt 11:14), John the Baptist, immersed Jesus of Nazareth in the Jordan River (cf. Matt 3:13–17; Mark 1:9–11; Luke 3:21–22).

> And John bore witness: "I saw the Spirit descend from heaven like a dove, and it remained on him. I myself did not know him, but he who sent me to baptize with water said to me, 'He on whom you see the Spirit descend and remain, this is he who baptizes with the Holy Spirit.' And I have seen and have borne witness that this is the Son of God." (John 1:32–34, ESV)

Two prophets at the Jordan, and in their passing through the waters the fullness of the Spirit comes upon the second. In John 3:34 the Baptist refers to "the Spirit without measure" (ESV) in the ministry of Jesus that transcends the double portion of the spirit of Elijah in Elisha's ministry. And as Elisha did twice as many mighty works as Elijah, Jesus speaks of how much greater the era he inaugurates will be in Matthew 11:11 (ESV), "Truly, I say to you, among those born of women there has arisen no one greater than John the Baptist. Yet the one who is least in the kingdom of heaven is greater than he.'"

§7.6 The Prophet like Moses

The New Testament presents Jesus in continuity with and fulfillment of what Moses and the prophets, including John, typified.

§7.6.1 Jesus and the Baptist

In the same way that Elisha continues and doubles the ministry of Elijah, Jesus can be seen to continue and transcend the ministry of the Baptist. Matthew summarizes the Baptist's preaching in the line, "Repent, for the kingdom of heaven is at hand" (Matt 3:2, ESV). After Jesus's baptism, temptation, and relocation to Capernaum, "From that time Jesus began to preach, saying, 'Repent, for the kingdom of heaven is at hand'" (4:17, ESV). Similarly, Jesus and his disciples extend and further the baptismal ministry of John the Baptist (John 3:22–4:1),[34] prompting the Baptist to declare, "He must increase, but I must decrease" (3:30).

§7.6.2 Jesus and Elijah

None of this should be taken as any kind of slight on Elijah. There are ways in which the New Testament authors understand him to typify not only John the Baptist but also Jesus.[35] For instance, Luke quotes the Greek translation of a phrase from the account of Elijah raising the widow's son from the dead when he recounts how Jesus raised the widow's son at Nain:

Luke 7:15, "And the dead man sat up and began to speak, and Jesus *gave him to his mother*." (ESV)

καὶ ἔδωκεν αὐτὸν τῇ μητρὶ αὐτου

LXX 1 Kgs 17:23, "And Elijah took the child and brought him down from the upper chamber into the house and *gave him to his mother*."

καὶ ἔδωκεν αὐτὸν τῇ μητρὶ αὐτου

---

34. Dale Allison presents two pages of side-by-side similarities between the Baptist and Jesus in the Gospel of Matthew (*The New Moses*, 137–39).

35. Cf. Leithart: "Elijah is a type of Jesus himself, and Elisha of the disciples who continued Jesus's ministry after his ascension." Leithart, *1 & 2 Kings*, 171.

§7.6.3 Jesus and Elisha

The quotation in Luke 7:15 connects the miracle of resurrection in Elijah's ministry to Jesus, the fulfillment prophet. Similarly, several of the miracles performed by Elisha prefigure things that Jesus would accomplish:

- presented with only "twenty loaves of barley and fresh ears of grain in his sack" in 2 Kings 4:42, Elisha is asked, "How can I set this before a hundred men?" The assumption is that there is not enough food, but Elisha announces, "Thus says the LORD, 'They shall eat and have some left'" (2 Kgs 4:43, ESV). On several occasions Jesus fed multitudes with small amounts of food, the disciples gathering up baskets of left-overs, twelve one time, seven another (see Matt 14:13–21; 15:32–39; Mark 6:30–44; 8:1–10; Luke 9:10–17; John 6:1–15).
- In 2 Kings 5:1–14 Elisha heals Naaman of leprosy, a feat only repeated by Jesus (Matt 8:2–4; Mark 1:40–44; Luke 5:12–16).
- Elisha knows where Gehazi went, what he said, and what he was think-ing (2 Kgs 5:25–27) in a way that presages the ability of Jesus to know what has just happened, been said, or even what people were thinking (e.g., Matt 17:24–27; Mark 2:7–8).
- Through Elisha's prayer his servant's eyes are opened to see spiritual realities, the Lord strikes the Syrian army with blindness, then opens their eyes again (2 Kgs 6:17–20). Jesus likewise grants spiritual sight and opens the eyes of the blind (esp. Mark 8:22–26; John 9).
- Like Elijah, and as discussed above, Elisha raises a boy from the dead. Not only that, however, but in death Elisha proves to be a life-giving prophet when a recently killed man is thrown into Elisha's grave and, having come in contact with Elisha's bones, rises from the dead (2 Kgs 13:20–21). Jesus not only raises the dead (Luke 7:11–17; John 11:38–44), he too proves to be life-giving in his death, as dead saints rise when he dies on the cross (Matt 27:51–53). Jesus also transcends anything Elisha accomplished in this regard when he himself rises from the dead (e.g., Matt 28:6).

§7.6.4 The Transfiguration

Having considered ways that Jesus fulfills what Elisha typified, there is more to be said along these lines with reference to Elijah, who typifies not only the Baptist but the Christ as well. As noted above, Elijah went to Sinai, to "the cave," where Yahweh passed by him just as he had Moses, whose face shone with reflected glory. The experience of Moses and Elijah at Sinai, and the shining face of Moses (Exod 34:29–33), informs the accounts of Jesus ascending "a high mountain" with Peter, James, and John, where "he was transfigured before them, and his face shone like the sun, and his clothes became white as light. And behold, there appeared to them Moses and Elijah, talking with him" (Matt 17:1–3, ESV). Luke's account specifies that they "spoke of his exodus, which he was about to fulfill at Jerusalem" (Luke 9:31).

Jesus brings about the typological fulfillment of what Moses and Elijah prefigured. He is the prophet whose face shines on the mountain; he will accomplish the salvation to which the deliverances wrought through the leadership of Moses and Elijah pointed; and like Elijah, taken to heaven on a whirlwind, Jesus will ascend to heaven on the clouds (Luke 24:51; Acts 1:8–11).

§7.6.5 The Two Witnesses in Revelation 11

That, however, is not the last we will see of Moses and Elijah. Their ministries symbolically inform the depiction of the two witnesses, who seem to symbolize the church's proclamation of the gospel, in Revelation 11:3–7.[36] On this reading, the church will be protected as Elijah was when the king sent the captain and fifty men, on whom fire came down from heaven to consume them (2 Kgs 1:9–16). Thus John writes, "if anyone would harm them, fire pours from their mouth and consumes their foes. If anyone would harm them, this is how he is doomed to be killed" (Rev 11:5, ESV).

Not only was Elijah protected to serve God's purpose in his generation, the drought that came by his prayer showed that Yahweh, God of Israel, not Baal the storm god, waters the earth by rainfall (1 Kgs 17–18). Along these lines, John writes that the two witnesses "have the power to shut the sky, that no rain may fall during the days of their prophesying" (Rev 11:6a, ESV). I take this to indicate that the church, with its verified witness to the truth (two witnesses), has Elijah-like power to demonstrate that the God of the Bible is the only living and true God, maker of heaven and earth, alone creator and savior of all men. And just as the plagues on Egypt were visited by Moses,

---

36. Rightly Bauckham, who writes of the two witnesses, "They are therefore the church insofar as it fulfills its role as faithful witness." Richard Bauckham, *The Theology of the Book of Revelation*, New Testament Theology (New York: Cambridge University Press, 1993), 85, cf. 84–88.

the two witnesses "have power over the waters to turn them into blood and to strike the earth with every kind of plague, as often as they desire" (Rev 11:6b, ESV). This seems to be a symbolic way of saying that the church has the power to bring to bear the fulfillment of the exodus from Egypt. The point is not plagues but the message of salvation to which the church testifies. Whether or not readers agree with my interpretation of the symbolism, it is beyond dispute that the ministries of Moses and Elijah foreshadow and typify not only what Christ himself fulfilled but also what John prophesies the two witnesses will accomplish before the final trumpet is blown in Revelation 11:15–19.

Much could be said about other prophets. We turn our attention to Isaiah and the way that he himself typifies what will be fulfilled in Christ.

§8 ISAIAH

This section examines the context of Isaiah 7–8 to understand what Isaiah meant by the statements in 8:17–18, and from there to seek to understand how the author of Hebrews employs that passage when he places it on the lips of Jesus in Hebrews 2:13.[37]

§8.1 Isaiah and His Sons

The prophet Isaiah has at least two sons with portentous names. We read in Isaiah 7:3, "And Yahweh said to Isaiah, 'Go out to meet Ahaz, you and Shear-jashub your son, at the end of the conduit of the upper pool on the highway to the Washer's Field." Then in 8:3 Isaiah writes, "And I went to the prophetess, and she conceived and bore a son. Then Yahweh said to me, 'Call his name Maher-shalal-hash-baz." Because of the similarities between 8:3–10 and 7:7–20, some have concluded that the child to be named Immanuel in 7:14 can be identified with Maher-shalal-hash-baz. I have argued elsewhere that the context of the prophecy of Immanuel in 7:14 requires that a child to be given that name be born in Isaiah's near future, and that Matthew claims typological fulfillment of Isaiah's prophecy when Jesus is born

---

37. For a wide-angle look at the way the author of Hebrews engages in typological interpretation, see James M. Hamilton Jr., "Typology in Hebrews: A Response to Buist Fanning," *Southern Baptist Journal of Theology* 24, no. 1 (2020): 125–36. For the most difficult to understand instances of the use of the Old Testament in Hebrews, see Aubrey Maria Sequeira, "The Hermeneutics of Eschatological Fulfillment in Christ: Biblical-Theological Exegesis in the Epistle to the Hebrews" (PhD diss., Louisville, KY, The Southern Baptist Theological Seminary, 2016).

(Matt 1:22–23).[38] At least Shear-Jashub and Maher-shalal-hash-baz are in view (if not also Immanuel), then, when Isaiah asserts in 8:18, "Behold, I and the children whom Yahweh has given me are signs and portents in Israel from Yahweh of hosts, who dwells on Mount Zion." In order to understand what the author of Hebrews means when he quotes parts of Isaiah 8:17–18 in Hebrews 2:13, we must understand Isaiah's statements in context.

In what sense are Isaiah and his children "signs and portents"? In Isaiah 7:1–2, Ahaz has been informed of the way that the Northern Kingdom of Israel has entered into a conspiracy with Syria to remove him and set up a puppet king in his place (7:5–6). He is likely inspecting Jerusalem's water supply in anticipation of a siege in 7:3, and his interchange with Isaiah in 7:10–13 indicates that he is not in the habit of responding positively to the prophet Isaiah. We also know from 2 Kings 16:5–20 that rather than heed Isaiah and trust Yahweh, Ahaz trusted Tiglath-pileser and worshiped his gods (2 Kgs 16:3, 7–14).

Ahaz made a deal with Tiglath-pileser so that the king of Assyria would help him against his enemies. He was trying to avoid being defeated by those enemies and taken captive by them into exile. As unhappy as he would have been to see Isaiah, that displeasure would only be increased when he learned the name of the son Isaiah was instructed to take along in 7:3. Isaiah's son, Shear-jashub, has a name that means "a remnant shall return," which implies that the people are going into exile. Isaiah faithfully proclaims the truth to Ahaz, king of Judah, but the king and his establishment are opposed to Isaiah's message and do not like what the name of Isaiah's son portends and signifies.

The naming of Maher-shalal-hash-baz in Isaiah 8 reflects a similar dynamic. Yahweh instructs Isaiah to write the child's name on a large tablet. Translated literally, the name means something like "hastening to the plunder, hurrying to the loot,"[39] and the name seems to imply "they're going to plunder us fast." That is, when the enemy army comes, the one that will take the people into exile, the victorious soldiers will be swift in their plundering, looting activity.

Both of Isaiah's sons, then, have names that imply exile. The remnant will

---

38. James M. Hamilton Jr., "The Virgin Will Conceive: Typological Fulfillment in Matthew 1:18–23," in *Built upon the Rock: Studies in the Gospel of Matthew*, ed. John Nolland and Daniel Gurtner (Grand Rapids: Eerdmans, 2008), 228–47. See also James M. Hamilton Jr., *God's Glory in Salvation through Judgment: A Biblical Theology* (Wheaton, IL: Crossway, 2010), 363–67. Similarly Andrew T. Abernethy and Gregory Goswell, *God's Messiah in the Old Testament: Expectations of a Coming King* (Grand Rapids: Baker, 2020), 88–89.

39. See the footnote on Isaiah 8:1 in the NET Bible.

return (Shear-jashub) after the exile, and the enemy will hasten to the plunder and hurry to the loot (Maher-shalal-hash-baz) when they take the people into exile. The exile comes as a curse of the covenant. The curse comes because the covenant has been broken. And the covenant has been broken because the people fail to respond to prophets like Isaiah, whose own name, Yeshayahu (יְשַׁעְיָהוּ), declares that Yahweh saves. Rather than believe the preaching of Isaiah and the prophets who preceded him, the non-remnant in Israel look to human solutions, typically political ones, to their problems, as they hope to be delivered by foreign powers, whether Egypt or Assyria.

The way that Isaiah and his small band of followers stand opposed to the broader populace and their dominant cultural perspective can be seen in what Isaiah writes in Isaiah 8:11–16. In verse 11 Isaiah recounts how Yahweh warned him "not to walk in the way of this people," and verse 12 specifies that he should neither indulge in their conspiracy theories nor "fear what they fear." The conspiracy in view likely involves the threat on Ahaz in chapter 7, and the people at large fear what foreign kings might do to them. In contrast to this, Isaiah teaches in 8:13 that "Yahweh of hosts, him you shall honor as holy. Let him be your fear, and let him be your dread." In verses 14–15 Isaiah explains that Yahweh will protect those who take refuge in him and judge those who spurn him. And then, reflecting the way that the general populace does not heed his prophetic ministry—though he does have a small group of followers that stands with him against establishment opinion—Isaiah asserts in 8:16–18,

> Bind up the testimony; seal the teaching among my disciples. I will wait for Yahweh, who is hiding his face from the house of Jacob, and I will hope in him. Behold, I and the children whom Yahweh has given me are signs and portents in Israel from Yahweh of hosts, who dwells on Mount Zion.

The Hebrew term rendered "teaching" in verse 16 is the word *Torah* (תּוֹרָה), which initially refers to the Torah of Moses and will eventually be used as a way of referring to all that Israel recognized as Scripture. With these words Isaiah identifies himself and his disciples with all before them who have, in the first phrase of verse 17, waited for Yahweh. When Isaiah goes on in verse 17 to speak of how Yahweh is "hiding his face," he picks up concepts from Deuteronomy 31:17–18 and 32:20, where Yahweh says that he will hide his face from his people when they break his covenant and are driven into exile (Deut 31:16–18).

§8.2 Jesus and His Disciples

Teaching the solidarity between Jesus and his people, urging those people to be faithful to Jesus in spite of the way the surrounding culture pressures them to abandon him, the author of Hebrews quotes from two Old Testament passages, Psalm 22 and Isaiah 8, to show that Jesus "is not ashamed to call them brothers" (Heb 2:11, ESV). I contend that the author of Hebrews sees in both David and Isaiah figures who typify Jesus. Having spoken of how Jesus, "he who sanctifies," and his followers, "those who are sanctified," are sons of God the Father, "all have one source," the author of Hebrews explains, "That is why he is not ashamed to call them brothers" (2:11, ESV). He then presents Jesus as the typological fulfillment of what David prefigured by placing Psalm 22:22 on the lips of Jesus.

David exclaimed in Psalm 22:22 (ESV), "I will tell of your name to my brothers; in the midst of the congregation I will praise you."[40] We recall the way that when David knew Saul meant to kill him, he fled to "the cave of Adullam. And when his brothers and all his father's house heard it, they went down there to him" (1 Sam 22:1, ESV). It would be natural for David to celebrate God's deliverance with his family and all those aligned with him, his "brothers."[41] This solidarity between David and his people in the face of opposition is fulfilled in the solidarity between Jesus and his people, and just as David called his people his "brothers,"[42] so the author of Hebrews refers to followers of Jesus as his "brothers" (Heb 2:11, 12).[43]

The author of Hebrews adds further support to this connection between Jesus and his people as they stand together against the seed of the serpent when he presents Jesus quoting Isaiah 8:17–18 as the typological fulfillment of what Isaiah prefigured. This is a particularly clear instance where we must understand the quotation of Isaiah 8:18 not as a predictive utterance where Isaiah declares the future but as an instance of the prophet's experience providing

---

40. We will discuss Psalm 22 more fully in §4.4 of Chapter 6. For exposition of the whole of Psalm 22, and discussion of the way David typifies Jesus, see my commentary, *Psalms*, and my essay, "Typology in the Psalms."

41. The term "brother" (אָח) can be used to refer to kinship ties broader than male siblings of the same parentage. For instance, though Laban is Jacob's uncle, he and Jacob refer to one another as "brother" (אָח, ESV renders "kinsman") in Genesis 29:12 and 29:15.

42. David addresses his fighting men as his "brothers" (אָח) in 1 Samuel 30:23 and calls Jonathan his "brother" (אָח) in 2 Samuel 1:26.

43. Jesus referred to his followers as family and specifically as "brothers" in a number of places, e.g., Matt 12:48–49; 23:8; 28:10; John 20:17, etc.

a typological pattern for which Hebrews claims fulfillment in Christ. Jesus fathered no biological children, but in the context of Isaiah 7–8, the prophet Isaiah speaks of the biological sons he fathered and the meaning of their names.

§8.3 Prosopology or Typology?

How, then, should we understand Jesus to be "saying" (first word of Heb 2:12) the words of Psalm 22:22 and Isaiah 8:17–18? Matthew Bates has argued that prosopological exegesis provides the key to understanding what the author of Hebrews has done here, but I contend that such a solution vitiates the meaning of the text in its Old Testament context. Bates acknowledges as much, offering no explanation of the context of Isaiah 7–8 as he writes,

> I would propose that the author of Hebrews determined that Isaiah had slipped into the guise of Jesus the Son, and that the Son was hereby speaking not to the Father but rather he was issuing *a warning to the theodramatic audience*, the ancient people of God.[44]

I have proposed a contextual understanding of Isaiah's words, and that context contains no indication that "Isaiah had slipped into the guise of Jesus the Son," which Bates proposes "the author of Hebrews determined." The suggestion Bates makes about the author of Hebrews entails that biblical author engaging in an arbitrary, non-contextual, exegetically unwarranted interpretive practice whereby he simply makes the text of the Old Testament say what he wants it to say. Since the author of Hebrews was trying to persuade people who could access the text of the Old Testament, and since both the author of Hebrews and his audience treated the Old Testament as authoritative, I do not think that either the author of Hebrews or his audience would have been convinced by claims about the meaning of the text that cannot be derived from the actual words of the text in context. The author of Hebrews does not overtly and directly state all that Bates claims. That is, the author of Hebrews presents Jesus speaking the words of Psalm 22 and Isaiah 8, but he does not spell out the rationale for that presentation.

Bates proposes a prosopological rationale that disregards the meaning of the Old Testament texts in their context. Such a proposal entails the author of

---

44. Matthew W. Bates, *The Birth of the Trinity: Jesus, God, and Spirit in New Testament and Early Christian Interpretations of the Old Testament* (New York: Oxford University Press, 2015), 142.

Hebrews engaging in a power play, whereby the quotation of an authoritative text can be used as an appeal to authority, even though the text in its original context does not mean what the author claims. This will only be convincing if the audience either does not think about the meaning of the text in context or has no access to that context. If the audience has access to the text in context, and if they think through the meaning of the text and compare that with the claims Bates proposes, their ability to see what the text means in context will undermine the authority of prosopological exegesis. Anyone who understands Isaiah chapters 7–8 will reject the idea that "Isaiah had slipped into the guise of Jesus the son"[45] because they will be able to see that Isaiah was talking about his sons Shear Jashub and Maher-shalal-hash-baz. Because I think the author of Hebrews was trying to persuade his audience to give full mental assent and loyal obedient allegiance to the actual meaning of the biblical text and the way it is fulfilled in Jesus the Messiah, I find a typological rationale for his presentation of Jesus speaking the words of Psalm 22 and Isaiah 8 more convincing than a prosopological one.

For Bates, the author of Hebrews identifies the speaker in Psalm 22 and Isaiah 8 as no longer being David and Isaiah, respectively, but actually Jesus.[46] Not only does this render the meaning of Psalm 22 and Isaiah 8 in context irrelevant to the argument the author of Hebrews makes, it also eviscerates the powerful typological connection between David, Isaiah, and Jesus that the author of Hebrews forges.[47]

Both David and Isaiah speak as the prophetic representative of God's elect remnant. That elect remnant represents the collective seed of the woman. The collective seed of the woman identify with God's prophetic spokesperson, whether David or Isaiah, both of whom typify the singular seed of the woman. This relationship between the people and God's prophet finds fulfillment in the relationship between Christ and his people, which is precisely how the author of Hebrews speaks of the relationship between Jesus and the prophets: "Long ago, at many times and in many ways, God spoke to our fathers

---

45. Ibid.

46. See ibid., 140–46.

47. Peter J. Gentry observes, "it is unlikely that the Apostles were aware of the methods [of prosopological exegesis] promoted in the rhetorical handbooks. This is anachronistic." Peter J. Gentry, "A Preliminary Evaluation and Critique of Prosopological Exegesis," *Southern Baptist Journal of Theology* 23, no. 2 (2019): 119. Cf. Gentry's discussion of "the sources often appealed to" in discussions of the technique (107–8).

by the prophets, but in these last days he has spoken to us by his Son . . ."
(Heb 1:1–2a, ESV).

§9 JESUS

Behold how great this man is: archetype and fulfiller of the patterns, Israel's
long history builds to him. He is the new Adam who obeyed where the first
Adam sinned. He was baptized in the floodwaters of God's wrath so that those
baptized into his death and resurrection might be saved. Abraham rejoiced to
see his day, and unlike Abraham who failed to protect his wife when he told
the sister-fibs, Christ stepped forward and said "take me, and let these go free"
(paraphrasing John 18:8). Abraham interceded for Lot and Sodom, and Christ
intercedes for all those whom the Father has given to him (John 17:6–9, 20;
Rom 8:34).

The remarkable birth of the Lord Jesus matches and exceeds that of Isaac,
and whereas a ram was provided as a substitute when Isaac was offered up
on the altar, Christ died as the substitute on the cross. Abraham figuratively
received Isaac back from the dead (Heb 11:19); Christ actually rose from the
dead. Jesus the man from Nazareth came as *the* prophet like Moses (John 6:14),[48]
and he himself will come again as a new Joshua to conquer the land. Fulfilling
everything typified by Elijah and Elisha, the Lord Jesus fed the multitudes,
healed hopeless women, and raised the dead son of a widow.

The Spirit of Yahweh was on Isaiah to proclaim the favorable year of
the Lord (Isa 61:1), and Jesus preached the fulfillment of that Scripture in
his hometown synagogue (Luke 4:16–21). Like Isaiah, he was rejected (Luke
4:28–30), but he stood—and stands—in solidarity with his disciples, whom
he is not ashamed to call brothers, just as Isaiah did when he called for the
teaching to be bound up among his disciples as he and his children with their
portentous names waited for Yahweh (Isa 8:16–18; Heb 2:11–13). At that
time God was hiding his face (Isa 8:17), but those who turn to God in Christ
have the veil removed (2 Cor 3:16) and behold the glory of God in the face of
Jesus Christ (3:18; 4:4, 6).

---

48. Allison, *The New Moses*, 97–106, 140–270.

KINGS

For the fragrance that came to each was like a memory of dewy mornings of unshadowed sun in some land of which the fair world in Spring is itself but a fleeting memory. . . . Suddenly Faramir stirred, and he opened his eyes, and he looked on Aragorn who bent over him; and a light of knowledge and love was kindled in his eyes, and he spoke softly. 'My lord, you called me. I come. What does the king command?'. . . . And soon the word had gone out from the House that the king was indeed come among them, and after war he brought healing; and the news ran through the City.

—J. R. R. TOLKIEN[1]

C hrist comes as the king of Israel, and for him to be king of Israel is for him to be son of David, son of man (Adam), son of God. This designation can be seen in the genealogies of Matthew and Luke, and also in the way Nathanael hails Jesus in John 1:49 (ESV), "you are the Son of God! You are the King of Israel!" God made Adam in his image and likeness as his son (Luke 3:38), then God announced that Israel was his son (Exod 4:22–23), before telling David that the seed he would raise up from his line would be a son to him (2 Sam 7:14).

The corporate personality discussed briefly in §3.1 of Chapter 2 is relevant here. The "son of God" that is the nation of Israel (Exod 4:22–23), the royal priesthood (19:6), now has a singular representative. In just the way that David went out to fight for Israel against Goliath in 1 Samuel 17, the people of Israel

---

1. J. R. R. Tolkien, *The Return of the King* (Boston: Houghton Mifflin, 1965), 142.

had insisted on having a king who would "go out before us and fight our battles" (1 Sam 8:20). In a real sense, Israel's king is her covenant head, or the *one* who stands for the *many*.[2]

In the Old Testament we find both promises of a future king and, in narratives describing historical people, patterns shaped by promises, so that the patterns typify the future king. All these find fulfillment in Christ, who in turn enables his people to reign with him (Rev 2:26–27; 5:10). This chapter and the next are intrinsically connected. The discussion of kingship-typology in this will prepare for the righteous-sufferer-typology in the next. Here we focus our attention on Adam and Abraham, leaving the discussion of the way David typifies the one to come for the chapter that follows.

§1 ADAMIC DOMINION

As has been noted, though Adam is not called "king," there are at least four indicators that he is treated as a king: (1) he is told to reign over God's creation; (2) he is made in God's image and likeness and implicitly God's son; (3) he is charged to serve and protect God's creation; and (4) he exercises God's own authority over God's world when he names what God has made. In these four ways Adam takes up the royal role in God's realm. The significance of each of these for what follows Adam in the Bible calls us to consider them in turn.

§1.1 Have Dominion

In Genesis 1:26 God says, "Let us make man . . . And let them have dominion," and then in 1:28, "God blessed them. And God said to them . . . have dominion." In both of these statements the verb the ESV renders "dominion" is רָדָה. This verb appears in some texts that promise and others that pattern, and the Adamic dominion is the archetypal basis for various synonymous descriptions of how kings are to reign (with verbs such as מָלַךְ or מָשַׁל), and the one God will raise up to reign, across the Old Testament.

---

2. Describing the way the "royal lament psalms" were "construed . . . as paradigmatic," Richard B. Hays writes, "Thus 'David' in these psalms becomes a symbol for the whole people and—at the same time—a prefiguration of the future Anointed One (ὁ Χριστός) who will be the heir of the promises and the restorer of the throne." Richard B. Hays, *The Conversion of the Imagination: Paul as Interpreter of Israel's Scripture* (Grand Rapids: Eerdmans, 2005), 110–11. Rather than saying that the David of the Psalms "becomes a symbol for the whole people," I think it more accurate to say that as king of Israel, David was the corporate head of the people, their individual representative, the ideal Israelite, or the national father-figure (i.e., patriarch).

§1.2 Patterned Promises of a King

To see the significance of the promissory use of this term in Numbers 24:19 (ESV), "And one from Jacob shall exercise dominion [רדה]," we need to consider how Moses deploys the Balaam oracles to bring earlier promises together to ensure that his audience rightly understands the story he is telling. Moses depicts Balaam uttering oracles that develop statements made earlier in the Torah. For instance, he presents Balaam tying Genesis 49:9 to 27:29 (with a loop in the knot from 12:3) to prophesy of Israel's future king in Numbers 24:9 (following the ESV in the Table below).

Genesis 49:9b	Numbers 24:9a
"He stooped down; he crouched as a lion and as a lioness; who dares rouse him?"	"He crouched, he lay down like a lion and like a lioness; who will rouse him up?"
כָּרַע רָבַץ כְּאַרְיֵה וּכְלָבִיא מִי יְקִימֶנּוּ	כָּרַע שָׁכַב כַּאֲרִי וּכְלָבִיא מִי יְקִימֶנּוּ
Genesis 27:29b	**Numbers 24:9b**
"Cursed be everyone who curses you, and blessed be everyone who blesses you!"	"Blessed are those who bless you, and cursed are those who curse you."
אֹרְרֶיךָ אָרוּר וּמְבָרְכֶיךָ בָּרוּךְ	מְבָרְכֶיךָ בָרוּךְ וְאֹרְרֶיךָ אָרוּר

In Genesis 27:29 Isaac thinks he is blessing Esau, but in reality he is passing the blessing of Abraham on to Jacob, disguised as Esau, in accordance with the oracle given to Rebekah when the twins struggled in the womb, "the older will serve the younger" (Gen 25:23). Even within the book of Genesis, Isaac's blessing of Jacob is tied to Jacob's blessing of Judah with repeated words and phrases from 27:29 lacing 49:8 (repeated phrases italicized).

Genesis 27:29a	Genesis 49:8
"Let peoples serve you, and nations bow down to you.	"your hand shall be on the neck of your enemies;
Be lord over your brothers, and may your mother's *sons* *bow down* *to you*."	your father's *sons* shall *bow down* *before you*."
הֱוֵה גְבִיר לְאַחֶיךָ וְיִשְׁתַּחֲווּ לְךָ בְּנֵי אִמֶּךָ	יָדְךָ בְּעֹרֶף אֹיְבֶיךָ יִשְׁתַּחֲווּ לְךָ בְּנֵי אָבִיךָ

The careful reader of Genesis, then, will have discerned that the blessing of Abraham was passed to Isaac then Jacob. When Jacob blesses Judah, speaking of "the scepter" and "the ruler's staff" (Gen 49:10), it appears that the blessing of Abraham will be brought to pass through the reign of the king from Judah's line. Abraham was, after all, promised that kings would come from him (Gen 17:6, 16). By presenting Balaam combining statements from Genesis 27 (Isaac passing the blessing of Abraham to Jacob) with statements from Genesis 49 (Jacob blessing Judah), Moses reiterates this point for his audience.

And that's not all. As just mentioned, the blessing of Judah speaks of a "scepter" (Gen 49:10, שֵׁבֶט), and Moses presents Balaam speaking of a "scepter" (Num 24:17, שֵׁבֶט) arising from Israel. Balaam's beautiful words in Numbers 24:17 flow directly into the future king of Israel exercising Adamic dominion in 24:19, and here too Moses puts the skeleton key for unlocking the relationships between promises into Balaam's hands.[3]

Balaam's first words in Numbers 24:17 indicate that the one of whom he speaks is not near in time or space: "I see him, but not now; I behold him, but not near" (Num 24:17a). In the next line of 24:17 he asserts, "a star shall come out of Jacob . . ." (ESV). Prior to Numbers 24:17, the term "star" (כּוֹכָב) has been used as follows:

- to speak of the creation of the stars (Gen 1:16);
- to show Abram the innumerable nature of his descendants (Gen 15:5);
- to promise Abraham what his multiplied offspring would be like (Gen 22:17);
- to promise Isaac how his seed would be multiplied (Gen 26:4);
- to symbolize Joseph's brothers bowing down to him (Gen 37:9);
- to remind the Lord how he promised to multiply the seed of Abraham, Isaac, and Jacob (Exod 32:13).

As this survey of usage shows, after the creation of the stars in Genesis 1:16, every subsequent reference to them prior to Numbers pertains to the seed of Abraham. Balaam's words about a star coming from Jacob in Numbers 24:17, then, point to the rise of one descendant of Abraham in particular. The next line of the verse says "a scepter shall rise out of Israel." This puts "star"

---

3. I want to thank my friend Alex Duke for this imagery.

in parallel with "scepter," doing the same with the verbs "come out of" and "rise" and the names "Jacob" and "Israel." As noted above, the use of the term "scepter" in Numbers 24:17 recalls the same term in Genesis 49:10.

Before commenting on how Balaam turns the key in Numbers 24:17, we should recall why he appears in the narrative in the first place: the king of Moab summoned him to curse Israel (Num 22). As we have discussed above, God cursed the serpent in Genesis 3:14, and then he promised to curse anyone who dishonored Abram in Genesis 12:3. The "curse" language identifies anyone who dishonors Abraham as seed of the serpent. In Genesis 3:15 God told the serpent that the seed of the woman would bruise his head. The fact that Moab seeks to have Balaam curse Israel identifies Moab with his father the devil, marking the next words of Numbers 24:17 as an interpretation of Genesis 3:15, "it [the star/scepter] shall crush the forehead of Moab and break down all the sons of Sheth" (ESV).

When Balaam throws open the door, Moses shows his audience that the blessing of Abraham (Gen 12:1–3) will be fulfilled through the king from Judah's line (Gen 49:8–12) when that king arises to crush the head of the serpent and his seed (Gen 3:15; Num 24:7, 9, 17). At that point Israel will conquer Edom and Seir (Num 24:18), "And one from Jacob shall exercise dominion and destroy the survivors of cities!" (Num 24:19).

The one Balaam prophesies will exercise Genesis 1:28 Adamic dominion (רָדָה). This new-Adam in Numbers 24:19 is the seed of the woman who will enact Genesis 3:15 in Numbers 24:17, in fulfillment of Genesis 12:1–3, 27:28–29, and 49:8–12 (Num 24:9).[4]

Numbers 24:19 is promissory, and the pattern of the dominion God granted Adam in Genesis 1:26 and 28 informs what people understand to have been promised. Thus when David prays for Solomon in Psalm 72:8 (ESV),[5] "May he have dominion [רָדָה] from sea to sea, and from the River to the ends of the earth," David likely envisions the future king from his line re-establishing Adamic dominion (and cf. Ps 8)—as granted in Genesis 1:26 and 28—over

---

4. Similarly Dempster, *Dominion and Dynasty*, 116–17.

5. Because the content of Psalm 72, where the prayer is for the "royal son" (72:1), joins the closing reference to the prayers of David (72:20), I take the superscription of Psalm 72, "Of Solomon," to mean that David prayed this prayer for Solomon. See further Hamilton, *Psalms* ad loc. So also Hensely, "In Ps 72 an aging David prays for his son and successor, through whom God would realize his Abrahamic covenantal promises." Hensely, *Covenant and the Editing of the Psalter*, 205. The interpretation, however, is not drastically altered if Solomon prays for his son, with his prayer included among the prayers of David.

God's world. The future king from David's line will be a new Adam, and he will succeed as king where the first Adam failed. Beetham observes, "Ps 72 begins to read like an entreaty for an Edenic kingdom, secured by Davidic vicegerency, in fulfillment of God's original intentions for creation."[6]

§1.3 Solomonic Promise-Shaped Patterns

In Solomon the patterns and promises come together. First, the pattern: when we read of Solomon in 1 Kings 4:24 (MT 5:4) that "he had dominion [רָדָה] over all the region west of the Euphrates from Tiphsah to Gaza, over all the kings west of the Euphrates" (ESV), the author of Kings likely means his audience to think of Solomon's dominion according to the pattern of what was granted to Adam (Gen 1:26, 28) and promised about the scepter/star (Num 24:17–19).[7] The next verse substantiates this understanding: 1 Kings 4:25 (MT 5:5) depicts Israel living under the blessed reign of the anointed king from the line of David: "And Judah and Israel lived in safety, from Dan even to Beersheba, every man under his vine and under his fig tree, all the days of Solomon" (ESV).

§1.4 Solomonic Patterned Promises

The pattern of Solomon's reign informs later promises, as both Micah and Zechariah point to a future day when it will again be as it was when Solomon reigned:

> Mic 4:4 (ESV), "but they shall sit every man under his vine and under his fig tree, and no one shall make them afraid"

> Zech 3:8, 10 (ESV), "I will bring my servant the Branch. . . . In that day, declares the LORD of hosts, every one of you will invite his neighbor to come under his vine and under his fig tree."

The Lord Jesus evoked the patterns and the promises when, in reply to Nathanael's question as to how Jesus knew him, Jesus declared, "Before Philip called you, when you were under the fig tree, I saw you" (John 1:48).

---

6. Beetham, "From Creation to New Creation," 249.
7. Similarly Leithart, *1 & 2 Kings*, 49. Leithart also notes the use of מוֹשֵׁל to describe how Solomon "ruled" in 1 Kings 4:21 (MT 5:1).

In response, Nathanael recognized him as "Son of God . . . King of Israel" (John 1:49).

The patterns and promises intermingle again with reference to Solomon in Zechariah 9:10. We have observed how Adamic dominion informs both 1 Kings 4:24 (MT 5:4) and Psalm 72:8. We see from the quotation of Psalm 72:8 in Zechariah 9:10 that David's prayer was not understood to be exhausted by Solomon. Using the language that David prayed for Solomon in Psalm 72:8, Zechariah prophesies, "his rule [מְשֹׁל] shall be from sea to sea, and from the River to the ends of the earth" (ESV).

וְיֵרְדְּ מִיָּם עַד־יָם וּמִנָּהָר עַד־אַפְסֵי־אָרֶץ, Ps 72:8

וּמָשְׁלוֹ מִיָּם עַד־יָם וּמִנָּהָר עַד־אַפְסֵי־אָרֶץ, Zech 9:10b

Zechariah's use of a different verb for "rule" shows the two Hebrew terms (רָדָה and מָשַׁל) to be synonymous—the one (מָשַׁל) is used for Solomon's reign in 1 Kings 4:21, the other (רָדָה) for the same in 4:24.

The preceding statement in Zechariah 9:9 (ESV), "Rejoice greatly, O daughter of Zion! Shout aloud, O daughter of Jerusalem! Behold, your king is coming to you; righteous and having salvation is he, humble and mounted on a donkey, on a colt, the foal of a donkey," seems to have been informed by Solomonic patterns. When Solomon's older brother Adonijah (1 Kgs 2:22) tried to set himself up as king (1:5), David settled the dispute by saying,

> "Call to me Zadok the priest, Nathan the prophet, and Benaiah the son of Jehoiada." So they came before the king. And the king said to them, "Take with you the servants of your lord and have Solomon my son ride on my own mule, and bring him down to Gihon. And let Zadok the priest and Nathan the prophet there anoint him king over Israel. Then blow the trumpet and say, 'Long live King Solomon!' You shall then come up after him, and he shall come and sit on my throne, for he shall be king in my place. And I have appointed him to be ruler over Israel and over Judah." (1:32–35, ESV)

These events are so significant that the author of Kings recounts the details three times in 1 Kings 1:32–35, 1:38–40, and 1:43–48. It seems that Solomon riding David's mule (1 Kgs 1:33, 38, 44) to be anointed as king provides the historical event that informed Zechariah's prophecy that the king would come "humble and mounted on a donkey, on a colt, the foal of a donkey" (Zech 9:9).[8]

The biblical authors appear to have interpreted the historical patterns of events they describe in light of the promises God made, and the patterns and the promises join together to point forward to the coming king. Then came one who, having announced "something greater than Solomon is here" (Matt 12:42, ESV), deliberately sent his disciples into Jerusalem that he might enact the fulfillment of Zechariah 9:9 (Matt 21:1–5).

Before leaving this discussion of Adamic dominion, allow me to note briefly some other ways to describe the reign of a king, in addition to the verb found in Genesis 1:26 and 28 (רָדָה). We have seen how Zechariah uses a synonymous term when he quotes Psalm 72:8 (מָשַׁל in Zech 9:10; also in 1 Kgs 4:21). The cognate verb appears in Psalm 8:6 (MT 8:7), as David there reflects on how God made man ruler over the works of his hands, commenting specifically on Genesis 1:26 and 28. Similarly, the Hebrew term "king" has a cognate verb built of the same consonants that means something like "reign as king" (מָלַךְ, e.g., Gen 37:8; 1 Sam 8:9; 2 Sam 5:4). Then, as we have seen, there are passages that do not directly use the word "king" but speak of things like scepters (Gen 49:8–12; Num 24:17). I would suggest that the statements about and to Adam in Genesis 1:26 and 28 make the initial deposit into the conceptual fund on which all the predictions of the future king will draw (cf., e.g., Ps 110:2).

§2 ADAMIC SONSHIP

We discussed the Adam—Israel—David—Son of Man dynamic in Chapter 2 above. There I argued that the logic of Genesis 5:1–3 implies that Adam is

---

8. So also Stephen Ahearne-Kroll, *The Psalms of Lament in Mark's Passion: Jesus' Davidic Suffering*, Society for New Testament Studies Monograph Series (New York: Cambridge University Press, 2007), 146. The Solomonic pattern could well have been laid across a prior Davidic one. Petterson writes, "the king is 'humble' (alternatively, the Hebrew can be translated 'afflicted'; cf. Isa. 53:4, 7, where Isaiah's suffering servant is 'afflicted' not for his own sins, like David, but for the sins of others). The background to Zechariah's picture seems to be the suffering David of 2 Samuel and the Psalms, along with the suffering servant of Isaiah. These have been woven together in Zechariah's portrait of the future king here and throughout chapters 9–14. This explains the . . . description of the king as 'mounted on a donkey.' During David's exile from Jerusalem, when he was nearly defeated by his enemies, he rode a donkey (cf. 2 Sam. 16:2)." Petterson, "Zechariah," 694.

God's son. To briefly rehearse: Genesis 5:3 presents Seth, Adam's son, in Adam's image and likeness, suggesting that Adam, likeness of God in 5:1, is therefore God's son, a conclusion reflected in Luke 3:38. God then identifies the nation of Israel as a new Adam when he refers to Israel as his son in Exodus 4:22–23, and when he says the seed of David who will be king will be a son to him in 2 Samuel 7:14, he identifies the future king as the new Adam covenant head of the nation. This section seeks to add a layer to the earlier discussion by considering the development of the new Adam son of God in Proverbs 30.

§2.1 What Is His Son's Name?
§2.1.1 Proverbs in Light of Deuteronomy 6 and 17

As we approach Proverbs 30, we should reflect briefly on its immediate (the chapter in the book of Proverbs) and broad (the book's place in the canon) contexts. The fact that in Proverbs King Solomon is the initial speaker addressing his son makes several features of Deuteronomy relevant. In Deuteronomy fathers are charged with the task of teaching Torah to their sons (Deut 6:6–7), and kings must copy Torah in their own hand and read it all their days (17:14–20). The book of Proverbs opens with the words, "The proverbs of Solomon, son of David, king of Israel" (Prov 1:1), and in the words of the book Solomon obeys Deuteronomy 6 and 17, as he instructs his son in the Torah he has thoroughly digested. Beetham comments, "The Wisdom literature provides training for royal administration in Judah. It is instruction for vicegerency."[9]

§2.1.2 Proverbs in Light of 2 Samuel 7:14

The teaching reflects not only Deuteronomy 6 (cf. esp. Deut 6:1–9 and Prov 3:1–10 and 6:20–23), but also the promise to David in 2 Samuel 7:14. Consider the lexical points of contact between 2 Samuel 7:14 and Proverbs 3:11–12.[10]

---

9. Beetham, "From Creation to New Creation," 249. Having just cited this reference to "Wisdom literature," I want to note my full-throated agreement with the rejection of the philosophical underpinnings of that genre label. On which, see Will Kynes, *An Obituary for "Wisdom Literature": The Birth, Death, and Intertextual Reintegration of a Biblical Corpus* (Oxford: Oxford University Press, 2019).

10. This point was brought to my attention by two presentations on Proverbs by Gwilym Davies at the Proclamation Trust's EMA Conference in the summer of 2018.

2 Samuel 7:14	Proverbs 3:11–12
אֲנִי אֶהְיֶה־לּוֹ לְאָב וְהוּא יִהְיֶה־לִּי לְבֵן אֲשֶׁר בְּהַעֲוֺתוֹ וְהֹכַחְתִּיו בְּשֵׁבֶט אֲנָשִׁים וּבְנִגְעֵי בְּנֵי אָדָם	מוּסַר יְהוָה בְּנִי אַל־תִּמְאָס וְאַל־תָּקֹץ בְּתוֹכַחְתּוֹ כִּי אֶת אֲשֶׁר יֶאֱהַב יְהוָה יוֹכִיחַ וּכְאָב אֶת־בֵּן יִרְצֶה
"I will be to him a **father**, and he will be to me a **son**.	"The correction of Yahweh, my son, do not reject, and do not abhor his discipline,
When he sins, I will **discipline** him with the rod of men, with the stripes of the sons of man."	For Yahweh **disciplines** the one he loves, even as a **father** the **son** with whom he is pleased."

Solomon, son of David, to whom the promises of 2 Samuel 7:14 were communicated, teaches his son, of the house of David Yahweh promised to build, in anticipation of the seed Yahweh promised to raise up from that house, both the terms of the Torah and the terms of the covenant-promise to David.

The book of Proverbs presents the son of David, whom God said would be a son to him, teaching the wisdom of Torah to his son. Near the end of the book, the teaching of Solomon (1:1; 10:1; 25:1) and of "the wise" (22:17; 24:23) is complemented by an oracle of Agur son of Jakeh (30:1), whose riddling question about the son of the one who established the ends of the earth (30:4) intrigues us here.

§2.1.3 Who Has Ascended?

After the opening statement identifying Agur as son of Jakeh and the chapter as a "burden" (הַמַּשָּׂא), Proverbs 30:1 reads, "The utterance of the man" (נְאֻם הַגֶּבֶר, ESV: "The man declares"). Christopher Ansberry notes, "With the exception of Proverbs 30:1, the expression נְאֻם הַגֶּבֶר occurs only three times in the Old Testament (Num 24:3, 15; 2 Sam 23:1)."[11] Remarkably, each of these passages pertains to the king of Israel:

- The "utterance of the man" Balaam in Numbers 24:3–9 states of Israel in 24:7, "his king shall be higher than Agag, and his kingdom shall

---

11. Christopher B. Ansberry, *Be Wise, My Son, and Make My Heart Glad: An Exploration of the Courtly Nature of the Book of Proverbs*, Beihefte zur Zeitschrift für die alttestamentliche Wissenschaft (New York: De Gruyter, 2010), 165 n. 9. I would note that whereas Proverbs 30:1 has נְאֻם הַגֶּבֶר, the three other texts (Num 24:3, 15; 2 Sam 23:1) have וּנְאֻם הַגֶּבֶר.

be exalted" (ESV), and then as we have discussed above, Balaam brings together the blessings of Abraham (Gen 12:1–3; 27:29) and Judah (Gen 49:8–12) in Numbers 24:9.

- Similarly, the "utterance of the man" Balaam in Numbers 24:15–19 contains the scepter that crushes the head of the Moabite seed of the serpent in 24:17, with the one from Jacob exercising Adamic dominion in 24:19.
- And "the utterance of the man" in 2 Samuel 23:1–7 is spoken by David, the prophet-king. He speaks of the just ruler who "dawns on them like the morning light" (2 Sam 23:4, ESV) before asking, "does not my house stand so with God? For he has made with me an everlasting covenant, ordered in all things and secure" (23:5, ESV). This statement about David's house and the covenant God made with him points back to the promises of 2 Samuel 7.

The usage of the phrase "the utterance of the man" (נְאֻם הַגֶּבֶר)[12] suggests that what Agur says in Proverbs 30 will also pertain to the king of Israel. The body of the book of Proverbs has called for the wisdom of Deuteronomy 4:6, the wisdom of keeping and doing the Torah of Moses, particularly by listening to parental instruction, avoiding forbidden women and criminal men, and not giving pledges to strangers (Prov 1–9). From there the book goes on to celebrate wise speech, diligent work, marriage, and the wisdom of walking humbly in the fear of God. Ansberry observes that though the Proverbs "convey a general, moral vision accessible to every member of the community, within the document, this vision is directed toward the noble youth."[13] This conclusion fits with the idea that Solomon seeks to prepare his son to ascend the throne of David.

The famous discrepancy between the teaching of Proverbs and the failures of Solomon, Rehoboam, and the kings who descended from them might explain Agur saying, "I am weary, O God; I am weary, O God, and worn out" (30:1, ESV). William Brown suggests: "Agur is a student of wisdom who vents his fatigue and frustration over the rigors of his discipline."[14] I would add that this fatigue and frustration might arise from the disconnects between the king's

---

12. Waltke renders this, "The inspired utterance of the man." See Bruce K. Waltke, *The Book of Proverbs, Chapters 15–31*, New International Commentary on the Old Testament (Grand Rapids: Eerdmans, 2005), 454–55 n. 6.

13. Ansberry, *Be Wise, My Son*, 189.

14. William P. Brown, "The Pedagogy of Proverbs 10:1–31:9," in *Character and Scripture: Moral Formation, Community, and Biblical Interpretation*, ed. William P. Brown (Grand Rapids: Eerdmans, 2002), 176.

teaching and the king's own life-story, a disconnect also seen in the king's sons.

Agur humbly communicates his lack of understanding in Proverbs 30:2–3, and then follow a remarkable set of questions in 30:4 (ESV),

> Who has ascended to heaven and come down?
>> Who has gathered the wind in his fists?
> Who has wrapped up the waters in a garment?
>> Who has established all the ends of the earth?
> What is his name, and what is his son's name?
>> Surely you know!

The first four questions pertain to heaven and earth, wind and water, and the fifth question hints at the answer to the first four. The first question recalls Deuteronomy 30:12 (ESV), "It is not in heaven, that you should say, 'Who will ascend to heaven for us and bring it to us . . . ?'"

Deut 30:12, מִי יַעֲלֶה־לָּנוּ הַשָּׁמַיְמָה וְיִקָּחֶהָ לָּנוּ

Prov 30:4, מִי עָלָה־שָׁמַיִם וַיֵּרַד

In all of the Old Testament, the question "who will go up/ascend" is only complemented by "to heaven" in these two places, Deuteronomy 30:12 and Proverbs 30:4. Psalm 24:3 is similar, and relevant, as it asks, "Who will ascend the mount of Yahweh?" Moses ascended Mount Sinai to receive the Torah, so the people need not do that for themselves (Deut 30:12).[15] The question posed in Psalm 24:3 and Proverbs 30:4, however, points beyond Moses's ascent to something only God himself could accomplish,[16] as the next three questions indicate.

These questions are like those posed to Job,[17] and in the Old Testament there is only one who has gathered the wind in his fists, wrapped up the waters

---

15. Commenting on Moses at Sinai, Morales writes, "Moses ascends in order to represent the people to God; Moses descends in order to represent God to the people." Morales, *Who Shall Ascend the Mountain of the Lord?*, 89.

16. Steinmann writes, "Centuries later Paul would make the same theological points as Agur as he too draws on Deut 30:11–14. The apostle states that Jesus Christ is the divine Word who has descended from heaven in order to reveal God's salvation to us. The preached and confessed Gospel of Christ brings us to the saving knowledge of God that we could never attain by our own efforts (Rom 10:6–17)." Andrew E. Steinmann, *Proverbs*, Concordia Commentary (Saint Louis: Concordia, 2009), 595.

17. In only Job 38:5 and Proverbs 30:4 do we find the exclamation, "surely you know!" כִּי תֵדָע.

in a garment, and established all the ends of the earth. The identity of that one is hinted at by the fifth question, "What is his name?" The question is worded in the same way that Moses articulated it when he anticipated what the people of Israel would want to know in Exodus 3:13, and this particular question is asked only in Exodus 3:13 and Proverbs 30:4.

Exod 3:13, מַה־שְּׁמוֹ
"what is his name?"

Prov 30:4, מַה־שְּׁמוֹ
"what is his name?"

Anyone who understands what the Old Testament teaches will know that his name is Yahweh, the only creator of heaven and earth, and the allusion to Exodus 3:13 in Proverbs 30:4 confirms that conclusion. The question that follows serves as our point of contact with the theme of this section, Adam's status as son of God: "and what is his son's name?" At the risk of belaboring the point, note that the first four questions in Proverbs 30:4 are creation-heavy—ascent to heaven, gathering of wind and wave, and establishment of the ends of the earth. The focus is on Yahweh as *maker* of heaven and earth. Then follow the queries about his name and that of his son.

The allusion to Exodus 3:13 establishes his name as Yahweh, and after the revelation of God's covenant with David in 2 Samuel 7, the answer to the question about his son's name is: the name of the one who will be a son to Yahweh is "seed of David." Here again Agur alludes to earlier Scripture to confirm the conclusion he wants his audience to draw about the identity of the son. Agur quotes Psalm 18:30, which can also be found in 2 Samuel 22:31 (ESV), "the word of the LORD proves true; he is a shield for all those who take refuge in him" (same wording in Ps 18:30 [MT 18:31]).

Ps 18:31, אִמְרַת־יְהוָה צְרוּפָה מָגֵן הוּא לְכֹל הַחֹסִים בּוֹ

Prov 30:5, כָּל־אִמְרַת אֱלוֹהַּ צְרוּפָה מָגֵן הוּא לַחֹסִים בּוֹ

This is the psalm that David sang to Yahweh on the day that Yahweh rescued him from the hand of all his enemies and from Saul (Ps 18:ss [MT 18:1]), and it concludes with the words, "Great salvation he brings to his king, and shows steadfast love to his messiah, to David and his seed forever" (18:50 [MT 18:51]). The quotation of Psalm 18:30 in Proverbs 30:5, "every word of God proves true; he is a shield to those who take refuge in him," indicates that the word that will prove true is the promise made to David regarding the future king from his line. This would resolve the frustration Agur articulates in Proverbs 30:1–2. Wearied and worn out by the discrepancy between Solomon's wisdom and Solomon's life, a discrepancy exacerbated when one considers the wisdom Solomon taught to his son in Proverbs and the way his sons lived, Agur is reminded who the creator is and what he has said about his son in 30:4, and that receives confirmation by the allusion to the promises to David in 30:5. Further, in view of texts like Psalm 2:12, "Blessed are all who take refuge in him," and Psalm 84:9, "Behold our shield, O God; look on the face of your messiah!," the one who "is a shield to those who take refuge in him" (Prov 30:5b) might indeed be the Davidic new Adam son of God.[18]

§2.2 When Jesus Answered Agur's Question

If we are uncertain about how specific Agur's understanding was, what Jesus reveals in his conversation with Nicodemus brings clarity and confirmation of the direction in which these reflections have been moving. In response to what Jesus said about the necessary new birth (John 3:3–8), Nicodemus asks, "How can these things be?" (3:9). Having marveled that Nicodemus does not understand (3:10) and asserted that he bears eyewitness testimony to the things he has said to Nicodemus (3:11), Jesus says in John 3:12, "If I have told you earthly things and you do not believe, how can you believe if I tell you heavenly things?" (ESV). Nicodemus did not receive Jesus's testimony (3:11) about how the Spirit's work in the new birth enables people to see and enter the kingdom of God (3:3–8). The words that Jesus spoke there (3:3–8) seem designed to provoke Nicodemus to see how everything Jesus has claimed is substantiated by the Old Testament.[19]

---

18. Cf. Hensley's conclusion: "The Psalter and its books are crafted around the hope of a coming 'David' through whom YHWH would renew his people and Zion (e.g., Pss 102–103) and lead them in the thanksgiving and praise of God (Ps 145 et al.). Announced as YHWH's 'anointed' and 'son' in Ps 2, the king both conquers his enemies (Pss 2, 101, 110, 118, cf. 143:12) and suffers as he identifies with the people as YHWH's servant (Pss 78, 86, 88–89, 102; cf. 18:1). This 'David' is instrumental in YHWH's fulfillment of his covenant promises to Abraham and exodus-like salvation of his people, announcing YHWH's grace and favor as YHWH himself had done before Moses (Ps 103)." Hensley, *Covenant and the Editing of the Psalter*, 271.

19. On which, see Hamilton, "John," 69–74.

The "heavenly things" Jesus references in John 3:12 would seem to explain the "how" that Nicodemus sought to understand ("how can these things be?" 3:9, ESV), and in John 3:13 Jesus appears to assert that he does indeed have access to those heavenly things, as he alludes to the first question in Proverbs 30:4 with the assertion, "No one has ascended into heaven except he who descended from heaven, the Son of Man."[20] The first part of the assertion about ascending and descending answers the riddle from Proverbs 30:4, and by appending "the Son of Man" to the end of his statement, Jesus forges a connection between the son of God in Proverbs 30:4, the Davidic king, and the one like a son of man, who is also the Davidic king, in Daniel 7:13–14 (see §5.1 in Chapter 2 above). In that passage the one like a son of man was already present in the heavenly throne room, from which, Jesus implies, he has descended, making him also able to ascend.

§3 ADAMIC KEEPING AND NAMING

The connection between the working and keeping that Adam was put in the garden to do (Gen 2:15), and the working and keeping the Levites did at the tabernacle (Num 3:8), has been discussed above. This section raises the following question: do the biblical authors intend their audiences to associate Adam's working and keeping of the garden with the work of the kings of Israel?

§3.1 The King Shepherds

Adam's role of working the garden (Gen 2:15) enacts his responsibility to subdue the earth (1:28), making the world productive for life as he cultivates the fruit of the land. As the working of the garden pertains to providing what is needed for life, the keeping of the garden (2:15) entails protecting and guarding. When joined with his responsibility to communicate the prohibition on eating from the forbidden tree (2:17), we see that fundamental to Adam's manhood were his responsibilities to lead, provide, and protect.

The two aspects of Adam's responsibility to work and keep, garden and shepherd, seem to have been divided between Cain and Abel. Cain worked

---

20. Commenting on Proverbs 30:4, Duane Garrett writes, "The Christian interpreter . . . cannot but think of the Son of God here and recall that he came down from above to reveal the truth to his people (John 3:31–33). Also, since 'God' is the only possible answer to the questions here, it is striking that the text speaks of his 'son.'" Duane A. Garrett, *Proverbs, Ecclesiastes, Song of Songs*, New American Commentary (Nashville: Broadman & Holman, 1993), 237.

the ground, while Abel was a shepherd (Gen 4:2). The description of Abel shepherding is similar to the descriptions of Joseph and Moses shepherding:

Gen 4:2, וַיְהִי־הֶבֶל רֹעֵה צֹאן

"And it came about that Abel was a shepherd of a flock."

Gen 37:2, הָיָה רֹעֶה אֶת־אֶחָיו בַּצֹּאן

"he was shepherding the flock with his brothers"

Exod 3:1, הָיָה רֹעֶה אֶת־צֹאן יִתְרוֹ

"he was shepherding the flock of Jethro"

Later David is brought in from shepherding the flock (רֹעֶה בַּצֹּאן) to be anointed as king (1 Sam 16:11), Solomon depicts an idealized version of himself as a shepherd in Song of Songs (Song 1:7–8), and Israel's prophets point to the day when God will raise up a good shepherd for his people (e.g., Ezek 34). In Zechariah 11, the prophet Zechariah himself patterns the promises, as he becomes a shepherd who is rejected by his people, bought off by them for thirty pieces of silver, which money is thrown to the potter in the house of Yahweh (Zech 11:4–14; cf. Matt 26:15; 27:9, 10). Jesus comes as the good shepherd (John 10:1–11) and the new Adam (10:36–38) who will give his life for the sheep (10:14–18) *and* be the true vine that God himself tends as gardener (15:1; cf. 20:15).

§3.2 The King Names

In Genesis 1 God called the world into being, seven times saying "Let there be . . ." Time and again, it was so, and then God named what he had made, along the lines of Genesis 1:3 and 1:5 (ESV), "And God said, 'Let there be light,' and there was light. . . . God called the light Day . . ." God here exercises his own authority over what he has made, and in Genesis 2 he allows the man to exercise that same authority:

> Now out of the ground the Lord God had formed every beast of the field and every bird of the heavens and brought them to the man to see what he would call them. And whatever the man called every living creature, that was its name. The man gave names to all livestock and to the birds of the heavens and to every beast of the field. (Gen 2:19–20, ESV)

We noted above the way that 1 Kings 4:24 (MT 5:4) portrays Solomon exercising Genesis 1:28 Adamic dominion, and shortly after that the author of Kings portrays Solomon taking up Adam's task of naming and classifying what God has made. In 1 Kings 4:33 (MT 5:13) we read of Solomon, "He spoke of trees, from the cedar that is in Lebanon to the hyssop that grows out of the wall. He spoke also of beasts, and of birds, and of reptiles, and of fish" (ESV). Strengthening the tie to the creation-setting in which Solomon speaks, the term rendered "reptiles" here is the same term rendered "creeping things" in Genesis 1 (רמש, Gen 1:24, 25, 26, 28, 30), and the other animals named match the lists of creatures over which God gave Adam dominion:

Gen 1:26	Gen 1:28	1 Kings 4:33 (MT 5:13)
fish, דָּגָה	fish, דָּגָה	beasts, בְּהֵמָה
birds, עוֹף	birds, עוֹף	birds, עוֹף
livestock, בְּהֵמָה	living thing that moves,	reptiles, רֶמֶשׂ
creeping thing, רֶמֶשׂ	חַיָּה הָרֹמֶשֶׂת	fish, דָּג

The reference to Solomon's dominion joins the description of him speaking of trees and animals to present him as a new-Adam king of Israel. After Adam named the animals, he named the woman God made to be his bride (Gen 2:23; cf. 3:20). This pattern of the Adamic king naming his beloved seems to find fulfillment when, having promised the right to eat of the tree of life (Rev 2:7), Jesus promises a new name to those who overcome (2:17).

What we have considered to this point is foundational for Israel's concept of kingship. Because of the way that Psalm 110 indicates that the future king from David's line will also be a priest according to the order of Melchizedek, we should ask what Genesis 14, where Abraham encounters Melchizedek, contributes to the Old Testament's typological development of royal expectations.[21]

§4 ABRAHAM'S CONQUEST OF THE KINGS

Abraham is never called a king, and yet he is told that kings will come from him (Gen 17:6) and Sarah (17:16). Abraham also conducts himself in kingly

---

21. Melchizedek is only mentioned in Genesis 14, Psalm 110, and Hebrews 5, 6, and 7.

ways in Genesis 14, and there are significant parallels, parallels that form a typological pattern, between Abraham, Gideon, and David. Like Abraham, Gideon is not officially a king, though he is said to resemble the son of a king (Judg 8:18), the people want him to reign (8:22–23), and he has a son named "Abimelech" ("my father is king," 8:31).

The relationship that I am proposing exists between Genesis 14, Judges 6–8, and 1 Samuel 30, could have developed as follows: First, Moses saw significance in what he narrates in Genesis 14, significance that warranted the inclusion of the account in the book of Genesis. His presentation of the event, moreover, highlights the fact that Abraham takes captivity captive (cf. Eph 4:8 KJV) when he rescues Lot from the coalition of the four Mesopotamian kings who defeated the five Canaanite kings, including the king of Sodom, and carried Lot off with the spoil (see Gen 14:1–16). Abram then interacts with two kings, the king of Sodom and the king of Salem (14:17–24). Moses builds the conceptual context for the promises that kings will come from Abraham and Sarah (17:6, 16) by presenting Abraham in kingly ways. The author of Judges then sees parallels between Abraham in Genesis 14 and the way that Gideon delivers Israel, and he presents Gideon in light of these parallels in Judges 6–8 (more on this shortly). Later, the writer of 1–2 Samuel, aware of the parallels between Abraham and Gideon, saw the similar sequences of events that he narrates in 1 Samuel 30.

Moses joins the pattern of Abraham's kingly behavior (Gen 14) to the promise that kings would come from him (Gen 17:6, 16) to produce a promise-shaped pattern for later biblical authors. The repeated pattern of events in Genesis 14, Judges 6–8, and 1 Samuel 30 also appears to have been recognized by David, so that in Psalm 110 he speaks of the future king from his line in ways that indicate that what was typified in these narratives will be fulfilled in him. With such a perspective the New Testament authors are in whole-hearted agreement. To establish these claims, I must establish historical correspondence and escalation in significance between Genesis 14, Judges 6–8, and 1 Samuel 30, and from there I need to show that Psalm 110 alludes to these passages. We will summarize Genesis 14 before drawing attention to the ways the later passages forge connections with it.

§4.1 Literary Structures in Genesis 14

The battle that results in Lot's capture is presented in Genesis 14:1–9, and the passage reflects a chiastic structure as follows:

14:1, Four Mesopotamian Kings
　14:2, Five Canaanite Kings
　　14:3, Gathering for Battle
　　　14:4, After Twelve Years of Service, Rebellion in the Thirteenth
　　　14:5–6, Attempt to Reestablish Control in Year Fourteen
　　14:7, After Conquest in Ham, Returning for Battle
　14:8, Five Canaanite Kings
14:9, Four Mesopotamian Kings

Rather than fight to the death to protect their people, the kings of Sodom and Gomorrah flee for their own lives, leaving those under their protection, including Lot, to be taken captive by the pirate kings (Gen 14:10–12). The turning point of this section of the narrative comes in the account of the fugitive who escapes to alert Abraham, who leads forth 318 trained men to rescue Lot (14:13–14). When we consider the fact that these 318 men are described as having been born in Abraham's house, we see this likely means that the parents of these men are in Abraham's employ, part of his expansive household operation. If, as was probably the case, each of these men's parents have other children, and assuming that there were others left to tend and protect Abraham's household and flocks and herds when he took the 318 in pursuit of Lot, then Abraham's household, which obviously numbers in the hundreds, might have encompassed thousands. Though Abraham is not referred to as a king, he is an ancient Near Eastern patriarch, a chieftain of sorts, a potentate. And he engages in a risky, determined effort to chase down four powerful kings who have defeated his neighbors and carried off his nephew. Abraham knows warfare: he divides his force by night, strikes the enemy, and chases the vanquished north of Damascus, driving them out of the land of Canaan, bringing back Lot, the women, the people, and the plunder that the kings had taken (14:15–16). This passage too appears to have a chiastic structure:

14:10, Kings of Sodom and Gomorrah Flee
　14:11–12, Enemy Plunders and Takes Lot
　　14:13, Fugitive Informs Abraham
　　14:14, Abraham Leads Forth His 318 Men
　14:15, Abraham Defeats and Drives Out the Enemy
14:16, Abraham Brings Back Lot, the People, and the Plunder

When Abraham returns, the king of Sodom and the king of Salem both come to meet him (Gen 14:17–18). The first word out of the mouth of Melchizedek, king of Salem, is "Blessed" (14:19–20). The first word out of the mouth of Bera, king of Sodom, is "Give" (14:21).[22] Abraham refuses to keep the plunder taken from the king of Sodom, though he does provide for his allies (14:22–24). Here again the passage has a chiastic structure:

14:17, The Victors in the King's Valley
    14:18, Melchizedek Brings Out Bread and Wine
        14:19–20, Melchizedek Blesses Abraham and Receives a Tithe
        14:21, King of Sodom Makes Demands and Offers Plunder
    14:22–23, Abraham Refuses the Offered Plunder
14:24, Abraham Provides for His Men and Allies

Much more could be said about this narrative, but we are now in position to consider parallels with later passages.

§4.2 Genesis 14 and Judges 6–8

Consider the following points of historical contact between Genesis 14 and Judges 6–8: Genesis 14:7 mentions the Amalekites, and the Mesopotamian kings that abduct Lot are from the east (14:1, 9). Judges 6:3 relates how "the Midianites and the Amalekites and the people of the East would come up against" Israel. There are strong points of contact with the exodus from Egypt in the near context of Genesis 14 (esp. in Genesis 12 and 15, see Chapter 8 below), and in Judges 6:8–10 a prophet sent from Yahweh reminds Israel of his work on their behalf at the exodus. Yahweh appeared to Abraham as he sat by the door of his tent by the oaks of Mamre in Genesis 18:1, and in Judges 6:11, "the angel of Yahweh came and sat under the terebinth at Ophrah" to summon Gideon to deliver Israel.

Once Gideon sets out to deliver Israel, his force is winnowed down from twenty-two thousand to ten thousand to three hundred. Gideon fights for Israel with a force of men remarkably close in number to the three hundred eighteen Abram took to recapture Lot. Interestingly, the number is brought down from ten thousand by means of the Lord revealing that those who kneel

---

22. Mathews, *Genesis 11:27–50:26*, 146.

down to drink are not to go, while the three hundred who will join the mission lap the water (Judg 7:4–8). Did they lift up their heads as they drank from the brook by the way (cf. Ps 110:7)?

Gideon does not yet receive intelligence from a fugitive as Abraham did (Gen 14:13), nor does he find a servant left for dead like David did (1 Sam 30:11), but he does overhear a key conversation that gives him confidence (Judg 7:9–14). Just as Abraham had done in the rescue of Lot (Gen 14:15), Gideon divides his force (Judg 7:16) by night (7:9) and ambushes the enemy (7:17–18). In the process of chasing the enemy, Gideon does capture a young man, from whom he gets key intelligence (8:14).

When the king of Sodom offered to let Abraham keep the plunder he recaptured from the eastern kings, Abraham refused to give the king of Sodom the chance to enrich him. Though Gideon declined the people's request that he become king, he received a perverted freewill offering of earrings captured from the defeated enemies, which he made into an ephod. Israel whored after the ephod, and it became a snare to Gideon and his people (Judg 8:22–28). The priestly character of the ephod recalls Abraham's encounter with Melchizedek, priest of God Most High (Gen 14:18), and Abraham's refusal of plunder (14:22–24) informs Gideon's misuse of the plunder to make the idolatrous ephod (Judg 8:27). Whereas Abraham acted wisely, Gideon not so much.

The lexical points of contact between Genesis 14 and Judges 6–8 include reference to the Amalekites (Gen 14:7; Judg 6:3), the force of roughly three hundred fighters (Gen 14:14; Judg 7:2–8), the "striking" of the enemy (נָכָה, Gen 14:5, 7, 15, 17; Judg 6:16; 7:13; 8:11), the "night" (Gen 14:15; Judg 7:9), and the pursuit of the defeated enemy (Gen 14:14–15; Judg 7:23, 25; 8:4, 5, 12).

The event sequence similarities include especially the division of the force of three hundred-ish fighters by night for an ambush of the enemy, the reception of information from a fugitive or a captive young man, the recovery of plunder from the enemy, and then the very different responses of Abraham and Gideon to the possibilities of that plunder (Abraham rejects it; Gideon makes an idolatrous ephod).

When we consider covenantal and salvation historical significance, the angel of Yahweh appears to both Abraham and Gideon, and Gideon clearly delivers the collective seed of Abraham, the people of Israel, just as Abraham had delivered his kinsman Lot.

Though I am not aware of quotations of lines or phrases of Genesis 14 in Judges 6–8, the other criteria for establishing historical correspondence seem more than sufficient to establish that the second narrative was intended to parallel the first.

§4.3 Genesis 14 and 1 Samuel 30

Lexical points of contact between Genesis 14 and 1 Samuel 30 abound, and many of the same events happen in the same order. As in Genesis 14:7 and Judges 6:3, Amalekites are mentioned in 1 Samuel 30:1. Here the Amalekites are the invading, plundering, kidnapping enemies who "strike" David's city Ziklag (1 Sam 30:1; Gen 14:7). In fact the "striking" is presented in the same way in Genesis 14:7 and 1 Samuel 30:1 (וַיַּכּוּ, "and they struck"). So also with the description of the kidnapping: the same verb used to describe Lot being "taken captive" is used to describe the women and all in Ziklag being "taken captive" (שָׁבָה, Gen 14:14; 1 Sam 30:2, 3, 5). Just as women were taken captive with Lot (Gen 14:16), so women were taken captive from Ziklag.

Like Abraham, who pursued the plundering pirate kings, so David pursues those who plundered Ziklag, and here again the same verb is used in both places (רָדַף, Gen 14:14–15; 1 Sam 30:8, 10). Though David set out in pursuit with a force of six hundred, when two hundred are too weary to continue, David's force of four hundred is only slightly larger than Abraham's of 318 (1 Sam 30:9–10; cf. Gen 14:14).

A fugitive had escaped to alert Abraham (Gen 14:13), and David and his men find an Egyptian left for dead, whom they nurse back to health, who takes them down to the Amalekites (1 Sam 30:11–16). Different terms are used to describe the spoil taken by the raiders, "possessions" in Genesis 14 (רְכֻשׁ, Gen 14:11, 12, 16, 21) and "spoil" in 1 Samuel 30:16 (שָׁלָל), but these are clearly synonymous ways to describe plunder taken by force.

In both cases, once Abraham and David have pursued the enemy, they strike the enemy, and the two narratives employ the same form meaning "and he struck them" (וַיַּכֵּם, Gen 14:15; 1 Sam 30:17). The two narratives also employ the same verb (שׁוּב) to describe the hero, Abraham and David, respectively, "bringing back" what had been taken (Gen 14:16; 1 Sam 30:19).

Having taken captivity captive, both Abraham and David interact with the righteous and the wicked and provide for their allies. Abraham interacts with the kings of Sodom and Salem and gives food to his men and a share of the spoil to his allies Mamre, Aner, and Eshcol (Gen 14:17–24). David rejects the objections of the "wicked and worthless" against those who had stayed with the baggage (1 Sam 30:22), ensures that all his men get their share of the recovered spoil (30:23–25), and sends gifts to the elders of Judah (30:26–31).

Unlike Gideon, who misused the spoil of his plundered enemies to make a priestly ephod, David stores up the plunder of his enemies for his son to build the temple (1 Chr 29:2–5), receiving freewill offerings for the same (29:6–9), donning a priestly linen ephod for the bringing of the ark of the covenant into Jerusalem (2 Sam 6:14).

The linguistic points of contact between Genesis 14 and 1 Samuel 30, the similarities in sequences of events, and the similar roles Abraham and David play in covenantal and salvation historical terms join together to establish the relationship between these texts. The repetitions cause a gathering and growing sense of the significance of the pattern, building toward Psalm 110 and beyond to the New Testament.

§4.4 Genesis 14 and Psalm 110

In Psalm 110, I would suggest that David, under the inspiration of the Holy Spirit, brings together the two prominent features of Genesis 14: the kingly conquest of Abraham and the priesthood of Melchizedek. Having realized the significance of his descent from Abraham and noted the parallels between Genesis 14, Judges 6–8, and the events of his own life in 1 Samuel 30, David understands that he himself typifies the future king from his line.

The defeat of the kings, as typified by Abraham in Genesis 14, Gideon in Judges 6–8, and David himself in 1 Samuel 30 and elsewhere, is promised in Psalm 110:1's reference to Yahweh making the enemies of David's Lord his footstool. He will rule in the midst of those enemies when Yahweh sends forth his mighty scepter from Zion in verse 2, when his people make freewill offerings of themselves (they themselves are the freewill offerings) in verse 3, as he shatters kings with Yahweh at his right hand in verse 5, judging the nations in verse 6.

Psalm 110:7 has puzzled interpreters: "He will drink from the brook by the way; therefore he will lift up his head" (ESV). Whereas in verse 6, Yahweh's king shatters the head (the Hebrew for "head," רֹאשׁ, being rendered "chiefs" by the ESV), in verse 7 he has his own head lifted up. More could obviously be said,[23] but here I want to highlight the fact that Gideon's force is winnowed down to three hundred at the water, and those three hundred were not those who "knelt down to drink" (Judg 7:4–8, ESV, esp. 7:5–6). The men who went with Gideon seem to be those who kept their heads up at the water. The "brook Besor" features prominently in 1 Samuel 30, as it was there that "those who were left behind stayed" (1 Sam 30:9–10, ESV, cf. 30:21). The reference in Psalm 110:7 to the conquering Melchizedekian king drinking from the brook by the way and therefore lifting up his head adds a subtle connection point to those earlier episodes.

It is not surprising that similarities between conquering warriors like Abraham and Gideon and David would be noticed, nor that these similarities would be understood by a biblical author to have been orchestrated by the sovereign God as types that point forward to the promised king from David's line. What is surprising is the way that the expectation of a future king is woven together with the announcement that the king will be a high priest according to the order of Melchizedek.

In Psalm 110, David brings together these two aspects of Genesis 14: Abraham's conquest of foreign kings in the rescue of Lot, and Melchizedek's role as king and priest in Salem, to whom Abraham gives a tithe. The wording of the announcement in Psalm 110:4, "The Lord has sworn and will not change his mind," recalls the way that God made promises to Abraham in Genesis 12:1–3, the way he alone passed through the pieces to make the covenant in Genesis 15, and the way that he swore by himself in Genesis 22:16, an oath on which he would not change his mind (Num 23:19; cf. Heb 6:13–18). The Psalm 110:4 oath is presented in a way that recalls the covenantal oaths to Abraham, reflecting the import of the link between Abraham and Melchizedek.

§4.5 Summary

To this point in this discussion of kingship we have considered Adamic dominion (Gen 1:28), Adam's role as son of God, Adam as the archetypal gardener-shepherd, and Adam's exercise of God's authority in naming God's creation. We considered how different aspects of these royal patterns were repeated in figures such as Joseph, the future king from Judah, Moses, David, and Solomon, to find

---

23. Elsewhere I have suggested that the water and "way" evoke Psalms 1 and 2, while the lifting up of the head recalls Psalm 3:3 (MT 3:4). For further discussion, see Hamilton, *Psalms*; and Matthew Habib Emadi, "The Royal Priest: Psalm 110 in Biblical-Theological Perspective" (PhD diss., Louisville, KY, The Southern Baptist Theological Seminary, 2015).

fulfillment in Christ. We then considered the way that Abraham's conquest of kings and rescue of Lot, followed by his interaction with Melchizedek, constitute a pattern repeated in the experiences of Gideon and David. Paul's presentation of Jesus in Ephesians brings all this together in eye-opening ways.

§5 CHRIST, FULFILLMENT KING, IN EPHESIANS

Having celebrated the ways that the church experiences the typological fulfillment of the promises God made to Israel in Ephesians 1:3–14 and prayed for the church in Ephesus in 1:15–20a, Paul describes the way Christ has been enthroned as king in 1:20b–23. Paul presents Jesus as the new-Adam Melchizedekian priest-king from the line of David who will accomplish what God set out to achieve at creation.

Asserting that God's power at work in believers is the same that raised Christ from the dead in Ephesians 1:19–20a, Paul alludes to Psalm 110:1 in Ephesians 1:20b (ESV in chart below).

Psalm 110:1	Ephesians 1:20b
"The LORD says to my Lord: 'Sit at my right hand, until I make your enemies your footstool."	"and seated him at his right hand in the heavenly places"

Paul elaborates on the exaltation of Christ over all in 1:21, before returning to the "footstool" idea from Psalm 110:1 in Ephesians 1:22a by means of a quotation of Psalm 8:6 (MT 8:7), "And he put all things under his feet."

Ps 8:7, כֹּל שַׁתָּה תַחַת־רַגְלָיו

LXX Ps 8:7 πάντα ὑπέταξας ὑποκάτω τῶν ποδῶν αὐτοῦ

Eph 1:22a, καὶ πάντα ὑπέταξεν ὑπὸ τοὺς πόδας αὐτοῦ

This citation of Psalm 8:6 (MT 8:7) in Ephesians 1:22 confirms the reading of Psalm 8 as a Davidic celebration of God's glory pursued by the new-Adam king of Israel (as discussed in §4 of Chapter 2 above).

The rest of Ephesians 1:22 and the first part of 1:23 present Christ as the head and the church as the body, before Paul speaks of how Christ has accomplished the Genesis 1:28 task of "filling" the earth in 1:23b, "the fullness of him who fills all in all."

The Old Testament texts we have examined in this chapter receive further development in Ephesians 4. We will return to Paul's use of Psalm 68:18 (MT 68:19) in Ephesians 4:8 when we consider the creation as a cosmic temple in Chapter 7 below (see Chapter 7 §2.3). In the context of Psalm 68 the statement, "You ascended on high, leading a host of captives in your train and receiving gifts among men, even among the rebellious, that the LORD God may dwell there" (Ps 68:18 ESV [MT 68:19]), celebrates the way that Yahweh led the captives, Israel, out of Egypt by the hand of Moses. At Sinai, Moses ascended the mount, received instructions for the tabernacle, took up freewill offerings of the plunder of Egypt for its construction, and then gave it to Israel as the place of Yahweh's dwelling. There Israel in turn gave Yahweh their sacrifices and offerings.

We have seen how Abraham, Gideon, and David overcame enemies, took captivity captive, and used the plunder for worship. Psalm 68 speaks of Moses bringing Israel out of Egypt in these terms, thus making Moses like Abraham, Gideon and David like Moses, and what Jesus fulfilled they all typified. Abram tithed enemy plunder to Melchizedek (Gen 14:20). Moses used enemy plunder to build the tabernacle. (Gideon used enemy plunder to make an idolatrous ephod). David stored up enemy plunder for Solomon to build the temple. And Jesus uses enemy plunder to build the church.

Whereas Moses ascended Mount Sinai (cf. Deut 30:12; Ps 24:3) and David ascended Mount Zion, the typological fulfillment Paul claims for Christ entails him having descended from the true place of ascent to which the Old Testament's holy mountains pointed: "(In saying, 'He ascended,' what does it mean but that he had also descended into the lower regions, the earth? He who descended is the one who ascended far above all the heavens . . .)" (Eph 4:9–10a). By emphasizing the descent and ascent of Christ, Paul calls to mind the riddle in Proverbs 30:4, "Who has ascended to heaven and come down? . . . What is his name, and what is his son's name?" (cf. Rom 10:6–8).

Like John, Paul presents Jesus as the new-Adam "son of man" (cf. Dan 7:13–14) who descended from heaven. The next words of Ephesians 4:10 confirm the connection with Adam as they return to the Genesis 1:28 commission to "fill the earth" with the words "that he might fill all things" (Eph 4:10b; cf. 1:23).

Above I suggested that Adam's role as gardener-shepherd was reprised in Israel's shepherd-kings, and in Ephesians 4:11 Paul details how Christ the King shepherds his church by giving them pastors, "shepherds." Paul mixes the "shepherding" metaphor with "temple-building" connotations as he speaks of the "building up" of the body (Eph 4:12, 16).

When Christ has completed his work in the church, he will have accomplished his Adamic task (Gen 1:28) of filling the earth, bringing about Christlikeness and causing the character of God to be known everywhere: "until we all attain to the unity of the faith and of the knowledge of the Son of God, to mature manhood, to the measure of the stature of the fullness of Christ" (Eph 4:13).

Jesus, the new-Adam Son of God, has been seated at God's right hand as the Melchizedekian high priest and king. Having descended from heaven to achieve redemption, he ascended to give gifts to his people as he builds them into the temple of the Holy Spirit, anticipating the day when all things will be under his feet. Paul interprets several Old Testament passages as he celebrates what God has done in Christ, and not all of these are directly promissory. Some are descriptive historical narratives, while others from the Psalms seem to commemorate what God did in the past. How does Paul understand these to find fulfillment in Christ? Are his interpretive conclusions valid and normative? When we understand the dynamic between the promises and the patterns, indeed, the way the promises shaped the patterns, we see that the patterns are understood to typify future fulfillment because they have been shaped by the promises. The Old Testament authors intended to communicate the very dynamic Paul claims has been fulfilled in Christ.

Though this chapter has focused on Adam and Abraham, with not so much of David, the one that follows pursues the way that David typifies and foreshadows, portends and patterns the king who is to come.

THE RIGHTEOUS SUFFERER

> For it was fitting that he, for whom and by whom all things exist,
> in bringing many sons to glory, should make the founder of their
> salvation perfect through suffering.
>
> —HEBREWS 2:10-11 ESV

§1 THE PATTERN: REJECTION THEN EXALTATION

How is it that a text like Psalm 41 can be cited as having been fulfilled when
Judas betrays Jesus in John 13:18? Psalm 41 is a "Psalm of David" (Ps 41:ss [MT
41:1]), and in it David speaks in the first-person singular about his own troubles
(41:4–12 [MT 41:5–13]). David prays in verse 9 (ESV; MT 10), "Even my close
friend in whom I trusted, who ate my bread, has lifted his heel against me."
The words of the psalm do not articulate the idea that the distant future is
being predicted. That is to say, Psalm 41 lacks the kinds of indicators we find
in the prophets when they predict the future, such as, "It shall come to pass in
the latter days" (Isa 2:2, ESV), or "the days are coming, declares the LORD" (Jer
31:31, ESV). How, then, can John present Jesus claiming that a statement in
Psalm 41 will be fulfilled when Judas betrays him (John 13:18)? To answer in
brief: a broader eschatological program at work in the canonical Psalter read
as a book joins with the typological pattern of the righteous sufferer seen in
David's experience, and for the program and the pattern John presents Jesus
claiming fulfillment when Judas betrays him.[1]

---

1. See esp. David C. Mitchell, *The Message of the Psalter: An Eschatological Programme in the Book of
Psalms*, Journal for the Study of the Old Testament Supplement Series 252 (Sheffield: Sheffield Academic
Press, 1997); Emadi, "The Royal Priest"; and Hamilton, *Psalms*.

The example of Psalm 41:9 in John 13:18 takes us right to the heart of the Old Testament theme of the righteous sufferer, a theme that begins with the death of Abel in Genesis 4 and continues to the murder of Zechariah in 2 Chronicles 24 (cf. Matt 23:34–36; Luke 11:49–51). This promise-shaped theme stems from the enmity between the seed of the serpent and the seed of the woman (Gen 3:15), and it can be stated plainly: those through whom God means to establish salvation first suffer rejection and persecution before being unexpectedly exalted to reign. In this chapter we will see this pattern of rejection then exaltation in the lives of Joseph, Moses, and David, and then their historical experience joins the prophecies of the future king from David's line in Isaiah as he projects the patterns into the future to make the promise-shaped pattern of the suffering servant, all this finding fulfillment in Christ, who was first rejected then exalted.

The words of judgment and promise in Genesis 3:15 shaped the perceptions of Moses and others, prompting the biblical authors to notice that the seed of the woman are consistently persecuted, opposed, even killed, by the seed of the serpent. As a result of the way the promise shaped their perception, the promise also shaped the patterns the biblical authors built into their presentations, so that across the Old Testament we find this theme building toward fulfilment in the death of Jesus, only to be continued (as Jesus said it would) in the persecution and not infrequent martyrdom of his people (e.g., Matt 5:11; 10:25; 23:34; 24:9; John 15:20; cf. Rev 6:11).

One aspect of the argument that Matthew Bates makes for prosopological exegesis is his rejection of typology because, as he puts it,

> the typological model as applied to the special case of Christ as one who speaks in the Old Testament, in my judgment, has decisive weaknesses— especially the lack of evidence that the earliest Christians had sufficient interest in the suffering of David so as to provide an imitative link.[2]

Though Bates speaks of "weaknesses" in the plural, he names only this alleged lack of interest in the suffering of David. Bates's argument is circular: he asserts that the New Testament quotations of David's suffering in the Psalms are examples of prosopological rather than typological interpretation, therefore these quotations do not evidence interest in David's suffering. He then argues

2. Bates, *The Birth of the Trinity*, 9.

that a typological understanding is weak because of "the lack of evidence that
the earliest Christians had sufficient interest in the suffering of David so as to
provide an imitative link."[3] I contend that evidence for the New Testament's
interest in the suffering of the Old Testament seed of the woman comes so
thick and fast in its pages as to be pervasive, and that the interest in David's
suffering is one aspect of that broader interest in the blood of all the martyrs
from Abel to Zechariah.

The New Testament presents the Old Testament faithful as those who
were rejected by the world (e.g., Heb 11:32–38)—precursors of the way the
world would reject the Christ and his followers (cf., e.g., Acts 7)—and it understands David this way too. When the New Testament claims that David's
suffering in the Psalms finds fulfillment in Christ, as John 13 does with Psalm
41 (and in other examples that will be discussed below), it does not disregard
the suffering of the historical David. The many texts considered here will
provide abundant evidence of significant interest not only in David's woes but
in those of all the Old Testament seed of the woman.

This chapter seeks to show that the theme of the righteous sufferer pervades the Old Testament. David's suffering makes a prominent installment in
the pattern, to be fulfilled in *the* righteous sufferer, Jesus the Messiah. In his
teaching, moreover, Jesus indicated that righteous suffering would be continued in the experience of those who follow him: "They will put you out of the
synagogues. Indeed, the hour is coming when whoever kills you will think he
is offering service to God" (John 16:2).

This chapter has a chiastic structure:

§1. The Pattern: Rejection Then Exaltation
    §2. Joseph Rejected Then Exalted
        §3. Moses Rejected Then Exalted
        §4. David Rejected Then Exalted
    §5. The Suffering Servant Rejected Then Exalted
§6. Jesus Rejected Then Exalted

Many chiasms place the most important unit in the center, but in this one
fulfillment stands at the end.

---

3. Ibid.

§2 JOSEPH REJECTED THEN EXALTED

Joseph received dreams in which his brothers and parents bowed down to him, then his brothers sold him into slavery. In Egypt as a slave, Joseph was falsely accused, thrown into prison, then unexpectedly exalted to the right hand of Pharaoh. And Joseph's experience matches the texture of earlier narratives in Genesis. In fact, all the major plotlines of Genesis come together in the Joseph narrative.[4]

We discussed the interconnectedness of Genesis 3–4 in Chapter 1 above with specific reference to the way that, after his murder of Abel, Cain is linked to the serpent by means of the phrase "cursed are you" (אָרוּר אַתָּה), which the Lord says to the serpent in Genesis 3:14 and to Cain in 4:11. This indicates that Moses intends his audience to understand the conflict between Cain and Abel as an outworking of the enmity between the seed of the woman and the seed of the serpent introduced in Genesis 3:15. The same link is established by Noah's cursing of Canaan in Genesis 9:25, and then when the Lord says to Abraham in 12:3 (ESV), "him who dishonors you I will curse," the audience of Genesis learns to associate anyone who opposes Abraham with the serpent: the seed of the serpent are at enmity with the seed of the woman.

The fact that Hagar "dishonors" Sarai, wife of Abraham, the same Hebrew verb (קלל) appearing in Genesis 12:3 and 16:4–5, indicates that Hagar and Ishmael will come under Yahweh's curse. Yahweh blesses Ishmael in 17:20 but not in a covenantal way (Gen 17:21). Later Ishmael dishonors Isaac by his laughter (21:9).

Rebekah inquires of the Lord regarding the children struggling in her womb and learns that "the older shall serve the younger" (Gen 25:23, cf. 21–26). This marks the younger son, Jacob, off as the one who will receive the blessing, through whom the line of descent will continue. Because of the way events play out, Esau wants to kill Jacob (27:41). Jacob has stolen Esau's birthright and blessing, making Esau's wrath understandable. Still, as God's mercy envelops Jacob, the repetitions of the choice of the younger son and the fraternal conflict

---

4. See Samuel Cyrus Emadi, "Covenant, Typology, and the Story of Joseph: A Literary-Canonical Examination of Genesis 37–50" (PhD diss., Louisville, The Southern Baptist Theological Seminary, 2016). A revised version of Emadi's dissertation is to be published in New Studies in Biblical Theology, and see now also Jeffrey Pulse, *Figuring Resurrection: Joseph as a Death and Resurrection Figure in the Old Testament and Second Temple Judaism*, Studies in Scripture and Biblical Theology (Bellingham, WA: Lexham, 2021).

provide another installment in the enmity between the seed of the woman and the seed of the serpent.

In addition to the manifestations of enmity between brothers, Abraham and Isaac suffer at the hands of the Egyptians (Gen 12:10–20) and the Philistines (20:1–18; 26:1–22). These patterns come together in the suffering of Joseph at the hands of his brothers, and once they sold him into slavery, the Egyptians (Gen 37, 39; Acts 7:9–16).

§3 MOSES REJECTED THEN EXALTED

The family of Moses resisted the Egyptian attempt to exterminate all the male children of Israel, Egypt playing the role of the seed of the serpent (Exod 1). As God providentially worked this together for good for his people, Moses was raised in Pharaoh's household and trained in all the wisdom of the Egyptians (Exod 2:1–10; Acts 7:17–22). Later Moses was rejected by his Hebrew kinsmen (Exod 2:11–14; Acts 7:23–29), and Pharaoh sought to kill him (2:15). Once Moses led Israel out of Egypt, they often grumbled against him, resisted his leadership, and even sought to put him to death. Even Aaron and Miriam opposed Moses in Numbers 12.

By means of the repeated installments in the pattern of fraternal conflict in the Pentateuch (Cain-Abel, Ishmael-Isaac, Esau-Jacob, brothers-Joseph, Aaron-Moses), Moses creates a context in which those who know the Scriptures will be familiar with the way that older brothers have brought suffering and difficulty into the lives of the younger brother who has been accepted by God (Abel), designated as the covenant child (Isaac), as the chosen one (Jacob), who will reign (Joseph) or deliver and lead (Moses). When David's brothers have gone off to war with Saul and Jesse sends David to see about them (1 Sam 17:12–18), we naturally think of the way Jacob sent Joseph to check on his brothers (Gen 37:12–17). When David's brother answers him harshly (1 Sam 17:28), we see David as a new Joseph,[5] a new installment in a pattern that will find fulfillment in future fraternal conflict (see John 7:1–9). Jesus is

---

5. For discussion of linguistic points of contact, event sequences, and similarity in covenantal and salvation historical significance between Joseph and David, see James M. Hamilton Jr., "Was Joseph a Type of the Messiah? Tracing the Typological Identification between Joseph, David, and Jesus," *The Southern Baptist Journal of Theology* 12 (2008): 52–77.

not the younger son, but he is both unexpected and, at least initially, rejected by his brothers (Mark 3:21, 31–35).

Promises such as Genesis 3:15, 12:1–3, 49:8–12, and Numbers 24:17 generate expectations about the line of descent being traced from the seed of the woman, and the promises cause the enmity between the seed of the woman and the seed of the serpent (Gen 3:15) to be recognized and noted, with the hope that the seed of the woman will crush the head of the serpent (Num 24:17). The pattern of fraternal conflict interweaves with the building promises and creates the interpretive matrix within which God's people understand themselves.

§4 DAVID REJECTED THEN EXALTED

Those who operate within this interpretive matrix, informed by the promises and the patterns, interpret subsequent events from this perspective. This does not result, however, in an uninteresting, predictable course of events. Though it has happened repeatedly before, because it goes against expectation, everyone is surprised by what happens when Samuel goes to anoint one of the sons of Jesse as king. The father, Jesse, was evidently so confident that David would not be God's choice that he didn't bother summoning him in from the flock (1 Sam 16:6–11). And then no sooner has another younger son been marked out as the one whom God accepts (like Abel), the one with whom God will enter into covenant (like Isaac), God's chosen (like Jacob) to reign (like Joseph) and deliver and lead (like Moses), but—as noted just above—his older brother answers him harshly in a scene starkly reminiscent of Joseph's father sending him to check on his older brothers (1 Sam 17:12–30; cf. Gen 37:2, 12–28).

Once the newly anointed David (1 Sam 16) has slain Goliath (1 Sam 17), his kinsman Saul begins to persecute him, initiating the period of suffering and difficulty in David's life narrated through the rest of 1 Samuel. Established as king over Israel and Judah (2 Sam 5), David receives God's covenant promises (2 Sam 7). He then begins to expand the borders of the kingdom in every direction (2 Sam 8–10) before his devastating sin with Bathsheba (2 Sam 11–12). Yahweh's judgment for this included his declaration that he would raise up evil against David out of his own house (2 Sam 12:11), portending Absalom's revolt (2 Sam 15), which causes a second period of massive suffering and difficulty in David's life.

The suffering of the key figures who preceded David created the context in which he could have interpreted his own suffering as an installment in the same pattern. The narratives of David's suffering in Samuel then provide the historical backdrop for interpreting David's own descriptions of his suffering in the Psalms. I would suggest that David understood his own suffering as an installation in the pattern of those who had preceded him, chiefly Joseph and Moses,[6] and that in the Psalms he presents himself as another installment in that same pattern. David does this because he expects the pattern to be fulfilled in the life of his descendent, his seed, whom God promised to raise up from his line, whose throne God promised to establish forever (2 Sam 7:13–14).[7]

Against the claim that Bates makes about "the lack of evidence that the earliest Christians had sufficient interest in the suffering of David so as to provide an imitative link,"[8] the authors of the New Testament quote the Psalms consistently and prominently. Bates claims that these quotations are not to be understood typologically, and argues that in cases such as Psalm 22,

> the earliest church did not read this psalm as if it was really about David at the first level, but secondarily about Jesus at a second deeper level as he fulfilled the Davidic pattern of suffering while serving as a symbol of corporate Israel. There is little evidence that the earliest Christians had much (if any) interest in this first level, and that is the principle mistake in how the significance of Psalm 21 LXX and other psalms featuring a righteous sufferer has been assessed for the earliest Christians by scholarship. On the contrary, the earliest church did not believe that this psalm was really about David's (or corporate Israel's) suffering because they believed that David's significance here was his prophetic capacity—that he was a willing and able prophet who had taken on a character, and thus he had spoken in the prosopon of the future Christ . . ."[9]

---

6. Cf. Psalm 40:2 (MT 40:3) with Gen 37:24, 28—in the narratives about David's life, we never read of him being in a "pit." Joseph, however, was put in a pit (Gen 37:24, 28), and it seems that when David speaks of the Lord drawing him up from the pit in Psalm 40:2, he presents himself in a way that reminds his audience of Joseph being drawn out of the pit. Similarly, while Moses was drawn out of the waters and named by the experience in Exodus 2:10, we never read of David having such an experience. In Psalm 18:16 (MT 18:17), however, David speaks of the Lord drawing him up from the waters in a way that reminds his audience of Moses.

7. See Hamilton, "Typology in the Psalms," and Hamilton, *Psalms*.

8. Bates, *The Birth of the Trinity*, 9.

9. Ibid., 127.

For Bates, the key question seems to be how the earliest church understood the psalm. I contend that the key question, rather, is how the author of the psalm intended it to be understood, and in addition how the final editor(s) of the canonical form of the Psalter intended it to function.[10] Bates may be correct that some individuals in the earliest church—not New Testament authors—understood Psalm 22 in the way he describes. When we consider the New Testament authors, however, again I contend that they have not disregarded what the Old Testament author intended to communicate. The New Testament authors do not claim to present *different* interpretations of these Old Testament texts but *fulfillments* of what their authors communicated. To claim that David was not speaking of his own experience but rather in the prosopon of Christ is to offer an *alternative interpretation*.[11] To claim that David spoke of himself and expected that the pattern of his experience would be repeated in and climactically re-lived in the seed of promise is to offer *fulfillment*.

Bates asserts that the earliest church was not interested in David's historical suffering, and then he explains that the quotations that reference that historical suffering present David speaking "in the prosopon of the future Christ."[12] If, however, those quotations are interpreted in a *typological* rather than a *prosopological* framework, then David's historical suffering, and the meaning of the statements of the Psalms in context, is affirmed, and the early church does in fact show quite a lot of interest in David's own suffering.

Bates's prosopological proposal *disregards* the Old Testament context and meaning of these statements. A typological understanding of the quotation of the Psalms in the New Testament, by contrast, would *depend upon* the meaning of the Old Testament text in context, respecting that meaning and seeing it fulfilled in accordance with what its Old Testament author intended to communicate.[13]

---

10. See the Introduction to my commentary, *Psalms*, along with the discussion of Psalm 22.

11. Gentry argues that the NT authors followed the interpretive methods modeled by the Old Testament authors (when later OT authors interpret earlier OT texts), that the OT authors do not model prosopological exegesis, and that—since the handbooks discussing prosopological exegesis come after the NT documents were written—claiming that the NT authors practiced prosopological exegesis is anachronistic. Gentry, "Prosopological Exegesis," 105–22, esp. 119–20.

12. Bates, *The Birth of the Trinity*, 127.

13. Moo writes, "It is the underlying typological identification of Jesus with David that legitimizes the transfer of language from the record of the Israelite King's experiences to the narratives of the sufferings of the 'greater Son of David.'" Douglas J. Moo, *The Old Testament in the Gospel Passion Narratives* (Sheffield: Almond Press, 1983), 300. Ahearne-Kroll's objections to the "characterization of the literary relationship between the two as typological" are unpersuasive. Ahearne-Kroll, *The Psalms of Lament in Mark's Passion*, 172–73.

The question is which interpretive proposal seems more preferable: one that allows the meaning of the Old Testament text in context to be preserved and fulfilled, or one that disregards the Old Testament context and asserts an alternative interpretation with no basis in that context? My conclusion on this matter will be obvious to anyone reading this book.

As I review some of the evidence regarding the righteous sufferer in the Psalms, and the quotation of these passages in the New Testament, I will seek to say enough about the quoted statements in their Old Testament context to show how a typological understanding of their fulfillment allows the original meaning to stand *and* be fulfilled in Christ.

Because I am interested in the meaning of the quoted statements from the Psalms in their context in the Psalter, I will proceed in canonical order.

§4.1 Psalm 2 in Acts 4

Though there is no superscription on Psalm 2, when Luke presents the early church praying its words in Acts 4:24–30, the quotation is introduced with the words, "Sovereign Lord . . . , who through the mouth of our father David, your servant, said by the Holy Spirit" (Acts 4:25, ESV). The prayer then quotes Psalm 2:1, points to its fulfillment when the gentiles raged, the peoples plotted, and the kings set themselves against Jesus (4:27); and the fact that the prayer responds to the persecution of Peter and John (4:13–24) and anticipates more of the same (4:29) indicates that the early church expects the enmity between the seed of the woman and the seed of the serpent to continue to be their experience. In the flow of thought in the Psalter, the interconnectedness of Psalms 2–3,[14] and really of the whole book, indicates that information gaps from Psalm 2 are intended to be filled from further information in Psalms 3 and following. This would suggest that the persecution initiated by Absalom in Psalm 3 illustrates the raging of the nations spoken of in Psalm 2. David's own historical suffering at the hands of Absalom, then, follows the pattern of those who have gone before and anticipates that of the seed God promised to raise up from his line. The suffering of Jesus fulfills the pattern, and in calling his disciples to take up the cross and follow him (Matt 16:24), Jesus indicated that his followers would suffer as he did. This way of looking at things seems to be reflected in the Acts 4:24–30 prayer that quotes Psalm 2:1 in Acts 4:25–26.

---

14. On which, see esp. Robert L. Cole, *Psalms 1–2: Gateway to the Psalter* (Sheffield: Sheffield Phoenix, 2013), who includes Psalm 3 in his discussion.

§4.2 Psalm 6 in John 12

The interconnectedness of Psalms 2–6 leads me to suspect that the same difficulty David faced in Psalm 3 (cf. the superscription, "when he fled from Absalom his son") prompts his prayer in Psalm 6.[15] David says in this context, "My soul also is greatly troubled" (Ps 6:3, ESV), and the phrasing used when this was rendered into Greek supplies the vocabulary for the statement that John presents Jesus making in John 12:27 (ESV), "Now is my soul troubled . . ."

LXX Ps 6:3 [MT 6:4], ἡ ψυχή μου ἐταράχθη σφόδρα

John 12:27, ἡ ψυχή μου τετάρακται

This passage in the context of the Psalter yields a meaning remarkably consistent with what John presents Jesus saying in John 12. When David says, "My soul also is greatly troubled" (Ps 6:3 ESV [MT 6:4]), the term rendered "troubled" is the same term employed in Psalm 2:5 (ESV) in the statement, "and terrify [trouble] them in his fury." In view of the claims I am making about David presenting himself in terms reminiscent of Joseph, note that the same verb is used when Joseph revealed himself to his brothers, and "they were dismayed at his presence" (כִּי נִבְהֲלוּ מִפָּנָיו, Gen 45:3, ESV).

Ps 6:3 [MT 6:4], וְנַפְשִׁי נִבְהֲלָה מְאֹד

Ps 2:5, וּבַחֲרוֹנוֹ יְבַהֲלֵמוֹ

On the basis of this and other connections with Psalm 2 in Psalm 6,[16] not least the confident assertion in 6:10 (MT 6:11) that his enemies will be ashamed

---

15. For the link word connections between Psalms 2–6, see the section entitled "Context: Verbal and Thematic Links with Surrounding Psalms" on each of these Psalms in Hamilton, *Psalms*.

16. Verbal connections between Psalms 2 and 6 include the following:

2:5, "he will speak to them in his wrath" (בְּאַפּוֹ, cf. 2:12).

6:1 (MT 6:2), "rebuke me not in your wrath" (בְּאַפְּךָ).

2:5, "in his fury he will terrify them" (יְבַהֲלֵמוֹ).

6:2 (MT 6:3), "my bones are terrified" (נִבְהֲלוּ).

6:10 (MT 6:11), "They will be . . . terrified" (וְיִבָּהֲלוּ).

2:10, "receive correction, O judges of the earth" (הִוָּסְרוּ).

6:1 (MT 6:2), "nor correct me in your rage" (תְיַסְּרֵנִי).

See further the discussion of Psalm 6 in my commentary.

and "troubled" (בָּהַל again), I would suggest that in Psalm 6:3 (MT 6:4) David feels that what was supposed to happen to his enemies is instead happening to him.

This connection is preserved in the Greek translation of the Psalter, which translates these uses of בָּהַל with ταράσσω:

Ps 2:5, καὶ ἐν τῷ θυμῷ αὐτοῦ ταράξει αὐτούς
"and in his wrath he will trouble them"

Ps 6:3 (LXX 6:4), καὶ ἡ ψυχή μου ἐταράχθη σφόδρα
"and my soul is troubled exceedingly"

Ps 6:10 (LXX 6:11), καὶ ταραχθείησαν σφόδρα
"and may they be troubled exceedingly"

David complains in Psalm 6 that he suffers as God said the enemies would in Psalm 2, but by the end of Psalm 6 David is confident that the Psalm 2:5 terror will indeed fall on those enemies (Ps 6:10 [MT 6:11]). Jesus faces the cross, where he will undergo exactly what his enemies deserve: the wrath of God. How fitting that he should quote Psalm 6, and like David there, he moves from distress to confidence in God's plan. Jesus announced that the hour had come (John 12:23), spoke of the grain of wheat dying to bear much fruit (12:24), and he went on to speak of his death in terms of his being lifted up to draw all men to himself (12:32–33). The use of the Greek phrasing of Psalm 6:3 indicates that in 12:27 John presents Jesus fulfilling the pattern of David's suffering. The meaning of Psalm 6 in the context of the Psalter fits John's presentation of Jesus perfectly.

Richard B. Hays observes another point of correspondence between Psalm 6 and John 12:27, but in my judgment he misinterprets it. Hays notes that in Psalm 6:4 David prays, "save me" (LXX 6:5, σῶσόν με). Having just used the language of Psalm 6:3 to speak of his soul being troubled in John 12:27, Jesus goes on to say, "And what shall I say? 'Father, save me from this hour'? But for this purpose I have come to this hour" (John 12:27 ESV, also σῶσόν με). Hays then writes,

Jesus echoes David in lamenting that his soul is troubled in a time of trial (Ps 6:3 LXX), but then ponders whether to continue to perform the Davidic script by joining in David's prayer for rescue ("Save me" [Ps 6:4 LXX]). In fact, John's Jesus rejects this option; he chooses instead to embrace the vocation of suffering for which he was sent into the world.[17]

For Jesus to do as Hays says would be for him not to pray that God would raise him from the dead. Hays's comment reflects a failure to appreciate the way that David suffers all through Book 1 of the Psalter (Pss 1–41), and then with the Psalms of the sons of Korah at the beginning of Book 2 (Pss 42–72) it seems that David has survived Saul's attempts on his life to be enthroned as king of Israel (see esp. Ps 45). David endures plenty of suffering in 1 Samuel 18–2 Samuel 5, and he famously refuses to lift his hand against the Lord's anointed (1 Sam 24:6, 10, 12; 26:9, 11, 23; 2 Sam 1:14). His prayer for salvation in Psalm 6:4 (MT 6:5) is not a rejection of his own "vocation of suffering" but rather reflects the kind of confidence he articulated when he refused to allow Abishai to strike Saul (1 Sam 26:8–9), saying in 1 Samuel 26:10 (ESV), "As the Lord lives, the Lord will strike him, or his day will come to die, or he will go down into battle and perish." David trusts that God will save him from the hand of Saul (cf. Ps 18:ss [MT 18:1]), and David trusts that God will be with him through the suffering he must endure until Saul's "hour" comes. Similarly, Jesus knows that he must suffer, that his "hour" has come, and he no more rejects David's prayer that God save him than David himself rejected the suffering he had to endure.

§4.3 Psalm 16 in Acts 2

As we consider the inner logic of the Psalter, we can interrogate the basis for David's prayerful confidence: what gives David the confidence from which he prays in a passage like Psalm 16:8–11? The Psalter's own flow of thought answers this question, as it has presented the blessed man who meditates on the Torah in Psalm 1, complemented by Yahweh's decree to the Davidic king in Psalm 2. If we supplement our understanding with the story of David's life as it is related in 1–2 Samuel, we can suggest that once the prophet Samuel anointed David to be king (1 Sam 16:12–13), David believed that God would preserve his life and establish him on the throne (see, e.g., 26:10). Similarly, once the prophet Nathan had delivered the promises recounted in 2 Samuel 7, David believed

---

17. Hays, *Echoes of Scripture in the Gospels*, 326–27.

that God would establish the throne of his seed forever. God's promises, therefore, prompted David's confidence. And for someone like David, whose line of descent could be traced back to Abraham through Judah, God's previous promises and the patterns they created would influence his perceptions. I want to set out two premises from which I will then draw a conclusion:

First, throughout the Psalter, as David speaks of his own experience, he does so believing that God will preserve him to keep the promises he made to him that he would be king, and he also believes that God will keep the promise to establish the throne of his seed.

Second, David understood that his own experience of being designated as God's chosen and attested by God's favor and blessing, only to be opposed and persecuted by the seed of the serpent, was an installment in a pattern of events seen in the lives of Joseph, Moses, and others, and David expected that pattern to be repeated in the life of the seed God promised to raise up from his line.

Therefore, as he wrote of his own experience, David understood himself as a type, an installment in a pattern that would be fulfilled in the future king God promised to raise up from his line, through whom God would accomplish salvation.

These two premises and the conclusion that follows from them put us in position to understand the use of Psalm 16:8–11 in Acts 2:25–33. Psalm 16 reads like a very personal prayer from David. From its opening words, "Preserve me, O God, for in you I take refuge" (16:1, ESV), to its concluding statement, "You make known to me the path of life" (16:11, ESV), David speaks throughout in the first-person singular. Unlike Psalm 110, where David presents what Yahweh said to his (David's) Lord (Ps 110:1), in Psalm 16 David speaks of himself and his own experience. The Old Testament context of David's statements weigh against the idea that David "cannot be the speaker of the psalm, and a different prosopon must sought [sic] out as the speaker."[18] For instance, in 16:4 (ESV), David asserts, "The sorrows of those who run after another god shall multiply; their drink offerings of blood I will not pour out or take their names on my lips." This statement fits perfectly in the Old Testament world, in which context David insists that he will be faithful and make sacrifices and offerings to Yahweh alone in distinction from the compromisers willing to sacrifice to other gods (see, e.g., 1 Kgs 11:6–8). Similarly, all the statements

---

18. Matthew W. Bates, *The Hermeneutics of the Apostolic Proclamation: The Center of Paul's Method of Scriptural Interpretation*, Reprint ed. (Waco: Baylor University Press, 2019), 213–14.

in Psalm 16:5–6 about David's "portion" and "lot" and where "the lines have fallen" for David's "inheritance" are informed by Israel's conquest of Canaan and the apportioning of the land by lot to the tribes as an inheritance. With this backdrop in view, David says that what he values and rejoices in is actually the inheritance that the Levites were given, Yahweh himself, rather than a plot of ground (cf. Num 18:20; Deut 10:8–9). These statements make sense in David's Old Testament context. It is true that Old Testament authors sometimes project old covenant realities into the new covenant future (e.g., Ezek 40–48; Zech 14), but when they do so they explicitly designate that they are speaking of the future with "days are coming" or "in the latter days" indicators.[19] Nothing in the text or context of Psalm 16 would indicate that someone other than David is the speaker in the Psalm.

In fact, when Luke presents Peter quoting Psalm 16 in Acts 2, he presents Peter affirming that David spoke the words of the psalm. Peter does not suggest that "a different prosopon must sought [sic] out as the speaker"[20] but explicitly affirms David as the speaker! In Acts 2:25 Luke presents Peter saying, "For David says concerning him . . ." After such an introductory statement, we might expect Luke to present Peter quoting one of the psalms that speak of the future king in statements about what "he" will do or how God will deliver "him," such as Psalm 21, "O Lord, in your strength the king rejoices, . . . he exults! You have given him his heart's desire . . . He asked life of you; you gave it to him, length of days forever and ever" (Ps 21:1–2, 4, ESV). If not these third-person statements (he, him), Peter could quote second-person (you, your) statements like those in Psalm 91, "For he will command his angels concerning you to guard you in all your ways" (91:11, ESV). Instead, Luke presents Peter quoting Psalm 16, in which David speaks in the first-person singular, "I saw the Lord always before me . . ." (Acts 2:25b, quoting Psalm 16:8).

The juxtaposition of these statements is jarring (following the ESV below):

Acts 2:25a, "For David says concerning him

Acts 2:25b, I saw the Lord always before me, for he is at my right hand that I may not be shaken . . ."

---

19. For example, Ezek 40:2, "In visions of God he brought me to the land of Israel . . ." and Zech 14:1, "Behold, a day is coming . . ." (ESV).

20. Bates, *The Hermeneutics of the Apostolic Proclamation*, 214.

Peter clearly affirms that David is the speaker in 2:25a, but he also affirms that David speaks *concerning* (εἰς) him, that is, Jesus. Peter then presents David speaking *of himself* in the *first-person singular (ESV)*:

Acts 2:25, "I . . . me, . . . my . . . I . . ."

Acts 2:26, ". . . my . . . my . . . my . . ."

Acts 2:27, ". . . my . . ."

Acts 2:28, ". . . me . . . me . . ."

How can Luke present Peter quoting David speaking *of himself* and claim that David speaks *concerning Jesus*? I have suggested above that the answer to this question is provided for us if we grant that *in speaking of himself* David intended to speak *concerning the future king God had promised to raise up from his line.* This suggestion entails embracing the idea that David understood the patterns we have pointed to in the lives of Joseph and Moses, that David saw repetitions of that pattern in his own life, and that thereby David consciously understood himself as a type, a prefiguring, foreshadowing installment in a pattern of experience that would be fulfilled in the seed of promise.

Luke's presentation of Peter's exposition of the quoted words from Psalm 16 in Acts 2:29–33 makes exactly these points. Luke does not present Peter explaining that David spoke in the prosopon of Christ. Rather, he has affirmed that David spoke concerning Christ (Acts 2:25), and he undertakes to prove this by pointing out that, while God kept David alive until he became king and preserved his line of descent down to the coming of Jesus, the words David spoke are fulfilled in Jesus in a way they were not in the life of David: "Brothers, I may say to you with confidence about the patriarch David that he both died and was buried, and his tomb is with us to this day" (Acts 2:29, ESV).

Luke next presents Peter continuing to affirm that David was the speaker (not some other face/prosopon), while explaining how David arrived at his position in Acts 2:30–31. I want to comment on what Luke presents Peter saying phrase by phrase. The first thing Peter says about David's comment is, "Being therefore a prophet" (Acts 2:30a, ESV). Here Luke presents Peter affirming that David spoke Spirit-inspired words from God.[21] This claim means that David's insight is not *merely* based on the information available to David's human intelligence, formidable as that intellect obviously was from the artistry of the Psalms. Rather, by affirming that David was a prophet, Peter asserts that God revealed otherwise inaccessible truth through David's prophetic insight.

Next, in Acts 2:30b (ESV), Luke presents Peter adding to the assertion that David was a prophet: "and knowing that God had sworn with an oath to him that he would set one of his descendants on his throne." Here Peter affirms that David was aware of the promises God delivered to him through the prophet Nathan in 2 Samuel 7. The knowledge of those promises, Peter claims, informs what David meant to communicate in Psalm 16.[22] Peter has affirmed that David was a prophet, that God made promises to him, and that David knew and understood those promises.

Out of the dynamic interaction between the prophet's own understanding and God's ongoing revelation, Peter asserts in Acts 2:31 (ESV) that David "foresaw and spoke about the resurrection of the Christ, that he was not abandoned to Hades, nor did his flesh see corruption." I submit that it was on the basis of (1) his perception of the patterns (which admittedly Peter does not mention) that (2) the *prophet* David (3) understood the relationships between the promises and the pattern, so that (4) he received divine revelation to understand that what he had experienced typified and thereby predicted what would take place in the life of his descendant.[23]

David's many near-death experiences, whether at the hands of Saul or Absalom, often result in him speaking of how the Lord rescued him from

---

21. Cf. Luke's similar presentation regarding David's words in Psalm 2 in Acts 4:24–25 (ESV), "Sovereign Lord . . . who through the mouth of our father David, your servant, said by the Holy Spirit." God spoke by the Spirit through David.

22. This does not necessarily entail that David received the promises *before* he wrote Psalm 16. Among other possibilities could be the following scenario: David receives the prophetic anointing by Samuel and, believing that God will establish him as king, writes Psalm 16 in the midst of Saul's attempts to kill him (cf. the superscription of Psalm 18). Later in his life, once God has established him as king and given him the promises recorded in 2 Samuel 7, David reflects on what he wrote in Psalm 16 and, with the additional promises of God fully in view, incorporates Psalm 16 into his own intentionally arranged collection of psalms, setting in motion the process that will culminate in the completion of the Psalter in its canonical form, as we now have it. I would suggest that the agenda reflected in the Psalter was David's idea, and that those who completed the project understood his intentions and honored them as they brought it to completion.

23. Contra Lindars, who writes, "There was no expectation of a dying and rising Messiah." Barnabas Lindars, *New Testament Apologetic* (Philadelphia: Westminster, 1961), 41. In his treatment of the use of the OT in the New, Lindars regularly fails to appreciate the biblical-theological context of the OT itself, which in turn results in a failure to appreciate the ways the NT authors understand and cite it.

death and Sheol (e.g., Pss 16:10a; 18:4–5). In fact, in Acts 2:31, Peter references the Greek translation of Psalm 16:10, which he had just quoted in Acts 2:27. Consider the ESV of the two verses together:

Psalm 16:10, "For you will not abandon my soul to Sheol, or let your holy one see corruption."

Acts 2:31, "he foresaw and spoke about the resurrection of the Christ, that he was not abandoned to Hades, nor did his flesh see corruption."

In his exposition of the verses quoted from Psalm 16 in Acts 2:29–33, Peter points to the *escalation* in significance of the antitype. That is, Peter assumes the points of historical correspondence between David and Jesus, and he points to the ways that the experience of Jesus *goes beyond* and thereby *fulfills* that of David:

- David enjoyed the Lord's presence *with* him (e.g., 1 Sam 18:12); the Lord protected David (e.g., 23:14); David rejoiced in the Lord (Ps 16:8–9; Acts 2:25–26, and see throughout David's psalms). Jesus too enjoyed God's ongoing presence and protection, rejoicing always in his Father in unbroken fellowship that transcended the experience of all sinners.
- David was kept from death, not abandoned to Sheol/Hades, in the sense that he was preserved alive to be enthroned as king (Ps 16:10; Acts 2:27).[24] Jesus was persecuted like David was, but Jesus was kept from death in the sense that he was resurrected.
- David died and was buried and his tomb remains, but Jesus has been raised (Acts 2:29).[25]

---

24. Cf. Levenson's comment, "When the psalmist says to the LORD, 'You will not abandon me to Sheol,/ or let Your faithful one see the Pit . . .'" (Ps 16:10), he is therefore not asserting the absurd notion that God will forever spare him from death. Rather . . . , he is expressing his faith that, 'You [God] will not let your faithful servant die an untimely, evil death.'" Levenson, *Resurrection and the Restoration of Israel*, 73.

25. Luke presents Paul making the same typological comparison and contrast in Acts 13:35–37, where having quoted Psalm 16:10 in Acts 13:35 (ESV), Paul explains that "David . . . fell asleep . . . and saw corruption, but he whom God raised up did not see corruption." Here Paul plays on the *historical correspondence*—both David and Jesus died (Acts 13:28–29, 36, and cf. 13:29 "laid him [Jesus] in a tomb" with 13:36 "David . . . was laid with his fathers")—and *escalation*—though there is a sense in which David's words are true about his own life (God preserved it for him to serve "the purpose of God in his own generation," 13:36), God brought out the deepest meaning of these words by fulfilling them through the resurrection of Jesus from the dead.

- David had near death experiences, close brushes that *almost* landed him in Sheol, from which God delivered him (2:31), but Jesus *actually* died. God raised Jesus (2:32), and he is not in the tomb but at the right hand of God (2:33).

- In the Psalter, the Psalm 16:8 reference to God being at David's right hand is like the statement in the final verse of Psalm 109, "he stands at the right hand of the needy one . . ." (Ps 109:31), which immediately precedes the Psalm 110:1 invitation from Yahweh for David's Lord to sit at his (Yahweh's) right hand, followed by the 110:5 statement to that future king, "The Lord is at your right hand . . ." All these references to the "right hand" would seem to connect Psalm 16 to Psalm 110, and the statements find fulfillment in the one at whose right hand Yahweh is throughout his life, who is then invited to sit at Yahweh's right hand when he ascends, namely Jesus (Acts 2:33).

§4.4 Psalm 22 in Hebrews and the Gospels

I am moving through the Psalms in canonical order, but here I discuss the use of Psalm 22:22 in Hebrews 2:12 before the use of Psalm 22 in the Gospels. I do this mainly because of the way that the quotation of Isaiah 8:17–18 in Hebrews 2:13 supports what I am arguing here. As discussed in §8.1 of Chapter 4 above, Isaiah actually had literal children, and in the context of Isaiah 7–8 their names signified portentous revelation from God through the prophet, revelation that the king and the establishment did not want to hear. Isaiah set himself at odds with the dominant unbelieving culture by warning that the people had broken covenant with Yahweh and faced exile, naming one son, "they're going to plunder us fast" (Maher-shalal-hash-baz), and another, "a remnant shall return" (Shear-jashub). Both names say: God's judgment will fall because we have broken the covenant, and he is sending us into exile, from which he will bring back a remnant. This message was not received by Ahaz and his court, but Isaiah stood fast with his disciples saying, "Behold, I and the children whom the LORD has given me are signs and portents in Israel . . ." (Isa 8:18, ESV).

Writing to persecuted Christians, urging them to keep the faith, the author of Hebrews puts Jesus in the place of Isaiah and the followers of Jesus in the place of Isaiah's children, quoting Isaiah 8:18 in Hebrews 2:13 to show that Jesus "is not ashamed to call" his followers "brothers" (Heb 2:11b). To show the solidarity between Jesus and his people, the author of Hebrews quotes David speaking of his "brothers" from Psalm 22:22 (Heb 2:12). He then quotes Isaiah speaking of the solidarity between himself and his children in Hebrews 2:13. Isaiah's role as rejected prophet like Moses finds fulfillment in Jesus, *the* rejected prophet like Moses, and the children of Isaiah find fulfillment in the new covenant children of God. The same kind of typological fulfillment at work in the quotation of Isaiah 8:17–18 in Hebrews 2:13 is at work in the quotation of Psalm 22:22 in Hebrews 2:12.

Much could be said about the placement of Psalm 22 in the Psalter and the literary structure of the psalm itself, realities that simultaneously bind Psalm 22 to its meaning as a psalm of David *and* join with statements from surrounding psalms to point beyond David to the seed promised to him (see esp. Ps 18:50 and 24:8–10). Throughout this discussion of the righteous sufferer in the Psalms, my contention is that a reading that maintains the meaning of the psalms in context, seeing that meaning fulfilled in the New Testament, should be preferred to a reading that disregards or nullifies the meaning of the Old Testament text in its Old Testament context.

With Psalm 22, then, I would propose that the psalm moves from David's feeling that God has forsaken him in 22:1 to a near-death experience that made the words of 22:15c a true description of his circumstances, "you lay me in the dust of death" (ESV), even though David was not literally dead (otherwise he could not have written the psalm!). David then celebrates the way that God delivered him from his plight in 22:21b. Having metaphorically depicted his enemies as animals attacking him (bulls, 22:12; a lion, 22:13; dogs, 22:16, 20; a lion, 22:21a), David exclaims in 22:21b, "You have rescued me from the horns of the wild oxen!" (ESV). In response to God's deliverance of him from "the dust of death" (22:15c), David asserts the words quoted in Hebrews 2:12, "I will tell of your name to my brothers; in the midst of the congregation I will praise you" (22:22, ESV), proceeding to call those who fear Yahweh to praise, glorify, and stand in awe of him (22:23), explaining that God did not abandon him in his own affliction (22:24), and continuing in praise through the end of the psalm (22:25–31). The "brothers" and "congregation" in which David praises the Lord for deliverance can easily be explained as those relatives and allies who remained loyal to him in most trying times (e.g., 1 Sam 22:1–2; cf. 2 Sam 15:13–37).

Does the author of Hebrews respect the context of Psalm 22? It seems that he means to match the suffering of David (and Isaiah) to the suffering of Jesus. The author of Hebrews presents Jesus first suffering and then receiving glory, the same pattern seen in David's life as he endured persecution at the hands of Saul on the way to being enthroned. In Hebrews 2:9 (ESV) we read of how Jesus is now "crowned with glory and honor because of the suffering of death," and then in 2:10 of how God made Jesus "perfect through suffering." He then points to the solidarity between the only-begotten of the Father, Jesus, and those born of God, believers (cf. 1 John 5:18), saying in Hebrews 2:11, "For he who sanctifies and those who are sanctified all have one source. That is why he is not ashamed to call them brothers" (ESV), before presenting Jesus saying the words of Psalm 22:22 in Hebrews 2:12, followed by the words of Isaiah 8:17–18 in Hebrews 2:13.

The typological logic at work in the quotation of Psalm 22:22 in Hebrews 2:12 entails historical correspondence and escalation as follows:

- Both David and Jesus suffered (Ps 22:15; Heb 2:9, 10).
- Both David and Jesus were surrounded by brothers and other followers (Ps 22:22; Heb 2:10, 11, 12).
- The near-death experience of David (Ps 22:15) escalates into the death of Jesus (Heb 2:9).
- The deliverance from near-death difficulty of David (Ps 22:21) escalates into the resurrection of Jesus from the dead (Heb 2:14).
- Just as the deliverance of David means victory for those allied with him (Ps 22:22), so the resurrection of Jesus brings salvation to the people of God (Heb 2:10, 12, 14–15).
- Just as David's experience is an outworking of the blessing of Abraham (cf. Ps 22:27; Gen 12:3), so also, and in fulfillment of the blessing of Abraham, Jesus "helps the offspring of Abraham" (Heb 2:16, ESV).

The historical context of David's Psalm 22 also finds typological fulfillment in the death of Christ on the cross.

Consider the words from Psalm 22 side by side with quotations or allusions to it in Matthew 27:35–46.

TABLE 6.1: Psalm 22 in Matthew 27 (ESV)

Psalm 22	Gospels
22:1, "My God, my God, why have you forsaken me?"	Matt 27:46, "'Eli, Eli, lema sabachthani?' that is, 'My God, my God, why have you forsaken me?'" (//Mark 15:34)
22:7, "All who see me mock me; they make mouths at me; they wag their heads;"	Matt 27:39, "And those who passed by derided him, wagging their heads"
22:8, "'He trusts in the Lᴏʀᴅ; let him deliver him; let him rescue him, for he delights in him!'"	Matt 27:43, "He trusts in God; let God deliver him now, if he desires him."
22:18, "they divide my garments among them, and for my clothing they cast lots."	Matt 27:35, "And when they had crucified him, they divided his garments by casting lots." (//Mark 15:24; Luke 23:34; John 19:24).

Whereas prosopological exegesis could only account for the quotation of Psalm 22:1 when Christ spoke those words from the cross, typological exegesis can account for all the references to Psalm 22 in the Gospels. Matthew, in particular, seems to want to remind his audience of David's suffering as he recounts the experience of Jesus being crucified.[26] Matthew does not simply lift words from Psalm 22 out of their context and claim that David did not speak them, rather Jesus did. No, Matthew presents Jesus suffering in accordance with the pattern of David's suffering. And by quoting Jesus himself saying the words of Psalm 22:1 on the cross, Matthew indicates that he himself, with the other followers of Jesus, learned to view the suffering of Jesus as a fulfillment of the pattern of David's suffering *from Jesus himself, because he viewed his suffering that way.*[27]

§4.5 Psalms 31:5 and 35:19

The words of Psalm 31:5, "Into your hand I commit my spirit . . . ," sit firmly in the context of the first five verses of Psalm 31. David has asserted in

---

26. Against the claim that "There is little evidence that the earliest Christians had much (if any) interest in" the psalm being "really about David." Bates, *The Birth of the Trinity*, 127.

27. For the argument that the NT authors learned their interpretive method from Jesus, see E. Earle Ellis, "Jesus' Use of the Old Testament and the Genesis of New Testament Theology," *Bulletin for Biblical Research* 3 (1993): 59–75.

verse 1 that he takes refuge in Yahweh, and in verse 2 he beseeches the Lord to be for him a rock of refuge, a stronghold, explaining that Yahweh is his rock and fortress in verse 3. In verse 4 he says that Yahweh is his place of strength, and in response to all these affirmations, he commits his spirit into Yahweh's hand in verse 5. Luke presents Jesus quoting these words from the cross (Luke 23:46), not because Jesus is to be understood as the real speaker in Psalm 31 but because the pattern of David's suffering is fulfilled in the suffering of the Christ.[28]

In Psalm 35:19 (ESV) David prays, "Let not those rejoice over me who are wrongfully my foes, and let not those wink the eye who hate me without cause." Once again these words fit naturally in the context of Psalm 35, and I have argued that the similarities—at the level of repeated words and phrases—between Psalms 35 and 40 relate to the intentional structuring of Psalms 34–41.[29] In my view, this makes it unlikely that any of these statements should be viewed as the kind of departures from context required by prosopological exegesis. David describes his own difficulties in Psalm 35:19, and those difficulties prefigure the experience of Jesus, as John presents him explaining: "But the word that is written in their Law must be fulfilled: 'They hated me without a cause'" (John 15:25, ESV).[30] In the immediate context John presents Jesus telling his disciples, "If they persecuted me, they will also persecute you" (15:20). This indicates that Jesus understands himself as *the* seed of the woman who is at enmity with the serpent and his seed, but he also sees his followers as the collective seed of the woman who will likewise face the same enmity (cf. Rev 12:1–6, 13–17).

§4.6 Psalm 69

The various statements from Psalm 69 that are quoted in the New Testament all make good sense in their Old Testament context. That is,

---

28. For my understanding of the way David interprets Exodus 12:46 in Psalm 34:20, and the way John understands this to be fulfilled in Christ's death in John 19:36, see Hamilton, *Psalms* ad loc., and Hamilton, "John," 289–90.

29. Cf. Psalms 35:4 and 40:14; 35:26 and 40:14; 35:21 and 40:15; and 35:25 and 40:15. See also my discussion of Psalms 35 and 40 in *Psalms*.

30. The phrase here rendered "who hate me without cause" (Ps 35:19, שֹׂנְאַי חִנָּם) also occurs in Psalm 69:4 (MT 69:5). What I have said about these words fitting the context of David's situation in Psalm 35 also applies to their context in Psalm 69. The words could have been cited in the New Testament to evoke either or both Psalms. Bates writes, "there is virtually no evidence that the earliest church found special significance in David's specific moments of suffering so that they were regarded as paradigmatic, as is required for a so-called 'typology,'" Bates, *The Birth of the Trinity*, 117. Bates can only say this, however, because he maintains that all the texts I am discussing here are to be understood prosopologically rather than typologically.

in every case it is easy to imagine how these words would have applied in David's own life. We will consider them in the order they appear in Psalm 69.

§4.6.1 Zeal for Your House

In Psalm 69:9a, quoted in John 2:17, David prays, "For zeal for your house has consumed me." Given David's well-known desire to build Yahweh's temple (2 Sam 7:1–7), David's intention was to communicate that his earnest concern for Yahweh's house has devoured him, so to speak, while those who hate God cause all the difficulty they can for him (cf. Ps 69:1–12). When Jesus cleanses the temple in John's Gospel, John relates that the disciples of Jesus remembered this line from Psalm 69 (John 2:17). The historical correspondence between Jesus and David is apparent: both David and Jesus were devoted to Yahweh and consumed with concern for Yahweh's temple. In David's case, as can be seen in Psalm 69, devotion to Yahweh put him at odds with the seed of the serpent. And so it proved to be with Jesus, as he cleansed the temple of those who had more concern for their own interests than Yahweh's. There is also escalation in significance as we move from David to Jesus, in two ways. First, the sense in which the zeal Jesus feels will "consume" him is that it will bring about his death—he is the fulfillment of the temple, and he will be "torn down" in the sense that he will be crucified and raised (2:17–22). Second, the new covenant temple for which Jesus feels this even-unto-death-concern is not a building but the new temple of the Holy Spirit, his people. There is no warrant for the idea that in Psalm 69, David in his prophetic capacity has "stepped into an alternative theodramatic character as he delivered his speech," as Bates contends.[31] Rather, Jesus is the typological fulfillment of what David understood himself to prefigure.

If we are to understand the Scriptures, we must maintain the contextual meaning of Psalm 69. The fullness of the Old Testament revelation will be vital for understanding the way that expectation builds toward Jesus, and we cannot afford to lose the Davidic contribution to that expectation. Bates's proposal would obscure the suffering of David, as would the proposal made by Richard B. Hays, who writes,

> What then, according to John 2:17–22, does a postresurrection reading of Psalm 69 discover in the text? It discloses, among other things, that *Jesus*

---

31. Ibid., 201.

himself is the speaker of Psalm 69:9, the praying voice who declares, "Zeal for your house will consume me." And that insight in turn opens the window on a fresh appropriation of the entire psalm—indeed, perhaps the entire Psalter—as a proleptic veiled revelation of the identity of Jesus.[32]

What Hays says here does not account for the intent of the human author of Psalm 69, and as a result it takes on the feel of an arbitrary assertion that appeals to the authority of the resurrection of Jesus. Because John and the other followers of Jesus were trying to convince people that Jesus was the Christ (John 20:30–31) and had been raised from the dead, I do not think it likely that they said, in effect, the persuasive power of our interpretations depend upon you granting that Jesus was raised—that was precisely the point in dispute. It seems more likely that John and the others would argue along these lines: *we are claiming that what the Old Testament actually says—what its human authors intended to communicate—has been fulfilled in Jesus.* Making that point would depend upon the meaning of Psalm 69 in context being fulfilled in Christ. To assert that Christ was the speaker of the Psalm, and that thereby the whole Psalter is a veiled revelation of his identity, seems in danger of asserting that Jesus is the answer before one has heard, or considered, the question.

I contend that there is a better way: it can be shown that the Psalter was written to promote the view that in the end times the promised king from David's line would accomplish salvation, but we have to allow the Psalter to teach us what it means by these ideas.[33] When we study the Psalter for itself to determine the meaning of its human authors, we put ourselves in position to understand how everything David presented himself to be typifying comes to fulfillment in Christ. Our appreciation of the depth and power of Psalm 69 gives validity to the fulfillment claimed in the New Testament, rather than Psalm 69 being stripped of its original meaning in context and the assertion that Christ is the actual speaker being foisted upon it.

§4.6.2 The Reproaches of Those Who Reproached You

David's original meaning in Psalm 69:9b, "the reproaches of those who reproach you have fallen on me," is crucial to understanding *both* the argument

---

32. Hays, *Echoes of Scripture in the Gospels*, 312.
33. See esp. Mitchell, *The Message of the Psalter*. I have also tried to demonstrate this in Hamilton, *Psalms*; and Hamilton, "Typology in the Psalms."

Paul makes in Romans 15 *and* his rationale for quoting Psalm 69:9b in Romans 15:3. First a word about this statement in the context of Psalm 69, then the contours of Paul's argument in Romans 15, which entails consideration of what Paul believed about Jesus that led him to put the words of David on his lips.

What does the context of David's statement, "the reproaches of those who reproach you have fallen on me," indicate that he meant by those words? That is, what light does the rest of Psalm 69 shed on 69:9b? The inner logic of Psalm 69 works as follows: David does not feel that he has wronged his enemies but rather that they hate him without cause, that they attack him with lies, and that they demand he restore what he did not steal (Ps 69:4). He also fully aligns himself with God's people (69:6) and confesses in his prayer that he bears hostility and dishonor from his enemies because of his relationship with Yahweh: "For it is for your sake that I have borne reproach, that dishonor has covered my face" (69:7, ESV). This indicates that David's enemies are in fact enemies of God, and that while David has not wronged them, they nevertheless hate him because they hate God. The enemies of God vent their fury at God on David. This results in David's alienation from his own family (69:8). It is based on his devotion to the building of a house for God's name (69:9a). And we can summarize the situation as follows: David's prominent position and evident commitment to Yahweh make him the earthly focal point where the enemies of God direct their hatred of Yahweh: "the reproaches of those who reproach you have fallen on me" (69:9b). More could be said about Psalm 69, but this suffices for our purposes here.

Turning to Paul's argument in Romans 15, he has dealt with the ways Christians of different religious backgrounds respond to food (Rom 14:1–4) and days of the week (14:5–9), explaining that Christians are not to judge one another because God is the judge (14:10–12), though all Christians should avoid causing other believers to stumble (14:13–23). To buttress this idea that Christians should not exercise their rights at the expense of other believers, in disregard of their concerns about clean and unclean food, drinking wine, and regarding every day the same (14:5, 14–17, 20–21), Paul asserts that the strong have an obligation to bear with the weak and not just please themselves (15:1). He summons all to love of neighbor, saying, "Let each of us please his neighbor for his good, to build him up" (15:2, ESV), and then he appeals to the example of the Lord Jesus in 15:3, "For Christ did not please himself, but as it is written, 'The reproaches of those who reproached you fell on me.'"

Paul's argument is that Christians of stronger conscience should not disregard the brethren of weaker conscience because Jesus did not disregard them. The argument appeals to the strong to be conformed to the image of Christ, the rich one who became poor that the poor might be made rich through his poverty (2 Cor 8:9). That is, Paul makes an analogy between the Lord Jesus and the strong of conscience who enjoy freedom from the law. Like the strong, Jesus was free from all obligation and enjoyed full satisfaction in the Father's presence prior to the incarnation. Jesus, however, did not disregard the needs of his people but humbled himself and took on the form of a servant to die for his people (Phil 2:5–11). And when he became incarnate, like David before him, Jesus became the focal point at which the God-haters aimed all their fury. The enemies of God made Jesus the target of their wrath. They hated Jesus because Jesus loved God. Their hatred of God manifested itself in their rejection of Jesus. And thus what was typified in David (and before David in Joseph, Moses, and others) was fulfilled in Christ: "the reproaches of those who reproached you fell on me" (Rom 15:3; Ps 69:9b).

Paul then makes a generalizing comment on the Old Testament that continues the argument in Romans 15:4 (ESV), "For whatever was written in former days was written for our instruction, that through endurance and through the encouragement of the Scriptures we might have hope." The encouragement of the Scriptures surely includes David's faithful endurance of the reproaches of the enemies of God in Psalm 69, in which he articulates both his love for God's people and his confidence that God would deliver him. Such encouragement pervades the Old Testament, available from the accounts of Joseph, Moses, Elijah and Elisha, Isaiah, and others. These righteous sufferers typified Christ, whose example Paul calls the Christians in Rome to follow.

§4.6.3 Poison for Food, Sour Wine to Drink

All four Gospels allude to Psalm 69:21 (ESV), "They gave me poison for food, and for my thirst they gave me sour wine to drink" (Matt 27:34, 48; Mark 15:23; Luke 23:36; John 19:29). Here again David's statements are right at home in the context of Psalm 69, preceded in verse 20 (ESV) by the words, "I looked for pity, but there was none, and for comforters, but I found none." It would be natural in the ancient world to find comforters among those offering hospitality, and even today people speak of "comfort-food." David, however, is surrounded by enemies who only offer him poison and sour wine (Ps 69:21), and in verse 22 (ESV) he prays that God would do justice on his unrepentant opponents, praying that the way they sought to entrap him by poisoning his food would rebound upon them: "Let their own table before them become a snare; and when they are at peace, let it become a trap" (69:22). They tried to entrap David at table through poisoned food, and David prays that they would fall into the hole they themselves dug (cf. Ps 7:15; 35:7–8).

The typological fulfillment of Psalm 69:21 in the crucifixion accounts can be traced as follows: the suffering of David is fulfilled in the suffering of Jesus; the God-hating enemies of David are likewise fulfilled in the God-hating enemies of Jesus; and in the same way that those enemies gave David sour wine when he needed comfort (Ps 69:20–21), those crucifying Jesus gave him sour wine when he cried out from thirst (Matt 27:34, 48; Mark 15:23; Luke 23:36; John 19:29).[34]

Understanding the role of the opponents of David as fulfilled in the role of the opponents of Jesus can also be seen in Acts 1:20 (ESV), where statements from two Psalms are cited in explanation of what took place with Judas. Having recounted how Judas met his end (Acts 1:16–19), in Acts 1:20 Luke presents Peter explaining how this fulfilled Psalms 69:25 and 109:8, "For it is written in the Book of Psalms, 'May his camp become desolate, and let there be no one to dwell in it;' and 'Let another take his office.'" In accordance with the prayer that another take his office, Peter goes on to argue that another be chosen to replace Judas (Acts 1:21–22).

What I have argued throughout this section is well summarized by Dale Brueggemann, quoting Delitzsch, "David becomes the prophet of Christ; but he speaks of himself, and what he says also found fulfillment in himself . . . his hope has found in Christ its full historical and redemptive realization . . ."[35]

§5 THE SUFFERING SERVANT

For the purposes of this project, my thesis about the suffering servant in Isaiah 52:13–53:12 is twofold: first, that within the book of Isaiah, what the servant suffers resolves the broader issue in the book, as he bears Yahweh's covenant

---

34. The Bible's imprecatory prayers ask that God not allow unrepentant sin to go unrequited. They call for God to do justice, and so it is with Psalm 69:22. David prayed that God would do justice against those who had rejected him, and Paul quotes this prayer with reference to "the rest" of Israel, the non-elect, who "were hardened" in Romans 11:7–9.

35. Dale A. Brueggemann, "The Evangelists and the Psalms," in *Interpreting the Psalms: Issues and Approaches*, ed. David Firth and Philip S. Johnston (Downers Grove, IL: InterVarsity, 2005), 272.

wrath against his sinful people, making it so that Yahweh can comfort his people and accomplish for them the new exodus and return from exile. Indeed, what he accomplishes can be seen as the salvific sacrifice of that new exodus. Second, virtually everything Isaiah says about the suffering servant is informed by earlier Scripture, as Isaiah prophesies a future figure who will suffer as those in Israel's history had before him. We will first consider the way Isaiah presents the servant in relationship to the new exodus before considering how the servant recapitulates typological patterns.

§5.1 The New Exodus Context

Isaiah everywhere compares Israel's sojourn in Egypt prior to the exodus to their exile to Babylon prior to the new exodus, and the leadup to Isaiah 53 is no different. In Isaiah 52:4 (ESV) the prophet declares, "For thus says the Lord God: 'My people went down at the first into Egypt to sojourn there, and the Assyrian oppressed them for nothing.'" In the same way that Yahweh made known his name at the exodus, he promises to make his name known in the new exodus (Isa 52:6). The good news of this salvation is proclaimed upon the mountains by those who have beautiful feet, and they proclaim that Yahweh reigns (52:7). The watchmen sing for joy because they see the return of Yahweh to Zion (52:8), Yahweh at last has comforted his people (52:9; 49:13; 40:1).

Yahweh saved Israel at the exodus by a mighty hand and an outstretched arm, and in the new salvation Isaiah prophesies, which all the ends of the earth will see, "Yahweh has bared his holy arm before the eyes of all the nations" (Isa 52:10). Thus just as Israel left Egypt, made the tabernacle and its implements at Sinai, then began the march on the land, so now God's people are called to depart, and those "who bear the vessels of Yahweh" are called to purify themselves (52:11). They fled Egypt in haste but will not do so this time: "For you shall not go out in haste, and you shall not go in flight" (52:12a, ESV). After the pillar of cloud and fire and the angel of Yahweh led them to the Red Sea, both the angel and the pillar stood between Israel and the chariots of Pharaoh (Exod 14:19), and so also this time: "for Yahweh will go before you, and the God of Israel will be your rear guard" (Isa 52:12b).

§5.2 The Suffering Servant Recapitulates the Patterns

When Yahweh says through Isaiah in 52:13a, "Behold, my servant shall act wisely," he employs two terms that have been used significantly in earlier

Scripture, "servant" (עֶבֶד) and "act wisely" (שָׂכַל). Stephen Dempster points out that Moses is called the "Servant of Yahweh" eighteen times. Joshua and David are so designated twice each. Moses, David, and Joshua are the only people referred to with this phrase in the Old Testament. When we consider the phrase "my servant," David is the servant twenty-three times, Jacob thirteen, Moses eight, Job six, and Israel three.[36] As we think about Yahweh's servant, then, Moses and David are prominent precursors.[37]

The verb "act wisely" (שָׂכַל) appears in the following places that seem relevant for this discussion:

- Joshua 1:7 and 1:8 (ESV), where Joshua is urged to keep the Torah that he "may have good success."
- David "was successful" in everything he did (1 Sam 18:5, 14, 15, 30, ESV).
- David charges Solomon to keep the Torah that he might "prosper" (1 Kgs 2:3, ESV).
- Yahweh was with Hezekiah, and "wherever he went out, he prospered" (1 Kgs 18:7, ESV).

More instances could be cited (e.g., Jer 23:5, cited in §5.3.5 of Chapter 3 above), but this is enough to suggest that there is a connection between keeping the Torah and thereby having success (cf. Ps 1:2–3; 2:10). These two terms, "servant" and "act wisely," join together to point to a Mosaic, Davidic figure who has success because he is faithful to Yahweh's Torah.

Isaiah then says that the servant "shall be high and lifted up and shall be exalted" (52:13b, ESV). This recalls how Isaiah said in 11:10 (ESV), "In that day the root of Jesse, who shall stand as a signal for the peoples—of him shall the nations inquire, and his resting place shall be glorious" (cf. 11:12). The Davidic character of the "servant" of Yahweh who "acts wisely" is thus confirmed by the link to Isaiah 11, which speaks of the future king from David's line.

Isaiah 53:1 reprises (cf. 52:10) the reference to the exodus-new exodus salvation by Yahweh's strong hand and outstretched arm with the question,

---

36. Stephen G. Dempster, "The Servant of the Lord," in *Central Themes in Biblical Theology: Mapping Unity in Diversity*, ed. Scott J. Hafemann and Paul R. House (Grand Rapids: Baker, 2007), 131.

37. Having summarized a number of points of contact between the suffering servant and Moses (see pp. 68–71), Allison writes, "Moses served the author of the [servant] songs as a type—one of several—for the suffering servant. . . . And what would have been more natural than to model the central figure of a second exodus upon the famous leader of the first?" Allison, *The New Moses*, 70.

"And to whom has the arm of Yahweh been revealed?" Both the imagery and the vocabulary of Isaiah 53:2 recall Isaiah 11. The prophet says in 11:1 (ESV), "There shall come forth a shoot from the stump of Jesse, and a branch from his roots [מִשָּׁרָשָׁיו] shall bear fruit." Then in 53:2a he declares, "For he grew up before him like a young plant, and like a root (וְכַשֹּׁרֶשׁ) out of dry ground." The imagery is the same, the term "root" is the same, and the term rendered "young plant" in 53:2 is the same rendered "nursing child" in 11:8 (יוֹנֵק). Isaiah identifies the Mosaic, Davidic servant who acts wisely by doing Torah (Isa 52:13) with the shoot from the stump of Jesse, even with the nursing child with nothing to fear from the venomous snake (53:2; 11:1, 8).

Isaiah 53:2b recalls the way that there was nothing impressive about David, at least, not when considered "as man sees" (cf. 1 Sam 16:7, ESV). Jesse did not even think it necessary to summon David from the flock when Samuel came to anoint one of his sons as king (16:11). And Isaiah likely has this kind of thing in mind when he writes, "he had no form or majesty that we should look at him, and no beauty that we should desire him" (Isa 53:2b, ESV). He was not like Saul, who was, according to externals, an obvious choice for a king: "There was not a man among the people of Israel more handsome than he" (1 Sam 9:2, ESV).

David speaks of himself in the Psalms with the same language seen in Isaiah 53:3 (ESV), which reads, "He was despised and rejected by men; a man of sorrows, and acquainted with grief; and as one from whom men hide their faces he was despised, and we esteemed him not." The term rendered "despised" (בָּזָה) occurs twice in Psalm 22, at 22:6 and 22:24 (MT 22:7, 25). These verses capture the way that in his own experience David prefigured what Isaiah says of the servant in Isaiah 53:3 (all texts here ESV).

> Psalm 22:6–7, "But I am a worm and not a man,
>> scorned by mankind and despised by the people.
> All who see me mock me;
>> they make mouths at me; they wag their heads."

> Psalm 22:24, "For he has not despised or abhorred
>> the affliction of the afflicted,
> and he has not hidden his face from him,
>> but has heard, when he cried to him."

Yahweh did not hide his face from David in Psalm 22:24 (וְלֹא־הִסְתִּיר פָּנָיו מִמֶּנּוּ, MT 22:25), but men hid their faces from the servant in Isaiah 53:3 (וּכְמַסְתֵּר פָּנִים מִמֶּנּוּ).

David looked particularly like "a man of sorrows" "acquainted with grief" (Isa 53:3) when his own son betrayed him and drove him from Jerusalem in 2 Samuel 15:30,

> But David went up the ascent of the Mount of Olives, weeping as he went, barefoot and with his head covered. And all the people who were with him covered their heads, and they went up, weeping as they went. (ESV)

The true king of Israel, like David before him, would exit Jerusalem, cross the Kidron Valley, ascend the Mount of Olives, there to weep with those loyal to him (Matt 26:30–46; Mark 14:32–42; Luke 22:39–46).[38]

Where could Isaiah have gotten the insight he begins to communicate in 53:4? To bring out the import of the question, consider the statements that go in this direction from Isaiah 53 (all texts here ESV):

- 53:4, "Surely he has borne our griefs and carried our sorrows . . ."
- 53:5, "he was pierced for our transgressions; he was crushed for our iniquities; upon him was the chastisement that brought us peace, and with his wounds we are healed."
- 53:6, ". . . the Lord has laid on him the iniquity of us all."
- 53:8, "who considered that he was cut off out of the land of the living, stricken for the transgression of my people?"
- 53:10, "it was the will of the Lord to crush him; he has put him to grief; when his soul makes an offering for guilt, he shall see his offspring; he shall prolong his days . . ."
- 53:11, "Out of the anguish of his soul he shall see and be satisfied; by his knowledge shall the righteous one, my servant, make many to be accounted righteous, and he shall bear their iniquities."
- 53:12, ". . . because he poured out his soul to death and was numbered with the transgressors; yet he bore the sin of many, and makes intercession for the transgressors."

---

38. Similarly Ahearne-Kroll, *The Psalms of Lament in Mark's Passion*, 167.

These statements all indicate that the righteous servant of Yahweh (53:11) will suffer for the sins of the people. Taking nothing away from the fact that Isaiah was a prophet, that he was inspired by the Holy Spirit, that God revealed the truth to him, I want to ask this question: is it possible to understand earlier Scripture to build toward Isaiah's insight, so that if we understand earlier Scripture as he did, we see that his conclusion was a natural one? If a dendrologist (someone who studies trees!) can reverse engineer an oak tree to an acorn, can we reverse engineer Isaiah 53 to understand the thought-world from which it sprang?

Isaiah seems to be saying that the way that the people's iniquity will be pardoned, the way they will receive double for all their sins (Isa 40:1–2), will be that the servant will drink the cup of wrath in their place (cf. 51:17, 22). We should also note the stress in the passage on the innocence from sin and righteous behavior of the servant (all texts here ESV):

- 52:13, "my servant shall act wisely."
- 53:9, "although he had done no violence, and there was no deceit in his mouth."
- 53:10, "the will of the Lord shall prosper in his hand."
- 53:11, "by his knowledge shall the righteous one, my servant, make many to be accounted righteous."

How did Isaiah arrive at these conclusions? I would submit that Isaiah anticipated in his own thinking much of what Paul articulates in Romans 5:12–21. We can break the key points down to a few simple sentences, each point arising from the Old Testament's own inner logic:

- Isaiah understood that because of Adam's sin, all people were born outside of Eden, transgressors against God, with Adam's guilt visited upon them because God visits "the iniquity of the fathers on the children and the children's children" (Exod 34:7; cf. 20:5).
- Isaiah understood that Adam was the son of God, that the nation of Israel was a new-Adam as the son of God (Exod 4:22–23), and that the king from David's line would be a new-Adam representative of Israel as the son of God (2 Sam 7:14).
- Isaiah understood that if sin and death were to be overcome, a righteous life would have to be lived and a full penalty for sin paid.

The patterns observable in the Joseph story likely played into Isaiah's thinking, along with the way Judah offered himself as pledge for and then substitute in place of Benjamin (Gen 43:8–9; 44:32–34). Joseph's own suffering, his affliction in being sold into slavery (37:28; 42:21–22), seem to be recalled by Isaiah in 53:8, "By oppression and judgment he was taken away . . ." There is a subtle tie to the Genesis narrative in the presence of the name of Joseph's mother, Rachel (רָחֵל), a name that means "ewe" and appears in the line, "and like a sheep [וּכְרָחֵל] that before its shearers is silent" (Isa 53:7, ESV). After mentioning the oppression and lack of justice by which he was taken away in 53:8a, Isaiah makes a statement reminiscent of the way Joseph's brothers callously went on with their lives, only realizing the guilt of what they had done to Joseph much later when they stood before him (Gen 37:31–36; 42:21–22; 45:3). In that narrative Joseph explained that he was sent by God away from Canaan to Egypt to preserve the life of a remnant (Gen 45:5–9, see "remnant," שְׁאֵרִית, in Gen 45:7). Isaiah presents the recapitulating fulfillment of all this in the words, "and as for his generation, who considered that he was cut off out of the land of the living, stricken for the transgression of my people" (Isa 53:8b, ESV). Just as the suffering of Joseph gave life to the seed of Abraham, the remnant, so the suffering of the servant in Isaiah 53 gives life and righteousness to his seed (53:10–11).[39]

Several indicators in the passage help us understand what Isaiah meant to communicate. The first of these concerns points of contact with 2 Samuel 7:14 (ESV), "I will be to him a father, and he shall be to me a son. When he commits iniquity, I will discipline him with the rod of men, with the stripes of the sons of men." Nathan's oracle concerns both David's house (2 Sam 7:11)—the line of kings that descends from him, and David's seed (7:13)—the one king whose throne Yahweh promised to establish forever. As the statement about discipline applies to David's house, Yahweh promises to discipline sinful kings who descend from David "with the rod of men" (7:14).

The servant of Isaiah 53, however, suffers not for his own iniquity but for that of his people (Isa 53:6). 2 Samuel 7:14 uses an infinitive construct verbal form in the phrase, "When he commits iniquity" (בְּהַעֲוֹתוֹ). Isaiah employs the cognate noun for "iniquity" (עָוֹן) three times to describe the sin of the people the servant will bear (texts here ESV):

---

39. So also Emadi, "The Story of Joseph," 82–102.

- Isa 53:5, "he was crushed for our iniquities."
- Isa 53:6, "the Lord has laid on him the iniquity of us all."
- Isa 53:11, "he shall bear their iniquities."

The servant in Isaiah 53 himself neither spoke nor did wrong (53:9) but was righteous (53:11). He will suffer for the sins of the people, and Isaiah signals that this is 2 Samuel 7:14 suffering by using the term rendered "stripes" in 2 Samuel 7:14 (נֶגַע) twice in Isaiah 53, at 53:4, "we esteemed him stricken," and 53:8, "stricken for the transgression of my people." 2 Samuel 7:14 spoke of this punishment as the Lord "disciplining" his son (the verb יָכַח). Isaiah does not deploy this term, but he does speak of the synonymous concept of "chastisement" (Isa 53:5, מוּסָר).

In 53:5 Isaiah also employs a term, "pierced" (חָלַל), that David used to describe his suffering in Psalms 69 and 109. Consider these statements:

- Ps 69:26 (MT 69:27), "the one you strike, they pursue. They recount the wound of those pierced by you."
- Ps 109:22, "Because afflicted and needy am I, and my heart is pierced within me."
- Isa 53:5, "But he was pierced for our transgressions . . ."

Another point of contact between Psalm 69:26 (MT 69:27) and Isaiah 53:4 exists with the phrase "smitten by God" in Isaiah 53:4 and "him whom you have struck" in Psalm 69:26 (MT 69:27). In both places God does the smiting, and Isaiah uses the same verb David had (נָכָה).

Isaiah has identified the suffering servant of Isaiah 53 with the future king from David of Isaiah 11. He has presented him suffering in terms used by David in Psalms 22, 69, and 109 (all psalms quoted in the NT). And I submit that he understood that the future king from David's line would be a new-Adam son of God who would be righteous where Adam was sinful, whose suffering unto death would pay the penalty for the sins of the people. As Adam was a covenant head who brought the people into sin, so the suffering servant would be a covenant head who would bear the sin of the people and suffer in their place. Because he committed no sin, death was not his consequence and could not therefore hold him.

A second set of indicators that gives insight into Isaiah's prophecy has to do with connections Isaiah forges between this passage, Isaiah 52–54, and the stories of Abraham and Isaac in Genesis 21–22. The statement "here I am" (הִנֵּנִי) occurs three times in Genesis 22, all on the lips of Abraham:

- Gen 22:1, God calls on Abraham, who replies, "Here I am."
- Gen 22:7, Isaac calls on Abraham, who replies, "Here I am."
- Gen 22:11, The angel of the Lord calls on Abraham, who replies, "Here I am."

In the narrative when God tested father Abraham by calling on him to offer his son, his only son, whom he loved, Isaac, as a burnt offering on one of the mountains of Moriah (Gen 22:1–2), the father replies, "Here I am" (22:1, 7, 11). Immediately prior to Isaiah 52:13–53:12, in which God the Father offers up his righteous servant, who appears to be the future king from the line of David and thereby God's son, the Lord says in Isaiah 52:6, "Therefore my people will know my name. Therefore on that day [they will know] that I am the one who says, 'Here I am'" (הִנֵּנִי). When joined with the other pointers to the narratives of Abraham and Isaac in the immediate context, this statement seems to be Yahweh telling his people that he will play the role of the father in the Genesis 22 narrative, saying as Abraham did, "Here I am."

If Abraham's "here I am" stands just prior to Isaiah 52:13–53:12 in 52:6, the rejoicing of Sarah at the birth of Isaac immediately follows the passage in 54:1 (ESV), "Sing, O barren one, who did not bear; break forth into singing and cry aloud, you who have not been in labor!" Confirming the allusion to the stories of Isaac in the rejoicing of the barren mother who gives birth in Isaiah 54:1 is the allusion to God's Genesis 22:17 statement to Abraham after the sacrifice of Isaac in 54:3, "and your offspring will possess the nations."

Gen 22:17, וְיִרַשׁ זַרְעֲךָ אֵת שַׁעַר אֹיְבָיו
"and your seed will possess the gate of those who hate him."

Isa 54:3, וְזַרְעֵךָ גּוֹיִם יִירָשׁ
"and your seed will possess the nations."

These allusions to the narratives dealing with Abraham and the birth and sacrifice of Isaac (Isa 52:6; 54:1–3) bracket the description of the servant in

52:13–53:12. This colors the passage with overtones of miraculous birth, ful-fillment of promise, faith that stares death in the face, even willing to offer up the beloved child of promise, believing that he would return from the slaughter alive (Gen 22:5, "we will return"), and that from the *one* seed would come *the many*, as numerous as the stars of heaven (cf. Isa 54:1).

Abraham was instructed to take Isaac and offer him up "on one of the mountains" (הֶהָרִים, Gen 22:2). In Isaiah 52:7 (ESV) the prophet exclaims, "How beautiful upon the mountains [הֶהָרִים] are the feet of him who brings good news . . ." On that mountain in Genesis 22 Abraham experienced the good news that he was not to harm the boy Isaac but instead offer the substitute ram as the sacrifice, naming the place, "God will see to it" (Gen 22:11–14). On the way up the mountain, Isaac said to his father, "'Behold, the fire and the wood, but where is the lamb for the burnt offering?' And Abraham said, 'God will see to it, the lamb for the burnt offering, my son.' And the two of them went together" (22:7b–8). The term rendered "lamb" twice in two verses (22:7, 22:8, שֶׂה), is the same term Isaiah uses when he compares the servant to a "lamb" (Isa 53:7). When Isaac asks about the lamb in Genesis 22, the realization has dawned upon him that they have everything necessary for the sacrifice but the animal to be slain. His father's answer places "the lamb for the burnt offering" in apposition with the words "my son." The phrasing is ambiguous. Abraham could simply be addressing his son with the statement that God will see to the lamb, or he could be saying that God is providing his (Abraham's) son as the lamb for the burnt offering.

The two go on together, and there is no indication that Isaac asked any further questions or offered any kind of objection as he was led to slaughter. Isaac was silent for the rest of the trip up the mountain (Gen 22:8b–9a), he was silent as his father bound him (22:9b), silent as his father laid him on the altar (22:9c), and silent as his father "reached out his hand and took the knife to slaughter his son" (22:10, ESV). At just that moment the angel of the Lord intervened, but Isaac's submission to his father and acceptance of his fate likely provides the typological pattern Isaiah says the servant will fulfill in 53:7b (ESV), "he opened not his mouth; like a lamb [שֶׂה] that is led to the slaugh-ter, and like a sheep [רָחֵל] that before its shearers is silent, so he opened not his mouth." We noted this above, but in Genesis 24 Jacob will marry Rachel, and her name is the term rendered "sheep" in Isaiah 53:7.

Isaac was, of course, the seed of Abraham, and the long wait for Isaac after

God's promise of seed is a central point of tension in the narrative from the making of the promise in Genesis 12:1–3 to its realization in 21:1–3. No sooner is the promise fulfilled than Abraham is called to sacrifice Isaac (22:1–2). For a barren woman to give birth is like resurrection from the dead, and for Abraham to take Isaac to the mountain to sacrifice him and bring him back alive (22:5) is also like resurrection from the dead (cf. Heb 11:19). Though the seed was to be sacrificed, he lived, and through that one seed, Isaac, came the rest of the seed of Abraham, until they were fruitful and multiplied and filled the land (Exod 1:7). Isaiah seems to speak of these patterns—of the one seed receiving life from the dead and thereby giving life to the rest of the seed— when he says, "when his soul makes an offering for guilt, he shall see his seed; he shall prolong his days" (Isa 53:10, ESV).

Isaiah speaks of the death of the servant (following the ESV below):

- Isa 53:8, "he was cut off out of the land of the living."
- Isa 53:9, "they made his grave with the wicked, and with a rich man in his death."
- Isa 53:10, "when his soul makes an offering for guilt" [אָשָׁם].
- Isa 53:12, "because he poured out his soul to death."

He was cut off, put in the grave, and his death was an *asham* (אָשָׁם), a guilt offering. He was slain as a sacrifice. How, then, can Isaiah say immediately after the phrase, "when his soul makes an offering for guilt," that, "he shall see his seed; he shall prolong his days" (Isa 53:10)? The answer is found in the fact that the logic of Genesis 22 is resurrection logic. Again, for Isaac to be born is for life to come from a dead corpse—make that two corpses—Paul says Abraham and Sarah were both as good as dead (Rom 4:17–19; cf. 1 Sam 2:5b–6). Similarly, Abraham took Isaac up the mountain to kill him and brought him back alive, and in the very next chapter, Genesis 23, the interest in a burial plot for a dead person seems to imply belief that God promised the land, so even if the land was not received during life, there will be a resurrection in which the promised land will be enjoyed (Gen 23, cf. 25:8–10; 35:29; 49:29–33; 50:24–26; Heb 11:22).[40]

The phrase "he will see his seed" in Isaiah 53:10 is reminiscent of Genesis

---

40. Chase, "Genesis of Resurrection Hope," 477–80.

50:23, "And Joseph saw Ephraim's children of the third generation. The children also of Machir the son of Manasseh were counted as Joseph's own." Joseph—who was thought to be dead but was in fact alive (Gen 37:33; 45:26–28)—saw his seed, and the killed but alive servant will see his.

The next phrase in Isaiah 53:10, "he shall prolong his days," exactly matches the purpose statement explaining why Israel's king should copy out the Torah in his own hand and study it always in Deuteronomy 17:20 (יַאֲרִיךְ יָמִים). Moses instructed Israel about how the king was to do this in Deuteronomy 17:14–20, and it is worth noting that Deuteronomy 17:20 also speaks of the king's sons (his seed). This phrase, "he shall prolong his days," only occurs four times in the Old Testament (Deut 17:20; Isa 53:10; Prov 28:16; Eccl 8:13), and it is likely that each instance alludes to the instructions for the king in Deuteronomy 17:20.

In spite of his death as a guilt offering for the sins of his people, the future king from David's line, Yahweh's righteous servant, will be like Isaac raised from the dead, firstborn, only begotten seed whose life promises seed that cannot be counted for multitude. His "acting wisely" in 52:13 is confirmed as Torah-obedient leadership by the next phrases of 53:10 (ESV), "the will of the LORD shall prosper in his hand." The reference to the "will of Yahweh" points to the king not being like Saul, who displeased Yahweh by disobedience, but like David, who loved the Torah and sang Yahweh's praises (cf. Hos 13:11; Acts 13:21–22). The statement that the good pleasure of Yahweh will "prosper in his hand" in 53:10 uses a verb (צָלֵחַ) that is a sister term to the one rendered "act wisely" (שָׂכַל) in 52:13. These terms appear in the following contexts that bring together leadership, the need for leaders to adhere to the word of God, and the wisdom and success that doing so causes:

- Gen 39:2, "And Yahweh was with Joseph, and he became a successful man (צָלֵחַ)" (cf. 39:3, 23).
- Josh 1:8, "This scroll of the Torah shall not depart from your mouth, but you shall meditate on it day and night, so that you may be careful to do according to all that is written in it. For then you will make your way prosperous (צָלֵחַ), and then you will have good success (שָׂכַל)."
- 1 Kings 2:3, "as it is written in the Torah of Moses, that you may prosper" (שָׂכַל).
- 2 Kings 18:6–7, "For [Hezekiah] held fast to Yahweh. He did not depart from following him, but kept the commandments that Yahweh

commanded Moses. And Yahweh was with him; wherever he went out, he prospered" (שָׂכַל).

- Ps 1:2–3, "his delight is in the Torah of Yahweh, and on his Torah he meditates day and night. . . . In all that he does, he prospers" (צָלַח).
- Ps 2:10, "And now, O kings, be wise" (שָׂכַל).

Isaiah prophesies that the future king from David's line will be righteous, no violence in his hands, no deceit in his mouth. This king will not suffer the discipline of 2 Samuel 7:14b for his own iniquity but for that of his people. Like David, he will be unexpected and surprising to those who think according to worldly standards, and like David he will be rejected, despised, and pierced. Like Joseph he will be oppressed and taken away, presumed dead, but in reality reigning over gentiles to give life to Israel. Like Isaac, he will be offered up as a sacrifice, silent like a lamb to slaughter, only beloved son, but through his death he will make many righteous (Isa 53:11), and through death and resurrection his seed will be multiplied (Isa 53:10). Because this future king will be fully devoted to Yahweh's will (53:10) as articulated in the Torah, he will act wisely (52:13), prosper (53:10), and prolong his days (53:10; cf. Deut 17:20).

Through the suffering servant of Isaiah 53, God will accomplish salvation.

§6 JESUS REJECTED THEN EXALTED

The Lord Jesus fulfills the role of the suffering servant. The repeated sequences seen in Joseph, Moses, and David join the patterned prophecy in Isaiah 53 to point forward to *the* suffering servant. The suffering of the Christ was hidden and is now revealed, and it is salvific and final. This section seeks to summarize the New Testament presentation[41] of Christ as the suffering servant by beginning and ending with texts that speak to the way Christ first suffered before entering into glory (Luke 24:26 and 1 Peter 1:10–11). From there we move to texts in John on how Christ was rejected, lifted up, and triumphant in the glorious defeat of the cross (John 1:10–11 and 3:14; 8:28; 12:32, 38). Luke has juxtaposed the patterns from the likes of Joseph and Moses in Stephen's

---

41. For extra-biblical "primary texts that have been cited in the scholarly literature as relevant for understanding Jesus' trial and crucifixion," see David W. Chapman and Eckhard J. Schnabel, *The Trial and Crucifixion of Jesus: Texts and Commentary*, Wissenschaftliche Untersuchungen zum Neuen Testament 344 (Tübingen: Mohr Siebeck, 2015) quote from p. v.

speech in Acts 7 with the prophecy arising from those patterns in Isaiah 53 in Acts 8:32–33. All of this grows out of the teaching of Jesus himself, who brought all these themes together in the parable of the wicked tenants (Mark 12:1–12). This section's chiastic structure seeks to summarize New Testament teaching, with Christ's own interpretive genius, humble lordship, and achievement through loss at the center.

§6.1 Luke 24:26, First Suffering Then Glory
   §6.2 John 1:10–11, They Received Him Not
      §6.3 Acts 7, Stephen's Speech
         §6.4 Mark 12:1–12, Parable of the Wicked Tenants
      §6.5 Acts 8:32–33, Quotation of Isaiah 53
   §6.6 John 3:14; 8:28; 12:32, 38, Isaiah's Servant Lifted Up
§6.7 1 Peter 1:10–11; 2:22–25, First Suffering Then Glory

§6.1 Luke 24:26, First Suffering Then Glory

Luke presents Jesus saying to the two men on the road to Emmaus, "O foolish ones, and slow of heart to believe all that the prophets have spoken! Was it not necessary that the Christ should suffer these things and enter into his glory?" (Luke 24:25–26, ESV). The disciples of Jesus were not expecting him to be crucified, in spite of the fact that he repeatedly told them he would be killed (Luke 9:22–27, 43–45; 18:31–34). The writers of the Gospels tell the story such that it rings true.[42] We understand that the disciples expect Jesus to conquer, how could he not if he could raise the dead and walk on water? And they tell us things like what we find in Luke 18:31–33, where Jesus plainly states that he will be killed but rise from the dead on the third day, and then Luke writes, "But they understood none of these things. This saying was hidden from them and they did not grasp what was said" (Luke 18:34, ESV).

In his words in Luke 24:25, Jesus rebukes the two men for not believing the prophets, calling them foolish and slow of heart to believe. When he then says that it was *necessary* for the Messiah first to suffer and then enter his glory, he indicates that the Old Testament teaches these themes. Apparently Jesus thought that his followers could have seen the prophecies and patterns, the suffering servants, the promises of redemption, and put it all together to arrive

---

42. On this see esp., Peter J. Williams, *Can We Trust the Gospels?* (Wheaton, IL: Crossway, 2018).

at something like what he accomplished. Luke's presentation of Simeon indicates that some in Israel were thinking in the right direction (Luke 2:34–35).

For the benefit of his two followers on the road to Emmaus, to help them understand, "beginning with Moses and all the Prophets, he interpreted to them in all the Scriptures the things concerning himself" (Luke 24:27, ESV). Later in the chapter Luke adds,

> Then he said to them, "These are my words that I spoke to you while I was still with you, that everything written about me in the Law of Moses and the Prophets and the Psalms must be fulfilled." Then he opened their minds to understand the Scriptures, and said to them, "Thus it is written, that the Christ should suffer and on the third day rise from the dead, and that repentance and forgiveness of sins should be proclaimed in his name to all nations, beginning from Jerusalem." (24:44–47, ESV)

§6.2 John 1:10–11, They Received Him Not

The theme of the righteous sufferer depends upon the rejection of the righteous one, which is always surprising and confusing. How could the people of Israel reject the Messiah? This mystery reaches back to Isaiah 6:9–10, a passage quoted in all four Gospels and Acts (alluded to in Romans), and still further to the teaching of Moses in Deuteronomy (e.g., Deut 29:4). John will both show Jesus being rejected (e.g., 5:1–18) and present Jesus teaching on why he has been rejected (e.g., 3:19–21), and he sets the story up in the prologue to his Gospel, plainly stating from the outset, "He was in the world, and the world was made through him, yet the world did not know him. He came to his own, and his own people did not receive him" (John 1:10–11, ESV).

§6.3 Acts 7, Stephen's Speech

In Acts 7 Luke presents Stephen answering the charges brought against him in Acts 6:8–14, "they secretly instigated men who said, 'We have heard him speak blasphemous words against Moses and God.' . . . and they set up false witnesses who said, 'This man never ceases to speak words against this holy place and the law, for we have heard him say that this Jesus of Nazareth will destroy this place and will change the customs that Moses delivered to us'" (Acts 6:11, 13–14, ESV).

Stephen's reply answers these charges by showing that God worked through the patriarchs and Moses *outside the land of Israel* (Acts 7:2–6, 9–15, 17–22). Even once they received the land and built the temple, Solomon confessed that it could not contain the living God (7:45–50). Along the way Stephen shows that the people of Israel rejected Joseph (7:9), rejected Moses in Egypt (7:25–29) and in the wilderness (7:35, 39–41), and this leads to his typological claim. The people of Israel and their fathers were not those who sided with Moses and the prophets but those who rejected and disobeyed them. In fact, Jesus and his followers are the heirs of Moses and the prophets. By rejecting Joseph, Moses, and the prophets, the people of Israel were resisting God and his Spirit's work, and the patterns in the Old Testament have now been fulfilled in Christ. Thus Stephen concludes,

> You stiff-necked people, uncircumcised in heart and ears, you always resist the Holy Spirit. As your fathers did, so do you. Which of the prophets did your fathers not persecute? And they killed those who announced beforehand the coming of the Righteous One, whom you have now betrayed and murdered, you who received the law as delivered by angels and did not keep it. (Acts 7:51–53, ESV)

What the seed of the serpent typified in rejecting Joseph, Moses, and the Prophets, they fulfilled in what they did to Jesus, and they keep right on doing the same with the followers of Jesus, as attested by the similarities between the death of Stephen and the death of Jesus (Acts 7:54–60).

§6.4 Mark 12:1–12, Parable of the Wicked Tenants

Mark 12 presents Jesus evoking Isaiah's love song for the vineyard of his beloved (Isa 5:1–7). As Jesus begins to speak "in parables" (Mark 12:1), the shared vocabulary and theme from Isaiah 5 quickly becomes obvious: both passages speak of a "vineyard" (ἀμπελών, Mark 12:1; Isa 5:1–2), both describe it being "planted" (φυτεύω, Mark 12:1; Isa 5:2) and surrounded by a fence (φραγμὸν περιέθηκα, Isa 5:2; περιέθηκεν φραγμὸν, Mark 12:1) with a wine press dug into it (προλήνιον ὤρυξα, Isa 5:2; ὤρυξεν ὑπολήνιον, Mark 12:1) and a watchtower built for it (ᾠκοδόμησα πύργον, Isa 5:2; ᾠκοδόμησεν πύργον, Mark 12:1). In both cases the vineyard is Israel (Isa 5:7; Mark 12:12), but Jesus develops the parable by adding in the Jewish religious leaders as the tenants and the servants sent by the landowner as the prophets. Whereas Isaiah simply uses the love song to speak of the fruit Yahweh wanted Israel to bear, Jesus develops it to summarize the history of Israel.

In this history the tenants, the people of God, do not respond well to those sent to them by the landowner, the Lord. With the first emissary, they "beat him and sent him away empty-handed" (Mark 12:3, ESV). This may allude to Jeremiah 37:15 (ESV), where "the officials were enraged at Jeremiah, and they beat him and imprisoned him." In the Greek translation of this verse, they "sent" him to the prison, using the same verb for the sending of the servant away empty in Mark 12:3 (ἀποστέλλω, LXX Jer 44:15; ET Jer 37:15).

When the second servant sent from the landowner arrived, "they struck him on the head and treated him shamefully" (Mark 12:4, ESV). The third "they killed. And so with many others: some they beat, and some they killed" (12:5). Jezebel "cut off the prophets of Yahweh," with one hundred being hidden by Obadiah, in 1 Kings 18:4. Elijah references the prophets being killed by the sword in 1 Kings 19:10. The murder of the prophet Uriah the son Shemaiah is recounted in Jeremiah 26:20–23. Zechariah the son of Jehoiada was stoned in 2 Chronicles 24:20–22. As the Levites confess the sins of Israel in Nehemiah 9:5–38, their summary of the treatment of the prophets is like that offered by Jesus: "they were disobedient and rebelled against you and cast your law behind their back and killed your prophets, who had warned them in order to turn them back to you, and they committed great blasphemies" (Neh 9:26 ESV). The mistreatment and murder of others is recounted in Hebrews 11:36–37.

When Jesus says in Mark 12:6 (ESV), "He had still one other, a beloved son," the term rendered "beloved" (ἀγαπητόν) is the same used in the Greek translation of the reference to Isaac as Abraham's beloved son in Genesis 22:2. The term also appears in the Greek translation of the description of the weeping over the death of the only, firstborn son in Zechariah 12:10 (a verse cited in John 19:37 and Rev 1:7). This phrase forges a connection within Mark's Gospel to the baptism of Jesus, where the voice from heaven said, "You are my beloved Son; with you I am well pleased" (Mark 1:11). In Mark 12:6, by means of the phrase "beloved son," Mark presents Jesus identifying himself with Isaac and the slain firstborn of Zechariah 12:10, and in the parable, moreover, Jesus presents himself as the culmination of those whom Yahweh has sent to Israel.

In the story Jesus tells, the response of the tenants when they see this beloved son is to say, "Come, let us kill him" (Mark 12:7). This Greek phrase (δεῦτε ἀποκτείνωμεν αὐτόν) was used to translate the response of Joseph's brothers when they saw him in Genesis 37:20, and aside from there the only place the phrase occurs in the Bible is in the parable of the wicked tenants (Mark 12:7; Matt 21:38). By means of this phrase, Mark presents Jesus identifying himself with Joseph, suggesting that the people of Israel are responding to him the same way the sons of Jacob responded to their brother Joseph. The pattern comes to its culmination in Jesus.

Jesus explains the motivation of the wicked tenants (Mark 12:7), their murder of the beloved son (12:8), and then warns that the landowner will come against them in judgment (12:9). He then quotes Psalm 118:22–23 as a summary of the theme, and the religious leaders know exactly what he means (Mark 12:12).

Mark does not include the "Abel to Zechariah" saying, but shortly after Matthew presents Jesus telling the parable of the wicked tenants in Matthew 21:33–46, he presents Jesus saying in 23:29–36 (ESV),

> "Woe to you, scribes and Pharisees, hypocrites! For you build the tombs of the prophets and decorate the monuments of the righteous, saying, 'If we had lived in the days of our fathers, we would not have taken part with them in shedding the blood of the prophets.' Thus you witness against yourselves that you are sons of those who murdered the prophets. Fill up, then, the measure of your fathers. You serpents, you brood of vipers, how are you to escape being sentenced to hell? Therefore I send you prophets and wise men and scribes, some of whom you will kill and crucify, and some you will flog in your synagogues and persecute from town to town, so that on you may come all the righteous blood shed on earth, from the blood of righteous Abel to the blood of Zechariah the son of Barachiah, whom you murdered between the sanctuary and the altar. Truly, I say to you, all these things will come upon this generation."

§6.5 Acts 8:32–33, Quotation of Isaiah 53

I argued above that Isaiah's prophecy in Isaiah 52:13–53:12 arose in part from the prophet's meditation on patterns in earlier Scripture. That understanding seems to be confirmed by Luke's account in Acts 8:26–40. In this passage the angel of the Lord directs Philip to join the chariot of an Ethiopian eunuch (Acts 8:26–29). Philip hears him reading Isaiah, engages the eunuch in conversation, and the eunuch invites Philip to sit with him (8:30–31). Luke then notes that the passage being read was Isaiah 53:7–8, and Luke's presentation of the text corresponds to the Greek translation of the passage (Acts 8:32–33).

The eunuch asks if the prophet speaks of himself or someone else, and Luke summarizes Philip's explanation of the passage with the words, "Then Philip opened his mouth, and beginning with this Scripture he told him the good news about Jesus" (Acts 8:35, ESV). Philip's explanation of how the gospel of Jesus fulfills what Isaiah prophesied was so compelling that,

> as they were going along the road they came to some water, and the eunuch said, "See, here is water! What prevents me from being baptized?" And he commanded the chariot to stop, and they both went down into the water, Philip and the eunuch, and he baptized him. (8:36–37, ESV)

§6.6 John 3:14; 8:28; 12:32, 38, Isaiah's Servant Lifted Up

We considered aspects of the discussion between Jesus and Nicodemus in John 3 with reference to the allusion to Proverbs 30:4 in John 3:13 above (see §2.1–2.2 in Chapter 5). As Jesus seeks to awaken in Nicodemus an understanding of how the signs he does signal that he brings the kingdom of God (John 3:2–5), he refers to the lifting up of the bronze serpent and says, "so must the Son of Man be lifted up" (3:14).

There is a verbal link between the lifting up of the bronze serpent in Numbers 21:8–9 and "the root of Jesse, who shall stand as a signal for the peoples" in Isaiah 11:10 (ESV). When Numbers 21:8–9 describe the bronze serpent being set on a "pole," the term for pole (נֵס) is the same term rendered "signal" in Isaiah 11:10 (also in Isa 11:12). Perhaps as Isaiah prophesied the new exodus in Isaiah 11 he meant to place the root of Jesse in the role of the bronze serpent, the one to whom the nations would look and be saved (cf. 45:22).

We have also seen above that there are numerous points of contact between Isaiah 11 and Isaiah 52:13–53:12. It is not surprising then that Jesus would connect the lifting up of the Numbers 21 bronze serpent to the lifting up of the Isaiah 53 suffering servant. The connection with Isaiah 52:13 in John 3:14 is in the phrase "so must the Son of Man be lifted up," where the verb for "be lifted up" is the same used to render Isaiah 52:13 into Greek (ὑψόω). The "it is necessary" (δεῖ) in John 3:14, rendered by the ESV "must," seems to indicate that because the Old Testament says the Son of Man will be lifted up, it is necessary for it to happen.

The connection between the bronze serpent, the Isaiah 11:10 root of Jesse, and the lifting up (ὑψόω) of the Son of Man in John 3:14 is reiterated in John 8:28, where Jesus declares, "When you have lifted up the Son of Man, then you will know that I am . . ." An even stronger link between John and Isaiah comes in John 12. The coming of Greeks to see Jesus prompts Jesus to declare that "the hour has come for the Son of Man to be glorified" (12:20–23), and the term rendered "glorified" also appears in the Greek translation of Isaiah 52:13 (passive forms of δοξάζω). Jesus then proceeds to talk about his death (12:24–31), concluding with the words, "And I, when I am lifted up from the earth, will draw all people to myself" (12:32, ESV). With these words Jesus presents himself as the Isaiah 11:10 "root of Jesse, who shall stand as a signal for the peoples," and he declares that the "lifting up" of the Son of Man like the bronze serpent on the pole will be realized as he is "glorified" by his death in fulfillment of Isaiah 52:13–53:12.

As if to make certain that his readers do not miss these connections with Isaiah, John quotes Isaiah 53:1 and 6:10 in John 12:38–40, prefacing the quotations with the words, "so that the word spoken by the prophet Isaiah might be fulfilled" (John 12:38a). The quotation from Isaiah 53:1 then asks who believed, to whom it was revealed (12:38b), and then the quotation from Isaiah 6:10 explains why "they could not believe. For again Isaiah said" that their eyes would be blinded and their hearts hardened (12:39–40). John seems to offer these texts to explain how the Jews could reject their Messiah so that he could fulfill the typological pattern of the suffering servant, writing in 12:41 (ESV), "Isaiah said these things because he saw his glory and spoke of him."

§6.7 1 Peter 1:10–11; 2:22–25, First Suffering Then Glory

Peter succinctly describes the righteous sufferer theme when he comments on the activity of the Old Testament authors with the words,

> Concerning this salvation, the prophets who prophesied about the grace that was to be yours searched and inquired carefully, inquiring what person or time the Spirit of Christ in them was indicating when he predicted the sufferings of Christ and the subsequent glories. (1 Pet 1:10–12, ESV)

In his mysterious providence, God sovereignly worked in history so that his people chose to reject those whom God raised up to accomplish their deliverance. Through that rejection—through Joseph being sold as a slave into Egypt, through Moses spending forty years in the wilderness, through David learning to trust the Lord through persecution, through the culminating crucifixion of the Messiah—God worked deliverance for his people. Betrayed, rejected, persevering in faith, the Lord's servant Jesus was exalted to reign like Joseph, refined in character like Moses and David, and then raised from the dead and seated at the right hand of power.

PART 2

EVENTS

The two events to be discussed in this section are creation (Chapter 7) and the exodus (Chapter 8), and a bit has been said about each already. God's works of creation and salvation are juxtaposed prominently in places like Psalm 136 and Hebrews 11 (and elsewhere). With both creation and the exodus, the event becomes a predictive paradigm and an interpretive schema. The original creation provides the pattern for the new creation (e.g., 2 Cor 5:17), and the way God worked at creation, accomplishing the work by his word, provides a paradigm for understanding how God saves (e.g., 2 Cor 4:6) and renews (cf. the term παλιγγενεσία, "regeneration," Matt 19:28 and Titus 3:5). Similarly, the exodus becomes a predictive paradigm: God will save in the future as he did in the past. And it is also an interpretive schema: in Psalms 18 and 34 David employs imagery from the exodus to describe the way God worked to deliver him, and the New Testament everywhere uses the concepts and terminology provided by the exodus to explain the salvation Jesus accomplished through his death and resurrection, opening the way to the new creation.

CREATION

The Old Testament, on the contrary, is dominated by an essen-
tially different form of typological thinking, namely, that of the
eschatological correspondence between beginning and end
(*Urzeit* und *Endzeit*).

— GERHARD VON RAD[1]

This chapter is in Part 2 of this book, which is concerned with Events,
because creation is an *event* accomplished by God. At the same time, once
God has accomplished the creation of the world, it becomes the setting for the
cosmic drama, the stage on which he tells his story. In this project's chiastic
structure, the current chapter on Creation stands across from Chapter 5 on
Kings because God made Adam king of creation, a role that the new Adam
will enact when God puts all his enemies under his feet (cf. 1 Cor 15:25–28).

The thesis of this chapter is that the original creation typifies the new creation,
and thus creation and new creation are the outer steps of the current chapter's
pedimental structure: for the world God created at the beginning portends the
new one at the end. The second and second to last stairs are the tabernacle and
temple on the front end and the church as the new temple on the back. At the
center of this chapter's structure stands Christ as the fulfillment of the temple:[2]

---

1. Gerhard von Rad, "Typological Interpretation of the Old Testament," in *Essays on Old Testament
Interpretation*, 19.

2. In my original plan for this book, a chapter on judgment as de-creation would follow this chapter
on creation. Time and space constraints prevented me from being able to write both that chapter and the
one that would stand across from it in the book's chiastic structure on the way false prophets typify and
build toward the antichrist (which would have gone between the chapters on prophets and kings). Thus
the chapter on those to be judged would stand across from the chapter on judgment, and the chapter on
judgment as de-creation would have pursued, among much else, Peter's presentation of the judgment of

§1 The Creation of the Cosmic Temple
    §2 The Tabernacle and Temple as Microcosms
        §3 Christ the Fulfillment of the Temple
    §4 The Church as the Temple of the Holy Spirit
§5 The Cosmic Temple of the New Creation

God made the world as a place where he would be known by and present with his creatures as they worship, enjoy, honor, and serve him. We have a word for a place where God dwells, where he is present, known, served, and worshiped. We call such a place a *temple*.

God created the world as a cosmic temple, and the rebellion of God's creatures brought defilement into the holy place. Our focus in this chapter is on the setting for the Bible's storyline: creation as a cosmic temple. From the archetypal creation narrated in Genesis 1–2, through the ectypal installments seen first in the tabernacle and camp of Israel and then in the temple and land, the creation of the cosmic temple creates a context in which God can walk with man, and man can walk with God (Gen 3:8; Lev 26:11–12; Deut 23:14).

In the garden, God is present and there is no sin. Once man sins, for God to be present atonement for sin must be made. These comprise the controlling realities for tabernacle and temple in the Old Testament: 1) God is present there; and 2) there sacrifice for sin is made. And thus Christ fulfills tabernacle and temple through his incarnation: he *is* the place where God is present and walks with man, and at the cross sacrifice for sin is made. When Jesus gives the Spirit to his disciples (John 20:22), he gives them authority to forgive sin and constitutes them as the new temple, indwelt by the Holy Spirit (1 Cor 3:16). Once all is accomplished, God will make the new creation a cosmic temple, and the dwelling place of God will be with man (Rev 21:3).

This chapter seeks a typological understanding of the answer to the question, "How do the biblical authors understand and portray the *setting* of the Bible's big story?" The short answer is: from cosmic temple, through literal tabernacle/temple to Christ as the fulfillment of the temple and then the church as the already/not yet temple, to consummation when the new creation will be the temple with Jerusalem as the holy of holies. In the beginning God typified the end.[3]

---

the world by water at the flood, to be matched by the judgment of the world by fire for the making of the new heavens and new earth (2 Pet 3:5–13).

3. Similarly Michael Morales, "Life with God in the house of God—this was the original goal of

§1 THE CREATION OF THE COSMIC TEMPLE

When God made the world he spoke his cosmic dwelling place into being. In my view Moses, author of Genesis, also wrote the narratives in Exodus concerning the instructions for and the building of the tabernacle, and he intended to communicate the correspondences we see in those narratives between creation and tabernacle. Later biblical authors noticed these correspondences and spoke of creation as a cosmic temple. For instance, in Psalm 78:69 (ESV), Asaph says of the Lord, "He built his sanctuary like the high heavens, like the earth, which he has founded forever." The comparison of the sanctuary (temple) with the heavens and the earth reflects the view that the temple (which replaced and was modeled on the tabernacle) is a small-scale replica of the cosmos, a microcosm. Similarly, Isaiah speaks as though the whole earth is the ark of the covenant in the holy of holies when he writes, "Thus says the Lord, 'Heaven is my throne, and the earth is my footstool; what is the house that you would build for me, and what is the place of my rest?'" (Isa 66:1, ESV).[4]

Isaiah 66:1 makes three points relevant for us here. First, the Lord asks what *house* (בית, i.e., temple, cf. 2 Sam 7:1–7) his people would build for him, and the question assumes that Yahweh has constructed creation as his temple. Second, the query about the *house* his people would build for him is set in parallel with a question about the *place of his rest*, indicating that God's cosmic temple is the place of his rest, which is exactly what we find in Genesis 2:1–4.[5] Having completed his cosmic palace, King Yahweh takes his repose in the *place of his rest*.[6] Third, the reference to the earth as Yahweh's footstool associates it with the ark of the covenant in the holy of holies, which is very suggestive when we consider questions such as *the purpose* of Yahweh's creation and *the requirements* for clean holiness in his presence. These questions reveal assumptions the biblical authors seem to reflect in their statements about the

---

the creation of the cosmos (which, as we will see, may be thought of as a house), and which then became the goal of redemption, the new creation." *Who Shall Ascend the Mountain of the Lord?*, 17.

4. For the ark as Yahweh's footstool, see Pss 99:5; 132:7; Lam 2:1; 1 Chr 28:2; (cf. 2 Chr 9:18). For the cherubim overshadowing the ark/mercy seat in the holy of holies, see Exod 25:20, 22; 37:9; 1 Chr 28:18; 2 Chr 5:8; Heb 9:5. For Yahweh enthroned above the cherubim, see Num 7:89; 1 Sam 4:4; 2 Sam 6:2 (//1 Chr 13:6); 2 Kgs 19:15; Isa 37:16; Ps 80:1; 99:1.

5. Beale discusses temples as places of rest in the Bible and in ancient Near Eastern literature in G. K. Beale, *The Temple and the Church's Mission: A Biblical Theology of the Dwelling Place of God*, New Studies in Biblical Theology 17 (Downers Grove, IL: InterVarsity, 2004), 60–66.

6. The same idea—of a king taking up residence in a place of rest after establishing his reign—can be seen in Isaiah 11:10 (ESV), ". . . and his resting place shall be glorious."

setting of their story. The biblical authors understand what God did at the beginning to indicate what he will achieve at the end.

§1.1 The Beginning a Preview of the End

God created the world, his cosmic temple, as the realm of life. Having made, formed, and filled the nonexistent, shapeless, void (Gen 1:2, 3–31), the temple teems with living things (1:20–21, 24–25), all of which are blessed by God and commanded to be fruitful and multiply (1:22, 28). All is very good (1:31), and in view of what develops, all being very good implies specifically that in God's cosmic temple there is no transgression, no rebellion, no sin against the holy creator: and if no sin then no death. All uncleanness flows from and is related to *contact with death*. Where there is no sin there is no death, and where there is no death there is no uncleanness. God created a clean realm of life.

In his clean and holy temple of life, God put his image and likeness (Gen 1:26–28). The image of God serves the same purpose in the cosmic temple that the forbidden images of false gods serve in temples devoted to their worship: the image represents the character, presence, authority, and reign of the unseen deity. God put man into the cosmic temple as his vice-regent: "You have given him dominion over the works of your hands; you have put all things under his feet" (Ps 8:6, ESV). With the woman, the man is to "be fruitful and multiply and fill the earth and subdue it, and have dominion" (Gen 1:28, ESV). The man is placed in the garden of Eden (2:15), and the command to "fill the earth and subdue it" (1:28) indicates that he is to make all the dry lands like the garden, a clean realm of life where God walks in the cool of the day with his image bearers (3:8). Obedience to God's commands will fill creation with the image and likeness of God, making it so that God's character, presence, authority, and reign are brought to bear in the whole of the cosmic temple. Thus will the glory of God cover the dry lands as the waters cover the sea (Hab 2:14).

§1.2 Correspondences between Eden and Tabernacle/Temple

The garden of Eden is almost like the holy of holies. The garden seems to be set within a wider region known as Eden, for the "river flowed out of Eden to water the garden" (Gen 2:10). Just as the camp of Israel centered on the holy of holies, with descending requirements for holiness as one moved out to the holy place and from there to the camp, so at the center of creation we have the garden holy of holies, the holy place of Eden, and outside the region of Eden all the dry lands.[7] Like the tabernacle and temple, where gold and precious stones were abundant, good gold and precious stones mark Eden (2:11–12). The lampstand of the tabernacle and temple seem to symbolize the sacred trees of Eden (2:8–9), and the showbread points to the abundant food of which the man could freely eat (2:16). The man's job in the garden is the same given to the Levites at the tabernacle: to work and keep it (2:15; cf. Num 3:8). And as Yahweh promised to walk among the people once they had the tabernacle (Lev 26:11–12; Deut 23:14), so he walked in the garden (Gen 3:8).[8]

There is, however, a prohibition that comes with a warning: "but of the tree of the knowledge of good and evil you shall not eat, for in the day that you eat of it you shall surely die" (Gen 2:17, ESV). Prohibition: do not eat of that tree; warning: if you do you die. Human sin will bring death into the world. Man sins, and death results. The man and woman die spiritually when they transgress, as evidenced by their hiding from God and one another (3:7–8). As God speaks words of judgment over them, he gives a promise of hope (3:15) but also states that they will die (3:19) and drives them out of the clean realm of life, the garden of Eden, into the unclean realm of the dead (3:22–23).

The cherubim and a flaming sword guarding the way to the tree of life in Genesis 3:24 anticipate the cherubim woven into the fabrics of the tabernacle and overshadowing the ark of the covenant. Similarly, Balaam encounters the angel with drawn sword, and Joshua meets the captain of Yahweh's hosts. In each case the one who encounters the cherubim or angel is coming toward Yahweh's place of rest from the east.

Because of what we will see regarding the "mountain of God" as we proceed, we should also note what Ezekiel says about the king of Tyre (Ezek 28:11–19). In this passage Ezekiel addresses the human king of Tyre, and he does so using imagery and terms that apply to "that ancient serpent, who is called the devil and Satan" (Rev 12:9, ESV). Ezekiel employs imagery having to do with heavenly beings (cherub) and the primordial garden (Eden) to speak of the king of Tyre to identify him with the rebellious heavenly being who introduced temptation into that pristine setting. The imagery marks the king of Tyre as the seed of the serpent, offspring of his father the devil (cf. John 8:44). In Ezekiel 28:13–14 (ESV) the prophet asserts:

---

7. Beale, *The Temple and the Church's Mission*, 74–75.
8. Wenham, "Sanctuary Symbolism."

You were in Eden, the garden of God; every precious stone was your covering, sardius, topaz, and diamond, beryl, onyx, and jasper, sapphire, emerald,
and carbuncle; and crafted in gold were your settings and your engravings.
On the day that you were created they were prepared. You were an anointed
guardian cherub. I placed you; you were on the holy mountain of God; in
the midst of the stones of fire you walked.

What Ezekiel says here to the king of Tyre reflects what he has learned
from earlier Scripture about the garden of Eden and Satan, and his application of this Satanic imagery to the king of Tyre reflects typological thinking:
the king of Tyre is the *type* of person Satan is.

What do Ezekiel's words to the king of Tyre show us about his father the
devil? This "anointed guardian cherub" (28:14) was "in Eden." As the cherub
was to guard Eden, so Adam and the priests were to guard Eden, tabernacle, and
temple. Second, this cherub was "anointed" (מִמְשַׁח) for his duties in Eden, just as
the priests were "anointed" (e.g., Exod 28:41, מָשַׁח) for their duties at tabernacle
and temple. Third, the list of stones that were the "covering" for this "cherub"
(28:13–14) are the same stones to be used for the priests' garments (Exod 28).

Ezekiel 28:13 (ESV)	Exodus 28:17–20 (ESV)
sardius, topaz, and diamond, beryl, onyx, and jasper, sapphire, emerald, and carbuncle; and crafted in gold were your settings and your engravings.	. . . sardius, topaz, and carbuncle . . . an emerald, a sapphire, and a diamond; . . . a jacinth, an agate, and an amethyst; . . . a beryl, an onyx, and a jasper. They shall be set in gold filigree.

Fourth, and most significant for this chapter, note that "in Eden, the
garden of God" (Ezek 28:13) this cherub was "on the holy mountain of God"
(Ezek 28:14). This indicates that when Ezekiel thought of the garden of Eden,
on the basis of the Scripture available to him, he thought of a mountain of God.

§2 THE TABERNACLE AND TEMPLE AS MICROCOSMS

The garden of Eden points to the new creation, but on the way we have ectypal
installments in the pattern. Here we consider the ways the tabernacle and the

temple point back to Eden and forward to the new creation as attempts to reestablish what was lost when man was driven from God's clean realm of life.

§2.1 The Tabernacle and Creation

Prior to sin, man was both clean and holy and could thus dwell in God's presence in his temple of life, the holy of holies of the garden of Eden. After sin, man filled the earth not with God's character but with violence (Gen 6:11). God did not renounce his program or destroy his world but chose Israel as a people for his own possession. His promise of land to Abraham and his seed in Genesis 12:7 (cf. 12:1–3) announces that through the blessing of Abraham God intends to reclaim the land cursed because of sin (3:17). God means to put his people in his place where they will enjoy fellowship with him as they live according to his law. In the same way that the storming of the beaches of Normandy was the beginning of the Allied capture of Fortress Europe, the promise of land to Abraham begins God's recapture of Fortress Earth, which he will take back from the prince of the power of the air.

To make it so that Israel could dwell in his presence, God gave them the tabernacle and the Levitical cult, whose function we will consider further in Part 3 (Chapter 9) of this book. Here we focus on the way that God's provision of tabernacle and sacrificial system makes the camp of Israel the realm of life where God dwells in the holy of holies.

In view of what we just observed regarding Eden as a holy mountain in Ezekiel 28:13–14, we note that the angel of Yahweh appears to Moses in the burning bush at "Horeb, the mountain of God" (Exod 3:1–2). Along these lines, as the people celebrate Yahweh's victory over Egypt in exodus and Red Sea (Exod 15:1–12), they turn to the conquest of Canaan (15:13–18). In Exodus 15:13 (ESV) the land is referred to as the Lord's "holy abode," and Exodus 15:17 speaks of it as a new garden of Eden:

> You will bring them in and plant them on your own mountain, the place,
> O Lord, which you have made for your abode, the sanctuary, O Lord, which
> your hands have established. (Exod 15:17, ESV)

Exodus 15:17 indicates that Yahweh made the land of promise the same way he made creation: as his mountainous sanctuary, his abode, the place his hands built where he would plant his people and make a home with them.[9]

---

9. So also Dempster, *Dominion and Dynasty*, 100.

Yahweh then meets with Israel at Mount Sinai/Horeb (Exod 19), where Moses ascends the mount and receives both the stipulations of the covenant and the instructions for the tabernacle. Once the tabernacle has been constructed, Yahweh takes up residence therein. The similarities in phraseology between the narratives of the creation of the world and the building of the tabernacle indicate that the author of the narratives intended his audience to associate the two building projects with one another.[10] Moses structures the presentation of the Lord's giving of the instructions for the building of the tabernacle such that his audience is reminded of the Lord's speaking creation into existence: as can be seen on Table 7.1, the seven *God said let there be* statements in the creation account are matched by the seven instances of *the Lord said to Moses* in the account of the instructions for the tabernacle (translations in Tables 7.1 and 7.2 follow the ESV).

TABLE 7.1: God Spoke Creation and Tabernacle Instructions

Genesis, Creation	Exodus, Tabernacle
1. Gen 1:3, "And God said, 'Let there be . . .'"	Exod 25:1, "The Lord said to Moses" וַיְדַבֵּר יְהוָה אֶל־מֹשֶׁה לֵּאמֹר
2. Gen 1:6, "And God said, 'Let there be . . .'"	Exod 30:11, "The Lord said to Moses" וַיְדַבֵּר יְהוָה אֶל־מֹשֶׁה לֵּאמֹר
3. Gen 1:9, "And God said, 'Let the waters be . . .'"	Exod 30:17, "The Lord said to Moses" וַיְדַבֵּר יְהוָה אֶל־מֹשֶׁה לֵּאמֹר
4. Gen 1:11, "And God said, 'Let the earth sprout . . .'"	Exod 30:22, "The Lord said to Moses" וַיְדַבֵּר יְהוָה אֶל־מֹשֶׁה לֵּאמֹר
5. Gen 1:14, "And God said, 'Let there be . . .'"	Exod 30:34, "The Lord said to Moses" וַיֹּאמֶר יְהוָה אֶל־מֹשֶׁה
6. Gen 1:20, "And God said, 'Let the waters swarm . . .'"	Exod 31:1, "The Lord said to Moses" וַיְדַבֵּר יְהוָה אֶל־מֹשֶׁה לֵּאמֹר
7. Gen 1:24, "And God said, 'Let the earth bring forth . . .'"[11]	Exod 31:12, "the Lord said to Moses" וַיֹּאמֶר יְהוָה אֶל־מֹשֶׁה לֵּאמֹר

---

10. For a similar discussion that makes many of the same points independently, see Morales, *Who Shall Ascend the Mountain of the Lord?*, 40–42, 100–103.

11. The phrase "And God said" appears ten times in Genesis 1. Only the first seven instances appear above because these seven are followed by the same kinds of statements while the last three (Gen 1:26, 28, 29) are followed by different phrases. These final three instances, moreover, all relate to God's creation of

Similarly, as can be seen on Table 7.2, Moses describes the completion of the tabernacle building project so that his audience is reminded of the completion of creation:

TABLE 7.2: Completion of Creation and Tabernacle

Genesis, Creation	Exodus, Tabernacle
Gen 1:31, "**And God saw everything** that he had **made, and behold**, it was very good. And there was evening and there was morning, the sixth day." וַיַּרְא אֱלֹהִים אֶת־כָּל־אֲשֶׁר עָשָׂה וְהִנֵּה־טוֹב מְאֹד	Exod 39:43, "**And Moses saw all** the work, **and behold**, they had **done** it; as the LORD had commanded, so had they done it. Then Moses blessed them." וַיַּרְא מֹשֶׁה אֶת־כָּל־הַמְּלָאכָה וְהִנֵּה עָשׂוּ אֹתָהּ
Gen 2:1, "**Thus the heavens and the earth were finished**, and all the host of them." וַיְכֻלּוּ הַשָּׁמַיִם וְהָאָרֶץ וְכָל־צְבָאָם	Exod 39:32, "**Thus all the work of the tabernacle of the tent of meeting was finished**, and the people of Israel did according to all that the LORD had commanded Moses; so they did." וַתֵּכֶל כָּל־עֲבֹדַת מִשְׁכַּן אֹהֶל מוֹעֵד
Gen 2:2, "And on the seventh day **God finished his work** that he had done, and he rested on the seventh day from all his work that he had done." וַיְכַל אֱלֹהִים בַּיּוֹם הַשְּׁבִיעִי מְלַאכְתּוֹ	Exod 40:33, "And he erected the court around the tabernacle and the altar, and set up the screen of the gate of the court. **So Moses finished the work**." וַיְכַל מֹשֶׁה אֶת־הַמְּלָאכָה
Gen 2:3, "**So God blessed the seventh day** and made it holy, because on it God rested from all his work that he had done in creation." וַיְבָרֶךְ אֱלֹהִים אֶת־יוֹם הַשְּׁבִיעִי	Exod 39:43, "And Moses saw all the work, and behold, they had done it; as the LORD had commanded, so had they done it. **Then Moses blessed them**." וַיְבָרֶךְ אֹתָם מֹשֶׁה

Within the instructions for the tabernacle, perhaps the most noticeable symbols from Eden were the bread of the presence (Exod 25:30), which

---

mankind. In the seven instances of "And God said" on the chart above, the phrases that follow are jussive singulars ("Let there be"). That pattern is broken in 1:26 when God for the first time utters a first-person plural cohortative ("Let us make").

matched the abundant food in the garden, the blossoming tree description of the lampstand (25:31–40), which matched the trees of the garden, recalling those of life and of the knowledge of good and evil, and of course the pervasive cherubim (e.g., 26:1).[12]

Once the tabernacle has been built, Yahweh takes up residence within it (Exod 40:34–35), previewing the way that he will fill the cosmic temple of the new creation with his glory (e.g., Num 14:21; Hab 2:14). Yahweh's presence requires the sanctification of the people, as he states plainly in Leviticus 11:44–45, offering his own holiness as the reason Israel must be holy:

> For I am the LORD your God. Consecrate yourselves therefore, and be holy, for I am holy. You shall not defile yourselves with any swarming thing that crawls on the ground. For I am the LORD who brought you up out of the land of Egypt to be your God. You shall therefore be holy, for I am holy. (Lev 11:44–45, ESV)

Yahweh made a holy and clean realm of life and put man over it as his vice-regent. Man sinned, defiled the holy place, and brought unclean death into God's realm. God banished man from Eden and initiated a program that would make the defiled clean, the impure holy, and the dead live. We will consider the function of the Leviticult and the Sinai covenant in Chapter 9, here we move from the way these considerations inform the tabernacle to the way they shed light on the camp.

§2.2 The Camp of Israel as a New Eden

From the way that the concept under discussion here—that the tabernacle and camp of Israel are a new garden of Eden—makes sense of what Moses narrates, it seems that Moses took this idea for granted, that the idea that a tabernacle or temple was a small-scale representation of the cosmos was so common in Moses's time that he had no need to spell it out. He could assume that all members of his audience would understand these ideas, and he could write his narrative taking the shared understanding for granted.[13]

Balaam will approach the camp of Israel from the east (Num 22:5), and

---

12. Cf. Dempster, *Dominion and Dynasty*, 102–3.
13. See Beale's discussion of temple symbolism in the ancient Near East in Beale, *The Temple and the Church's Mission*, 50–60.

on the way he encounters "the angel of the LORD standing in the road, with a drawn sword in his hand" (22:23, 31, ESV). This angel recalls the cherubim and flaming sword placed at the east of Eden to guard the way to the tree of life in Genesis 3:24. Balaam's description of the camp of Israel in Numbers 24:5–6 moves along similar Eden-tabernacle-imagery lines. In verse 5 Balaam exclaims, "How lovely are your tents, O Jacob, your encampments, O Israel!" And then in verse 6 Balaam compares those tents and encampments to a garden planted by Yahweh: "Like palm groves that stretch afar, like gardens beside a river, like aloes that the LORD has planted, like cedar trees beside the waters." The terminology of Numbers 24:6 recalls that of Genesis 2:8–10 (ESV).

Genesis 2:8, 10	Numbers 24:6
"And the LORD God **planted** (נָטַע) a **garden** (גַּן) in Eden, in the east, . . . A **river** (נָהָר) flowed out of Eden to water the **garden**, and there it divided and became four rivers."	"Like palm groves that stretch afar, like **gardens** (גַּנָּה) beside a **river** (נָהָר), like aloes that the LORD has **planted** (נָטַע), like cedar trees beside the waters."

When he took up residence in the tabernacle, Yahweh constituted the camp of Israel as the realm of life, just as Eden had been at the beginning. This understanding is reflected in Leviticus 26:11–12 and Deuteronomy 23:14, both of which describe Yahweh walking in the camp of Israel as he walked in the garden (with the verb הָלַךְ in the *hithpael* stem, texts here ESV):

Gen 3:8, "And they heard the sound of the LORD God walking (מִתְהַלֵּךְ) in the garden."

Lev 26:12, "And I will walk (וְהִתְהַלַּכְתִּי) among you."

Deut 23:14 [MT 23:15], "Because the LORD your God walks (מִתְהַלֵּךְ) in the midst of your camp."

The idea of the Lord walking in the midst of his people (again the verb הָלַךְ in the *hithpael* stem) reappears when David wants to build the temple in 2 Samuel 7:6–7 (ESV), where the Lord is presented saying, ". . . I have been moving about (מִתְהַלֵּךְ) in a tent for my dwelling. In all places where I have moved (הִתְהַלַּכְתִּי) with all the people of Israel . . ." These references in 2 Samuel 7 point to the way God has related to his people while dwelling in the tabernacle (even after they have conquered the land), and we find similar references regarding his presence among the people once the temple has been built.

§2.3 The Land of Israel as a New Eden

Moses not only speaks of the garden of Eden and the camp of Israel as the land of life where Yahweh dwells, he speaks the same way of the land of promise. How does the promise of land function in the Bible's story? The territory pledged to Abraham is the place where God means to resume fellowship and dwell among those with whom he has entered into covenant, beginning the process of regaining what was lost when mankind was driven from the garden of Eden. God works toward the solution to the problem of his image-bearers being driven from the land of life at expulsion from Eden by vouchsafing the land to Abraham—a strip of ground that points beyond itself to the recapture of the whole world (cf. Rom 4:13).

In the Exodus 15 Song of the Sea, Moses makes a statement that connects the land of promise with Yahweh's other mountain redoubts: "You will bring them in and plant them on your own mountain, the place, O LORD, which you have made for your abode, the sanctuary, O Lord, which your hands have established" (Exod 15:17, ESV). The garden of Eden was a mountain sanctuary (Ezek 28:13–14). Altars, ziggurats, and other "tower" like structures (such as the one at Babel, Gen 11) were likely attempts to recreate access to God through his mountain. Something like this seems to have been Jacob's experience when he saw the angels of God ascending and descending on a "ladder" (so ESV, NIV: "stairway") with Yahweh himself there (Gen 28:12), in response to which he exclaimed, "Surely Yahweh is in this place . . . How awesome is this place! This is none other than the house of God, and this is the gate of heaven" (28:16–17). Moses and the nation of Israel met Yahweh at Horeb, the Mountain of God (Exod 3, 19). Exodus 15:17 identifies the land of promise as Yahweh's "own mountain," and once they enter the land, the temple is built on Mount Zion.

Yahweh was specially present at Mount Sinai—it was the mountain of God—when Moses received the Ten Commandments, the instructions for the building of the tabernacle, and the teaching in Leviticus (cf. Exod 19:1–2; Num 10:11–12). Once Israel entered the land and the threshing floor of Araunah was identified as the place where the temple would be built (2 Sam 24:15–25), that location became the place where Yahweh was specially present. Because the Torah of Moses, and probably the growing collection of sacred writings, were likely kept at the temple,[14] just as the word of the Lord went forth from Mount Sinai (cf. Exod 19–20), so it went forth from Mount Zion (cf. Isa 2:3). This means that what Sinai signified was transferred to Zion, so that David can assert in Psalm 68:17 (ESV), "Sinai is now in the sanctuary." The most significant thing about Mount Sinai—that it was the place at which God's people encountered him, from which he announced his Torah to his people—now accrues to Mount Zion and the temple to be built there. After the assertion that "Sinai is now in the sanctuary" in 68:17, David says words that recall Moses leading Israel out of Egypt to Mount Sinai, where the freewill offerings were used to build the tabernacle: "You ascended on high, leading a host of captives in your train and receiving gifts among men, even among the rebellious, that the LORD God may dwell there" (Ps 68:18, ESV).

The host of captives seems to be the nation of Israel, and the one leading them and ascending on high and receiving gifts could be either Yahweh or Moses, Yahweh's representative. The reception of the gifts is "that the LORD God may dwell there," seeming to point to the use of the plunder taken from Egypt in the building of the tabernacle, God's dwelling place.

Why would David juxtapose Psalm 68:17 with 68:18? We get help answering this question from 1 Chronicles 29:1–6, where David details how he has provided for the building of the temple and calls for and collects freewill offerings from Israel:

And David the king said to all the assembly, "Solomon my son, whom alone God has chosen, is young and inexperienced, and the work is great, for the palace will not be for man but for the LORD God. So I have provided for the house of my God, so far as I was able, the gold for the things of gold, the silver for the things of silver, and the bronze for the things of bronze, the iron for the things of iron, and wood for the things of wood, besides great quantities of onyx and stones for setting, antimony, colored stones, all sorts

---

14. Milton C. Fisher, "The Canon of the Old Testament," in *The Expositor's Bible Commentary*, ed. Frank E. Gaebelein, 12 vols. (Grand Rapids: Zondervan, 1979), 1:387; Roger T. Beckwith, *The Old Testament Canon of the New Testament Church and Its Background in Early Judaism* (Grand Rapids: Eerdmans, 1985), 80–86.

of precious stones and marble. Moreover, in addition to all that I have provided for the holy house, I have a treasure of my own of gold and silver, and
because of my devotion to the house of my God I give it to the house of my
God: 3,000 talents of gold, of the gold of Ophir, and 7,000 talents of refined
silver, for overlaying the walls of the house, and for all the work to be done
by craftsmen, gold for the things of gold and silver for the things of silver.
Who then will offer willingly, consecrating himself today to the LORD?"
Then the leaders of fathers' houses made their freewill offerings, as did also
the leaders of the tribes, the commanders of thousands and of hundreds, and
the officers over the king's work. (1 Chr 29:1–6, ESV)

Where did David get all this wealth? At least some of it came from the
plunder of his enemies (cf., e.g., 1 Sam 30:26). This passage from Chronicles
indicates that just as Israel plundered Egypt at the exodus and made freewill
offerings for the building of the tabernacle, David plundered his enemies and
stored up the wealth that Solomon might build the temple.

Thus, having spoken of how "Sinai is now in the sanctuary" in Psalm
68:17, David alludes to the freewill offerings made from the plunder of Egypt
in 68:18 because he too has plundered his enemies and made provision for
the building of the temple. As God walked with man in the garden on the
mountain in Eden, so God met Israel at Mount Sinai, before bringing them to
his own mountain, Zion, where he planted his people in the land, as though
they themselves were trees in his holy preserve.

Paul quotes Psalm 68:18 in Ephesians 4:8, and whereas Psalm 68:18 speaks
of the "receiving" of gifts, Ephesians 4:8 speaks of the "giving" of gifts. This
discrepancy is insignificant: Moses received the gifts on Yahweh's behalf, and
the craftsmen built the tabernacle, which was then entrusted, i.e., given, to
Israel. The points of contact between tabernacle, temple, and church in the
quotation of Psalm 68:18 in Ephesians 4:8 fall out as follows.

- After the exodus, Israel plundered Egypt, and at Mount Sinai the people
  gave freewill offerings from the plunder of the enemy for the building
  of the temple.
- Along similar lines, David gave victory to Israel over all her surrounding enemies, plundering the enemies and amassing great wealth for
  Solomon to use in the building of the temple.

- Jesus Christ came as the typological fulfillment of Moses, David, and Solomon, and in his death and resurrection he accomplished the new and greater exodus, binding the strong man and plundering his house. The plunder of the enemy that Christ took was *people*, and those people give themselves as freewill offerings on the day of his power (cf. Ps 110:3). Christ gives them gifts—and gives them as gifts (Eph 4:8, 11)—and they give themselves, and the plunder of the enemy is used for the building of the temple of the Holy Spirit, the church (4:12, 16).

§2.4 The Temple and Creation

The vast topic of the correspondence between Israel's temple and creation will be simplified into five points for this discussion. First, we see creation imagery in the account of the building of the temple in 1 Kings 6–8. Second, in texts like Psalm 29, the Lord's "temple" seems to be all creation. Third, there are passages that speak of a new creation and passages that speak of dwelling in Yahweh's "house" forever (Ps 23:6), and the idea that the creation is the Lord's house would make sense of these statements. Fourth, the "tent" and "room" imagery for creation (Ps 104:2–3) fits with this way of thinking. And fifth, again, the promises of a new creation fit with Old Testament indications that Yahweh will fill his temple with glory (Hag 2:7). These five points form a chiasm:

§2.4.1 Creation Imagery and Temple Filled with Glory in 1 Kings 6–8
   §2.4.2 All Creation God's Temple in Psalm 29
      §2.4.3 To Dwell in God's House Forever in Psalm 23
   §2.4.4 Tent and Room Imagery for Creation in Psalm 104
§2.4.5 I Will Fill This House with Glory in Haggai 2:7

A brief word on each of these:

§2.4.1 Creation Imagery and Temple Filled with Glory in 1 Kings 6–8

In the narrative of the building of the temple we read of cherubim (e.g., 1 Kgs 6:23–28), palm trees and open flowers (6:29, 32, 35), pomegranates and lily-work (7:18–19, 20, 22, 42), a massive "sea" (7:23–25), gourds (7:24), the flower of a lily (7:26), lions and oxen (7:25, 29, 36, 44), more palm trees (7:36), more flowers (7:49), and of course the tree-like lampstands (7:49). In addition to all this creation imagery, Solomon was exactly seven years in building the temple (6:37–38). Once built, as with the tabernacle so with the temple: the glory of Yahweh filled the house so the priests could not stand to minister (8:10–11).[15]

§2.4.2 All Creation God's Temple in Psalm 29

With the voice of Yahweh over the waters (Ps 29:3) and Yahweh enthroned over the flood (29:10), Psalm 29 reads like a description of God's judgment of the world at the flood of Noah. As Yahweh's majestic voice (29:4) breaks cedars (29:5), making shattered tree trunks from cedars of Lebanon skip around like calves (29:6), making the very wilderness shake (29:8) and panicking deer so they go into labor and give birth (29:9a), David summarizes all creation's response to Yahweh's powerful voice with the words, "and in his temple all cry, 'Glory!'" (29:9b, ESV). In context, the "all" who are "in his temple" crying "glory" are the waters and cedars, the calves and deer—all affected by the floodwaters of Yahweh's almighty justice.

§2.4.3 To Dwell in God's House Forever in Psalm 23

Within the book of Psalms we find indications that Yahweh will accomplish a new creation. For instance, in 102:25 he laid the foundations of the earth, and the heavens are the work of his hands. Then in 102:26, the heavens and earth will perish, while Yahweh remains. The verse goes on to say that the creation will wear out like a garment and be changed like a robe. This seems to indicate that in the same way an old garment wears out and is replaced by a new, so also creation will wear out and be made new. When we combine the indications of a new creation in Psalm 102:25–26 with David's words in Psalm 23:6 (ESV), "and I shall dwell in the house of the LORD forever," it seems that the new creation will be a new temple.

§2.4.4 Tent and Room Imagery for Creation in Psalm 104

Psalm 104 poetically re-presents Yahweh creating the world, speaking of him covering himself with light as with a garment (104:2a), and then the

---

15. Gary Millar writes of the imagery, "This may well be part of a broader Eden symbolism in the entire temple complex, but it is impossible to be dogmatic about this." A bit later he notes, "Again, the decorative elements . . . are modeled on the natural world. . . . seems to point to the connection between Eden and the temple." Millar, "1–2 Kings," 560, 562.

heavens are depicted as a tent curtain that Yahweh stretched through the skies (104:2b). The earth is spoken of as a house, the rooms of which are built on beams that Yahweh laid on the waters (104:3a). The imagery seems informed by the idea that creation is a house, a palace, that is to say, a cosmic temple Yahweh built as the place of his rest.

§2.4.5 I Will Fill This House with Glory in Haggai 2:7

Yahweh filled the tabernacle and temple with his glory (Exod 40:34–35; 1 Kgs 8:10–11), and in a number of places he promises to fill a new temple with glory:

- Isa 60:7, "and I will beautify my beautiful house."
- Hag 2:7, "I will fill this house with glory."
- Zech 2:5, "I will be to her a wall of fire all around, declares Yahweh, and I will be the glory in her midst."

On that day the inscription on the headpiece of the high priest of Israel, "Holy to Yahweh," will be "on the bells of the horses," and everything in the city will be holy (Zech 14:20–21). The imagery suggests that all things will be fit for the holy of holies, because Yahweh will inhabit the city as he formerly inhabited the temple.

These five points about the temple's correspondence to creation can be complemented by five on how Christ fulfills the temple:

§3 CHRIST THE FULFILLMENT OF THE TEMPLE

How is it that a *person* can be the fulfillment of a *building*, and why am I discussing the question in a part of this book dealing with *events*? When God created it was an event, and the key things about the temple were that it was the place where God was present and the place where atonement for sin was made. Christ fulfills the temple because he is the place where God is present and the place where atonement for sin is accomplished, and that took place at the event of his crucifixion. The preceding section on the temple and creation had five subsections, and the five subsections on Christ as the fulfillment of the temple match those:

§3.1 The Word Tabernacled

    §3.2 Angels Ascending and Descending

        §3.3 Destroy This Temple

    §3.4 In My Father's House Are Many Rooms

§3.5 I Am Glorified in Them

The Word became flesh and tabernacled among men, and those who walked with him saw his glory (John 1:14). Having shown forth the glory of the Father, he gave that glory (17:22) to his people in whom he would be glorified (17:10). The glory of God tabernacling in Christ and being seen in his followers matches the way God filled tabernacle and temple with glory, promising to do so in the new temple.

God built the world as his cosmic temple, and the temple imagery informs Jesus saying that the angels will ascend and descend on him as they did when Jacob saw the "ladder" at the place he named "Bethel," house of God, gate of heaven (Gen 28:10–22; John 1:51). That same imagery comes into play when Jesus says there are many rooms in the house of his Father where he goes to prepare a place for his disciples (John 14:2). At the center of all things is the death of Christ on the cross, the destruction of the fulfillment of the temple under Yahweh's covenant wrath, that sinners might dwell in his house forever (cf. 2:19–22).

§3.1 The Word Tabernacled

Having introduced the Word who was with God and was God in the opening statement of his Gospel (John 1:1–2), John announces that "the Word became flesh and tabernacled among us, and we have seen his glory, glory as of the only begotten from the Father, full of grace and truth" (1:14).[16] John's statement that Jesus is "full of grace and truth" (πλήρης χάριτος καὶ ἀληθείας) aptly renders Yahweh's assertion of himself that he is "abounding in steadfast love and truth" (רַב־חֶסֶד וֶאֱמֶת, Exod 34:6). When we look to the Old Testament for the use of the Hebrew noun "tabernacle" (מִשְׁכָּן) and its cognate verb (שָׁכַן), often rendered "dwell," we find a number of statements about Yahweh dwelling among his people in glory.

---

16. For book length treatments of the temple in John, see Mary L. Coloe, *God Dwells with Us: Temple Symbolism in the Fourth Gospel* (Collegeville, MN: Glazier, 2001); Paul M. Hoskins, *Jesus as the Fulfillment of the Temple in the Gospel of John,* Paternoster Biblical Monographs (Waynesboro, GA: Paternoster, 2006); and Alan R. Kerr, *The Temple of Jesus' Body: The Temple Theme in the Gospel of John* (London: Sheffield Academic Press, 2002).

For instance, Yahweh's glory fills the tabernacle upon its construction: "Then the cloud covered the tent of meeting, and the glory of the Lord filled the tabernacle. And Moses was not able to enter the tent of meeting because the cloud settled on it, and the glory of the Lord filled the tabernacle" (Exod 40:34–35, ESV). Later biblical authors naturally say things like what we find in Psalm 26:8 (ESV), "O Lord, I love the habitation of your house and the place where your glory dwells" (מִשְׁכַּן, "the place of the tabernacle of your glory").

The Hebrew verb *shachan* (שָׁכַן) appears in a number of statements about Yahweh dwelling in the midst of Israel (following the ESV in the texts below):

- Exod 25:8, "And let them make me a sanctuary, that I may dwell in their midst."
- Exod 29:45, "I will dwell among the people of Israel and will be their God."
- Exod 29:46, "And they shall know that I am the Lord their God, who brought them out of the land of Egypt that I might dwell among them. I am the Lord their God."

The same verb (שָׁכַן) is used in Deuteronomy in the statements where Yahweh says he will "make his name dwell there" (לְשַׁכֵּן שְׁמוֹ שָׁם, Deut 12:11; 14:23; 16:2, 11; cf. also 12:5). In Deuteronomy 33:16 this verb is used to refer to Yahweh as "him who dwells in the bush," meaning the burning bush, in which Yahweh appeared to Moses (cf. CSB, NIV, "burning bush"), and it is used to describe Israel causing the tent of meeting to tabernacle at Shiloh (Josh 18:1).

Yahweh inhabited the tabernacle and then the temple. His dwelling among his people gave them the opportunity to experience his glory at the temple, and Psalm 85:9 (ESV, MT 85:10) celebrates God's saving presence and his glory: "Surely his salvation is near to those who fear him, that glory may dwell in our land." The one who dwells "in thick darkness" (1 Kgs 8:12), in "the high and holy place, and also with him who is of a contrite and lowly spirit" (Isa 57:15, ESV), also promised to "dwell in their midst forever" (Ezek 43:9, ESV), a promise that follows the glory of Yahweh entering the eschatological temple (43:4; cf. Joel 3:17 [MT 4:17]).

John evokes all this Old Testament background when he says, "the Word became flesh and tabernacled among us, and we have seen his glory"

(John 1:14). In the Old Testament God's glory was seen when he filled the temple with the cloud of his glory. In the incarnation, Jesus takes up "the temple of his body" (John 2:21), fills it with God's glory "as the only begotten from the Father" (1:14), causing it to abound with God's own רַב־חֶסֶד וֶאֱמֶת ("abounding in steadfast love and truth," Exod 34:6) character, being "full of grace and truth" (John 1:14). By his description of the Word as *tabernacling* among us, John indicates that in the same way God dwelt among Israel in the temple in the Old Testament, God dwelt among his people in the temple of Jesus' human body during the incarnation.

§3.2 Angels Ascending and Descending

Shortly after announcing that in Jesus God dwells among his people as he indwelt the temple in John 1:14, John presents him telling Nathanael in 1:51 (ESV), "you will see heaven opened, and the angels of God ascending and descending on the Son of Man." In these words John presents Jesus alluding to God's revelation of himself to Jacob in Genesis 28. As Jacob fled from Esau (Gen 27:41–43) to Laban for a wife (27:46; 28:1–2), Isaac transmitted to him the blessing of Abraham (28:3–5). On the way, Jacob had a dream in which Yahweh revealed himself standing above (or perhaps *by*, עָלָיו, 28:13) a ladder on which angels were ascending and descending (28:12–13). The Lord then reiterated the blessing of Abraham to Jacob and promised to bring him back to the land (28:13–15). On waking, Jacob exclaimed that he had not been aware of Yahweh's presence, which made the place awesome, and identified it as the "house of God" (בֵּית אֱלֹהִים) and the "gate of heaven" (28:17).

With his terse statement in John 1:51, Jesus evokes the whole scene and puts himself in the place of the ladder, or "flight of steps" (Gen 28:12, HALOT, s.v. סֻלָּם). It seems likely that the ladder/steps that Jacob saw comprised the ascent of the holy mountain, atop which, in the assumed symbolism, sat the house of God, or temple, prompting Jacob's comment about the house of God and the naming of the place "Bethel" (בֵּית־אֵל, Gen 28:17, 19). By saying that the angels will ascend and descend "on the Son of Man" (John 1:51), Jesus identifies himself as the true Bethel, the house of God (cf. 2:21).

In the literary structure of John's opening chapter, the first (1:1–18) and last (1:43–51) units identify Jesus with the dwelling place of God: he is the true tabernacle in 1:14 and the true house of God in 1:51. The chiastic structure of John 1 can be depicted as follows:

John 1:1–18, The Word Tabernacled in Glory
John 1:19–28, The Voice Crying in the Wilderness
John 1:29–34, The Descent of the Spirit to Remain on Jesus
John 1:35–42, The Baptist's Disciples Follow Jesus
John 1:43–51, The True Bethel of Whom Moses and the Prophets Wrote

In chiastic structures such as these, not only will the beginning and ending correspond to one another, often the turning point in the central section will recall the beginning and anticipate the end. In this case, the descent of the Spirit to remain upon Jesus at the midpoint of the chapter recalls him as tabernacle in 1:14 and anticipates him being the house of God in 1:51. As the Spirit of God hovered over the waters at creation, as the Lord filled tabernacle and temple with his glory, so the Spirit comes down upon Jesus to remain upon him (John 1:33).

§3.3 Destroy This Temple

Why would John in his Gospel present Jesus as the fulfillment of the temple, and where would he get such an idea? John's own testimony is that the concept came from Jesus himself. John presents Jesus cleansing the temple (John 2:13–17), and when he is asked for a sign to demonstrate his authority to have done so (2:18), he makes a symbolic reference to his own crucifixion and resurrection as a destruction and rebuilding of the temple (2:19–21). Only after his resurrection, according to John, did his disciples remember and believe both the Scripture and what Jesus said (2:22).

It seems that John learned from Jesus that Jesus came as the fulfillment of the temple (John 1:51; 2:19–21), prompting John to present Jesus this way. Why would Jesus teach this idea?

Already in 2 Samuel 7 we see a dynamic relationship between the house of Yahweh that David wants to build (2 Sam 7:1–7) and the house of David that Yahweh promises to build (7:11, 16). Yahweh also promises to raise up the seed of David who will build a house for Yahweh's name (7:13), whose suffering is intimated as well (7:14, see Chapter 6). Christ comes as the heir of the house of David that Yahweh built, and he is simultaneously the fulfillment of the house for Yahweh David wanted to build.

The connection between the destruction of the temple and the crucifixion of Jesus makes both covenantal and salvation-historical points. The sacrificial rites and the need for the temple itself to be cleansed on the Day of Atonement imply that with the sprinkling of the blood of the sacrifices, Yahweh himself bore the sins of his people.[17] Christ comes as the incarnation of Yahweh, bearer of the sins of his people, and his death puts an end to the sacrifices that transferred the sins of the people to the house of their God. The destruction of the temple, moreover, marks the moment when the curse of the covenant falls with finality. That "day of the LORD" finds fulfillment as Christ dies on the cross, with the heavens black, the mountain shaking, and the veil rent in two.

All this Jesus intimates when he offers as the sign to authorize his cleansing of the temple, "Destroy this temple and in three days I will raise it up" (John 2:19, ESV). As so often in John, Jesus makes a symbolic statement that is initially misinterpreted in a literal direction only to be clarified as the narrative continues.[18] John presents the Jews objecting that the temple has been under construction for forty-six years, incredulous that Jesus could claim to raise it in three days (2:20), before explaining, "But he was speaking about the temple of his body" (2:21). The resurrection is the key for the disciples being able to remember and believe both "the Scripture and the word that Jesus had spoken" (2:22).

§3.4 In My Father's House Are Many Rooms

Having announced to his disciples that one of them will betray him, and having dismissed Judas to do the deed (John 13:21–30), Jesus announced that the hour had come for the Son of Man to be glorified, commanded his disciples to love one another, and prophesied Peter's threefold denial (13:31–38). He then urged his disciples not to be troubled of heart but to trust God and him (14:1), explaining in 14:2 (ESV), "In my Father's house are many rooms. If it were not

---

17. Roy Gane, *Cult and Character: Purification Offerings, Day of Atonement, and Theodicy* (Winona Lake, IN: Eisenbrauns, 2005), 99–105, 334–37. Also, when Yahweh identifies himself in Exodus 34:6–7 as one who is "forgiving iniquity and transgression and sin" (Exod 34:7), the term rendered "forgiving" could also be rendered *bear,* or *carry* (נשׂא). It is as though he is able to *forgive* the sins because he himself *bears* them through the sacrificial system. Cf. the parallel expressions for "bearing iniquity" in Lev 10:17 and 16:22 and discussion in Gane, ibid., 100 n. 35, 104, 262–63, and esp. 299–300, where Gane writes of "YHWH, who bears moral evils when he extends pardon" (citing Exod 34:7). See also ibid., 322: "A judge who forgives a guilty person is responsible for such a ruling. But YHWH does precisely that: he forgives guilty people and therefore incurs judicial responsibility, which constitutes a cost of kindness that he chooses to bear. This helps to explain why he bears (נשׂא) sins when he forgives (Exod 34:7), as represented in the ritual system by the fact that his sanctuary and priesthood, representing his administration, carry חטאת, expiable sin (Lev 16:16), and עון, culpability (10:17)." Cf. ibid., 334–35, 343.

18. Cf., for instance, the new birth (John 3:3–8), the living water (4:13–26), and the bread of life (6:32–40).

so, would I have told you that I go to prepare a place for you?" The expression "my Father's house" in 14:2 matches the same in 2:16 except for the necessary adjustments of case because of the different statements:

John 2:16, "my Father's house"
τὸν οἶκον τοῦ πατρός μου

John 14:2, "my Father's house"
τῇ οἰκίᾳ τοῦ πατρός μου

The house of the Father in John 2:16 is the physical temple in Jerusalem. The house of the Father in 14:2, by contrast, is not the physical temple in Jerusalem but the house Jesus goes to the cross to prepare.

To this point Jesus has affirmed the legitimacy of the Jerusalem temple (John 2:16), but even as he affirmed to the Samaritan woman that "we worship what we know, for salvation is from the Jews" (4:22, ESV), he also said to her, "the hour is coming when neither on this mountain nor in Jerusalem will you worship the Father" (4:21). He went on to say, "the hour is coming, and is now here, when the true worshipers will worship the Father in spirit and truth, for the Father is seeking such people to worship him. God is spirit, and those who worship him must worship in spirit and truth" (4:23–24). These statements indicate that the time of worship at the temple in Jerusalem has come to an end ("the hour is coming, and is now here," 4:23) now that Jesus has come to fulfill and replace it.

John presents Jesus telling his disciples in 16:7 that if he does not go away, the Helper, the Holy Spirit, will not come to them, but if he goes, he will send him to them. To this point God has inhabited the temple in Jerusalem, and it has been possible for the holy God to live among the sinful people because of the sacrifices associated with the Levitical cult. Jesus fulfills the temple as the place where God is present and the place where atonement for sin is made as he dies on the cross.

The Spirit coming to the disciples will constitute the followers of Jesus as the place where God is present and the place where forgiveness for sins can be found (see §4 below). What Jesus says in John 16:7 indicates that if he does not put an end to the sacrificial system by his death on the cross, the Spirit cannot take up residence in a temple (believers) where no sacrifice for sin is made.

The house where Jesus goes to prepare a place for his disciples in John 14:2 is the one he will take them to when he returns for them in 14:3. This would seem to indicate that they will be taken by Jesus to that house upon his return, and the return in view does not seem to be his resurrection from the dead (cf. 16:19–22). It would appear that the many-roomed Father's house in John 14:2 is the cosmic temple of the new creation, of which the post-resurrection church is an inaugurated experience.

§3.5 I Am Glorified in Them

Christ tabernacled in the flesh and showed the glory of his self-giving love to his disciples (John 1:14). Also displayed was the glory of his commitment to the Father, the glory of his ability to satisfy the Father's justice, the glory of his ability to fulfill the temple, and his ability to make the disciples into a new temple where God's glory is displayed. Jesus prays to the Father in John 17:10 (ESV), "All mine are yours, and yours are mine, and I am glorified in them." He then goes on to pray in 17:22, "The glory that you have given me I have given to them, that they may be one even as we are one."

The oneness that Jesus seeks for the disciples is a oneness possible because he will give them the Spirit to be in them (John 14:17). The Spirit will teach them the truth Jesus taught (14:26), bear witness to them about Christ (15:26), and bring conviction concerning sin, righteousness, and judgment (16:8–11), guiding the disciples into truth and exalting Jesus (16:13–14). Note the similarity between 16:14b and 17:10a (ESV).

John 16:14b, "He will take what is mine and declare it to you."

John 17:10a, "All mine are yours, and yours are mine."

The mutual self-giving concern among the members of the Godhead, Father, Son, and Spirit, seems to be extended to the disciples of Jesus so that they love as he loves. When the Spirit unites the disciples in the truth and common purpose, the disciples will be unified. As the Spirit produces self-giving Christlike love in the disciples, they will love one another as Christ has loved them (13:34), and all will know they are disciples of Jesus (13:35), glorifying him (12:28; 13:31–32; 16:14).

Jesus went to the cross, fulfilling the sacrificial system and the ministry of the temple, suffering in himself the culmination of the covenant wrath of God against sin, bearing it for his people. On the day of the resurrection (John 20:1, 19) he imparted the indwelling Spirit to his disciples, constituting them the new temple of the Holy Spirit, the place where God is present, and granting them authority to forgive and retain sin: "he breathed on them and said to them, 'Receive the Holy Spirit. If you forgive the sins of any, they are forgiven them; if you withhold forgiveness from any, it is withheld'" (20:22–23, ESV).[19]

Jesus made the church the place where God is present by giving them the indwelling Spirit, and he made them the place where forgiveness for sin can be granted by giving them the keys to the kingdom of heaven (cf. Matt 16:19). In that church Christ is glorified (John 17:10, 22).

§4 THE CHURCH AS THE TEMPLE OF THE HOLY SPIRIT

In a chapter on creation, why so much focus on the temple? Again, because when God created the world he constructed a cosmic temple. How does the church fit into that? In the old covenant God indwelt the tabernacle, but in the new covenant God indwells his people by his Spirit, making them his temple. The corollary of this is that those who are in Christ are even now part of the new creation (2 Cor 5:17; Gal 6:15). The whole world was made for God to be present with his people, imaged by his people, known, served, and worshiped by his people. These realities will be fully enjoyed in the new heaven and new earth, and the church experiences an inauguration of the new creation through the regenerating and indwelling Spirit.

The church is the place where the omnipresent God is covenantally present, the place of the people with the authority to give assurance of forgiveness of sin, the place where God is known and served, and the place of the people who live out the inauguration of the new creation. The movement of thought in this subsection matches that of the previous two, beginning and ending with glory, moving then to God's presence with his people, centering on the death of Christ for the sins of his people and the forgiveness thereby enjoyed.

---

19. See further James M. Hamilton Jr., *God's Indwelling Presence: The Holy Spirit in the Old and New Testaments*, NAC Studies in Bible and Theology 1 (Nashville: Broadman & Holman, 2006).

§4.1 Pentecost, Acts 2:1–4

Once constructed, tabernacle and temple were filled with the glory of God (Exod 40; 1 Kgs 8). The Baptist said that Jesus would baptize with the Holy Spirit and fire (Luke 3:16). At his own baptism, "the heavens were opened, and the Holy Spirit descended on him in bodily form, like a dove; and a voice came from heaven, 'You are my beloved Son; with you I am well pleased'" (Luke 3:21–22, ESV). After his resurrection, Jesus told his disciples, "not to depart from Jerusalem, but to wait for the promise of the Father, which, he said, 'you heard from me; for John baptized with water, but you will be baptized with the Holy Spirit not many days from now'" (Acts 1:4–5, ESV).

Jesus imparted the indwelling Spirit to his disciples on the day of the resurrection (John 20:22), but he baptized them with the Holy Spirit in a public manifestation of God's approval, with audible and visible evidence of the Spirit's coming upon them, on the day of Pentecost (Acts 2:1–4).[20] In biblical-theological terms, the baptism of the church in the Spirit on the day of Pentecost functions like the glory of God filling tabernacle and temple and the Spirit coming on Jesus at his baptism.[21]

§4.2 Temple of the Holy Spirit, 1 Corinthians 3:16

Believers in Jesus are individually indwelt by the Holy Spirit, as statements in the singular show. Paul writes in Romans 8:9b (ESV), "Anyone who does not have the Spirit of Christ does not belong to him," and in 1 Corinthians 6:19 (ESV), "do you not know that your body is a temple of the Holy Spirit within you, whom you have from God?" There are also statements in the plural asserting that the church as a whole is God's temple:

---

20. For the different verbs used to describe the coming of the Spirit in Acts, see James M. Hamilton Jr., "Rushing Wind and Organ Music: Toward Luke's Theology of the Spirit in Acts," *Reformed Theological Review* 65, no. 1 (2006): 15–33, which also appears as Appendix 3 in Hamilton, *God's Indwelling Presence*, 183–203.

21. See further G. K. Beale, "The Descent of the Eschatological Temple in the Form of the Spirit at Pentecost: Part 1: The Clearest Evidence," *Tyndale Bulletin* 56 (2005): 73–102.

"Do you not know that you are God's temple and that God's Spirit dwells in you?" (1 Cor 3:16).

Paul fleshes out the idea that the church is God's temple by applying it to his appeal that the Corinthian church not tolerate false teachers. He calls them not to be unequally yoked with unbelievers (2 Cor 6:14, ESV), rhetorically asking, "What agreement has the temple of God with idols? For we are the temple of the living God." He then quotes Leviticus 26:12, because the Lord inhabiting the tabernacle in the midst of Israel's camp is typologically fulfilled in the church being indwelt by the Spirit.

This application is like that in 1 Corinthians 3, where to teach in accordance with the gospel foundation Paul laid in the church is to build with gold, silver, and precious stones—to adorn the temple of the Holy Spirit in a fitting way (1 Cor 3:10–12a). If, on the other hand, people depart from the true gospel Paul taught, they build with wood, hay, and stubble that fires of judgment will consume, even if they themselves might be true believers (3:12b–15). Paul teaches at length in Romans 8 on the need to set the mind on the Spirit (Rom 8:5–11) and employs temple imagery as he describes the Son and the Spirit interceding for believers (8:26, 34).

§4.3 Forgiveness of Sins, John 20:22–23

God made provision for sin under the old covenant through the sacrificial system operative at the temple. God was present there, and there they could offer sacrifice for the forgiveness of sin.[22] When Jesus breathed on his disciples (overtones of Gen 2:7, new life for a new humanity in a new creation) and imparted the indwelling Spirit to them in John 20:22, he went on to say to them in 20:23 (ESV), "If you forgive the sins of any, they are forgiven them; if you withhold forgiveness from any, it is withheld." This statement recalls what Matthew records Jesus saying after Peter's confession of him as the Christ: "I will give you the keys of the kingdom of heaven, and whatever you bind on earth shall be bound in heaven, and whatever you loose on earth shall be loosed in heaven" (Matt 16:19, ESV).

The giving and withholding of forgiveness in John 20:23 is another way of describing the binding and loosing on earth and in heaven in Matthew 16:19. What does it mean? It means that the church has the authority to assure those

---

22. Cf. Gane, *Cult and Character*, 335–37, 343.

who repent of their sin and trust in Christ that their sins are forgiven, and the church has authority to say to those who do not repent and believe that they are not part of the church and have no reason to think that their sins have been forgiven (cf. Matt 18:15–20; John 3:16–21, 36). The church has the ability to assure those who believe Jesus and repent of sin that they are indwelt by the Spirit and thus part of the temple of God. Likewise, the church warns those who do not repent and believe that they are not part of the temple, have not the Spirit, and are without God in the world (Eph 2:12).

§4.4 Living Stones in a Spiritual House, 1 Peter 2:5

The idea that the church is the temple of God where the Holy Spirit dwells crops up regularly and informs architectural imagery across the New Testament. For instance, Matthew presents Jesus, who comes in fulfillment of the 2 Samuel 7:13–14 promise of a temple-building ("house for my name") seed of David, saying that he will "build" his church (Matt 16:18).

The false charges against Jesus in Mark 14 included the claim, "We heard him say, 'I will destroy this temple that is made with hands, and in three days I will build another, not made with hands" (Mark 14:58, ESV). A similar charge comes against Stephen, alleging that was speaking against the temple, including the allegation, "we have heard him say that this Jesus of Nazareth will destroy this place" (Acts 6:14). These charges likely stem from teaching along the lines of Jesus saying in John 2:19, "destroy this temple, and in three days I will raise it up."

The warning that the man of lawlessness will take "his seat in the temple of God" in 2 Thessalonians 2:4 (ESV) probably indicates that this figure will be a wolf in sheep's clothing who has infiltrated the church. Paul speaks of the church as "the household of God" and calls it "a pillar and buttress of the truth" (1 Tim 3:15). The author of Hebrews likely refers to the fulfillment of the tabernacle/temple in the church when he says in 3:6, "Christ is faithful over God's house as a son. And we are his house if indeed we hold fast . . ." John in Revelation presents Jesus promising that the one who overcomes will be "a pillar in the temple of my God" (Rev 3:12).

The imagery communicates God's presence and the way that his people were made to enjoy knowing him, walking with him, serving him, and worshiping him. Peter explains that Christ is the living stone (1 Pet 2:4), because of whom believers, like Christ living stones themselves, are built into a spiritual temple to offer spiritual sacrifices acceptable to God through Christ (2:5). In this house, Peter the rock (Matt 16:18) asserts, Christ is the cornerstone (1 Pet 2:6), the one the builders rejected (2:7), over whom the disobedient stumble (2:8). Believers, by contrast, are like Israel in reception of the dwelling place of God—tabernacle, temple, presence of the holy one—which makes them the chosen race, the royal priesthood, the holy nation, the people for God's own possession to praise him (2:9) and walk in holiness before him (1:15–16).

Between the incarnation, in which Christ fulfilled the temple, and the new creation, which itself will be a cosmic temple, the church is an inaugurated (already/not yet) typological fulfillment of the temple. The church enjoys the presence of God through the indwelling Spirit, and the church administers forgiveness of sins through the gospel, experiencing a foretaste of the age to come, having been made a regenerated (Matt 19:28; Titus 3:5) new creation (2 Cor 5:17; Gal 6:15) by the life-giving Spirit.

§4.5 A Dwelling Place for Glory, Ephesians 2:19–22; 3:10

God will fill the new creation cosmic temple with his glory, and to that end the church pursues the Great Commission task of making disciples of all nations (Matt 28:18–20). For this great endeavor Jesus took captivity captive and, like Moses and David before him, ascended on high, leading captives, giving gifts (Eph 4:8). To fill all things with his glory (4:10), he gave the apostles, prophets, and evangelists to found the church, and he gifts pastors and teachers for the ongoing equipping of believers for ministry (4:11–12). This is to produce unity in faith and knowledge of Jesus, to bring all to the fullness of who Christ is (4:12), growing everyone in every way into Christ (4:15).

In Ephesians 4:8–16 Paul explains what it means to be part of the "household of God" (Eph 2:19), the foundation of which Christ is cornerstone. In true line with him, the apostles and prophets provide the foundational deposit of revelation for the church (2:20; 3:5), and the "holy temple in the Lord" on that foundation rests (2:21). As churches are built up, they are joined together as God's temple, "a dwelling place for God by the Spirit" (2:22).

As God's glory was manifested at the beginning of the church when the temple was baptized in the Holy Spirit on the day of Pentecost, so the end of the church is glory: "so that through the church the manifold wisdom of God might now be made known to the rulers and authorities in the heavenly places" (Eph 3:10, ESV).

§5 THE COSMIC TEMPLE OF THE NEW CREATION

Isaiah presents the Lord making a new heavens and a new earth, replete with a new Jerusalem (Isa 65:17–18), and in the near context he speaks of heaven as his throne and the earth as his footstool, asking what house man would make for him (66:1), implying that the new creation is his temple. Ezekiel's new temple (Ezek 40–48) is to be understood in this context: not as a literal building to be built in Jerusalem but as a visionary symbol of the new heaven and new earth, as John interprets it in Revelation 21–22.[23]

§5.1 The End a Fulfillment of the Beginning

God created a clean realm of life in Genesis 1–2, and when all is fulfilled, John depicts a clean realm of life in Revelation 21–22. As there was no death in God's cosmic temple prior to sin in Genesis 3, so there will be no death in the cosmic temple after the first heaven and earth passes away and the sea is no more (Rev 21:1, 4). As there were no transgressors in Genesis 1–2, so there will be none in the new Jerusalem (21:8). No sin and no death means that there will be nothing unclean, as it was in the beginning (21:27). As Adam was God's son, granted dominion over God's realm as vice-regent, so those who overcome will be granted sonship that fulfills that given to new-Adam Israel and new-Israel king from David's line, so that God's temple will be served by God's royal priesthood: "The one who conquers will have this heritage, and I will be his God and he will be my son" (21:7, ESV).

§5.2 Correspondences between Eden and the New Creation

John's depiction of the new Jerusalem shows it to be a new and better Eden city, where "the dwelling place of God is with man. He will dwell with them, and they will be his people, and God himself will be with them as their God," (Rev 21:3, ESV), in fulfillment of God's purposes in creation and redemption. John depicts a new and better Eden, a cosmic temple, in the new creation by showing points of historical correspondence and escalation in Revelation 22:

---

23. See Beale, *The Temple and the Church's Mission*, 335–64.

- A river flowed out of Eden to water the garden in Genesis 2:10, and the river of the water of life flows "from the throne of God and of the Lamb" in Revelation 22:1.
- The tree of life was in the garden in Genesis 2:9, but it is even better in the new Eden as it is on both sides of the river, for the healing of the nations (Rev 22:2), for those who enter the city by the gates (22:14).
- Whereas the unclean serpent was able to infiltrate the garden and induce God's people to sin (Gen 3:1–7), nothing accursed will be in the city (Rev 22:3). All evildoers will be outside (22:15).
- Whereas Adam was to work and keep the garden but failed (Gen 2:15; 3:6), in the new and better future God's priestly servants will experience him and serve him: "the throne of God and of the Lamb will be in it, and his servants will worship him" (Rev 22:3, ESV).
- God walked in the garden in the cool of the day (Gen 3:8), but in the new Jerusalem the "temple is the Lord God the Almighty and the Lamb" (21:22, ESV), there he will be enthroned (22:3), his radiance such that no sun moon or lamp is necessary (22:5).

God made the world as a cosmic temple, and when he has accomplished his purposes, it will be just that.

EXODUS

When I tread the verge of Jordan,
Bid my anxious fears subside.
Death of death, and hell's Destruction,
Land me safe on Canaan's side.

—WILLIAM WILLIAMS[1]

God delivered his people at the exodus from Egypt, and we can see how important Moses thought this was from the way he previews the exodus in his accounts of Abraham and Jacob, narrates the exodus itself, and then indicates that God will save his people in the future the way he saved them at the exodus. Proof that later biblical authors understood that Moses meant to present the exodus as both an interpretive schema and a predictive paradigm can be seen in the way that they, in turn, deploy it. Joshua presents the conquest of the land and the salvation of Rahab as installments in the exodus pattern (see below). The prophets pointed forward to a future day when God would do a new and greater exodus, eclipsing it in significance (e.g., Isa 11:15–16; Jer 16:14–15; 23:5–8). The Psalms celebrate the exodus (e.g., Pss 74:12–15; 78; 136) and join the Prophets in pointing to a new exodus and conquest (e.g., Ps 106:47–107:3; 108; 110; 135:14; 137:7–9). In the Gospels, the evangelists present Jesus recapitulating the history of Israel and bringing exodus patterns to fulfillment in both his life and in his death and resurrection, which fulfills the Passover. Paul and Peter use the exodus pattern of events as an interpretive schema for understanding Christian experience and shaping Christian

---

1. "Guide Me, O Thou Great Jehovah." I wish to thank Matt Damico for bringing this hymn's typological truth to my attention.

identity. Then in Revelation John indicates that the end of all things will yet again recapitulate and fulfill the exodus pattern of salvation.

This chapter cannot begin to exhaust the Bible's treatment of the exodus motif.[2] The installments in the pattern discussed below seek to show how Moses previewed it, then it happened, and later Old Testament authors made further installments in the pattern, showing that they understood what Moses intended to teach. Jesus then fulfilled the exodus in life and death, and Paul used it to teach Christians what Christ had done for them, before John in Revelation prophesies a future exodus. To put manageable constraints on the discussion that follows, regretting not being able to discuss everything (but gladly operating within the constraints of this project), we pursue a sampling of exodus typology as follows:

§1 The Exodus in the Torah
§2 The Exodus in Joshua
§3 The Exodus in the Gospels
§4 The Exodus in Paul
§5 The Exodus in Revelation

This chapter puts forward the idea that beginning with Moses, the biblical authors present what God did for Israel at the exodus from Egypt as the kind of thing God does when he saves his people.[3] The following three points summarize the argument:

1. That Moses established that the historical event of the exodus is a *type* by presenting previews of it in the lives of Abraham and Jacob.
2. He then recorded the historical event of the exodus itself, establishing the pattern by presenting it being repeated.
3. And even within the book of Exodus itself, once the event of the exodus is recorded, there are indications that the pattern will be repeated in the future.

---

2. For book length treatments, see esp. Morales, *Exodus Old and New*; Rikki E. Watts, *Isaiah's New Exodus in Mark* (Grand Rapids: Baker, 2000); David W. Pao, *Acts and the Isaianic New Exodus* (Grand Rapids: Baker, 2002).

3. Similarly Francis Foulkes, "The Acts of God: A Study of the Basis of Typology," in *The Right Doctrine from the Wrong Texts? Essays on the Use of the Old Testament in the New*, ed. G. K. Beale (Grand Rapids: Baker, 1994), 343, 352.

Moses thus establishes the events of the exodus as a type, and later biblical authors show in their work that they have learned from Moses that the exodus is both an *interpretive schema* and a *predictive paradigm*.

§1 THE EXODUS IN THE TORAH

This section seeks to show that there are author-intended parallels between the exodus from Egypt and key events in the narratives of Abraham and Jacob, so that the patriarchs preview the exodus. There are also statements made that indicate that what happened at the exodus will be repeated at the conquest. Those are the facts, and here is my interpretation of them: Moses noticed the parallels that God sovereignly built into the outworking of history, understood them under the inspiration of the Holy Spirit, and wrote the narratives so that the exodus pattern is typified in the lives of Abraham and Jacob, then the exodus itself happened when God brought Israel out of Egypt, and Moses indicated that his audience could expect God to continue to act in the same way in the future.

§1.1 Abraham

There is a preview of the exodus from Egypt in Abram's life. That Moses intended to establish this parallel can be seen from the way he uses the same words and even whole lines in the two narratives, presents matching sequences of events, and all this with characters advancing the same salvation-historical plotline in covenant with God. Taking the latter first, God made promises to Abraham about his seed, entering into covenant with him. The nation of Israel is the collective seed of Abraham, and once God did for them what he had done for Abraham, which he also promised Abraham he would do (Gen 15:13–16), he entered into covenant with the nation. Moses signals the preview of the exodus from Egypt in Abram's life by means of Yahweh's statement in Genesis 15:7, "I am Yahweh who brought you out . . . ," which Moses later presents Yahweh saying to Israel in Exodus 20:2, "I am Yahweh your God, who brought you out . . ."[4] We see common terminology describing similar events

---

4. In conjunction with what we will see of Jacob and the way Hosea interprets his story below, there may be a preview of the new exodus: The statement in Genesis 15:7 (ESV) ends with the phrase, "from Ur of the Chaldeans to give you this land to possess." At the exodus from Egypt, Yahweh brought Israel out of Egypt and gave them the land of Canaan. At the new-exodus from the Babylonian exile, Yahweh brought his people out of the land of the Chaldeans to give them the land of Canaan.

when the term "plague" (נֶגַע) describes what God does to Pharaoh to liberate Sarah in Genesis 12:17 and Israel in Exodus 11:1. The parallel event sequences between the exoduses of Abraham and Israel are presented in Table 8.1.

TABLE 8.1: Parallel Event Sequences in the Exoduses of Abraham and Israel from Egypt[5]

Abraham	Israel
Gen 12:10, Descent into Egypt Because of Famine	Gen 46, Descent into Egypt Because of Famine
Gen 12:15, Sarah Seized by Pharaoh	Exod 1, Israel Enslaved by Pharaoh
Gen 12:16, Pharaoh Enriches Abraham	Exod 12:35–36, Israel Plunders Egypt
Gen 12:17–20, Yahweh Liberates Sarah by Plagues	Exod 7–12, Yahweh Liberates Israel by Plagues
Gen 14, Defeat of Kings to Rescue Lot	Num 21, Defeat of Sihon and Og
Gen 14:17–24, Melchizedek, Priest-King of Salem	Exod 18, Jethro, Priest of Midian
Gen 15:7, "I Am Yahweh Who Brought You out . . ."	Exod 20:1, "I Am Yahweh Who Brought You out . . ."
Gen 15:12–17, Theophany: Smoke, Fire, Darkness	Exod 19:16–18, Theophany: Thick Cloud, Smoke, Fire
Gen 15:13–14, Prophecy of the Exodus from Egypt	Exod 15:5, 16, Prophecy of Exodus-Like Conquest of the Land

In addition to pointing forward, the narrative dealing with Abraham's descent into Egypt also points backward. Mathews catalogs an impressive number of verbal and sequential parallels between the temptation narrative in Genesis 3 and Abram's exodus-preview in Genesis 12, and his summary puts the matter well:

---

5. This table updates the one in James M. Hamilton Jr., "The Exodus Motif in Biblical Theology," in *The Law, The Prophets, and the Writings: Studies in Evangelical Old Testament Hermeneutics in Honor of Duane A. Garrett*, ed. Andrew M. King, William R. Osborne, and Joshua M. Philpot (Nashville: Broadman & Holman, 2021), 80.

Both accounts involve the backdrop of food (plenty or famine), depend on
the idea of deception, and portray the wife in a critical role. Following the
discovery of the deception, there is the interrogation of the parties (by God/
Pharaoh), admission of the deed (by Adam/Abram), and expulsion of the
parties (from Eden/Egypt). Also the subsequent stories tell of family schism
(Cain-Abel/Lot-Abram).[6]

We have seen above how Abraham's sister-fib in Genesis 12:10–20 is
repeated in 20:1–18, and then Isaac does the same in 26:6–11. The connections
between Abraham's sin in Genesis 12 and Adam's sin in Genesis 3 also anticipate connections between the sin of Jacob and that of Adam.

§1.2 Jacob

Before looking at the way the Jacob narrative foreshadows the exodus,
we begin with ways it links up with Adam's sin. This enables us to see the
connections Moses has forged within Genesis, as both Abraham and Jacob
point back to Adam, and as Adam, Abraham, and Jacob all experienced exile
from God's presence in anticipation of salvation and return.

The narrative of Jacob's deception of Isaac when he stole Esau's blessing
contains remarkable event-sequence parallels with Genesis 3, and we will point
out the way Moses redeploys language as we survey these:

- The serpent deceived the woman (Gen 3:1–5), who took of the forbidden fruit and ate, "and she also gave some to her husband who was with
  her, and he ate" (3:6, ESV). Just as the woman gave the fruit to the man
  in Genesis 3, initiating the transgression, so in Genesis 27:5–6 Rebekah
  initiates the plan to deceive Isaac.
- In Genesis 3:17 the LORD begins his words of judgment: "Because you
  have listened to the voice of your wife." In Genesis 27:13 Rebekah tells
  Jacob to listen to her voice (שָׁמַע "listen, hear, obey" + קוֹל "voice").
- In Genesis 3:6 the woman "took" the "fruit," and in Genesis 27:14 Jacob
  "took" the goats and his mother prepared the "food."
- Adam did not answer God truthfully when he was called to account
  (Gen 3:8–11), and Jacob repeatedly lied to Isaac (27:19–20, 24).

---

6. Mathews, *Genesis 11:27–50:26*, 123.

- God cursed the serpent and spoke words of judgment over the woman and the man in Genesis 3:14–19. Rebekah tells Jacob in Genesis 27:13, "upon me be your curse" (עָלַי קִלְלָתְךָ).
- After the transgression, in Genesis 3:21 God "clothed" (לָבַשׁ) the man and woman with "garments" (כְּתֹנֶת) of "skin" (עוֹר). As part of the deception, in 27:15–16 Rebekah "clothed" (לָבַשׁ) Jacob with Esau's garments (בֶּגֶד), and with "skins" (עוֹר) she "clothed" (לָבַשׁ) his hands and the smooth part of his neck.
- After the transgression in Genesis 3, God spoke judgment over the serpent (Gen 3:14–15). After the transgression in Genesis 27, Isaac spoke judgment over Esau (27:39–40).
- God blessed the man and woman with words of hope (Gen 3:15), and that hope is extended through Isaac's blessing of Jacob (27:27–29; 28:1–4).
- It is also interesting to observe that whereas the Lord said the serpent would bruise the heel (עָקֵב) of the seed of the serpent (Gen 3:15), Jacob's name is built off the term "heel" because of the way the "heel grasper" (יַעֲקֹב) had hold of his brother's at birth (25:26).
- After Genesis 3, Cain murders Abel (Gen 4:8), and after Jacob steals his blessing, Esau wants to kill him (27:41–42).
- Because of their sin, the man and woman are driven from the garden (Gen 3:22–24). Because of his sin (and to keep him from intermarrying with the Canaanites), Jacob is driven from the land of promise (27:43–46; 28:1–2).

These points of contact present Jacob as a new Adam. After his twenty-year exile from the land (Gen 31:41), Jacob experienced an exodus from captivity and returned to the land of promise (33:18), implying that the exile from Eden would also be remedied by an exodus from captivity and a return to the clean realm of life.

The evidence that Moses means for his audience to connect Jacob's exodus from Paddan-aram with Israel's exodus from Egypt includes lexical points of contact, quotation of phrases, similarities in event sequence, and analogous covenantal and redemptive-historical significance. Isaac passes the blessing of Abraham to Jacob in Genesis 28:3–4, and Jacob's name is changed to Israel, which becomes the name by which his seed, the nation, are called. This establishes similarity in covenantal/redemptive historical significance. The reuse of language, quotations, and similar event sequences are as follows:[7]

- When Jacob goes to Laban he initially receives a warm welcome (Gen 29:13–14). Similarly, when Jacob goes to Egypt, Pharaoh welcomes him with respect (47:5–12).
- Laban subjects Jacob to hard labor (Gen 29:15, 27; 31:38–41), just as the Pharaoh who knew not Joseph did to the Israelites (Exod 1:8–14).
- In Paddan-aram Jacob was fruitful and multiplied (Gen 28:3; cf. 1:28), and he "increased abundantly" (Gen 30:30, 43 ESV, פָּרַץ). In Egypt also Israel was fruitful and multiplied (Exod 1:7, 10, 12) and "spread abroad" (1:12 ESV, פָּרַץ).
- Laban sought to deter the multiplication of Jacob's flocks by removing the animals that would populate Jacob's holdings (Gen 30:35), and Pharaoh sought to deter the multiplication of the people of Israel (Exod 1:15–22).
- In both cases God identifies himself: "I am the God of Bethel" (Gen 31:13, אָנֹכִי הָאֵל בֵּית־אֵל); "I am the God of your father" (Exod 3:6, אָנֹכִי אֱלֹהֵי אָבִיךָ).
- And then he explains how he "sees" the mistreatment of his people and instigates the exodus: "I have seen all that Laban is doing to you. . . . Now arise, go out from this land and return to the land of your kindred" (Gen 31:12–13, ESV, ‫רָאִיתִי אֵת כָּל־אֲשֶׁר לָבָן עֹשֶׂה לָּךְ. . . . קוּם צֵא מִן־‬ ‫הָאָרֶץ הַזֹּאת וְשׁוּב אֶל־אֶרֶץ מוֹלַדְתֶּךָ‬); "I have surely seen the affliction of my people . . . , and I have come down to deliver them out . . . and to bring them up out of that land to a good and broad land, flowing with milk and honey . . ." (Exod 3:7–8, ESV, ‫רָאֹה רָאִיתִי אֶת־עֳנִי עַמִּי‬).
- In both cases the Hebrews ask for their own release (Gen 30:25; Exod 5:1 etc.).
- With each narrative God's people plunder their enemies, "stripping" them of spoil (piel forms of נָצַל in Gen 31:9 and Exod 3:22).
- Jacob escapes (Gen 31:20–21), as do the Israelites (Exod 14:5).
- The same language is used to inform Laban and then Pharaoh that Israel has fled: "When it was told Laban on the third day that Jacob

---

7. My attention was drawn to these by a presentation made by Jeffrey Timmons, "New Exodus," in Old Testament Colloquium at Southern Seminary on November 4, 2020. Timmons cited David Daube, *The Exodus Pattern in the Bible* (London: Faber & Faber, 1983); and Yair Zakovitch, *"And You Shall Tell Your Son—": The Concept of the Exodus in the Bible* (Jerusalem: Magnes, 1991).

had fled" (Gen 31:22, ESV, וַיֻּגַד לְלָבָן . . . כִּי בָרַח יַעֲקֹב); "When the king of Egypt was told that the people had fled" (Exod 14:5, ESV, וַיֻּגַד לְמֶלֶךְ . . . כִּי בָרַח הָעָם).

- Both Laban and Pharaoh pursue Israel: "he took his kinsmen with him and pursued him" (Gen 31:23, ESV, וַיִּקַּח אֶת־אֶחָיו עִמּוֹ וַיִּרְדֹּף); "he took six hundred chosen chariots. . . . and he pursued the people of Israel" (Exod 14:7–8, ESV, וַיִּקַּח שֵׁשׁ־מֵאוֹת רֶכֶב בָּחוּר . . . וַיִּרְדֹּף).

- "And Laban overtook Jacob" (Gen 31:25, וַיַּשֵּׂג לָבָן אֶת־יַעֲקֹב), and Pharaoh said, "I will pursue, I will overtake" (Exod 15:9, אֶרְדֹּף אַשִּׂיג).

- Whereas Yahweh appears to Laban and warns him not to attack Jacob (Gen 31:24, 29, 31, 42), he throws Pharaoh and his host into the sea (Exod 14:27; 15:4; cf. 14:23–29).

When he returned to the land, Jacob's way followed in the footsteps of Abraham's journey to the land of promise. Abraham started in Ur of the Chaldees near Babylon, and from there went to Haran (Gen 11:28, 31; 15:7). He then went from Haran (11:31; 12:4) to Shechem (12:6), where he built an altar, before going on to Bethel/Ai (12:8), where again he built an altar. This progression is later matched by Jacob, whose parents sent him to Haran to find a wife (27:43; 28:10; 29:4). From Haran Jacob returned to Shechem (33:18–20), where he built an altar, before moving on to Bethel (35:14–15, 27), where again he built an altar.[8]

Moses thus forges connections between Adam and Abraham, Jacob and Adam, Jacob and Abraham, and between Abraham and Jacob and the exodus from Egypt. Hosea appears to have understood the relationship Moses established between Jacob and the exodus, prompting him to follow a verse about Jacob going to Laban for a wife with a verse about Moses leading Israel out of Egypt: "Jacob fled to the land of Aram; there Israel served for a wife, and for a wife he guarded sheep. By a prophet the LORD brought Israel up from Egypt, and by a prophet he was guarded" (Hos 12:12–13, ESV [MT 12:13–14]).

§1.3 The Exodus from Egypt

Here is a proposal regarding how Moses arrived at what he presents: having experienced the exodus, Moses reflected on and intended to signal the

---

8. These parallels were brought to my attention by Mathews, *Genesis 1–11:26*, 52.

way that what happened to Abraham typified the exodus. Moses did not, of course, experience the new exodus and return from exile, but he did speak of it repeatedly (Lev 26; Deut 4:25–31; Deut 28–32). The prophet Hosea seems to connect Jacob's exile to the land of Aram and the exodus from Egypt (see esp. Hos 12:12–13, cf. 12:2–14).[9] The idea that the experiences of Abram and Jacob typify both the exodus *and* the new exodus could be informing Hosea on these points. We could say that one patriarch, Abraham, was brought out of Egypt in anticipation of the exodus, and the other, Jacob, was brought home from Paddan-aram in anticipation of the new exodus.

Every detail in Scripture matters, and the biblical authors have made more connections with other passages than we can begin to recognize. What follows highlights features of the exodus narrative that will be reprised by later passages:

- Moses's sons were circumcised on the way into Egypt (Exod 4:24–26), and the wilderness generation was circumcised on the way into Canaan (Josh 5:2–9). Heart circumcision is promised at the restoration (Deut 30:6; cf. Col 2:11, 13).
- Pharaoh's heart was hardened (Exod 4:21; 7:3), as were the hearts of the kings of Canaan (Deut 2:30; Josh 11:20).
- As God told Abraham, he brought judgment on the oppressing enemy (Gen 15:14; Exod 7:4).
- As God told Abraham, and as Jacob did to Laban, Israel plundered the enemy (Gen 15:14; 31:9; Exod 3:22; 11:2; 12:35–36).
- Israel followed the pillar of fire and cloud through the wilderness (Exod 13:21–22; cf. Isa 52:12).
- The people went through the sea on dry ground (Exod 14:16), as Joshua would lead the people across the Jordan (Josh 4:23; cf. 2 Kgs 2:8, 14).
- The Lord intervened at night and kept Laban from attacking Jacob (Gen 31:24, 29, 42), and at the exodus, the angel of the LORD encamped around those who feared him and delivered them (Exod 14:19–20; cf. Ps 34:7 [ET 34:8]).

---

9. See further Derek Drummond Bass, "Hosea's Use of Scripture: An Analysis of His Hermeneutic" (PhD diss., Louisville, The Southern Baptist Theological Seminary, 2008), 236–42.

- Yahweh became the strength, song, and salvation of his people (Exod 15:2), and Isaiah and the psalmist sang the same words (Isa 12:2; Ps 118:14; both quoting Exod 15:2).
- At the blast of his nostrils Yahweh parted the Red Sea for his people (Exod 15:8), figuratively doing the same for David when he delivered him from the hand of all his enemies and from Saul (Ps 18:15; cf. 18:ss [MT 18:16; 18:1]).
- Yahweh gave his people manna from heaven to eat (Exod 16), anticipating the way later prophets such as Elisha (2 Kgs 4:42–44) and Jesus (e.g., John 6:4–13) would feed multitudes, culminating in Jesus giving himself as the bread of life to his people (John 6:33).
- The Lord twice gave water from the rock (Exod 17:6; Num 20:11), and when he came he called the thirsty to come to him to drink and receive something better than water, the Holy Spirit (John 7:37–39).
- At Mount Sinai Israel met Yahweh and entered into covenant with him on the third day (Exod 19–20), and after three days they crossed the Jordan (Josh 1:11; 3:2).
- The covenant was inaugurated, and not without blood (Exod 24; Heb 9:18).
- At Sinai Moses was shown the pattern of the tabernacle on the mountain, and at Sinai they built it for Yahweh to fill with his glory (Exod 25–31, 35–40).
- At Sinai also Israel built the golden calf and broke the covenant, showing that a law that could give life had not been given (Exod 32–34; Gal 3:21; cf. Exod 32:4, 8 and 1 Kgs 12:28).
- Only the intercession of Moses kept the Lord from destroying them, and when he looked to him he was radiant (Exod 32:11–14; 33:12–23; 34:29–35; cf. Ps 34:5 [MT 34:6]).
- On the way to Canaan, to deliver the people, Moses lifted the bronze serpent as a signal for the nations, that they might look unto it and be saved (Num 21:4–9; same term for "signal" [נֵס] used in Isa 11:10, 12; cf. Isa 45:22; John 3:14; 12:32).

The repetition of the pattern of events seen in the lives of Abraham and Jacob adds significance, and with all this Moses also indicates that when Israel enters the land of Canaan to conquer it, they will do so after the pattern of the exodus. That is to say, the conquest will be a new exodus.

§1.4 The Exodus and the Conquest

As Moses celebrates the defeat of Pharaoh in the Red Sea, he recounts how Pharaoh's chariots and his host "went down into the depths like a stone" (Exod 15:5, ESV). Later in the victory song, at 15:16, he uses the same imagery to describe the Canaanite kings that he prophesies Israel will conquer as they "pass over," saying: "they are still as a stone, till your people, O LORD, pass by (עָבַר), till the people pass by (עָבָר) whom you have purchased" (15:16, ESV). That Joshua understood this and presented the conquest of the land as an installment in an exodus-style pattern of events will be evident in the next section.

§2 THE EXODUS IN JOSHUA

We saw in §6 of Chapter 4 above that Joshua is presented as a prophet like Moses. Here I want to suggest that the book of Joshua means to present the conquest of the land as an installment in the exodus pattern of events. The exodus pattern was previewed in the narratives of Abraham (Gen 12–15) and Jacob (Gen 27–32), happened in full when Israel came out of Egypt and made their way through the wilderness (Exod–Num), and Moses suggested that the conquest would be like the exodus in the Song of the Sea (Exod 15), establishing the connection by comparing the host of Pharaoh to a "stone" in Exodus 15:5 and the inhabitants of Canaan to a "stone" in 15:16.

The repetitions of the exodus pattern throughout the Torah create an *escalation* in its significance that increases still more when the narratives of Joshua make more deposits into the imagery-account. We will first consider the conquest in general before reflecting on the deliverance of Rahab in particular.

§2.1 Israel's New-Exodus Conquest of Canaan

The criteria for establishing historical correspondence between the exodus and the conquest are abundant in the book of Joshua: linguistic points of contact, quotations and references back to earlier material, similarities in sequences of events, and continuity of covenantal import. This last is easiest to establish in this case: the people whom Yahweh saved at the exodus and covenanted with at Sinai are the people to whom he gives the land of promise at the conquest, and these are the people who renew the Abrahamic covenant of circumcision in Joshua 5:2–9, who celebrate the Passover in Joshua 5:10, and who renew the Mosaic covenant on Mounts Gerizim and Ebal in Joshua 8:30–35. The redemptive historical and covenantal significance of the conquest in relationship to the exodus is readily apparent.

The historical correspondences between exodus and conquest are likewise abundant: Joshua is like a new Moses (Josh 1). The salvation of Rahab has features that re-enact the Passover (Josh 2, for discussion see under the next subtitle below, "Rahab's Passover"), and then the Red Sea crossing is re-enacted as Israel crosses the Jordan River "on dry ground" (Josh 3, esp. 3:17; 4:23).

In a context reminiscent of the way that the exodus would be educational for coming generations, the crossing of Jordan and Red Sea are directly compared in Joshua 4:21–24 (ESV),

> When your children ask their fathers in times to come, "What do these stones mean?" then you shall let your children know, "Israel passed over this Jordan on dry ground." For the LORD your God dried up the waters of the Jordan for you until you passed over, as the LORD your God did to the Red Sea, which he dried up for us until we passed over, so that all the peoples of the earth may know that the hand of the LORD is mighty, that you may fear the LORD your God forever.

Compare the similar setup for the rehearsal of events in Exodus 12:26 (ESV), "And when your children say to you, 'What do you mean by this service?'" The context of Exodus 12 then rehearses the events of the night of Passover. Note from the quotation above that Joshua 4:23 directly compares the Jordan and Red Sea crossings. We should also observe the repetition in this quotation of the phrase "passed over" (עָבַר once in 4:22, twice in 4:23), which employs the same Hebrew verb used to speak of the night of Passover (עָבַר, Exod 12:12, 23). This verb appears so frequently in the early chapters of Joshua that the "Passover" note is like a steady bass line for the narrative's melody (Josh 1:2, 11, 14, 15; 2:10, 23; 3:1, 2, 6, 11, 14, 16, 17; 4:1, 3, 5, 7, 8, 10, 11, 12, 13, 22, 23 etc.).

We can also observe that the stated purpose of the crossing of the Jordan River in Joshua 4:24 (ESV), "so that all the peoples of the earth may know that the hand of the LORD is mighty, that you may fear the LORD your God forever," is the same purpose stated for the exodus from Egypt in, for instance, Exodus 9:14, 16; 14:4, 17–18.

Some of these points of correspondence were bullet-pointed above, but they bear repeating with others here:

- Just as Moses circumcised his sons on his way back to Egypt before the exodus (Exod 4:24–26), Joshua circumcised the wilderness generation on their way into the land for the conquest (Josh 5:2–9).
- Just as Moses met the angel of the LORD at the burning bush and was told to remove his sandals because the ground was holy (Exod 3:1–6), Joshua met the commander of the army of the LORD and was told to remove his sandals because the ground was holy (Josh 5:13–15).
- Israel plundered Egypt (Exod 3:21–22; 11:3; 12:36), and Israel plundered Jericho (Josh 6:19, 24).
- Just as Yahweh hardened Pharaoh's heart at the exodus (Exod 4:21; 7:3; 9:12; 10:1 etc.), so we read of the kings of Canaan and their people in Joshua 11:20 (ESV), "For it was the LORD's doing to harden their hearts that they should come against Israel in battle, in order that they should be devoted to destruction and should receive no mercy but be destroyed, just as the LORD commanded Moses" (cf. Deut 2:30).
- Just as Yahweh rested when he completed his work of creation in Genesis 2:2–3, so the land had rest when the promises were fulfilled and the conquest was complete (Josh 11:23).
- Just as Adam was to rule and subdue (כָּבַשׁ) the land (אֶרֶץ) in Genesis 1:28, so the new Adam, God's son (Exod 4:22–23), the nation of Israel, sets up the tent of meeting at Shiloh, and "the land (אֶרֶץ) lay subdued (כָּבַשׁ) before them" (Josh 18:1, ESV).

As we saw in the preview of the exodus in Abraham's life, the same events are repeated, and while there is broad correspondence there is not always an exact match in the sequence of the events. Here again this attests to the historical veracity of the accounts. The biblical authors are not inventing stories that match each other but noticing similarities and presenting them for their audiences to notice.

The continuation of the salvation-historical and covenantal significance of Israel from exodus to conquest is clear, as are the similarities in sequences of events, and there are plenty of lexical points of contact and references back to what happened at the exodus in the narratives of the conquest. *Historical correspondence* between exodus and conquest abounds. I submit, then, that Joshua intended to present the conquest of Canaan as an installment in the exodus pattern. The repetition of the pattern creates *escalation* in significance, reinforcing the conclusion that what God did at the exodus is the *type* of thing he does when he intervenes on behalf of his people to save them. This is the *type* of thing that we see at the conquest, and this is the *type* of thing Moses and the prophets who followed him, the first of those being Joshua, led Israel to expect God to do for them in the future.

§2.2 Rahab's Passover

Does the salvation of Rahab typify the salvation of the church? The scarlet cord sometimes features as a parade example of fanciful typological and allegorical excess. The cord was red, the blood of Christ was red, *voila!* The deliverance of Rahab points to the deliverance of Christ's gentile bride at the cross.

Is this suggestion—that what happens with Rahab points to salvation in Christ—totally illegitimate? The validity of the conclusion depends upon what evidence is used to establish it, how that evidence is interpreted, and the quality of the argument made upon the basis of the interpretation of the evidence.

Using the criteria for establishing *historical correspondence* discussed in Chapter 1, this section proposes that the author of the book of Joshua intended to present Rahab's deliverance as an installment in a Passover-like pattern of events. My first premise, then, is that the biblical author meant for his audience to think of the Passover and the exodus from Egypt when he presented his account of the deliverance of Rahab. The second premise is that the Passover and the exodus point forward to the salvation that would be fulfilled in Christ, and that when this pattern of events is repeated in the account of Rahab's deliverance, there is an author-intended *escalation* in the audience's perception of the significance of the pattern. Therefore, as an installment in the Passover-exodus pattern, Rahab's deliverance typifies the way God saves his people in Christ.

For this argument to work, my premises must be valid, and the first one requires historical correspondence between the salvation of Rahab and Passover. To establish that historical correspondence, we need similarities in sequences of events, points of lexical contact, quotation of earlier material, and similarities in redemptive-historical import. Joshua gives us exactly what we need.

Like the midwives who "feared God and did not do as the king of Egypt commanded them, but let the male children live" (Exod 1:17, ESV), Rahab fears Yahweh (Josh 2:9–11) and refuses to cooperate with the king of Jericho's attempt to seize the spies from Israel (2:2–7). This action forges *both* an event-sequence *and* a salvation-historical import correspondence between Rahab and the midwives: in both cases the women recognized that to be faithful to the seed of the serpent would amount to *un*faithfulness to the seed of the woman, and to be righteous in the eyes of the king would be *un*righteous in the sight of God. Like the midwives, who were called to account by Pharaoh and answered shrewdly (Exod 1:18–19), Rahab speaks shrewdly to the king of Jericho (Josh 2:3–7). Like the midwives who were active at the time of the birth of Moses the delivering prophet (Exod 2:1–2), Rahab became part of the line of descent of *the* delivering prophet (Matt 1:5).

In an account intended to evoke the events of the exodus (see §2.1 in this chapter above), Joshua embeds a recitation from Rahab of exactly what Yahweh did for Israel at the exodus: "For we have heard how the LORD dried up the water of the Red Sea before you when you came out of Egypt" (Josh 2:10, ESV). This not only rehearses what happened at the exodus but fulfills prophecies made to Pharaoh as the events of the exodus were being played out: "for this purpose I have raised you up, to show you my power, so that my name may be proclaimed in all the earth" (Exod 9:16, ESV). Here again we see the dynamic relationship between promise and pattern. Yahweh promises that the events of the exodus will result in his name being proclaimed in all the earth, and informed by the promise, Joshua recognizes that even a prostitute living in the wall at Jericho has heard Yahweh's great name. Joshua's interpretation, reflected in his narrative, of what happened with Rahab has been shaped and informed by earlier Scripture.

Rahab has even come to know what Moses taught in Genesis 1–2, which is that Yahweh alone is God: "for the LORD your God, he is God in the heavens above and on the earth beneath" (Josh 2:11, ESV). Not only does she know Yahweh's uniqueness as creator, she knows the unique character of Yahweh, his "lovingkindness" (חֶסֶד), and she asserts that she has acted in accordance with that and calls on the spies from Israel to give her a sure sign that they will treat her according to the character of their God in Joshua 2:12.

The presentation of the plan the spies communicate to Rahab about how her household will be delivered also factors into this interpretation. Joshua's audience would be thoroughly familiar with the events of the Passover, so when he presents the spies instructing Rahab to put a scarlet cord in her window—the one through which they exited her dwelling (Josh 2:18), he seems to mean for them to think of the lamb's blood on the lintel at Passover (Exod 12:7). Just as the LORD passed over the homes with "the blood on the lintel and the two doorposts" and did "not allow the destroyer to enter" the homes of the Israelites to strike them (Exod 12:23), so when Israel struck Jericho they would see the scarlet cord and pass over her house (Josh 2:19). Just as Israel was instructed that on the night of the Passover, "None of you shall go out of the door of his house until the morning" (Exod 12:22, ESV), so Rahab was told,

> you shall gather into your house your father and mother, your brothers, and all your father's household. Then if anyone goes out of the doors of your house into the street, his blood shall be on his own head, and we shall be guiltless. But if a hand is laid on anyone who is with you in the house, his blood shall be on our head. (Josh 2:18–19, ESV)

Just as Israel was saved by lamb's blood on lintel, so Rahab and her household were saved by scarlet cord in window (Josh 6:22–23, 25).

It seems to me that the suggestion that Rahab and the scarlet cord points forward to deliverance in Christ has failed to convince because of the way the point has been argued: some who have proposed it move directly from Rahab to Christ. If, on the other hand, we do not only go forward from Rahab to Christ, but first go back from Rahab to the exodus, and only then go forward to Christ, we arrive at an interpretation that accords with the intentions of both Moses and Joshua. Moses intended the exodus as a type, and he expected further installations in the typological pattern before it was fulfilled. Joshua understood the exodus as a type, and he presented installations in the typological pattern, the conquest in general and the salvation of Rahab in particular. By pointing back to the exodus, the salvation of Rahab points forward to Christ, who fulfilled the exodus in life and death.

§3 THE EXODUS IN THE GOSPELS

This very selective discussion of the presentation of the fulfillment of exodus typology in the Gospels will focus on a few instances in the accounts of Matthew and John. Each author presents Jesus fulfilling the exodus in both the course of his life and in his Passover-fulfilling death.

§3.1 In the Life of Jesus

Matthew and John tell their respective stories in different but complementary ways. We consider them in canonical order.

By means of the genealogy, Matthew presents Jesus as the long-promised seed (Matt 1:1–17). He then embarks on a journey through the early life of Jesus that shows him recapitulating the history of Israel, fulfilling promises and repeating patterns. This begins with the father of Jesus, whose name is Joseph, whose father's name was Jacob, reminding us of the father who gave his son the special coat (Gen 37:3), and the son who had the special dreams (37:5–11). Joseph, son of Jacob, father of Jesus, also received a special dream (Matt 1:20), this one informing him that Mary would bear a son, that he would be the Savior, in fulfillment of Isaiah 7:14 (1:21–25).[10] The context of the Isaiah 7:14 prophecy deals with the exile of the people from the land, the promise that God would preserve the holy seed, and the hope that the child to be born, the shoot from the stump of Jesse, would fulfill the exodus from Egypt, surpassing it with a new and greater exodus (Isa 6:11–13; 8:16–9:7; 11:1–16).

Matthew subtly evokes the Numbers 24:17 prophecy regarding the "star" when he narrates how the wise men saw it rise and came to worship (Matt 2:2), and then he recounts that the birth of Jesus in Bethlehem accords with Micah's prophecy (Mic 5:2). Like the context of Isaiah 7:14, the context of Micah 5:2 deals with the exile of the people from the land and their return when the future king from David's line is born. Micah describes the exile and the failure of Israel's line of kings as a woman being in labor, groaning from birth pains (Mic 4:9–10), and the people will "go to Babylon" (4:10) "until the time when she who is in labor has given birth" (5:3, ESV). The birth of the ruler from Bethlehem (5:2) will bring about the rescue and redemption of the people (4:10).

---

10. These parallels were brought to my attention by Mathews, *Genesis 1–11:26*, 52.

Because of his dreams, Joseph son of Jacob takes his family to Egypt (Matt 2:12, 13). Having recapitulated the descent of the patriarchs of Israel into Egypt (cf. Gen 37–50), after the death of Herod, in fulfillment of Israel's exodus, Matthew cites Hosea 11:1, "Out of Egypt I called my son" (Matt 2:15, ESV). Like Isaiah and Micah, Hosea prophesied that Israel would go into exile to Babylon/Assyria, which would parallel the descent of the people to Egypt: "They shall not return to the land of Egypt, but Assyria shall be their king, because they have refused to return to me" (Hos 11:5, ESV). Like Isaiah and Micah, Hosea prophesied that God would bring his people back from exile in an act of salvation like the exodus from Egypt: "as at the time when she came out of the land of Egypt" (Hos 2:15, ESV, cf. 2:14–23). Hosea has established this paradigm so that a reference to the exodus from Egypt, in context, implicitly points to the new exodus. God's "son" in Hosea 11:1 is the nation of Israel (cf. Exod 4:22–23). So having spoken of the exile of the nation and the cutting off of Israel's king (Hos 10:13–15), the reference back to the exodus in 11:1 also points forward to the new exodus, as can be seen from 11:5–11.

Matthew then narrates a point of correspondence between the birth of Jesus and the birth of Moses. Whereas Pharaoh tried in vain to stamp out the seed of the woman by having all the male children born to Israel murdered by the midwives, and that failing, commanding they be cast into the Nile (Exod 1:15–22), Herod slaughters the male children born in Bethlehem (Matt 2:16). Just as Pharaoh failed to kill Moses, Herod failed to kill Jesus. The Lord has ordained praise from babies to defeat his enemies (cf. Ps 8:2). Matthew's quotation of Jeremiah 31:15 fits because there Jeremiah spoke of the pain the people would feel when their sons were killed in battle and they went into exile, but the exile would give way to the new exodus and new covenant (Jer 31:31–34).

Matthew thus presents Jesus fulfilling prophecies and patterns in the buildup to his ministry, which only broadens and deepens as Jesus goes public. We have seen above how the Jordan River crossing was part of Joshua's succession of Moses, and then Elisha received a double portion of Elijah's spirit, with both crossing the Jordan on dry ground. John the new-Elijah (Matt 3:4; 11:14) comes proclaiming the new exodus and return from exile prophesied in Isaiah 40:3 (3:3), then he baptizes Jesus in the Jordan (3:13–17). Just as Israel crossed the Red Sea into the wilderness where they were tempted and failed repeatedly (Exod 14–Num), having been baptized in the Jordan Jesus enters the wilderness to overcome temptation (Matt 4:1–11).

Matthew notes that Jesus beginning his ministry in Galilee fulfills the new exodus and return from exile prophecy in Isaiah 9:1–2 (Matt 4:14–16), and he calls his disciples to be fishers of men in fulfillment of Jeremiah 16:9–16, where the Lord promised to bring all the exiles home at the new exodus (Matt 4:19). Jesus then ascends the mountain as a new Moses giving a new Torah to his people in the Sermon on the Mount (Matt 5–7), and he does this in fulfillment of the Torah itself (5:17). Whereas through Moses the Lord visited ten plagues on Egypt and then gave the law at Sinai, Jesus gives the Sermon on the Mount and then validates his teaching with the ten mighty works in Matthew 8–10. More could be said, but this is enough to show that Matthew presents Jesus fulfilling exodus patterns in his life.

John does the same, as can be seen from the way he presents Jesus as the fulfillment of the manna from heaven (John 6:32–35) and the fulfillment of the rock from which the water flowed (7:37–39). Jesus not only presents himself as corresponding to these life-giving provisions of God in the wilderness, he presents escalation as he claims to transcend them, saying that the one who believes in him will never hunger or thirst (6:35). John also explains that whereas water flowed from the rock, the Holy Spirit flows from Jesus, the rock who will be struck (7:39; 19:34). And as Israel was led by the pillar of fire in the wilderness, Jesus says that whoever follows him will not walk in darkness because he is the light of the world (8:12). Jesus fulfills the lifting up of the bronze serpent (3:14; 12:32), for he is the Lamb of God, who takes away the sin of the world (1:29).

§3.2 In the Death and Resurrection of Jesus

According to the authors of the Gospels, Jesus himself taught that his death would bring to fulfillment what was typified in the exodus from Egypt. One prominent way that Jesus taught this was through the transformation of the Passover meal on the night in which he was betrayed. Celebrating the Passover with his disciples (Matt 26:17–19), Jesus transformed the symbolism of the commemorative feast. The Passover was instituted for Israel to celebrate the exodus from Egypt, but Jeremiah prophesied that a day would come when God's people would no longer identify him by the exodus but by the new exodus (Jer 16:14–15; 23:7–8). Jesus declared that time had come as he re-signified the elements of the Passover meal. The unleavened bread formerly symbolized Israel's hasty departure from Egypt, when they had not time to allow the leaven to work through the bread. Jesus took that bread, broke it, and declared that it now symbolized his body, broken on behalf of his disciples at the cross (Matt 26:26). Jesus then took the cup that celebrated God's redemption of his people from Egypt when the old covenant was made and declared that day to be over. Jesus announced that the cup now symbolized the new covenant, inaugurated by his blood, poured out on the cross for the forgiveness of sins (26:27–28). In the rest of the New Testament, we never read of the church celebrating the Passover. We do, however, read in Acts of them partaking of the Lord's Supper (e.g., Acts 2:42, 46; 20:7, 11), and Paul gives instructions on it in 1 Corinthians (1 Cor 10:16; 11:17–34). Jesus declared that in his death he was the fulfillment of what the Passover meal celebrated, and his disciples learned that from him, recorded it in the Gospels, enacted it in Acts, and explained it in the Epistles.

Along these lines, when Jesus was on the cross, the soldier did not break the legs of Jesus because he was already dead, and John writes, "these things took place that the Scripture might be fulfilled, 'Not one of his bones will be broken'" (John 19:36, ESV). John is well aware that passages such as Exodus 12:46 and Numbers 9:12 do not prophesy that the bones of the Messiah will not be broken. Those passages, rather, describe what Israel was to do with the Passover lamb—they were not to break any of its bones when they slew it and prepared it for the feast. John says that the way Jesus died fulfills the Scripture on these points because what Jesus accomplished in his life and death fulfills the exodus-pattern of salvation. The role that Jesus played in his death is the role that the Passover lamb played, as Paul also taught.

§4 THE EXODUS IN PAUL

In 1 Corinthians Paul repeatedly applies exodus typology to the formation of Christian identity and the understanding of Christian experience. Several features of Paul's references to the exodus suggest that Paul expected the Corinthians to be thoroughly familiar with *both* what took place when God brought Israel out of Egypt *and* with the idea that the events pertained to the Christian life. If Paul had thought that he needed to establish and explain what happened at the exodus and how it applies to Christians, perhaps he would have felt the need to retell the whole story or at least mention its components in the order they actually took place. And then if he had not assumed that his audience would know the story and its application, perhaps he would have provided a more elaborate justification of his use of the story, and perhaps that justification would have come earlier in the letter. To illustrate what I mean regarding the order of the events of the exodus as they are presented in 1 Corinthians, see Table 8.2, where the left side presents the order of events in the Old Testament, and the right side puts them in the order they appear in 1 Corinthians:

TABLE 8.2: The Exodus in the Old Testament and in 1 Corinthians

The Exodus in the Old Testament		The Exodus in 1 Corinthians	
Passover	1 Cor 5:7; 11:23–26	1 Cor 3:16	Tabernacle/ Temple
Redemption	1 Cor 6:20; 7:23	1 Cor 5:7; 11:23–26	Passover
Red Sea	1 Cor 10:2	1 Cor 6:20; 7:23	Redemption
Manna/Water	1 Cor 10:3–4	1 Cor 9:21	New Law (Sinai)
Sinai Law	1 Cor 9:21	1 Cor 10:2	Red Sea
New Covenant	1 Cor 11:25	1 Cor 10:3–4	Manna/Water
Tabernacle/ Temple	1 Cor 3:16	1 Cor 11:25	New Covenant

And as for explanatory comments on how he applies these realities to Christian identity and life, the closest Paul comes to offering a justification comes only in 1 Corinthians 10. In what follows we briefly discuss the way Paul employs exodus typology to address who the Corinthians understand themselves to be and what that implies about how they should live.

Paul's use of the categories and concepts rooted in the exodus from Egypt teach Christians how to think about themselves. Because the church is a new dwelling place of God by means of the indwelling Spirit (1 Cor 3:16), Paul speaks of it as a "building" (3:9) and of himself as a skilled master builder who laid its foundation, Jesus Christ (3:10). There are ways of building that accord with the temple and ways that do not. Paul refers to ways of doing ministry in the church that preach nothing but Christ and him crucified (2:2) as "gold, silver, and precious stones" (3:12). Those ways of doing ministry, by contrast, that exalt the minister and create factions (1:12–13; 2:1, 5; 3:5–7) are but wood, hay, and stubble (3:12). The temple will survive the flames of judgment (3:13–15), but God will destroy those who destroy his temple (3:17), which consists of those indwelt by his Spirit (3:16). Ministry must be done in a way that exalts not the human minister but Christ and the gospel.

As Paul addresses sexual immorality within the church in 1 Corinthians 5:1–6a, he argues that the unrepentant offender should be disciplined out of church membership, employing Passover imagery in explanation:

> Do you not know that a little leaven leavens the whole lump? Cleanse out the old leaven that you may be a new lump, as you really are unleavened. For Christ, our Passover lamb, has been sacrificed. Let us therefore celebrate the festival not with the old leaven, the leaven of malice and evil, but with the unleavened bread of sincerity and truth. . . . not even to eat with such a one. (1 Cor 5:6b–8, 11b ESV)

Paul's argument is that because Christ died in fulfillment of the Passover lamb, the church should remove from its midst the leaven, that is, the unrepentant sinner. At the exodus from Egypt, the lamb died to free Israel from literal slavery. At the new exodus Christ accomplished, he died to free his people from sin, liberating them from its leavening power. The celebration of the festival to which Paul refers in verse 8 is not the Passover but the Lord's Supper, which the church is to share only with those who show they belong to Jesus by repenting of their sin and trusting in him (cf. 1 Cor 11:27). When Paul calls the church not even to eat with the unrepentant who claims to be a brother in Christ in 5:11, he calls the church not to welcome the unrepentant to the Lord's Supper. The church has been liberated from the power of sin and must walk in repentance pursuing holiness. Just as Israel would not celebrate the Passover with Pharaoh, who wanted to keep Israel enslaved, so the church should not celebrate the Lord's Supper with those who want to maintain slavery to sin and so refuse to repent.

The same dynamic is at work when Paul applies exodus typology to the fact that some Corinthian men were visiting prostitutes, and apparently trying to justify it (1 Cor 6:12–20).[11] Having addressed their argument (6:12–18), Paul

---

11. See esp. Denny Burk, "Discerning Corinthian Slogans through Paul's Use of the Diatribe in 1 Corinthians 6:12–20," *Bulletin for Biblical Research* 18 (2008): 99–121; and Jay E. Smith, "The Roots of a Libertine Slogan in 1 Corinthians 6:18," *Journal of Theological Studies* 59 (2008): 63–95.

concludes with two comments that shape Christian identity by conforming it to the exodus narrative: Israel was redeemed from Egypt, freed from slavery and given the tabernacle, by means of which they could maintain a clean and holy status—in spite of their sin—through the sacrificial system, so that God could dwell in their midst. Christians, likewise, have been redeemed by the death and resurrection of Jesus, freed from slavery to sin and given the indwelling Spirit, making them God's temple. Just as the Israelites should neither attempt to live on their own in the wilderness outside the camp—nor should they have decided to go back to slavery in Egypt—so Christians should stay "within the camp," so to speak, by living within the boundaries set up by the Bible's prohibitions and instructions and repenting of all known transgressions. And thus Paul clinches his argument that the Christians in Corinth should not think they can go on visiting prostitutes with a rhetorical question and an assertion: "Or do you not know that your body is a temple of the Holy Spirit within you, whom you have from God? You are not your own, for you were bought with a price. So glorify God in your body" (1 Cor 6:19–20, ESV).

Paul seems to suggest in 1 Corinthians 7:17–24 that Christians are to so inhabit this new narrative understanding of themselves that it shapes their identity in spite of their circumstances. Circumcision was apparently so distinctive that some Jews sought to remove the evidence that they had been circumcised that they might fit into Greek culture more naturally (1 Macc 1:14–15; 1 Cor 7:18). Paul dismisses such cultural distinctives as not counting for anything. What matters is keeping God's commands (1 Cor 7:19; cf. discussion of 9:21 below). Paul goes so far as to say, "Were you called while a slave? Do not worry about it; but if you are able also to become free, rather do that. For he who was called in the Lord while a slave, is the Lord's freedman; likewise he who was called while free, is Christ's slave" (1 Cor 7:22 NASB). Though Christians might be slaves, they are to find their identity in the narrative that tells them they have been freed from slavery to sin and enslaved to Christ to live for righteousness. Thus Paul again employs exodus typology to frame what happened when Christ died for his people. Just as God redeemed Israel for himself through the death of the lamb at Passover, so God redeemed Christians—bought them with the price of Christ's blood—at the cross: "You were bought with a price; do not become slaves of men" (7:23). Paul teaches God's ownership of his people through Christ because of redemption to shape their self-conception and guide their behavior.

As Paul explains his freedom, he reveals his own conformity to Christ as, though free, he made himself a slave to all to win them to Christ (1 Cor 9:19; cf. 2 Cor 8:9). With Jews he lives as a Jew to avoid unnecessary offense and gain a hearing for the gospel, and with gentiles he does likewise, articulating this with reference to the law of Moses:

> To those under the law I became as one under the law (though not being myself under the law) that I might win those under the law. To those outside the law I became as one outside the law (not being outside the law of God but under the law of Christ) that I might win those outside the law. (1 Cor 9:20–21, ESV)

Paul is not under the law of Moses because Christ brought an end to the time in which the old covenant was the operative arrangement between God and his people (Rom 10:4; Gal 3:19–4:7). In the making of the new covenant, as with the making of the old covenant, a deposit of revelation is given, and Paul calls this "the law of Christ" (9:21).[12] Just as the deliverance accomplished at the exodus from Egypt was accompanied by covenant and law, so the deliverance that fulfills the exodus is accompanied by covenant and law. Paul is not under the old but the new.

Exodus typology is prominent in 1 Corinthians 10, as Paul responds to objections to his teaching that he has either heard about or anticipates.[13] Paul has addressed Corinthian sexual immorality (1 Cor 5–7) and idolatry (1 Cor 8–10), and it seems some in Corinth thought that the fact that they were baptized and partaking of the Lord's Supper meant they could ignore Paul's concerns. The redefinition of Christian identity is apparent in Paul's address—he calls the Corinthian Christians "brothers," and then he identifies the nation of Israel as "our fathers" (10:1). Paul treats the passage through the Red Sea as a type of baptism, and he treats the manna from heaven and the water from the rock as typifying the Lord's Supper.

Paul says that Israel was baptized into Moses (1 Cor 10:1–2), and he says that they partook of the old covenant type of the Lord's Supper when they ate

---

12. For extensive discussion, see Chester, *Messiah and Exaltation*, 537–601.

13. Contra Bell, who writes, "I believe 1 Cor. 10.1–13 does have some typological significance but any typology is a by-product of something more fundamental: myth." Bell, *The Irrevocable Call of God*, 186.

manna from heaven and drank water from the rock (10:3–4). These assertions are likely based on the teaching of Jesus in John 6–7. Anticipating what he would do at the Last Supper, Jesus identified himself as the bread of life that fulfills the manna from heaven in the bread of life discourse (John 6:25–59). Jesus then identified himself as the fulfillment of the rock from which the water flowed, John explaining that Jesus would give what is even better than water—the Holy Spirit (7:37–39). Paul's reference to the rock following the people and being Christ, then, likely weaves several threads together:[14]

- In the original provision of water from the rock, Yahweh himself stood before Moses on the rock, so that for Moses to strike the rock would seem to entail him striking Yahweh, resulting in the flow of water (Exod 17:6).
- Yahweh is also regularly identified as his people's rock (e.g., Deut 32:4, 13, 18).
- Yahweh manifested himself in both the angel of the Lord and the pillar of fire and cloud (e.g., Exod 14:19).
- Other New Testament teaching plainly asserts the identity between Yahweh and Jesus, saying that Jesus led his people out of Egypt (Jude 5).
- The blood and water flowing from Jesus when he was struck, when his side was pierced on the cross (John 19:34), would seem to enact a typological fulfillment of the striking of the rock in the wilderness.

As these points simmer together in the mind, we also note the function of the Lord's Supper in the narratival fulfillment of the exodus pattern of events in the New Testament: just as Israel was sustained by manna from heaven and water from the rock in the wilderness as they made their way to the land of promise, so Christians are sustained by the Lord's Supper as they make their way to the new and better Jerusalem in the fulfillment of the promised land. Just as Israel celebrated the Passover yearly to enter into the salvation that they had experienced, to grind for themselves Passover-prescription-lenses through which to view the world and their own lives, so Christians break bread on the first day of the week (Acts 20:7), when they come together as a church (1 Cor 11:17, 18, 20, 33, 34), to remind themselves that the body of Jesus was broken for

---

14. Cf. Basil of Caesarea: "'the Rock was Christ' typologically . . . The manna was a type of the living bread, which came down from heaven." Basil, *On the Holy Spirit*, 53.

their redemption (11:24), to eat the bread and drink the cup in remembrance of him (11:24–25).

Paul, then, tells the Corinthians that the types of baptism (Red Sea crossing) and the Lord's Supper (manna from heaven, water from the rock) did not protect Israel from God's wrath when Israel committed sexual immorality and idolatry in the wilderness, saying in 1 Corinthians 10:5 (ESV), "Nevertheless, with most of them God was not pleased, for they were overthrown in the wilderness." Paul's point is that no Corinthian claiming to be a Christian should think that baptism and the Lord's Supper prevent God's wrath on idolatry and sexual immorality. He explains that God made Israel typify the church's experience to teach believers to desire holiness rather than sin in 1 Corinthians 10:6, "Now these things took place as types [τύποι] for us, that we might not desire evil as they did." Flowing out of the statement "that we might not be those who desire evil," Paul adds four more things Christians should not be (all beginning with the same "nor" conjunction, μηδὲ), and each comes with a comparison (καθώς in the first three, καθάπερ in the fourth) to the way some in Israel did those very things:

> nor be idolaters
> > as some of them were . . .
> nor may we be sexually immoral
> > as some of them were . . .
> nor may we test Christ
> > as some of them tested . . .
> nor grumble
> > as some of them grumbled . . . (1 Cor 10:7–10)

It seems from Paul's list that the first thing, worded "that we may not be those who desire evil," manifests itself in the four things worded "nor be." If this is correct, desiring evil results in idolatry, immorality, testing Christ, and grumbling. Paul has grounded all this in the Old Testament narratives dealing with the exodus and wilderness wandering: 10:1–5 gets the people out of Egypt into the wilderness, and then Paul punctuates the statements of what Christians must not be/do with references to Israel's wilderness failures in 10:7–11. In 10:7 Paul quotes Exodus 32:6 referring to Israel's sin with the golden calf. In 10:8 he seems to bring together Numbers 25 and 26, before referencing the fiery serpents of Numbers 21:5–9 in 10:9 and concluding, it seems, in 10:10 with a reference to the destroying plague of Numbers 14 after the people grumbled in response to the report of the spies (Num 14:2, 36–37). Paul then returns to the idea he had stated in 10:6, that these Old Testament events were types from which Christians are to learn to desire holiness, in 10:11, "Now these things happened to them typologically [τυπικῶς], but they were written down for our instruction, on whom the end of the ages has come."

In 1 Corinthians 10:6 and 10:11 Paul states explicitly the implicit rationale that results in all his references to Christians thinking of themselves as those who have experienced the fulfillment of what Israel's experience of the exodus typified. Paul's view is that God caused those events to happen to typify what he would bring to pass in the church, and this was for the instruction of Christians (cf. 1 Cor 9:10, ESV, "It was written for our sake," and Rom 15:4, ESV, "whatever was written in former days was written for our instruction").

In 1 Corinthians, Paul speaks of Christians experiencing the typological fulfillment of Israel's experience at the exodus: their experience of redemption by means of Passover, the institution of the feast to commemorate it, their baptism in the cloud and in the sea, their eating of the spiritual food and drink, and their reception of law, tabernacle, and covenant at Sinai, and their many failures in the wilderness. All this, Paul asserts, happened typologically and was written to teach Christians who they are, what they should desire, and how they should live.

§5 THE EXODUS IN REVELATION

The Bible's exodus typology works at a number of different levels. The overarching story begins with Adam and Eve exiled from Eden, and through the new exodus and return from exile, God will finally bring his people home to himself. Within this broad story of all humanity, the Old Testament focuses on a national story dealing with the house of Israel. Jacob and his children first sojourn in Egypt, where they are eventually enslaved, and God delivers them at the exodus and brings them back to the land of promise. Because they broke the covenant, however, Israel was exiled to Babylon, and Israel's prophets announced that God would do a new exodus and bring his people back to the land of promise. The whole of what the prophets pointed to included the reign of a new king from David's line, a return to Edenic conditions, the removal of death, a complete change of the hearts of God's people producing obedience, and the nations streaming to Zion to worship Yahweh (e.g., Isa 2:1–4; 11:1–16; Amos 9:11–15; Mic 5:2–4; Dan 9:24; Zech 14:16–20).

When Babylon fell to Persia in 539 BC, Yahweh "stirred up the spirit of Cyrus, king of Persia, so that he made a proclamation" allowing the Jews to return to their land and rebuild the temple (Ezra 1:1b, 2–4, ESV). Ezra directly states that these things took place "that the word of Yahweh by the mouth of the prophet Jeremiah might be fulfilled" (1:1a). As Ezra tells the story of the people leaving Babylon, he presents it as an installment in the exodus pattern of events.[15] For Ezra, Israel experienced a fulfillment of the prophesied new exodus and return from exile, but it was an inaugurated fulfillment not a final one, for though Ezra states that prophecies were fulfilled, he also shows that many prophecies were not fulfilled: only a small number of God's people returned, certainly not all the lost sheep of the house of Israel (cf. Jer 16:16). The wilderness of Zion did not become like Eden (cf. Isa 51:3; Ezek 36:35). No Messiah arose, no lions ate straw instead of lambs, no nursing children played over the hole of the cobra, and Yahweh's glory did not cover the dry lands as the waters cover the sea (Isa 11:1–9). Far from it. God's people had not experienced the pervasive heart change, and they were so at home among idolaters that they intermarried with them, committing anew the very sins that got them exiled in the first place (Ezra 9–10; Neh 13). Israel had returned to the land of promise from the exile to Babylon, but they had not returned to Eden from the exile from God's presence. Promises remained unfulfilled.

Then at the appointed time, God sent forth his son, born of a woman, born under law (Gal 4:4). The Lord Jesus enacted a recapitulation of the history of Israel in his life and death, bringing to fulfillment all that was prophesied and all that was typified by the exodus from Egypt. The death of Christ opened the way to the garden of Eden and the presence of God. With the *already* of Christ's finished work, however, comes a *not yet* on the full reception of the promise, "since God had provided something better for us, that apart from us they should not be made perfect" (Heb 11:40, ESV).

From what John presents in the book of Revelation, it seems that we can say the following about exodus typology in the Bible: the archetypal exile from Eden awaits the antitypical return from exile that will be accomplished

---

15. See further James M. Hamilton Jr., *Ezra and Nehemiah*, Christ-Centered Exposition Commentary (Nashville: Broadman & Holman, 2014).

through the consummation of exodus typology. The ectypal installments in the exodus pattern of salvation include the anticipations of the exodus in the lives of Abraham and Jacob, the exodus from Egypt, the new exodus and return from exile to Babylon, all coming to fulfillment in the exodus Jesus accomplished in Jerusalem. The exodus from Egypt restored God's people to the land of promise. The exodus Jesus accomplished in Jerusalem freed his people from their sins. The exodus John depicts in Revelation will liberate God's people from bondage to corruption. The way that God saved his people at the exodus from Egypt and in its fulfillment on the cross is the way that God will save his people in the future.

How does John present this in the book of Revelation?

To answer this question I will survey the ways that John deploys exodus typology in Revelation in the order of events as they occurred in the Old Testament.[16] John has his own literary reasons for putting this in the order in which we find them.[17]

Just as Joseph's dreams and his descent into Egypt provide the setup for the exodus from Egypt, so John presents a "sign" that reminds readers of Joseph dreaming that the sun, the moon, and eleven stars were bowing down to him in Genesis 37:9. John presents the mother of Jesus symbolically "clothed with the sun, with the moon under her feet, and on her head a crown of twelve stars" (Rev 12:1, ESV). Joseph's descent into Egypt prepares for the exodus in the same way that the birth of Christ puts things in motion for its fulfillment.

At the exodus from Egypt a number of things happened: God visited plagues on Egypt, plagues that did not touch his own people (Exod 8:22; 9:20–21, 26; 10:23). In Revelation, the plagues that accompany the trumpets and bowls of wrath match the plagues on Egypt (see Rev 8–9, 15–16), but before they fall God seals his servants (Rev 7:1–4) to protect them from the wrath (9:4). Like the magicians of Pharaoh imitating Moses but failing, the beast tries to imitate God's seal with his mark (13:16–18). Whereas the beast's mark does not protect his worshipers from the wrath of God, God's seal protects his

---

16. Cf. Bauckham's discussion of "the eschatological exodus" in *The Theology of the Book of Revelation*, 70–72.

17. For my attempt to trace these, see Hamilton, *Revelation*. Note esp. the chiastic structure of the whole book proposed on p. 165. Bauckham's discussion of the "Structure and Composition" of Revelation is magnificent. See Richard Bauckham, *The Climax of Prophecy: Studies on the Book of Revelation* (Edinburgh: T&T Clark, 1993), 1–37.

servants, and even when Satan kills them for not having the mark, God raises them from the dead (13:15; 20:3–4).

Through the final plague, the death of the firstborn, with the Passover, God liberated his people from slavery in Egypt. At the cross, Christ freed his people from their sins by his blood (Rev 1:5; 5; 9). As the Passover lamb was slain for Israel, Jesus was slain for his people but stands alive (5:6, 12). The resurrection of his people and their entrance into the new Jerusalem in Revelation 20–22 shows that the final installment in the exodus pattern of salvation will consummate salvation.

Just as Israel sang the Song of Moses after leaving Egypt and crossing the Red Sea in Exodus 15, so God's people celebrate his salvation with a new song (Rev 14:1–3), which at the same time is the old song, the Song of Moses (15:3).

God told Moses to say to Israel, "You yourselves have seen what I did to the Egyptians, and how I bore you on eagles' wings and brought you to myself" (Exod 19:4, ESV). This is the Lord's own description of how he led Israel through the wilderness by the pillar of fire and cloud, sustaining them with manna from heaven and water from the rock as they made their way from the Red Sea to Sinai. Isaiah prophesies that those who hope in Yahweh will experience the same at the new exodus: "they who wait for Yahweh shall renew their strength; they shall mount up with wings like eagles; they shall run and not be weary; they shall walk and not faint" (Isa 40:31). As John depicts the church likewise being led through the wilderness to a new and better land of promise, an angel brings John a scroll that he is to eat and then prophesy to God's people (10:8–11), and this angel is "wrapped in a cloud" and "his legs like pillars of fire" (10:1). This indicates that the leading Israel experienced typifies the way the church is led by the apostolic word John prophesies. Israel had manna from heaven and water from the rock, and the church is symbolically nourished by God in the wilderness (Rev 12:6), being rescued from Satanic attacks by "the wings of a great eagle" (12:13–14).

As Israel met Yahweh at Sinai with thunder, lightning, smoke, and earthquake marking the theophany (Exod 19:16–20), John sees the one seated on the throne, from which come "flashes of lightning, and rumblings and peals of thunder" (Rev 4:5, ESV), with earthquakes in later manifestations of God's judging presence (8:5; 11:19; 16:18). The revelation made to Moses at Sinai is fulfilled in the revelation made to John in the Apocalypse.

God's purpose was to make Israel "a kingdom of priests and a holy nation"

(Exod 19:6). Jesus fulfilled that purpose with the people of God: he "made us a kingdom, priests to his God and Father" (Rev 1:6, ESV; 5:10). At Sinai Israel received the tabernacle (Exod 25–40), but now Christ tabernacles over his people (Rev 7:15). Moses shepherded the people through the wilderness, and that role is fulfilled by the Lamb shepherding his people and seeing that they no more hunger or thirst (7:16–17). Israel was endangered by the teaching of Balaam in the wilderness after the exodus (Num 22–31), and the church is confronted with similar false prophets and teachers (Rev 2:14).

Moses promised the people a land flowing with milk and honey. In fulfill-ment of that good land, Jesus promises his people the right to eat from the tree of life (Rev 2:7), and what John sees and writes shows Jesus able to make good on that promise (22:2). The exodus is fulfilled in Christ's first coming, and the fact that the plagues accompanying the trumpets and bowls of Revelation 8–9 and 15–16 precede his return in Revelation 19 shows that God's future salva-tion will be according to the pattern of the past. Jesus has destroyed the devil and delivered "all those who through fear of death were subject to lifelong slavery" (Heb 2:14–15, ESV). The exodus will be fulfilled in the resurrection of the dead, when all creation and all God's people will be liberated from "bondage to corruption" to enjoy "the freedom of the glory of the children of God" (cf. Rom 8:21, ESV; Rev 18:2–4; 20:11–21:4).[18]

---

18. Cf. Morales' discussion of "Egypt as Sheol," *Exodus Old and New*, 50–54.

PART 3

INSTITUTIONS

I f typology deals with people, events, and institutions, how do institutions typify what God does for his people in Christ? For our consideration of "institutions," it will be helpful to clarify what an institution is. The Oxford English Dictionary's entry 6.a. on "institution" describes it as

> An established law, custom, usage, practice, organization, or other element in the political or social life of a people;
>> a regulative principle or convention subservient to the needs of an organized community or the general ends of civilization.[1]

As we move into Part 3 of this book, the goal is to explore and exposit the ways that certain institutions create and/or contribute to patterns that typify the way that God delivers his people, forges relationships (i.e., covenants) with them, and continues in ongoing intimacy between himself and his beloved. In this section we will consider marriage and the Leviticult. As we consider marriage and the Levitical cult, we bear in mind that we are dealing with *texts* about these things, not the things themselves. As Mary Douglas has written, "Literature is institutional; institutions establish stereotyped forms

---

1. "Institution, n.," in *OED Online* (Oxford University Press), http://www.oed.com/view/Entry/97110.

of behavior, and literature itself contributes to the selection and stereotyping process."[2]

A fascinating feature of both of these institutions is the way that the eschatological and heavenly reality seems to cast its earthly shadow backwards through history. With marriage, Paul seems to indicate in Ephesians 5:31–32 that God created marriage to give human experience categories that would enable understanding of the relationship between Christ and the church. The heavenly reality in this case is the Savior's love for his covenant people, and its eschatological consummation will take place at the marriage feast of the Lamb. The shadow of that great day stretches all the way back to Genesis 2:24, cited in Ephesians 5:31, in response to which Paul asserts, "This mystery is profound, and I am saying that it refers to Christ and the church" (Eph 5:32, ESV).

The Levitical cult centered on the tabernacle and temple presents a similar case, with the author of Hebrews indicating that the heavenly tabernacle provided the pattern for the one made under Moses (Heb 8:5), which would then be fulfilled in Christ (9:23–26).

---

2. Mary Douglas, *Thinking in Circles: An Essay on Ring Composition* (New Haven: Yale University Press, 2010), 17.

LEVITICULT

The gospel points out with the finger what the law foreshadowed under types.

—JOHN CALVIN[1]

G od provided the Levitical cult to Israel to reinstitute the most important aspect of the garden of Eden: God's ability to fellowship with man without the man being struck dead because of God's holiness.[2] This chapter begins by considering the tabernacle and the temple as the context of the cult and ends with God's presence as the goal of the cult. Within the cosmic temple God put man, and after sin and redemption at the exodus, God meant Israel to be a kingdom of priests. In place of the firstborn he redeemed for himself at the exodus (Num 3:11–13), God took the Levites as his own, establishing priests from the line of Aaron to offer the sacrifices made necessary by sin and its resulting uncleanness. All this is laid out in the Torah of Moses, which provides both needed instruction that must be believed and indications of a coming redeemer-king. The hope for that redeemer motivates the people to keep the instructions of the Torah, which also tells of him. And all these things center on the covenant, into which Yahweh entered with Israel at Sinai. The chiastic structure of this chapter, described in the preceding sentences, is as follows:

---

1. John Calvin, *Institutes of the Christian Religion*, ed. John T. McNeill, trans. Ford Lewis Battles (Philadelphia: Westminster John Knox, 1960), 2.9.3, 426.

2. In the Introduction to his commentary on Leviticus, Nobuyoshi Kiuchi writes, "Other links to Gen. 3 are noted throughout the commentary, all of which convey the message that holiness is what the first man and woman had before the fall, and that the various rules in Leviticus aim to lead the Israelites, as it were, back to this existential condition." *Leviticus*, Apollos Old Testament Commentary (Downers Grove, IL: InterVarsity, 2007), 29.

§1 Temple
 §2 Priests and Levites
  §3 The Torah of Moses
   §4 The Covenant
  §5 The Coming King
 §6 Sin, Sacrifices, and Feasts
§7 God's presence

The foundation for these seven aspects of the cult is laid in the garden of Eden,[3] will find fulfillment in Christ and the church, and then in turn the new and better Eden of the new creation, the new heaven and new earth, with Jerusalem as the holy of holies in the cosmic temple, will bring the institution of the Levitical cult to its ultimate fulfillment. The church experiences inaugurated fulfillment of every aspect of the cult discussed in this chapter, as can be seen from Table 9.1, "The Leviticult and Its Fulfillments."

TABLE 9.1: The Leviticult and Its Fulfillments

§1 Temple	The Church
§2 Priests and Levites	Priesthood of Believers
§3 The Torah of Moses	The Law of Christ
§4 The Covenant	The New Covenant
§5 The Coming King	King Jesus
§6 Sin, Sacrifices, and Feasts	Baptism and Eucharist
§7 God's Presence	God's Presence

§1 TEMPLE

We looked at the relationship between creation, the tabernacle and temple, Christ, the church, and the new creation as a cosmic temple in Chapter 7 above.

---

3. Morales explains, "With the Eden narratives serving to inform the symbolism of the cultus, including its rituals, being clean may have been understood in terms of admittance to Eden, while being banished from Israel's camp would have been a sort of 'reenactment of the fall, when Adam and Eve were expelled from Eden.... As Adam and Eve experienced a living death when they were expelled from Eden, so every man who was diagnosed as unclean suffered a similar fate.'" Morales, *Who Shall Ascend the Mountain of the Lord?*, 166; citing Gordon J. Wenham, *The Book of Leviticus*, New International Commentary on the Old Testament (Grand Rapids: Eerdmans, 1979), 201, 213.

In this section we focus on how the tabernacle and temple functioned in relationship to the institution of the Levitical cult.

In the instructions for the tabernacle, which overflow to the temple, we see graded holiness, moving outward from the most holy place where God dwells, to the clean realm of the camp, and then outside the camp is the unclean realm of the dead. Only the high priest can enter the holy of holies, and he can only go there once a year on the day of atonement (Lev 16:15, 34; Heb 9:7). Moving outward in decreasing gradations of holiness, only priests can enter the holy place, and they do so only at appointed times (Num 18:2–6; 28:3; Heb 9:6).

When the tabernacle was instituted, Moses and Aaron and Aaron's sons "were to camp before the tabernacle on the east, before the tent of meeting toward the sunrise . . . guarding the sanctuary itself, to protect the people of Israel. And any outsider who came near was to be put to death" (Num 3:38, ESV). These guardians of the tabernacle are there to prevent what happened to Nadab and Abihu in Leviticus 10, when they offered unauthorized fire and were struck dead by an outbreak of Yahweh's holiness (Lev 10:1–3). So much of the Leviticult is informed by this reality: God is holy, and if the holy comes into contact with the unclean, death results. As Michael Morales has written,

> Holiness, properly conceived, pertains to fullness of life, a perspective that will be grasped more clearly when we consider . . . the correspondence between the holy of holies and the garden of Eden. Suffice it to say here that the holy of holies derives its status from being the locale of God's Presence on earth, and, so, from God's nature as absolute life, the fountain of life—the God of the living. Understood in this manner, *the tabernacle's grades of holiness are seen rather as grades of life*, with *the holy of holies representing fullness of life*.[4]

Uncleanness results from death. Death results from sin. Sin brought death into the world, and contact with death makes unclean. For the holy God to dwell among a sinful people, the Levitical cult is necessary. For the sinful people to stay alive with Yahweh inhabiting the holy of holies, Moses, Aaron, Eleazar, and Ithamar were to guard God's dwelling place for the protection of the people against God's wrath. It was so important that any non-priest who attempted to draw near was to be put to death (Num 3:38).

---

4. Morales, *Who Shall Ascend the Mountain of the Lord?*, 31.

As additional protection, the Levites were to encamp around the tabernacle, between Moses, Aaron, and the sons of Aaron at its entrance and the broader camp of Israel. The Levites served as a kind of protective buffer zone between tabernacle and people. The description of their duty is very much like that of Moses and Aaron and Aaron's sons: "the Levites shall camp around the tabernacle of the testimony, so that there may be no wrath on the congregation of the people of Israel. And the Levites shall keep guard over the tabernacle of the testimony" (Num 1:53, ESV). The Levites were to guard God's dwelling place to prevent unauthorized intruders, so that God's holiness did not break out against the people. Aaron and his sons were charged with guarding what was within the tent, and while the priests were ministering within, the Levites were to guard the tent (Num 18:1–7). If a priest was ministering within and an unauthorized intruder broke through, death could fall on intruder, Levite, and priest (18:3). Intruders, therefore, were to be put to death (18:7).

Outside the Levite buffer zone the tribes of Israel encamped around the tabernacle, three tribes per side, north, south, east, west (Num 2:1–31). Outside the camp was the unclean realm of the dead.

As the tabernacle and temple gave to Israel a clean realm of life that sought to recapture undefiled creation after sin, so the church is a sanctified space (cf. 1 Cor 7:14). As the priests and Levites were to guard the sanctuary, so the priesthood of all believers is to guard the gospel (Gal 1:1–2; Eph 5:6; Col 2:8; 2 Tim 1:14; Titus 1:9).

§2 PRIESTS AND LEVITES

In Chapter 3 on Priests above we looked at Adam as a royal priest, Melchizedek as a king-priest, Israel as a royal priest, the Aaronic priesthood, and the Old Testament promises of a faithful priest. This section focuses on the priesthood's function within the Levitical cult, and I will take my cues from the author of Hebrews, who details points of correspondence between the Levitical priesthood and Jesus, pointing out how the significance of these points is transcended by the "great priest over the house of God" (Heb 10:21). The previous section of this chapter noted how the priests were to guard the tabernacle and temple, and in that role of guardian, the Lord Jesus promised to be always with his people to the end of the age (Matt 28:20). This section looks first at how Christ fulfills the priesthood, then briefly at how he makes his people priests.

§2.1 Christ Fulfills the Priesthood

The author of Hebrews sees a number of points of historical correspondence and escalation between the Levitical priesthood and the Melchizedekian high priesthood of Jesus. These include appointment to the priesthood, what was attainable by the ministry of the priesthood, and the offerings made by the priesthood.

§2.1.1 Appointment to the Priesthood

The author of Hebrews explains that "every high priest chosen from among men is appointed to act on behalf of men in relation to God, to offer gifts and sacrifices for sins" (Heb 5:1, ESV), and then adds that "no one takes this honor for himself but only when called by God, just as Aaron was" (5:4, ESV). Drawing out the historical correspondence between the high priests and Jesus, he states in the next verse, "So also Christ did not exalt himself to be made a high priest, but was appointed by him who said to him, 'You are my Son, today I have begotten you'" (Heb 5:5, ESV), quoting Psalm 2:7.

The author of Hebrews sees the appointment of the Messiah to the high priesthood in the words of Psalm 2:7. How does he arrive at this conclusion? He cites Psalm 110:4 in the very next verse, so it seems that the author of Hebrews has read Psalms 2 and 110 together. In doing this, our author has drawn a connection between the poetic re-presentation of 2 Samuel 7:13–14 in Psalm 2:7 and the announcement made to the promised seed from David's line, David's Lord, in Psalm 110:4.[5] Further, understanding the connection between *Adam* as son of God and *David* as new-Adam son of God (discussed in §4 of Chapter 2 above) also helps to establish this reality. As God's son, Adam is a priest-king. As a new-Adam representative of Israel, the son of David will be son of God (2 Sam 7:14), and his role as priest-king has been prefigured by Melchizedek (Ps 110:4; Gen 14:18–20).

For Jesus to be appointed as the new-Adam son of God is for Jesus to be appointed to Adam's roles, which were embodied in Melchizedek, passed to Israel, then to the future king from David's line: the roles of priest and king.[6]

---

5. This kind of connection validates the reading of the Psalter *as a book*, verifying the relationship between Psalms 2 and 110 as one intended by those who put the Psalter into its final canonical form. For discussion of the relationship between Psalms 2 and 110, see Emadi, "The Royal Priest." For an attempt to read the whole Psalter as a book, see Hamilton, *Psalms.*

6. Cf. Morales's comments on "the high priest, whose role was that of Adam," in *Who Shall Ascend the Mountain of the Lord?*, 153.

Having established the historical correspondence between the Levitical priests and the high priesthood of Jesus, the author of Hebrews adds the escalation in significance when he points out that, because it came with an oath, Christ's appointment is superior:

> those who formerly became priests were made such without an oath, but this one was made a priest with an oath by the one who said to him: "The Lord has sworn and will not change his mind, 'You are a priest forever.'" This makes Jesus the guarantor of a better covenant. (Heb 7:20–22, ESV)

He then points to another way that Christ's priesthood transcends that of the former priests. Explaining that the Levitical priests had to offer sacrifices for their own sins on a daily basis (7:27)—a need they had because of their weakness (7:28a; cf. 5:2), the author celebrates the Psalm 110:4 oath made to the perfect Psalm 2:7 son: "the word of the oath, which came later than the law, appoints a Son who has been made perfect forever" (7:28b, ESV).

The author of Hebrews does not mention this, but it is also the case that as the priests of Israel began their service at the age of thirty (Num 4:3, 30), Jesus began his ministry at "about" that age (Luke 3:23).

§2.1.2 What Was Attainable

Hebrews seems to understand the failure of the Aaronic priesthood and the promises of a future faithful priest[7] to be resolved in the Melchizedekian high priesthood of Jesus. The author discusses these points as he deals with the fact that whereas the law established priests from the line of Levi, Jesus arose from the line of Judah (Heb 7:4–15). He takes it for granted that his audience will agree with him that the Old Testament itself showed the failure of the Mosaic law and its priesthood when he writes,

> Now if perfection had been attainable through the Levitical priesthood (for under it the people received the Law), what further need would there have been for another priest to arise after the order of Melchizedek rather than one named after the order of Aaron? (Heb 7:11, ESV)

---

7. These were discussed in Chapter 3 above, on Priests, which corresponds to this one in the chiastic structure of this study.

Perfection is a key issue throughout the discussion, and the perfection in view pertains to both the priests and the worshipers. As can be seen from 7:11, the author of Hebrews assumes that the Levitical priesthood could not bring about perfection, nor could the law, as he states in 7:19 (ESV), "for the law made nothing perfect." The priests themselves were not perfect but sinful and weak (5:2–3; 7:27–28). Christ, by contrast, was shown to be perfect as he endured temptation and suffered faithfully unto death, completing his appointed course and being made "perfect through suffering" (2:10; 5:8–9; 7:28).

The priests were not perfect, and the "gifts and sacrifices" they "offered" could not "perfect the conscience of the worshiper" (Heb 9:9). The author explains that the Levitical priests

offer gifts according to the law. They serve a copy and shadow of the heavenly things. For when Moses was about to erect the tent, he was instructed by God, saying, "See that you make everything according to the pattern that was shown you on the mountain." (Heb 8:4–5, ESV)

In this case, then, it seems that Moses was shown the heavenly tabernacle, which provided the pattern according to which he was to construct the earthly tabernacle. That earthly tabernacle and its worship provided "a copy and shadow of the heavenly things" (Heb 8:5). These "copies of the heavenly things" (9:23) prescribed by the law had "but a shadow of the good things to come instead of the true form of these realities" (10:1, ESV). Jamieson observes,

The point in 10.1 is to assert the inadequacy of the law, but it is striking that the author does so by saying that the law possesses a shadow of good things *to come*. The shadow in this case is not cast from heaven to earth (as in 8.5), but from the future to the past. . . . Jesus' heavenly, eschatological sacrifice is prefigured in the earthly Levitical cult. The Christ-event, as it were, cast a shadow backwards, determining the form of the first covenant's cult.[8]

Moses seems to have been shown the real thing on the mountain, and then he instructed Israel to make its shadow, which pointed forward to what Christ would accomplish in the real thing.

---

8. R. B. Jamieson, "Hebrews 9.23: Cult Inauguration, Yom Kippur and the Cleansing of the Heavenly Tabernacle," *New Testament Studies* 62 (2016): 583.

Accordingly, while the copy and shadow could "sanctify for the purification of the flesh," so that the worshiper could dwell in the clean realm in the presence of God (Heb 9:13), "it can never, by the same sacrifices that are continually offered every year, make perfect those who draw near" (10:1, ESV). The continual need to offer the sacrifices shows that they are not able to cleanse the conscience: "Otherwise, would they not have ceased to be offered, since the worshipers, having once been cleansed, would no longer have any consciousness of sins?" (10:2, ESV; cf. 9:14). The author of Hebrews puts this plainly: "For it is impossible for the blood of bulls and goats to take away sins" (10:4, ESV); and again, "every priest stands daily at his service, offering repeatedly the same sacrifices, which can never take away sins" (10:11, ESV).

To summarize what we have seen thus far: the Levitical priests were not perfect, their sacrifices were not perfect, and what they did could not perfect the worshiper. Because the law has only a shadow of what Christ would do, "it can never . . . make perfect those who draw near" (Heb 10:1, ESV).

The author of Hebrews puts all this in service of highlighting the glory of what Christ accomplished. He writes of the true priest, "And being made perfect, he became the source of eternal salvation to all who obey him, being designated by God a high priest after the order of Melchizedek" (5:9–10, ESV). The old covenant Levitical priests were not perfect (5:1–3; 7:27–28a), but Jesus was perfect (5:9; 7:28b). The Levitical priests died and had to be replaced by others (7:23), but Jesus has indestructible life and so holds his priesthood permanently, continuing forever (7:16, 24). The old covenant Levitical high priest had "to offer sacrifices daily, first for his own sins and then for those of the people" (7:27; 9:6–7; 10:11), but Jesus saves to the uttermost having offered himself once for all (7:25, 27, 28). Along these lines, too, the old covenant high priests entered the earthly holy of holies, which are but "copies of the heavenly things" (9:23–24). Jesus, by contrast, entered into the heavenly holy of holies to offer himself once for all (8:2–5; 9:25–28).

Jamieson writes, "Jesus is the true priest and true sacrifice, and the Levitical sacrifices were patterned in advance on Christ's eschatological achievement."[9] Whereas the atonement attainable under the old covenant was at best provisional ("For it is impossible for the blood of bulls and goats to take away sins," Heb 10:4), Christ "by a single offering . . . perfected for all time those who are

---

9. Ibid., 583.

being sanctified" (10:14). This perfection, moreover, purifies the "conscience from dead works to serve the living God" (9:14, ESV).

§2.1.3 The Offerings Made

The author of Hebrews presents what Christ accomplished in his sacrifice and offering against the backdrop of what the high priest was to do on the day of atonement.[10] The day of atonement, modeled on what Christ would do in the future, also typified and pointed forward to him. Michael Morales has suggested that Leviticus is central to the whole of the Pentateuch, and that Leviticus 16 stands at the center of the whole of Leviticus,[11] structural realities that highlight the significance of both the Day of Atonement and Christ's fulfillment thereof.

On the tenth day of the seventh month, Israel's high priest offered "the bull as a sin offering for himself" and made "atonement for himself and for his house" (Lev 16:6, 11). For this action the Lord Jesus had no need (Heb 7:26). Two goats were then placed before Yahweh "at the entrance of the tent of meeting" (16:7), and lots were cast over them, one for Yahweh, the other for Azazel (16:8). The goat for Yahweh was offered as a sin offering (16:9), the other being sent away into the wilderness (16:10).[12] The high priest was then to go "inside the veil and put the incense on the fire" to create the cloud that would shield Yahweh and keep the priest alive (16:12–13). He then sprinkled the blood of the bull (16:14). Next came the killing of the goat for Yahweh and the taking of its blood "inside the veil" to sprinkle it likewise (16:15). All this was to make atonement for the high priest and his house, for the holy place and the tent of meeting (16:16), and no one was to enter until he came out, having "made atonement for himself and for his house and for all the assembly of Israel" (16:17, ESV). He was then to make atonement for the altar (16:18). Having confessed the iniquity of the people over the live goat, it was sent into the wilderness (16:21–22).[13]

The important things to note for our purposes here are that the sacrifices take place outside, with the blood then being brought into the holy places to be sprinkled. As Jamieson notes, "Hebrews describes the high priest's

---

10. R. B. Jamieson, *Jesus' Death and Heavenly Offering in Hebrews*, Society for New Testament Studies Monograph Series 172 (New York: Cambridge University Press, 2019), 35.

11. Morales, *Who Shall Ascend the Mountain of the Lord?*, 25, 29.

12. Morales writes: "In relation to the atoning death of the cross, note that Jesus is led outside the gates of Jerusalem to suffer the wrath of God for his people's sins. It is as the resurrected righteous one that he afterwards enters the heavenly holy of holies. In this manner Jesus fulfils the pattern of both goats on the Day of Atonement." Ibid., 128 n. 35.

13. See further Ibid., 167–84.

inner-sanctum blood manipulation as an 'offering.'"[14] This highlights the difference between what the high priest offered and what Jesus offered. The Levitical high priest offered "blood not his own" (Heb 9:25) but that of "bulls and goats," and it is "impossible" for such "to take away sins" (10:4). Jesus, by contrast, "entered once for all into the holy places, not by means of the blood of goats and calves but by means of his own blood, thus securing an eternal redemption" (9:12, ESV).

The sacrifice of Christ took place when he died on the cross. The offering of the blood took place when he entered "the greater and more perfect tent (not made with hands, that is, not of this creation)" (Heb 9:11, ESV). The author of Hebrews seems to understand Jesus entering the true temple in heaven, the pattern of which Moses was shown on the mountain, according to which the tabernacle was to be constructed (8:5). That earthly tabernacle was a copy and shadow of the heavenly one, and it thereby typified and foreshadowed what Christ would accomplish when, having been sacrificed on the cross, he entered the heavenly holy of holies to make atonement. Because the old covenant was inaugurated with blood (9:18), and because purification and forgiveness come by means of the shedding of blood (9:22),

> it was necessary for the copies of the heavenly things to be purified with these rites, but the heavenly things themselves with better sacrifices than these. For Christ has entered not into holy places made with hands, which are copies of the true things, but into heaven itself, now to appear in the presence of God on our behalf. (9:23–24, ESV)

Jamieson comments on this passage, "Yom Kippur is the only rite on whose sequence the author plots point-for-point correspondences with the self-offering of Jesus."[15] He then nicely summarizes the way Hebrews presents the points of contact:

> The author has carefully crafted the narration of Yom Kippur in 9:6–10 so that each detail will find its contrastive fulfillment in the work of Christ expounded chiefly in 9:11–10:18. The high priest entered the earthly Holy of Holies; Christ entered the heavenly one (6:20; 9:12, 24; cf. 10:12–13, 20).

---

14. Jamieson, *Jesus' Death and Heavenly Offering in Hebrews*, 39.
15. Ibid., 36.

The high priest entered once a year; Jesus once for all (9:12, 25–26; cf. 10:12, 14). The high priest entered with the blood of animals; Christ by means of his own blood (. . . , 9:12; cf. 9:14, 25).[16]

Even within the Old Testament itself, there were patterns germinating in seed form that would come to full flower in Christ. For instance, Morales comments on the different direction the characters go in Leviticus 16 and Genesis 3: "On the Day of Atonement Adam's eastward expulsion from the garden of Eden was reversed as the high priest, a cultic Adam, ascended westward through the cherubim-woven veil and into the summit of the cultic mountain of God."[17]

The author of Hebrews explains the achievement of the "fitting" high priest, the one who is "holy, innocent, unstained, separated from sinners, and exalted above the heavens" (Heb 7:26). Jesus has "sanctified" his people through his offering (10:10), and he gives "confidence to enter the holy places by [his] blood" (10:19, ESV). Jamieson puts it well:

> Hebrews is not cherry-picking convenient details, but is employing the logic of the whole rite. The high priest cleanses the tabernacle and the people by offering blood in the Holy of Holies; . . . Hebrews' Jesus does precisely the same. . . . Hebrews preserves intact the ritual logic of Yom Kippur whereby blood manipulation in the Holy of Holies purges God's people and place.[18]

§2.2 Christ Makes His People Priests

Having fulfilled the Levitical sacrificial system, the Lord Jesus achieves God's purpose of a new-Adam priestly humanity, a new-Israel priestly nation, by making his people a kingdom of priests (1 Pet 2:9; Rev 1:6; 5:10). Like Jesus the great high priest whom they follow, the priestly people of Jesus are called to be both priest and sacrifice, as they offer the living sacrifices of their own bodies, pursuing lives of consecrated worship to the living God (Rom 12:1–2). Paul also presents the mediatorial intercession between God and people who do not know him, the nations, in the act of evangelism, as priestly activity (1:9; 15:16).

---

16. Ibid., 38.
17. Morales, *Who Shall Ascend the Mountain of the Lord?*, 177.
18. Jamieson, *Jesus' Death and Heavenly Offering in Hebrews*, 47.

§3 THE TORAH OF MOSES

When God revealed himself to Israel at Sinai through Moses, the people recognized that God himself was speaking to them:

> Moses came and told the people all the words of the LORD and all the rules. And all the people answered with one voice and said, "All the words that the LORD has spoken we will do." And Moses wrote down all the words of the LORD. (Exod 24:3–4a, ESV)

The main point of this section is that for the Levitical cult to operate, the people had to respond to the word of God through Moses in faith. They had to believe what Moses was telling them. The Levitical cult was no works-based legalistic ladder the people were to climb into heaven. That had been tried and rejected at Babel (Gen 11:1–9). The Leviticult was God's gracious gift to a redeemed people, and it only worked by faith.

Since the rationale for the whole thing is the dangerous holiness of God (Heb 12:29), who was to take up residence in the holy of holies, the people had to believe "that he exists" (Heb 11:6). They had to believe that Yahweh really was everything Moses said: that he made the world by his word as Moses described in Genesis 1–2 (Heb 11:3), that his holiness would break out against transgressors, as it did against Nadab and Abihu (Lev 10), and that what put people in danger was their sin and its resulting uncleanness (cf. Gen 2:17; 3:8).[19]

The people had to believe that Yahweh was really there in the holy of holies, and they had to believe that the instructions Moses was giving them really worked. They had to trust what Moses told them about what pleased and displeased God, about what was clean and unclean, about how things defiled by sin and death could be made clean again and safely reenter the camp. They had to believe Moses when he explained to them that if God's holiness came into contact with anything unclean, death would result.

Only by believing that Yahweh was there, that he was holy, that what he identified as sinful really was an outrage against holiness, and that the actions Moses prescribed would work, would they ever do the things required.

---

19. Rightly Morales: "while YHWH has opened a way for humanity to enter his Presence, the only way to avoid danger is to enter through obedience to his torah, walking *positively* in that way." Morales, *Who Shall Ascend the Mountain of the Lord?*, 147.

The economy of ancient Israel did not work like today's, but they had things of value. The animals they were called upon to sacrifice were valuable, and the people had the ability to calculate whether or not they deemed a sacrifice worth making.

Why would someone slaughter an animal and offer it up on the altar unless he believed that doing so was to be preferred to the alternative? The alternative, in this case, was being in proximity to the holy one in an unclean state, risking death. The one who worshiped Yahweh in a way pleasing to Yahweh had to believe all that Moses had taught, and his calculation was that the sacrifice was a small price to pay for the blessing of life in the presence of God.

§4 THE COVENANT

As will be seen in the next chapter, the covenant between Yahweh and Israel is like a marriage. This means that the instructions of the Levitical cult are like the ways a husband and wife relate to one another. The goal of the cult, like the goal of marriage, is intimacy, communion, fellowship, life, joy, and love (cf. Hos 2:19–20 [MT 2:21–22]).

In the same way that some view marriage as a mere transaction, as a means of coercion or oppression,[20] some view the covenant Yahweh made with his people as transactional, coercive, or oppressive. None of these negatives capture any part of God's intention for either marriage or his covenant with Israel.[21] Timothy Keller explains that a covenant is

> a stunning blend of both law and love. It is a relationship much more intimate and loving than a mere legal contract could create, yet one more enduring and binding than personal affection alone could make. It is a bond of love made more intimate and solid because it is legal. It is the very opposite of a consumer-vendor relationship, in which the connection is maintained only

---

20. So Karl Marx and Friedrich Engels, *The Communist Manifesto* (New York: Penguin, 2002), 240, 268 n. 38.

21. It is a misreading of Paul's statement "But the law is not of faith" (Gal 3:12) that leads to the conclusion that Moses was a legalist who taught works-based salvation to Israel. Paul's comment pertains not to the old covenant situation but to new covenant believers tempted to add legalistic requirements to faith in Christ. See James M. Hamilton Jr., "The One Who Does Them Shall Live by Them: Leviticus 18:5 in Galatians 3:12," *Gospel Witness*, August 2005, 10–14. Available online, https://www.academia.edu/30691342/The_One_Who_Does_Them_Shall_Live_by_Them_Leviticus_18_5_in_Galatians_3_12.

if it serves both parties' self-interest. A covenant, by contrast, is the solemn, permanent, whole self giving of two parties to each other.[22]

God made the world a certain way. God's holy character has definite consequences for those who transgress. And in the covenant God made a way for a sinful people who deserve death to have hope and life in his presence. God's covenant with Israel arose from his mercy, communicated his grace, and offered the way to life (Deut 30:15–20).

The covenant came with promises of blessing for its keeping and cursing for its breaking (Lev 26; Deut 28). It also came with indications that it would in fact be broken (Deut 30:1), but that God would keep the promises he made to the patriarchs (see further discussion in Chapter 10 on Marriage, esp. §3). Though the covenant made at Sinai would come to an end because of the sin of his people, its intentions would be fulfilled through the Messiah, in whom God would keep the covenants he made with Abraham and David.

§5 THE COMING KING

In the chiastic structure of this chapter, this section on the king stands across from the section on the Torah because of the silent centrality of the king to the Leviticult. The silent part is this: there are not overt mentions of the king in the instructions for the operation of the Levitical cult. I contend, however, that the implicit hope that informed those who by faith lived in the covenant by the cult was that a king would arise who would reopen the way to Eden. God promised Abraham that kings would come from him and Sarah (Gen 17:6, 16), and the blessing of Judah reads as though the king lives in an Edenic land (Gen 49:8–12). The enmity between the seed of the serpent and the seed of the woman would be resolved when the king crushed the head of those who sought to curse the seed of Abraham (Num 24:17), resulting in blessing for all nations (Gen 12:3; 22:17–18).

The king was to be the exemplary Israelite, the man of Torah (Deut 17:14–20).[23] He was to be a father to his people, teaching them the word of God

---

22. Timothy Keller, *Preaching: Communicating Faith in an Age of Skepticism* (New York: Viking, 2016), 104.

23. Jamie A. Grant, *The King As Exemplar: The Function of Deuteronomy's Kingship Law in the Shaping of the Book of Psalms*, Academia Biblica 17 (Atlanta: Society of Biblical Literature, 2004).

(Deut 6:4–7), a role Solomon models as he teaches his son the Torah in the book of Proverbs.[24] Indeed, he was to be the blessed man, whose life would be like a tree in Eden (Ps 1), who would know the perfect, soul-reviving power of God's wisdom-giving word (19:7–14). Because the king would know God and love him, because he would understand that God's instructions for holiness point the way to fullness of life, he would love the Bible like the author of Psalm 119.[25]

The Leviticult gave God's people a way to live while they awaited the coming of the one who could ascend the hill of the Lord (Ps 24:3). When he of clean hands and pure heart, genuine worship and true word arose (24:4), God's blessing and salvation would be given (24:5), and the forbidding gates, the ancient doors would open for the king of glory to enter (24:7). The generation of those who seek Yahweh would then celebrate that opening of the long closed way to the very presence of God (24:6, 8–10). They would fling wide the gates of righteousness for the king, the one to whom they say, "Blessed is he who comes in the name of the Lord," to enter through them (Ps 118:19, 26; cf. Matt 21:9; 23:39).

Love for Torah rises from love for God (Deut 6:5–6). And love for God springs from the revelation of his character, the experience of his goodness (Exod 34:6–7), and the hope for what he has promised (Isa 26:8). Everything he promised hinges on the king-priest for whom the gates would lift up their heads, for whom the ancient doors would be lifted up, that he might enter in (Ps 24:7).

§6 SIN, SACRIFICES, AND FEASTS

The institution of the Levitical cult not only typified what Christ would accomplish on the cross and in the heavenly holy of holies, as we saw in §2 above, it also typified what Christ would provide for his people through the feasts, how Christians would worship God, and how Christians would experience forgiveness for sin in relationship to God.

§6.1 Christ Fulfills the Feasts for His People

Deuteronomy 16:16 states, "Three times a year all your males shall appear before Yahweh your God at the place that he will choose: at the Feast of Unleavened Bread, at the Feast of Weeks, and at the Feast of Booths . . ." (ESV).

---

24. Ansberry, *Be Wise, My Son.*
25. Grant, *The King as Exemplar.*

The Feast of Unleavened Bread is Passover, celebrating the way God delivered his people from Egypt, when they left Egypt in haste, with no time for leavening bread. We saw in §3 of Chapter 8 how Christ presented his death as the fulfillment of the exodus from Egypt and instituted the Lord's Supper as the fulfillment of Passover.

The Feast of Weeks is also known as Pentecost, and it came to be associated with the giving of the law at Mount Sinai.[26] In view of what happens on the day of Pentecost in Acts 2, when the church was baptized in the Spirit (cf. §4.1 in Chapter 7 above), perhaps Pentecost celebrated the filling of the newly constructed tabernacle with the glory of God. If so, Christ brings it to fulfillment when, in the words of Peter in Acts 2:33 (ESV), "being . . . exalted at the right hand of God, and having received from the Father the promise of the Holy Spirit, he has poured out this that you yourselves are seeing and hearing."[27]

The Feast of Booths is Tabernacles, and we saw in §3.1 of Chapter 7 above that the Word became flesh and tabernacled among his people (John 1:14). John also describes Jesus tabernacling over the redeemed in Revelation 7:15. The Feast of Tabernacles celebrated God's provision for Israel in their time living in tabernacles or booths as they journeyed through the wilderness. A significant lighting the menorah and water pouring ritual (m. Sukkah 4:9–5:3), probably commemorating the pillar of fire and water from the rock, accompanied the feast. Jesus announces himself the light of the world, saying that those who follow him will not walk in darkness (John 8:12). He presents himself as the fulfillment of the rock from which water flowed, but gives the better provision of the Holy Spirit (7:37–39; thus Paul's comment "the rock was Christ" in 1 Cor 10:4). And Jesus is the bread of life, come down from heaven to give life to the world (6:33, 35).[28]

---

26. Jeffrey Tigay writes, "At least since Second Temple times the Feast of Weeks has served to commemorate the giving of the Torah, which began with the revelation of the Ten Commandments at Mount Sinai. . . . This function of the festival was based on the calculation that its date coincides with the date which Exodus 19 implies for the revelation." Jeffrey H. Tigay, *The JPS Torah Commentary: Deuteronomy* (Philadelphia: Jewish Publication Society, 1996), 156.

27. As argued by Beale, "The Descent of the Eschatological Temple in the Form of the Spirit at Pentecost: Part 1."

28. For more on these points, see Hamilton, "John," 133–34, 155–56, 160–61.

§6.2 The Sacrifice of Praise

The New Testament authors see the sacrifices of the Levitical cult fulfilled in the Christian life of faithful worship and living as priests in the world (see §2.2 of this chapter). The author of Hebrews calls his audience to this way of life, saying, "Through him then let us continually offer up a sacrifice of praise to God, that is, the fruit of lips that acknowledge his name" (Heb 13:15, ESV). Peter speaks of Christians as "living stones . . . being built up as a spiritual household, to be a holy priesthood, to offer spiritual sacrifices acceptable to God through Jesus Christ" (1 Pet 2:5, ESV). Such statements present believers typologically fulfilling the Leviticult through lives of worship and service (cf. Rom 12:1).

§6.3 Forgiveness and Cleansing

Levitical concepts of the way sin defiles and renders unclean are evident in 1 John 1:9, where John declares, "If we confess our sins, he is faithful and just to forgive us our sins and to cleanse us from all unrighteousness" (ESV). Repeatedly in Leviticus the one who would make a sin offering for atonement is said to "come to know" his sin when he "realizes his guilt," and he then "confesses the sin he has committed," offering the prescribed sacrifice for atonement (Lev 5:4–6, ESV, cf. 4:13–20; 5:17–18; 6:4, 6–7). The author of Hebrews says that these sacrifices could "sanctify for the purification of the flesh" (Heb 9:13), though they could never "take away sins" (10:4). Their fulfillment in Christ, however, is able to "purify our conscience from dead works to serve the living God" (9:14, ESV). Coming to know one's sin, realizing its guilt, confessing it, and being forgiven and cleansed: all this happened under the old covenant for those who believed what Moses taught, and under the new covenant it happens in a full and final way for those who repent of sin and trust in Christ in accordance with the New Testament's teaching.

§7 GOD'S PRESENCE

The goal of the tabernacle and temple as they functioned in the context of the Levitical cult was to enable the people to enjoy the presence of God. Many statements in the Psalms indicate that God's people realized this to some degree (texts here ESV):

- Psalm 16:11, "You make known to me the path of life; in your presence there is fullness of joy; at your right hand are pleasures forevermore."
- Psalm 73:25, 28, "there is nothing on earth that I desire besides you. . . . But for me it is good to be near God."
- Psalm 84:4, "Blessed are those who dwell in your house, ever singing your praise!"
- Psalm 100:2, "Serve the LORD with gladness! Come into his presence with singing!"

What was available to Israel through the Levitical cult, by means of God's presence in the holy of holies, believers in Jesus experience through the indwelling Spirit, which constitutes them as God's temple (see §4 of Chapter 7 above).

Before departing, Jesus promised to give the Spirit, who would be in his disciples (John 14:17, 26; 15:26; 16:7). The final words Matthew presents him saying are, "And behold, I am with you always, to the end of the age" (Matt 28:20, ESV). And Paul asserts that the presence of Christ by the Spirit is the mark of the true believer: "Anyone who does not have the Spirit of Christ does not belong to him" (Rom 8:9, ESV). Under the old covenant God took up residence in the house his people built for his name. In the new covenant, Jesus, the promised seed of David, builds the church as the house for God's name, the temple of the Holy Spirit.[29]

In Christian experience, the church enjoys an inaugurated fulfillment of God's presence as the temple of the Holy Spirit, relishing the fulfillment of the feasts and sacrifices through the forgiveness of sins that Jesus the great high priest makes possible for his kingdom of priests, treasuring the word of God in hope for the day that the king will reign in righteousness, living in relationship with God the Father in the new covenant. Believers in Jesus experience the reality of Psalm 25:14 ("The friendship of the LORD is for those who fear him, and he makes known to them his covenant" [ESV]) through Christ, who told his followers, "I have called you friends, for all that I have heard from my Father I have made known to you" (John 15:15b, ESV).

---

29. Cf. Hamilton, *God's Indwelling Presence*; and Beale, *The Temple and the Church's Mission*.

MARRIAGE

The Church's one foundation
is Jesus Christ her Lord;
she is His new creation
by water and the Word:
from heav'n He came and sought her
to be His holy Bride;
with His own blood He bought her,
and for her life He died.

—SAMUEL JOHN STONE[1]

This chapter will work canonically[2] through relevant passages dealing with marriage in an attempt to show how the institution of marriage comes to typify the covenant relationship that God will enter into with his people. How does an *institution*, in this case marriage, prefigure a pattern of events that will be fulfilled in the relationship between Christ and the church? Did the Old Testament authors intend to communicate this?

The covenantal creation ordinance of marriage exists to be fulfilled at the marriage feast of the Lamb. The spiritual fidelity needed for covenantal marriage will be enacted when the bridegroom comes, and the Bible's story is told in terms of Yahweh's marital covenant with Israel, a story of marital union, only to have the covenant broken and ended by divorce and separation,

---

1. "The Church's One Foundation" (1866).
2. I refer by this term to the arrangement of the biblical books in the canonical text. See James M. Hamilton Jr., "Canonical Biblical Theology," in *God's Glory Revealed in Christ: Essays in Honor of Tom Schreiner*, ed. Denny Burk, James M. Hamilton Jr., and Brian J. Vickers (Nashville: Broadman & Holman, 2019), 59–73.

but because of God's love carrying promises of a new covenant reunion. The statements in this paragraph preview the contents of this chapter, which comprise a chiasm:

§1 Marriage as a Covenantal Creation Ordinance
　　§2 Marriage and Spiritual Fidelity
　　　　§3 Divorce and Remarriage: Exile and New Covenant Return
　　§4 The Bridegroom Cometh
§5 The Consummation of Marriage at the Wedding Feast of the Lamb

§1 MARRIAGE AS A COVENANTAL CREATION ORDINANCE

The story begins at the beginning, in the garden of Eden, where prior to sin, prior to judgment, as part of the original, very good creation (Gen 1:31) God instituted marriage. Moses narrates the way that God, having created the helper suitable to the man to address his not-good loneliness (2:18–21), brought the woman to the man in Genesis 2:22, and from the beginning marriage is covenantal. We have observed above (see discussion in Chapter 2, §2.3.2) that Moses forges an association between this narrative and the covenant into which God entered with Abraham in Genesis 15 by noting the "deep sleep" (תַּרְדֵּמָה) that God caused to fall on both Adam and Abraham (Gen 2:21; 15:12). Anyone familiar with the use of the term תַּרְדֵּמָה in Genesis 15:12 instinctively perceives the way light from each passage shines on the other, adding covenantal color from Genesis 15 to the radiant institution of marriage in Genesis 2.

On the basis of the use of this key term תַּרְדֵּמָה ("deep sleep") in Genesis 2:21 and 15:12, it seems that Moses intended his audience to associate the covenant of marriage, depicted in Genesis 2, and the covenant into which Yahweh entered with Abraham, depicted in Genesis 15.[3] This conclusion receives verification from the way that, as will be discussed below, Moses goes on to use marital terms and imagery with reference to Yahweh's covenant with Israel. Following Moses and embracing his worldview, Israel's prophets and later authors of Scripture do the same.

---

3. On different grounds, Gordon P. Hugenberger argues that we should understand "The paradigmatic marriage of Adam and Eve as a 'covenant'" in *Marriage as a Covenant: Biblical Law and Ethics as Developed from Malachi* (Leiden: Brill, 1994), 156–67, quote from 156.

We see that marriage is a "creation-ordinance" (something instituted by God as part of creation) from the way Genesis 2:24 draws conclusions about what took place between the first man and woman, conclusions that are applied to all their descendants. Neither Adam nor his wife had a father or mother, but because of what took place between the first man and woman, Genesis 2:24 says that a man—any man who descends from the first couple—will leave father and mother and cleave to his wife, and the two become one flesh. This means that the marriage between the first man and woman has implications for all people in all places at all times. In Matthew 19:4–5, Jesus attributes the words of Genesis 2:24 to the creator: ". . . he who created them from the beginning made them male and female. And said, 'Therefore a man shall leave his father and his mother and hold fast to his wife, and the two shall become one flesh'" (ESV).

Marriage, then, was instituted by God in the garden of Eden as part of the very good creation. Moses teaches his audience its covenantal character by means of a lexical link with a key text on God's covenant with Abraham (Gen 2:21; 15:12). As we continue through the books of Moses and the rest of the Old Testament, the biblical authors apply marital and covenantal concepts in ways that lay the groundwork for marriage to typify its fulfillment in Christ.

§2 MARRIAGE AND SPIRITUAL FIDELITY

The first marriage between the first man and woman became the prototype. In later texts Moses extends the significance of marriage from its concrete origin into metaphorical applications. Specifically, Moses uses imagery drawn from human marriage to speak figuratively about the relationship between Yahweh and his people. In the Torah this use of marital language and imagery mainly concerns calls to faithfulness: Israel must not play the whore—commit adultery—against Yahweh.

As we continue through the Old Testament into the Latter Prophets, Isaiah, Jeremiah, and Hosea all extend the marital language further, taking the concepts in new figurative directions.[4] All three of these prophets either speak directly of or symbolically depict Yahweh's *divorce* of Israel. When they

---

4. This discussion will not be an exhaustive consideration of what the Old Testament says on this theme. Similar points could be made from, e.g., Ezekiel 16.

speak (or in Hosea's case, act) this way, the prophets are saying that the covenant has been broken, warning that its curses cannot be avoided.

These prophets not only depict Yahweh's *divorce* of Israel, however, they also speak of a *covenant renewal*, and in various ways they point to the fulfillment of the covenant with Abraham as a new and lasting marital relationship between God and his people. What the Lord reveals through Hosea is perhaps most startling.

The Lord calls the prophet to enact in his own marriage a parabolic depiction of the relationship between Yahweh and Israel. This involves Hosea marrying a prostitute (Hos 1:1–3), separating from her when she returns to her adulterous ways (1:8; 2:2), and then buying her out of slavery with a view to renewing the marital covenant with her (3:1–5).

If the negative portrayal takes place in the book of Hosea, the positive is likewise portrayed in the Song of Songs. I will argue that in the Song, the king represents Yahweh, the bride Israel, and the marriage betwixt them twain points to the new covenant to be inaugurated through the future king from David's line.[5]

The pattern provided by the institution of marriage will be fulfilled in the covenant between Christ and his bride, the church. We turn to the way Moses in the Torah extends the creation ordinance of marriage metaphorically to apply its categories to God's relationship with his people.

§2.1 Spiritual Adultery in the Torah

In Exodus 34:14–16 we encounter the first explicit indication that Moses conceives of the Sinai covenant in marital terms. Moses admonishes Israel with the words,

> (. . . you shall worship no other god, for the Lord, whose name is Jealous, is a jealous God), lest you make a covenant with the inhabitants of the land, and when they whore [זָנָה] after their gods and sacrifice to their gods . . . and you take of their daughters for your sons, and their daughters whore after their gods and make your sons whore [זָנָה] after their gods. (ESV)

---

5. I want to acknowledge, however, that the interpretation of the Song of Songs is disputed, and this chapter's presentation of the institution of marriage typifying the relationship between God and his people does not stand or fall with this reading of the Song.

For the sons of Israel to worship other gods would be to commit spiritual adultery against Yahweh. This imagery functions on the assumption that the covenant between Yahweh and Israel is like a marital covenant.[6] Just as spouses in a marriage are to be faithful to one another, Yahweh and Israel—the partners to the covenant—are to be faithful to one another. Yahweh and Israel have responsibilities to one another, and they have privileges they are to share only with one another. As in a marriage, the privileges and responsibilities shared by the covenant-participants are to be exclusive. These things with one another and no one else. Just as sharing the intimacies of the covenant with someone other than one's spouse is adulterous, so doing what one should only do for Yahweh—in this case worship and offer sacrifice—is adulterous.

In a marital conception of the covenant, Yahweh is the husband and Israel is the bride. The covenant is like a marriage. An adulterous spouse not only engages in acts of intimacy with someone other than the covenant partner, intimate acts create expectations and obligations that have to do with hopes for the future and the commitments that intimacies necessarily entail, whether these are stated or only implied.[7] And so it is with acts of worship and sacrifices offered to other gods. The one who worships an idol comes with expectations, which will not be met, and leaves with obligations, which inexorably enslave. By contrast, Yahweh and Israel have pledged themselves to one another, entered into covenant with solemn words, clearly stated commitments, and fully understood blessings and curses.[8]

To worship other gods by offering sacrifice to them is to seek from those gods what Yahweh has pledged to provide. The adulterous act of idolatry indicates dissatisfaction with the covenant partner.[9] The idolatrous adultery makes the offensive declaration that Yahweh himself is not enough for Israel.

---

6. See further Raymond C. Ortlund, *God's Unfaithful Wife: A Biblical Theology of Spiritual Adultery*, New Studies in Biblical Theology (Downers Grove, IL: InterVarsity, 2003).

7. Similarly Dempster, *Dominion and Dynasty*, 73.

8. Jonathan Gibson cites Roger Beckwith's definition of "covenant": "a league of friendship either between man and man or between God and man, solemnly inaugurated, either by words alone or by words and symbolic ceremonies, in which obligations are undertaken on one or both sides. The obligations are often accompanied by an oath, and have the character of solemn promises." Gibson, *Covenant Continuity and Fidelity*, 1 n. 1; citing Roger T. Beckwith, "The Unity and Diversity of God's Covenants," *Tyndale Bulletin* 38 (1987): 96.

9. This reality is poignantly illustrated in Vladimir Nabokov's novel, *Lolita*, wherein the protagonist has everything that should satisfy him, but he desires only perversity with a continual lust for more. See Vladimir Nabokov, *Lolita*, ed. Alfred Appel Jr, Revised, Updated, Annotated Edition (New York: Vintage, 1991).

But not only does an adulterous wife demean her husband; adultery costs the wife as well. The acts of sacrifice are just that: sacrificial. The worshiper offers something of value, often at great personal cost, in the hope that the sacrifice will yield things of even more value than what was sacrificed. Instead of receiving returns on the investment, however, for idolaters the debts only deepen. Israel had pledged exclusive loyalty, obligation, privilege, and responsibility to Yahweh alone. To go outside the covenant was to commit adultery, to declare Yahweh insufficient for their needs, to seek fulfillment from other lovers, even to engage in prostitution.

§2.2 What Spiritual Adultery Entails in Torah

Moses does not explicitly articulate the consequences of Israel's spiritual adultery in the immediate context of Exodus 34. In the broader context of the Torah, however, Moses is clear that covenant-breaking sin will lead to exile (see Lev 26; Deut 4:25–31; Deut 28–32). The metaphor of whoring after other gods communicates the spiritual infidelity that results in a broken covenant, which in turn brings down the curses of the covenant, which include exile from the land.

§3 DIVORCE AND REMARRIAGE: EXILE AND NEW COVENANT RETURN

Chronologically, Solomon precedes Hosea, Isaiah, and Jeremiah in Israel's history. Solomon was active in the 900s BC, Hosea and Isaiah in the 700s, Jeremiah in the late 600s and 500s. In this chapter we are moving canonically through the Old Testament, however, which means we encounter these in reverse order: through the Latter Prophets to the Writings. We will proceed in canonical order through the contributions that Isaiah and Jeremiah, Hosea and the Song of Songs make to the typological understanding of the institution of marriage as a covenant between God and his people.

§3.1 In the Latter Prophets: Isaiah, Jeremiah, and Hosea

Both Isaiah and Jeremiah speak of Israel's covenant breaking sin resulting in "a decree of divorce" (סֵפֶר כְּרִיתֻת, Isa 50:1; Jer 3:8; cf. Deut 24:1). Prophesying at the time of the destruction of the Northern Kingdom, calling Judah in the south to repent and return to Yahweh, Isaiah both warns of divorce (Isa 50:1) and points to a future marriage like Abraham's, in which the barren wife will be the mother of children (Isa 54:1–3). For his part, Jeremiah will announce that at the exile Yahweh divorced his people (Jer 3:8), but he will also prophesy a new covenant (31:31–34). For Isaiah and Jeremiah, then, the curse of the Mosaic covenant, exile, is like divorce, but the keeping of the covenant with Abraham in the new covenant will have Yahweh rejoicing over his people like a bridegroom over his bride (Isa 62:5).

§3.1.1 Isaiah

Isaiah prophesies that when the enemy army comes (Isa 8:7), breaks down the walls of Jerusalem (22:5), burns down the temple (44:28), kills the men (4:1), humiliates the women (3:18–26), and exiles the people from the land (5:13), Israel will be like a woman whose husband has divorced her (50:1), mourning the death of her children (49:20–21). Several of these realities are communicated as Isaiah prophesies of the restoration. For instance, in Isaiah 50:1 (ESV) the prophet declares, "Thus says the LORD: 'Where is your mother's certificate of divorce, with which I sent her away?'" It is clear from this verse that Israel has indeed been sent away for their transgressions, and yet now the Lord comes to take his bride back to himself, asking in 50:2,

> Why, when I came, was there no man . . . ? Is my hand shortened, that it cannot redeem? . . . Behold, by my rebuke I dry up the sea, I make rivers a desert; their fish stink for lack of water and die of thirst. I clothe the heavens with blackness and make sackcloth their covering. (ESV)

The Lord's outstretched hand to redeem recalls the strong arm and outstretched hand by which he brought Israel out of Egypt at the exodus (Exod 3:19; 6:6; Ps 136:12). The references to the crossing of Red Sea and Jordan River, and to the plagues visited upon Egypt, likewise recall the exodus: through Isaiah the Lord says that though his adulterous people have been sent away like a divorced woman, he will save them after the exile in the way that he saved them after their sojourn in Egypt. The rhetorical question of why there was no man when Yahweh arrived indicates that the gods with whom Israel committed adultery are not faithful providers who have stayed to protect her.

To communicate the poignant pain the Lord will visit upon his people when he exiles them, Isaiah makes the judgment personal. He does this by personifying the nation as a tender mother mourning the loss of her children: "I was bereaved and barren, exiled and put away" (Isa 49:21, ESV). The putting away of this woman signifies Israel's exile from the land because they broke the covenant. As a man divorces his wife and sends her away as a result of her devastating unfaithfulness, Yahweh declares the covenant to have been broken and sends away his disobedient people. The bereavement of this woman speaks to the way the children of Israel will be cut down by the enemy army that exiles them from the land.

Isaiah connects the future salvation after exile to resurrection from the dead and the fulfillment of the Abrahamic covenant. The exile results from the breaking of the Sinai covenant, for neither the Abrahamic nor the Davidic covenants came with curses threatening exile. With the Sinai covenant broken and exile on the horizon, the future covenant of which Isaiah prophesies is spoken of as though it will be a new marriage.

The Abrahamic, Mosaic, Davidic, and new covenants stand in relationship to one another as follows: Yahweh made a covenant with Abraham, and then, as Paul explains in Galatians 3–4, to preserve Israel until the coming of Christ, Yahweh instituted the Mosaic covenant, marrying Israel. Israel broke the Mosaic covenant and was exiled, but Isaiah prophesies that Yahweh will keep the Abrahamic covenant. When Yahweh keeps the Abrahamic covenant, it will be as though he has remarried his people.

The exile from the land is likened to divorce, and it is also likened to death. The restoration of the marriage will entail new life, like new birth, even for those who have died. We see indications that the return from exile will result in resurrection from the dead in Isaiah 49:19–21. Prophesying of the way God will restore his people, Isaiah says in 49:19 (ESV) that the "desolate places" (שְׁמֵם) will be "too narrow." As if in answer to this dilemma, the call comes in 54:2 for the too-small tent to be enlarged, stretched out, lengthened, and in 54:3 the "desolate cities" (שְׁמֵם) will be peopled.

Returning to the flow of thought in Isaiah 49:19–21, Isaiah writes in verses 20–21 (ESV),

> The children of your bereavement
>   will yet say in your ears:
> "The place is too narrow for me;
>   make room for me to dwell in."

Then you will say in your heart:
   "Who has borne me these?
I was bereaved and barren,
   exiled and put away,
     but who has brought up these?
Behold, I was left alone;
   from where have these come?"

The phrase at the beginning of 49:20, "children of your bereavement" (ESV, בְּנֵי שִׁכֻּלָיִךְ), seems to mean "children of whom you were bereaved" (NASB, CSB).[10] The word "bereavement," which occurs only here in the Old Testament, seems to point to the mourning of a mother on the death of her children. These children who died, of whom their mother was bereaved, will live again to speak in the ears of their mother. Even if Oswalt is correct that the figure of speech "should not be pressed,"[11] it remains suggestive. Isaiah has asserted that the dead will rise (Isa 26:19), and at certain points a close association is made between resurrection from the dead and barren mothers giving birth (see 1 Sam 2:5–6; Rom 4:17–19).[12]

As we continue in Isaiah 49, it seems that the mother has been "bereaved" of her children because they have been carried into exile, taken into the unclean realm of the dead. This seems to be the import of the return of the children from exile in 49:22 (ESV), "they shall bring your sons in their arms, and your daughters shall be carried on their shoulders." Then when Isaiah speaks of the "captives of the mighty" and the "prey of the tyrant" in 49:24–25, he seems to be speaking of the children who have been taken into captivity, for the Lord asserts at the end of 49:25 (ESV), "I will contend with those who contend with you, and I will save your children." When the Lord brings his exiled people back into the realm of life—where he dwells—from the unclean realm of the dead, it will be as though they have been resurrected from the dead.

---

10. NIV and KJV interpret the phrase to mean "children born during your bereavement." This rendering indicates that the mother has given birth to children during the time of her mourning. The ESV's straightforward rendering can be understood either way. Though I favor the interpretation of the NASB and CSB, on either understanding the passage celebrates new life after death. The focus of this discussion is on the mother's marital status.

11. John N. Oswalt, *The Book of Isaiah, Chapters 40–66*, New International Commentary on the Old Testament (Grand Rapids: Eerdmans, 1998), 308.

12. Cf. also Gen 30:1. Jon Levenson writes, "birth is the reversal of death and thus to a large degree the functional equivalent of resurrection." *Resurrection and the Restoration of Israel*, 116.

With life abounding in the renewal after the death of the exile, the too narrow place will be made larger in 49:20 (cf. 54:2), and the one who was "bereaved and barren, exiled and put away" in 49:21 (ESV) will be amazed that she has children. As noted above, divorce is mentioned in 50:1, then after the servant suffers in Isaiah 53, the barren woman is called upon to sing and rejoice over her children in 54:1. Isaiah's prophecy evidences strategic arrangement, so we should not fail to note the relationship between the suffering servant in Isaiah 53 and the symbolic depiction of the fulfillment of the Abrahamic covenant in Isaiah 54. The fact that this newly married and newly fertile mother has not always been so can be seen from the second half of Isaiah 54:1 (ESV), "'For the children of the desolate [שׁוֹמֵמָה] one will be more than the children of her who is married,' says the Lord."

Isaiah figuratively presents God's people as a formerly bereaved (Isa 49:20–21), formerly desolate, formerly divorced (50:1), formerly barren woman, and Isaiah's assertion that "the children of the desolate one will be more than the children of her who is married" (54:1, ESV) implies that now she has a husband again. The bride, Israel, was in covenant with her husband, Yahweh, but was divorced and sent away because of her adultery. Now the formerly shamed woman is being brought back: she is married again, and once again she becomes fruitful and multiplies. The tent is to be enlarged in 54:2, and then in 54:3 Isaiah signals the fulfillment of the Abrahamic covenant by using language from Genesis 22:17, "and your offspring [seed] will possess the nations" (Isa 54:3, ESV). With these words Isaiah evokes the major "seed" theme from Genesis (cf. Gen 3:15; 12:1–3; 18:18; 22:17; 24:60; 27:29; 28:14, etc.), establishing that Isaiah's intent is to depict the fulfillment of the Abrahamic covenant.[13]

The language Isaiah employs in 54:5 makes plain the marital significance of the fulfillment of the Abrahamic covenant in the new covenant: "For your Maker is your husband [כִּי בֹעֲלַיִךְ עֹשַׂיִךְ], the Lord of hosts is his name; and the Holy One of Israel is your redeemer [גֹּאֲלֵךְ], the God of the whole earth he is called" (ESV). Here "husband" is set in parallel with "redeemer," a term familiar from the way Boaz "redeemed" Ruth when he married her (Ruth 2:20; 3:9, 12–13; 4:1, 3–4, 6, 8, 14). As Isaiah continues, he alludes to the "divorce" when the covenant breaking people were exiled for their sin in 54:6–8,

---

13. Similarly Gentry and Wellum, *Kingdom through Covenant*, 495–97.

> For the LORD has called you
>> like a wife deserted and grieved in spirit,
> like a wife of youth when she is cast off,
>> says your God.
> For a brief moment I deserted you,
>> but with great compassion I will gather you.
> In overflowing anger for a moment
>> I hid my face from you,
> but with everlasting love I will have compassion on you,
>> says the LORD, your Redeemer. (ESV)

That the new covenant is indeed in view, though Isaiah does not use that phrase, can be seen in Isaiah 54:13, where the prophet asserts, "All your children shall be taught by the LORD" (ESV). This line is not only functionally equivalent to Jeremiah saying that God's people will have the law on their hearts and know Yahweh (Jer 31:33), it is quoted by Jesus to speak of those whom the Father draws to him in John 6:45.

The way that God "married" Israel at Sinai will be typologically fulfilled when he "husbands" his people in the new covenant (Isa 54:5, 13). Isaiah declares that when the Lord restores his people,

> You shall no more be termed Forsaken,
>> and your land shall no more be termed Desolate,
> but you shall be called My Delight Is in Her,
>> and your land Married;
> for the LORD delights in you,
>> and your land shall be married.
> For as a young man marries a young woman,
>> so shall your sons marry you,
> and as the bridegroom rejoices over the bride,
>> so shall your God rejoice over you. (Isa 62:4–5, ESV)

What does Isaiah employ the institution of marriage to communicate about God's covenant with his people? Isaiah teaches that when God fulfills the covenant with Abraham, he will be like the bridegroom rejoicing over his bride. That bride will be like a formerly divorced and barren woman whose never-born-in-the-first-place children lived only to die, but now she is a joyful mother of children, children raised from the dead to speak in her ears (cf. 2 Kgs 4:11–37).

For a culture that values marriage and sexual purity within marriage, likening idolatrous unfaithfulness to adultery produces a visceral response. Isaiah not only uses marriage to communicate the emotional impact of Israel's unfaithfulness and Yahweh's steadfast love, however, with it he also communicates a *pattern of events* that plays out across Israel's history: covenant made, covenant broken, new covenant promised.

§3.1.2 Jeremiah

The divorce of God's covenant-breaking bride, of which Isaiah spoke, receives further consideration from Jeremiah, who famously engages the divorce law of Deuteronomy 24:1–4 to show the extravagance of Yahweh's love for his people. Deuteronomy 24:1–4 states that if a man sends his wife away with a writ of divorce, she remarries, but that marriage ends, the divorced wife may not return to the first husband. For that to happen would be "an abomination before the LORD" (Deut 24:4, ESV).

What Jeremiah prophesies is that Yahweh's love is shocking, abominable in its lawless prodigality. In the process of calling the Southern Kingdom of Judah to return to Yahweh, the prophet references the Deuteronomy 24:1–4 law in Jeremiah 3:1. He then presents the LORD speaking of the exile of Israel, the Northern Kingdom, with the words, "I sent her away, and I gave her a certificate of her divorce," and though Judah saw this, "she too went and played the whore" (Jer 3:8). In spite of her sin, Yahweh calls his bride back to himself in Jeremiah 3:12 with the words, "Return, faithless Israel, declares the LORD. I will not look on you in anger, for I am merciful, declares the LORD; I will not be angry forever" (ESV).[14]

Here again, as with Isaiah, the institution of marriage is deployed to help Jeremiah's audience understand the relationship between Yahweh and Israel. In this case, the patterns and norms stipulated for marriage in the Torah of Moses are engaged to illustrate the enduring love Yahweh has for his beloved. Once again the exile of the people, the sending of the covenant partner away

---

14. Derek Kidner, *The Message of Jeremiah: Against Wind and Tide* (Leicester: InterVarsity, 1987), 35–36.

from the place where the covenant is enjoyed, comes with a "certificate of divorce" (Jer 3:8), a formal announcement that the covenant has come to an end.

If the people will repent, however, acknowledging their guilt, rebellion, and faithless disobedience (Jer 3:13), and return to Yahweh (3:12, 14), then he will give them a king like David (3:15), they will be fruitful and multiply in the land (3:16), and Yahweh himself will be enthroned in Jerusalem (3:17). The promise of the future Davidic king in Jeremiah 3:15 builds on the covenant God made with David in 2 Samuel 7 (cf. Ps 89). The promise that the people will be fruitful and multiply in the land indicates that what God charged Adam to do (Gen 1:28) will be accomplished. What Jeremiah prophesies in chapter 31 indicates that these, too, are promises of a new marital covenant between Yahweh and his people.

In Jeremiah 31:31–32 the prophet speaks directly of the new covenant:

> Behold, the days are coming, declares the LORD, when I will make a new covenant with the house of Israel and the house of Judah, not like the covenant that I made with their fathers on the day when I took them by the hand to bring them out of the land of Egypt, my covenant that they broke, though I was their husband, declares the LORD. (ESV)

The new covenant here is contrasted with the old, the one made at Sinai when Israel came out of Egypt. Israel broke that covenant though Yahweh played the part of a husband to them. Once again, Yahweh married his people when he entered into the Sinai covenant with them, but that marriage ended because the people broke the covenant. The Lord promised through Isaiah that he would rejoice over them again as a bridegroom over his bride, with the result that the land would be regarded as married (Isa 62:4–5), and what Isaiah implies Jeremiah explicitly states: Yahweh will make a new covenant between himself and his people. Jeremiah also makes statements that indicate that when God makes the new covenant with his people he will be fulfilling the promises made to Abraham (see esp. Jer 33:25–26). The Mosaic covenant has been broken, but the Abrahamic covenant will be fulfilled in the new marriage between Yahweh and his people.

Like Isaiah, Jeremiah uses the institution of marriage to depict the relationship between Yahweh and his people. Both Isaiah and Jeremiah use the institution of marriage as a *type* in the sense that the pattern of events in a broken and remade marriage corresponds to the way Yahweh's people have broken the covenant, but Yahweh will nevertheless renew intimacy of relationship with them. Presenting the covenant breaking people as a divorced wife (Jer 3:8), Jeremiah says that after God has visited the curses of the covenant by exiling the people from the land (e.g., 16:11–13), the Lord will make a new covenant with them. The broken covenant was one in which Yahweh was a husband to his people, so the promise of a new covenant points to a new marital covenant, a renewal of the relationship, between the Lord and his people.

Like Isaiah and Jeremiah, Hosea uses marital terms and categories to speak of the end of the old covenant and the promise of the new.

§3.1.3 Hosea

In the book of Hosea we have an allegory that makes a contribution to the use of the institution of marriage as a typological pattern for understanding the relationship between God and his people. In what Yahweh commissions Hosea to do, "Go, take to yourself a wife of whoredom and have children of whoredom," the explanation as to why Hosea should do this establishes an allegorical relationship between God's people and Hosea's wife to be: "for the land commits great whoredom by forsaking the LORD" (Hos 1:2, ESV). In this relationship, then, Hosea represents the Lord himself, and Gomer Israel.

As the marriage between Hosea and Gomer progresses, Yahweh tells Hosea to give his children portentous names. The first child receives the name "Jezreel" (Hos 1:4–5), which also referred to the site of an awful massacre in Israel's history (2 Kgs 10:11). The second child's name, "No Mercy," points to the merciless justice God will visit upon the house of Israel (Hos 1:6–7). Then Hosea has a child he is to name "Not My People," announcing that the covenant between God and his people has come to an end: "for you are not my people, and I am not your God" (1:8–9, ESV).

When we read of the end of the marriage in Hosea 2:2 (MT 2:4), the point is that the covenant is over: "Plead with your mother, plead—for she is not my wife [אִשְׁתִּי], and I am not her husband [אִישָׁהּ] . . ." (ESV).

Hosea, like other prophets, moves freely back and forth between the coming judgment and the eventual restoration. After the naming of "Not My People" in 1:9, Hosea immediately quotes Genesis 22:17 in 1:10 to assert that though the Sinai covenant comes to an end, God will keep the covenant he made with Abraham: "Yet the number of the children of Israel shall be like the sand of the sea, which cannot be measured or numbered . . ." (Hos 1:10, ESV). The husband-prophet alludes to Exodus 1:10 in Hosea 1:11 (MT 2:2), indicating that just as God saved Noah at the flood then made a covenant with him, saved Israel at the exodus then made a covenant with them, he will save his people again at the new exodus then make covenant with them:

Exod 1:10, וְעָלָה מִן־הָאָרֶץ
"and go up from the land"

Hos 1:11 [MT 2:2], וְעָלוּ מִן־הָאָרֶץ
"and go up from the land"

After the description of judgment, in which the nation of Israel is often personified as an individual human woman who has been an adulterous wife (Hos 2:2–13), Hosea begins to describe the new exodus and return from exile in terms of a new marriage in 2:14–23.[15] Hosea recalls the way Yahweh brought Israel out of Egypt to Mount Sinai when he writes of the way Yahweh will save his people in the future in 2:14 (ESV), "Therefore, behold, I will allure her, and bring her into the wilderness, and speak tenderly to her." He makes a comment about the new conquest of the land in 2:15a,[16] before continuing with another reference to what happened when he spoke tenderly to the people at Mount Sinai in 2:15b, "And there she shall answer as in the days of her youth, as at the time when she came out of the land of Egypt" (ESV).

The Lord speaking tenderly to Israel in 2:14, and her answering positively in 2:15b, recalls the way that Yahweh spoke the ten words to Israel in Exodus 20. The positive answer from Israel in 2:15b seems to speak of the event recounted in Deuteronomy 5:22–29, where the people assert that they will do

---

15. I am using the enumeration of the verses of Hosea 2 found in English translations. Hebrew texts start enumerating the verses of chapter 2 at 1:10, so that 2:1 in an English translation is 2:3 in a Hebrew text. For the Hebrew verse number add 2 to the English.

16. The Valley of Achor was the place where Achan was executed after his sin of taking forbidden things (Josh 7:24–26). No sooner had Israel entered the land than they showed they had not the heart to keep it (cf. Deut 29:4 [MT 29:3]). Thus understood, the Valley of Achor was a portent of doom, testifying that Israel would break the covenant and be exiled. As Hosea prophesies of the new exodus and return from exile, he announces a reversal of the significance of the place. Because the Lord will have changed the hearts of his people, they will not defile the land, nor will they take forbidden things at the new conquest. The place will be like the garden of Eden, and the people will be fit to work and keep it. Thus Hosea 2:15a (ESV), "And there I will give her her vineyards and make the Valley of Achor a door of hope."

everything Yahweh commands (esp. Deut 5:27 [ESV], "speak to us all that the LORD our God will speak to you, and we will hear and do it").

As Hosea continues, the marital overtones of the immediate and wider context of these statements make it sound as though at Sinai Israel was a bride at the altar saying "I do" in the wedding ceremony. The infidelity that resulted in the end of the old covenant, the divorce, will have been banished when the new exodus and return from exile see the new covenant inaugurated. Hosea writes in 2:16 (ESV), "And in that day, declares the LORD, you will call me 'My Husband [אִישִׁי],' and no longer will you call me 'My Baal [בַּעְלִי].'"

When Hosea 1:10 (MT 2:1) quoted Genesis 22:17, notes resonant of the fulfillment of the Abrahamic covenant were added to the music of the new covenant. In a similar way the language of Hosea 2:18 causes the new covenant to sound like the Adamic covenant: "And I will make for them a covenant on that day with the beasts of the field, the birds of the heavens, and the creeping things of the ground" (Hos 2:18a, ESV). This new covenant will see an end to the enmity between the seed of the woman and the seed of the serpent (Gen 3:15), for as God promised to David in 2 Samuel 7:10 (ESV), "violent men shall afflict them no more as formerly." Hosea prophesies in 2:18b (ESV), "And I will abolish the bow, the sword, and war from the land, and I will make you lie down in safety."

The new marital covenant that Hosea prophesies will fulfill the Adamic, Abrahamic, and Davidic covenants, and it will be inaugurated after the failure of the Mosaic. That is to say, when the Mosaic covenant was broken, Yahweh divorced his people. With the making of the new covenant, however, the Lord entered into a new marital covenant between himself and his beloved, just as Hosea prophesied he would in 2:19–20,

> "And I will betroth you to me forever. I will betroth you to me in righteous-
> ness and in justice, in steadfast love and in mercy. I will betroth you to me
> in faithfulness. And you shall know the LORD." (ESV)

The names of Hosea's children are reprised in 2:21–23, with No Mercy receiving mercy and Not My People being called "my people."

The marital significance of what Yahweh has promised to do for his people at the end of Hosea 2 is then revisited in what happens between Hosea and Gomer in Hosea 3. Gomer has committed adultery and been enslaved

(Hos 3:1), but Hosea buys her back for himself (3:2), and they begin the long process of restoration that corresponds to the nation's long wait for the restoration of the throne of David (3:3–5). What Hosea prophesies in chapter 3 appears to correspond to the way the nation was able to return to the land, at which point they continued to operate under the Mosaic covenant, as they would until the time of the events narrated in the New Testament.[17]

God instituted marriage in the garden in Genesis 2. Then Moses used marital terms and concepts to call Israel to faithfulness to the Sinai covenant. When that covenant had been broken, Isaiah, Jeremiah, and Hosea used the language of divorce to speak of its end, the sending away of a divorced wife corresponding to Yahweh's sending of his people into exile. And as they point to the future, when Yahweh will again save his people as he did when he brought them out of Egypt, when he will again meet their every need as he did when he provided for them in the wilderness, when he will again enter into a new and better covenant than the one made at Sinai, Isaiah, Jeremiah, and Hosea all speak of a new marital covenant into which Yahweh will enter with his renewed people. The institution of marriage provides a set of concepts and patterns for relationships that typify the relationship between Yahweh and his people.

§3.2 In the Writings: The Song of Songs

We have seen that Moses used marital language and imagery to speak of the covenant between Yahweh and Israel. We have also seen how the prophets, specifically Isaiah, Jeremiah, and Hosea, developed that imagery to point to the end of the covenant and exile, and beyond that disruption to a new covenant that would be like a new marriage. Between Moses, around 1400 BC, and

---

17. The metaphors are direct, but the situation is complex. Hosea definitely points to the failure of the marriage (the Sinai covenant), and he definitely points to the fulfillment of the Adamic, Abrahamic, and Davidic covenants. Israel was exiled from the land in 586 BC, but starting in 539 BC they were allowed to return to the land. They rebuilt the temple in 516 BC, and then when Ezra (458 BC) and Nehemiah (445 BC) returned to the land, they eventually entered into covenant with one another to keep the provisions of the Mosaic covenant (see Neh 10). This may correspond to the way that in Hosea 3, after Hosea buys Gomer out of slavery in Hosea 3:2, he tells her in 3:3–5 (ESV), "'You must dwell as mine for many days. You shall not play the whore, or belong to another man; so will I also be to you.' For the children of Israel shall dwell many days without king or prince, without sacrifice or pillar, without ephod or household gods. Afterward the children of Israel shall return and seek the LORD their God, and David their king, and they shall come in fear to the LORD and to his goodness in the latter days." This passage seems to indicate that as Hosea and Gomer have been reunited but their covenant not yet renewed, so the people of Israel will be brought back but have to await the coming of the king who will inaugurate the new covenant "afterward" and "in the latter days" (Hos 3:5).

Isaiah and Hosea in the 700s BC, Solomon ruled Israel in the 900s BC.[18] My working hypothesis is that Solomon's worldview was shaped by the Torah of Moses, and that thereby he had enough information and sophistication to put the following together.

First, as the king from David's line, he stood in the line of descent of the seed of the woman from Adam through Noah to Abraham to Judah to David, and I assume he would have known the remarkable promises made to David about his seed in 2 Samuel 7. Solomon is not *the* expected seed, but he is in the line of descent and typifies the one to come (Matt 12:42; and see discussion of Solomon in Chapter 5 on Kings above). I would suggest that Solomon understood himself as the new-Adam representative of Yahweh, king from David's line, anticipating the one who would uniquely and ultimately fulfill what he typified as *the* new-Adam, *the* king from David's line, *the* earthly representative of Yahweh.

Second, understanding what Moses had done with marital imagery in the Torah, Solomon would have had the conceptual categories for understanding human marriage as an allegorical representation of the covenant between Yahweh and Israel. If Hosea can depict the marital covenant between Yahweh and Israel with its tragic infidelity, Solomon can do the same, with the spotlight on the glorious restoration of intimacy.[19]

---

18. I am assuming that Solomon is the Song's author, and that in the Song he presents an idealized version of himself. That is to say, the Song of Songs, in my view, does not depict a historical relationship but an idyllic one meant *both* to depict allegorically the relationship between Yahweh and Israel *and* to inspire his audience to love more deeply and pursue greater intimacy in their own marriages. See further James M. Hamilton Jr., "The Messianic Music of the Song of Songs: A Non-Allegorical Interpretation," *Westminster Theological Journal* 68 (2006): 331–45; and James M. Hamilton Jr., *Song of Songs: A Biblical-Theological, Allegorical, Christological Interpretation*, Focus on the Bible (Fearn: Christian Focus, 2015). Iain Duguid interprets the Song very differently than I do, and he does not think Solomon wrote it. Yet he too can write, "Marriage is designed by God to give us language and experiences that are not merely satisfying and delightful in themselves, but out of which we learn to understand our relationship with God more fully.... To miss that connection between human and divine love, which allegorical interpretation makes instinctively, even if sometimes inappropriately, is to miss something profound and important.... This same intimacy will ultimately be extended to the bride of Christ by her Saviour; as a result, application to the relationship of Christ and the church flows naturally from the Song of Songs, in a metaphor designed by God himself (Eph. 5:22–33)." Iain M. Duguid, *The Song of Songs: An Introduction and Commentary*, Tyndale Old Testament Commentaries (Downers Grove, IL: InterVarsity, 2015), 48–49. For convincing arguments for Solomonic authorship, see Duane A. Garrett and Paul R. House, *Song of Songs, Lamentations*, Word Biblical Commentary (Nashville: Thomas Nelson, 2004); and Duane A. Garrett, *Proverbs, Ecclesiastes, Song of Songs*, New American Commentary (Nashville: Broadman & Holman, 1993).

19. Similarly Christopher W. Mitchell, *The Song of Songs*, Concordia Commentary (Saint Louis: Concordia, 2003), 44–45. There is much wisdom in Mitchell's 1,300 page (!) commentary on the Song, the Introduction of which comprises the first 553 pages. For his history of interpretation, see 451–510, but

It is not uncommon for the Song to be read as a piece of wisdom literature meant to celebrate and inspire better human marriages. For the Song to function this way, however, it must grow out of and feed back into the broader biblical worldview, with its particular understanding of marriage. My reading of the Song holds that Solomon understood his status as the king from David's line, seed of the woman descended from Adam, and that in the Song he presents a glorious renewal of intimacy achieved by the Davidic King as a symbolic and allegorical depiction of the salvation God will accomplish when he initiates the new covenant with his people. This reading would only increase the exemplary power of what the Song depicts. People should pursue greater harmony and intimacy in marriage not as goods in themselves but as a display of the very love of God (cf. Song 8:6 [ESV], ". . . love is strong as death . . . the very flame of the LORD").

In Song 3:11 Solomon has come to Jerusalem for his wedding. As he approaches the Holy City in the Holy Land, those who see him coming ask, "What is that coming up from the wilderness like columns of smoke . . . ?" (Song 3:6a, ESV). The columns of smoke recall the pillar of cloud, making the coming of the king reminiscent of the way Israel came up from the wilderness. Song 3:7 then announces, "Behold, it is the litter of Solomon!" This "litter" is a "sedan chair," or "palanquin," which is a box, carried on poles, in which the important person sits. Solomon approaches Jerusalem being carried on something like the ark of the covenant, and Israel's king sits enthroned where Yahweh sat, surrounded by warriors (Song 3:7–8), just as Yahweh made his way through the wilderness with Israel "in martial array" (Exod 13:18 NASB). Solomon is depicted as having made the carriage with the same material used for the building of the temple: "from the wood of Lebanon" (Song 3:9). Like tabernacle and temple, Solomon's carriage has silver, gold, and purple (3:10).

Solomon, royal representative of Yahweh, arrives in Jerusalem to enter into covenant, marriage, with his bride (Song 3:11). As he encounters his bride, it is as though the two of them are in the garden of Eden, naked and unashamed in the cool of the day (4:1–6), and as the relationship is consummated it is as though the bride is the very garden itself (4:12–5:1).

In the Song of Songs, the idealized king from David's line overcomes

---

I would especially commend the sections on his hermeneutical approach (14–66) and his discussion of marriage in relationship to allegory, typology, sacramental considerations, prophetic signs, and analogy (67–97).

barriers to intimacy, removes hostility, and loves his bride in such a way that together the two enter covenant and enjoy unashamed vulnerability and trust, not only in a lush garden but in Jerusalem, city of the great king. The glory of this relationship points forward to a time when by his king Yahweh will renew the covenant with his people, having removed everything that separates them from himself. The everlasting covenant love is "the very flame of the LORD" (Song 8:6, ESV).

The wedding of the king of Israel celebrated in texts like the Song of Songs (and in Psalm 45) points beyond human marriage to the new covenant into which the Lord will enter with his people. As elsewhere in the Old Testament, the institution of marriage presents a typological pattern that points backward and forward—backward to the covenant into which Yahweh entered with his people, forward to that of Christ and the church.

§4 THE BRIDEGROOM COMETH

To this point in this chapter, we have briefly surveyed the way Old Testament authors, beginning with Moses, make typological use of the institution of marriage. The expectations, norms, patterns, concepts, and terminology of marriage were established by Moses in the Torah, where we saw the covenantal quality of the relationship and the expectation of pure fidelity. To commit idolatry is to commit spiritual adultery because Israel's covenant with Yahweh is marital. The marital quality of the covenant was then extended by later Old Testament authors, who spoke of the end of the Sinai covenant as a divorce, even as they looked forward to remarriage in the new covenant.

Along with the expected new marital covenant between God and his people, the authors of the Old Testament point forward to a future king from David's line, and at key points the new Davidic king and the new marital covenant are brought together. I would suggest this happens in the Song of Songs, but even if that argument is rejected, we still see it in places like Hosea 3:5. In addition, if "the days are coming" when the Davidic king will reign (e.g., Jer 23:5–7), and if the new covenant will be inaugurated at the same time ("days are coming," 31:31), "in that day" (e.g., Hos 2:16, 21), then both new covenant and future king pertain to the "latter days" (3:5; Jer 30:24), the time after the purging judgment of exile when Yahweh will restore the fortunes of his people. It is natural to bring together the various things promised of the future salvation: new exodus, new David, new Eden, new covenant, new life from the dead.

Understanding the association of these Old Testament expectations helps us make sense of things said by and about Jesus in the New Testament.

§4.1 The Bridegroom

I distinctly remember years ago sitting in church, listening to the preacher emphasize how significant it was that Jesus came as the bridegroom. Unfortunately, I was ignorant of the Old Testament teachings explored here, and the preacher had not explained them. Perhaps he knew them and took them for granted. While I suspected he was right about the significance of Jesus coming as the bridegroom, I was at a loss as to *why* it was significant or *what* precisely the significance was.

Those who authored the Gospels, however, show themselves to have been steeped in Old Testament expectation. The same can be said about many in their audience, and those members of their audience who were not would naturally be encouraged to search the Scriptures for themselves (Acts 17:11). The New Testament authors expected their audiences to know the Old Testament.

In view of what we have seen from the Old Testament, we are positioned to perceive what Matthew presents Jesus asserting about himself in response to a question from the disciples of John about why the disciples of Jesus do not fast. Matthew 9:15 states, "And Jesus said to them, 'Can the wedding guests mourn as long as the bridegroom is with them? The days will come when the bridegroom is taken away from them, and then they will fast'" (ESV, cf. parallel accounts in Mark 2:19 and Luke 5:34). Jesus does not directly assert: *I am the Messiah, the future king from David's line, and my disciples are not fasting because I have come to inaugurate the new covenant between Yahweh and his people, making it time to celebrate rather than fast. But I will ascend to heaven after being crucified and raised from the dead, then my disciples will fast.* Something amounting to all this, however, seems to be what Matthew, Mark, and Luke present Jesus saying.

For those who understand the Old Testament's typological development of the institution of marriage, Jesus' designation of himself as the bridegroom sends a coded signal that he has come to inaugurate the prophesied new covenant. As for his being taken away and then his disciples fasting, the Gospel writers expect their audiences to read to the end of the story, whereby they will understand what Jesus meant (see Matt 28:16–20; cf. Luke 24:50–53; Acts 1:9–11). The parable of the ten virgins in Matthew 25:1–13 likewise presents Jesus as the bridegroom whose coming inaugurates a covenant that brings about the kingdom of heaven.

The same encrypted assertions are at work when the Gospel of John presents John the Baptist saying of Jesus, "The one who has the bride is the bridegroom. The friend of the bridegroom, who stands and hears him, rejoices greatly at the bridegroom's voice. Therefore this joy of mine is now complete" (John 3:29, ESV). The Baptist has already been portrayed asserting, "I am not the Christ" (1:20), and in this statement about being the friend of the bridegroom he indicates that the one who is the Christ has come to enter into a covenantal marriage with his bride, God's people.

These identifications of Jesus as the bridegroom find symbolic purchase because of the way the Old Testament authors made typological use of the institution of marriage. To identify Jesus as the bridegroom is to identify him as the expected king from David's line through whom Yahweh will betroth himself to his people in fulfillment of Hosea 2:19–20, making good on the promise to cut a new covenant with his people (Jer 31:31–34).

In addition to the overt identifications of Jesus as the bridegroom and the suggestive imagery of the parable of the virgins, we also find in John 4 the story of Jesus meeting the Samaritan woman at the well. The repeated pattern in the Old Testament establishes a pattern that gathers significance and increases expectation: Abraham's servant met a wife for Isaac, Rebekah, at a well (Gen 24:11–15); Jacob met Rachel at a well (29:2–9); and Moses met Zipporah at a well (Exod 2:15–21). John presents the meeting of Jesus with the Samaritan woman such that earlier parallel episodes are recalled by means of the mention of Jacob (John 4:5–6), with the woman asking Jesus if he is greater than the patronym of the people of God (4:12). The conversation touches on husbands (4:16–18), by which the woman perceives that Jesus is a prophet (4:19), and he reveals himself as Messiah (4:25–26). John is not suggesting that Jesus will marry this particular woman, but coming as the bridegroom of God's people, as the Baptist identified him in 3:29, he comes to inaugurate a covenant that extends beyond the boundaries of ethnic Israel to include Samaritans and gentiles (cf. 10:16). The inclusion of non-Israelites might even be hinted at by a precursor, when Moses married the daughter of the priest of Midian, whom he met at a well.

§4.2 I Am Saying That It Refers

Paul speaks of how Christ loved the church at the end of Ephesians 5:29, explains that he does so because we [those who belong to the church] are members of his body in 5:30, before quoting Genesis 2:24 in Ephesians 5:31, "for this reason a man shall leave father and mother and cleave to his wife, and the two shall be one flesh," and then asserting in 5:32, "This mystery is profound, and I am saying that it refers to Christ and the church" (ESV). Paul here seems to indicate that the mystery of marriage, alluded to by the quotation of Genesis 2:24, refers to Christ and the church. This suggests that God created marriage so that people would be able to understand the relationship between Jesus and the church. To put it another way, God created the *institution of marriage* to give the world a covenantal relationship that would depict the relationship between God and his people.

God related to Israel as a husband to a bride, entering into covenant and faithfully leading, protecting, and providing for his people. That covenant was broken by the adulterous wife, but God promised a new covenant that would be inaugurated by a new Moses who would be a new king from the line of David. Jesus came as that bridegroom to inaugurate that new covenant, and this deepest meaning of marriage enriches the marriages of the people of God. The best art points beyond itself to the real thing, and in this case, the art that a married couple produces together in marriage points beyond itself to the real thing, the holy intimacy Christ the bridegroom has with his church.

John Gill wrote of these glorious realities:

> . . . the man cleaving to the wife very aptly expresses the strong affection of Christ to his church, and the near communion there is between them; and indeed, the marriage of Adam and Eve was a type of Christ and his church; for in this the first Adam was a figure of him that was to come, as well as in being a federal head to his posterity . . .[20]

§4.3 The Whore of Babylon

In Revelation 17:1–3 John presents the whore of Babylon in a way that closely parallels his presentation of "the Bride, the wife of the Lamb" in 21:9–10.[21] The matching statements can be seen on Table 10.1 (ESV).

---

20. John Gill, *Exposition of the Old and New Testaments*, 9:106. Cited from Matt Haste, "A Type of the Marriage of Christ: John Gill on Marriage," *Puritan Reformed Journal* 6 (2014): 296–97.

21. Bauckham, *The Climax of Prophecy*, 4.

TABLE 10.1: The Whore and the Bride

Revelation 17:1–3	Revelation 21:9–11
Then one of the seven angels	Then came one of the seven angels
who had the seven bowls came	who had the seven bowls full of the seven last plagues
and said to me,	and spoke to me, saying,
"Come, I will show you the judgment of the great prostitute who is seated on many waters, with whom the kings of the earth have committed sexual immorality, and with the wine of whose sexual immorality the dwellers on earth have become drunk."	"Come, I will show you the Bride, the wife of the Lamb."
And he carried me away in the Spirit	And he carried me away in the Spirit
into a wilderness,	to a great, high mountain,
and I saw a woman sitting on a scarlet beast that was full of blasphemous names, and it had seven heads and ten horns.	and showed me the holy city Jerusalem coming down out of heaven from God, having the glory of God, its radiance like a most rare jewel, like a jasper, clear as crystal.

These parallel statements serve a significant structural function in the book of Revelation, but here my interest is in what they communicate about the marital covenant between Christ and his people. John intends his audience to ponder the metaphors he uses to depict the unfaithful, who use the prostitute, and the faithful, who are pure virgins (Rev 14:4) like a bride.

Why is it that a person would make recourse to a prostitute? Those who do so seek the privileges of the covenant of marriage—pleasure, companionship, intimacy, union—apart from the commitments and responsibilities of that covenant. Why is it that a prostitute would be willing to sell those privileges for money? Some who do so are physically enslaved and coerced. Others are emotionally manipulated to the point that they believe they have no other choice. However they got there, a prostitute sells for money things that cannot truly be given in a financial transaction. The realities sought from prostitutes are priceless, and they cannot be faked in exchange for cash. True love, true companionship, true intimacy, is only possible in the context of the marital covenant, the comprehensive interpersonal union between one man and one woman that is to be exclusive, monogamous, permanent, and productive of children.[22]

To gain the privileges of marriage, to enter into this love, a man must love as Christ loved the church, and a woman must submit to her husband as the church does to Christ. In the same way that soldiers who have been through war together have a unique bond, spouses that have committed, covenanted, sacrificed, wept, rejoiced, and in a word, loved one another, have a union that cannot be play-acted in exchange for mammon. And so it is with Christ and the church.

What the world offers to people in exchange for money, Christ gives freely to those who give everything they are to him. What the world offers, however, is not what Christ freely gives, for though Satan attempts to provide his pseudo-version of the Way, he is not God and can only imitate the one who is alive and reigns. Satan can offer his false trinity (Rev 16:13), but his "godhead" remains a dragon, a beast, and a false prophet. He can put forward his fake Christ, with his faked death and resurrection (13:1–3), but the beast did not die, did not stand in anyone's place, and so does not achieve atonement for anyone. He can send out his false prophet to deceive with signs and wonders (13:11–14), but though he looks like a lamb he speaks like a dragon (13:11). And so it is with the whore. She may go through the motions of acting like a wife, but there is no covenant and there is no love. There is only the certainty of the arrow through the liver (Prov 7:23).

§5 THE CONSUMMATION OF MARRIAGE AT THE WEDDING FEAST OF THE LAMB

To what shall we liken the consummation of the ages? What will it be like when the Lord Christ comes for his people? It will be like a king, whose resources are limitless and whose love for his son is unbounded, preparing a lavish wedding feast for that beloved son, at long last come of age to marry his betrothed (Matt 22:2). It will be like wise virgins, who have made preparation

---

22. Sherif Girgis, Robert George, and Ryan T. Anderson, "What Is Marriage?," *Harvard Journal of Law and Public Policy* 34 (2010): 245–87.

and kept themselves pure, hearing the long anticipated shout, "Behold, the bridegroom cometh" (25:6 KJV). Like the best wine from water (John 2:1–11), like faithful people, beloved of God and one another, clothed with fine white linen that somehow depicts the best and truest and most loving things they ever did: their righteous acts (Rev 19:8). It will be like Yahweh delighting in his people as a husband delights in his bride (Isa 62:4). It will be like Adam and Eve in the garden before sin, but better. Like Song of Songs 4, like liberated slaves singing the Song of the Sea (Exod 15; Rev 15:3), like the high priest entering the holy of holies on the great day. Like Jerusalem adorned as a bride for the wedding day (Rev 21:2), like Solomon wearing the crown with which his mother crowned him (Song 3:11).

For this the world was made. For the bride to make herself ready. For Jesus to love her unto death, and then rise. For him to go to the Father to prepare the rooms the new born family will inhabit forever. For him to come, for whom they longed who loved his appearing.

Amen. Maranatha (1 Cor 16:22). "The Spirit and the Bride say, 'Come.' And let the one who hears say, 'Come.' And let the one who is thirsty come; let the one who desires take the water of life without price" (Rev 22:17, ESV).

CONCLUSION TO PROMISE-SHAPED TYPOLOGY

Macro-Level Indicators for Determining Authorial Intent

> Why is ring composition practiced all over the world? What is it for? So many people! So many epochs! They could not all have learned it from one another. Its robustness over thousands of years supports the theory that something in the brain preserves it, and yet we know that it can fade out so completely that new readers miss it altogether.
>
> —MARY DOUGLAS[1]

In the Introduction to this book in Chapter 1 we looked at micro-level indicators that demonstrate that the biblical authors intended to forge typological connections: lexical points of contact (reuse of terms), quotations of phrases or lines, similarities in event sequence, and consonance in covenantal or salvation-historical import. In this Conclusion to the book we examine macro-level indicators that demonstrate that biblical authors intended to forge typological connections. Because of the foundational character of the book of Genesis for everything that follows in the Bible, this chapter will examine it as a

---

1. Douglas, *Thinking in Circles*, 12. This exclamation responds to the studies Douglas documents of ring composition in Homer, in the Bible, in Zoroastrian literature, in eleventh millennium BC Chinese divination, in the medieval Chinese novel, and in the thirteenth century Persian poet Rumi (4–12).

primary example. My working hypothesis is that later biblical authors learned the literary strategies employed by Moses and imitated his methodology, but demonstrating that to be the case is beyond the scope of this chapter.

The claim of this chapter is that the micro-level indicators work with macro-level indicators to communicate an author's intended message. In Genesis, Moses has structured his narrative to provoke recognition of similarities between people and events, creating typological patterns that later biblical authors develop. This chapter has a chiastic structure as follows:

§1 What Chiasms Are and Do
    §2 The Chiastic Structure of the Whole Book of Genesis
        §3 The Chiastic Structure of the Subunits of Genesis
    §4 Themes Derived from Comparison of the Subunits
§5 Chiastic and Typological Structures

§1 WHAT CHIASMS ARE AND DO

Chiasms are (1) an extension of parallelism, and (5) they provide a vehicle for artistic beauty, even as they (2) provide structure and boundaries for a presentation and (4) create synergy between corresponding units of text. Central to chiastic structures, (3) authors employ them to give their audiences an aid to memory.[2] The enumerated statements in this paragraph correspond to the following chiastic structure for this subsection:

§1.1 An Extension of Parallelism
    §1.2 Providing Structure and Boundaries
        §1.3 An Aid to Memory
    §1.4 Creating Synergy
§1.5 A Vehicle for Artistic Beauty

§1.1 An Extension of Parallelism

Parallelism is a well-known and widely recognized feature of Hebrew poetry, and a chiastic literary structure simply extends that parallelism to units of text of varying length. Mary Douglas writes,

---

2. See also Wayne Brouwer, "Understanding Chiasm and Assessing Macro-Chiasm as a Tool of Biblical Interpretation," *Calvin Theological Journal* 53 (2018): 99–127.

Ring composition is found all over the world, not just in a few places stemming from the Middle East, so it is a worldwide method of writing. It is a construction of parallelisms that must open a theme, develop it, and round it off by bringing the conclusion back to the beginning.[3]

The biblical authors could employ chiastic parallelism in the artistry of a single Hebrew line, such as we see in Psalm 2:10,

And now O kings	וְעַתָּה מְלָכִים
be wise	הַשְׂכִּילוּ
be warned	הִוָּסְרוּ
O judges of the earth	שֹׁפְטֵי אָרֶץ

We see the same device, extremely common in the Psalter, in Psalm 18:4 (MT 18:5),

Encompassed me	אֲפָפוּנִי
the cords of Death,	חֶבְלֵי־מָוֶת
and the torrents of Belial	וְנַחֲלֵי בְלִיַּעַל
startled me.	יְבַעֲתוּנִי

The kinds of chiastic structures I will propose for the book of Genesis simply extend these grammatically parallel chiastic structures[4] through the narrative. Commenting on the use of small-scale chiastic structures in the parallelism that pervades Hebrew poetry, Douglas writes, "What I have in mind when I refer to ring composition is the large-scale, blow-up version of the same structure."[5]

§1.2 Providing Structure and Boundaries

Chiastic structures operate like other literary forms that both structure presentations and set limits within which authors work. For instance, some psalms and the book of Lamentations employ the acrostic format, whereby the lines of the poetic work begin with successive letters of the Hebrew alphabet.

---

3. Douglas, *Thinking in Circles*, x.
4. On which, see further Wilfred G. E. Watson, *Classical Hebrew Poetry: A Guide to Its Techniques* (New York: T&T Clark, 2001), 201–7.
5. Douglas, *Thinking in Circles*, 2.

This creates an A-to-Z effect: the poet can create the impression of having addressed everything pertaining to a topic—which is never possible with finite words—by going through the whole alphabet. Similarly, writers who employ chiastic structures can cover a range of topics in a way that satisfies their audience as the presentation comes full circle. As Watson notes, "A very common way of expressing *merismus* or a totality is to use chiasmus."[6]

The discussion you are now reading provides an example: this section does not account for everything that chiasms do, but the chiastic structure of the presentation sets this discussion of structure and boundaries across from the discussion of the way that chiasms create synergy between sections. In effect, the form causes more meaning to be generated than could be accounted for by the sum of its parts. I hope, too, that this discussion of what chiasms are and do feels complete, even though it cannot hope to be exhaustive.

§1.3 An Aid to Memory

In his entertaining book *Moonwalking with Einstein: The Art and Science of Remembering Everything*, Joshua Foer discusses the "memory palace," an ancient and still widely used technique of associating things to be remembered along a route through a large palace, so that when one wants to recall the list to be memorized, he simply takes a walk through the palace, metaphorically picking up the items to be remembered as he passes from room to room.[7] Chiastic structures function similarly, as they provide an architectural superstructure that enables those who recognize it to recall where topics are in relation to one another.[8] As Victor Wilson explains,

> The *mnemonic* advantage may be the most compelling reason for the longevity of the chiasm and the universality of its use. Here is a mechanism that responds to the listener's need for a generic frame of reference to guide the memory in the process of recollection. The chiasm is self-tutoring, prodding the memory to fill in the elements of the form with balanced pairs . . .[9]

---

6. Watson, *Classical Hebrew Poetry*, 205.

7. Joshua Foer, *Moonwalking with Einstein: The Art and Science of Remembering Everything* (New York: Penguin, 2011), 1–2, 89–105.

8. On this point see also David M. Carr, *Writing on the Tablet of the Heart: Origins of Scripture and Literature* (New York: Oxford University Press, 2005), 98–99.

9. Victor M. Wilson, *Divine Symmetries: The Art of Biblical Rhetoric* (Lanham, MD: University Press of America, 1997), 51.

§1.4 Creating Synergy

The synergy created between corresponding units in a chiastic structure is one of the most important exegetical payoffs of a chiasm.[10] By setting this discussion of synergy across from the discussion of structure and boundaries, I can also justify saying the following here: chiasms often place their most important points at the center of the chiastic structure.[11] The synergy created by this technique has to do with the way the reader is brought up the mountain to its peak, from which the discussion also descends in corresponding steps on the other side. I could easily have made that point about centering the main point the centerpoint of my chiastic structure in this discussion, but my preference—and prerogative as author—was to use it to illustrate the relationship between structure and boundaries and synergy. To reiterate: as with synergy, so with structure and boundaries—understanding the chiastic form proves exegetically productive as it allows readers to determine what the author has presented as central. And here again, the synergy and the structure work together to create the impression of a comprehensive discussion.

§1.5 A Vehicle for Artistic Beauty

Chiastic structures provide those who employ them with a form that produces of itself balance, proportion, harmony, symmetry, and in the hands of an artist, radiance.[12] Wilson puts it well,

> ... note the *aesthetic* attraction of the chiasmus. The pattern conveys the cyclic orderliness of a perceived reality. ... As the artist seeks a visual balance in composition, the chiasm obliges an oral world with an aural balance. So, in a chiasm's return to its point of departure a resolution satisfies the ear's anticipation, like music's return to the opening key.[13]

---

10. Douglas, *Thinking in Circles*, 14.

11. So also Douglas, *Thinking in Circles*, 7; Wilson, *Divine Symmetries*, 49.

12. Commenting on James Joyce's novel, Stuart Gilbert writes, "*Ulysses* achieves a coherent and integral interpretation of life, a static beauty according to the definition of Aquinas (as abridged by Joyce): *ad pulchritudinem tria requiruntur: integritas, consonantia, claritas.*" In a footnote Gilbert directs his readers to "*A Portrait of the Artist as a Young Man*, page 248; Stephen, who aligned his aesthetic views with those of St. Thomas Aquinas, translates these words: 'three things are needed for beauty: wholeness, harmony and radiance.'" Stuart Gilbert, *James Joyce's Ulysses* (New York: Vintage Books, 1959), 9 n. 1.

13. Wilson, *Divine Symmetries*, 51.

Many times has it been my joy to engage in close study of the text of Scripture, feel that I am picking up the clues the biblical author has laid down, that I am on his trail, so to speak, and when I have arrived at what he seems to have done, I have sat back in wonder at the beauty of the literary artistry. But it is far more than mere art: the form functions to communicate meaning, and if we do not see the form we will not feel the force of the truth the author presents. Often those who do not perceive the beautiful chiastic structures in biblical texts will allege that the statements are arranged in a haphazard, disjointed, unorganized, repetitive way.[14] These judgments say more about the failure of such readers to understand than they do about what the biblical authors communicated.

§2 THE CHIASTIC STRUCTURE OF THE WHOLE BOOK OF GENESIS

When we consider Genesis as a literary whole, suggestive themes begin to emerge. One way to structure the material in chiastic fashion would be as follows:

Gen 1–11, Creation to Abraham
    Gen 12–22, Abraham to Isaac: Abraham's Faith
        Gen 23–25, Sarah Dies, A Wife for Isaac, Abraham Dies
    Gen 25–36, Jacob to Joseph: Jacob Wrestles with God
Gen 37–50, Joseph to Judah: Forgiving Brothers, Blessing Nations,
    and the Lion

A few thoughts on what emerges from such a structure, directed by its corresponding units: the first unit introduces the problem, human sin that defiles the world, results in fraternal conflict (Cain/Abel), and fills the world with violence (Gen 6:11); and the last section presents Joseph as a type of one who will bring about the solution—a seed of the woman who forgives his brothers

---

14. Douglas (*Thinking in Circles*, 1) writes, "Many fine old texts have been disdained and disrespectfully mauled in the effort to get to the sense. What a shame, and what dull and trivial interpretations have been piously accepted in default! And how ready the commentators were to lay the perceived incoherence to the door of weak writing skills, or even weak intelligence. Writings that used to baffle and dismay unprepared readers, when read correctly, turn out to be marvelously controlled and complex compositions. Learning how they were structured is like a revelation, with something of the excitement of hidden treasure. Now is a good moment for the effort of rereading."

and blesses the nations. The second and second to last sections, dealing with Abraham and Jacob respectively, contrast Abraham's willing obedience of faith with Jacob's self-centered wrestling with God, and significantly, both men experience anticipations of the exodus from Egypt (see §1.1 and §1.2 in Chapter 8 above). At the center of the whole of Genesis stand three chapters that present the hope for the seed of the woman to overcome death: in the outer rings of chapter 23 and the first part of chapter 25 we read of the deaths of Sarah and Abraham; these narratives of death bracket the story of Abraham sending his servant to acquire a wife for Isaac. The line of descent of the seed of the woman will continue. Death will not extinguish hope.

Not only do these subunits create a chiastic structure for the whole of Genesis, they are chiastic structures themselves. In the discussion that follows I will first deal with the four units that surround the centerpiece of the book, Genesis 23:1–25:11, referring to these as the Creation-chiasm (Gen 1:1–11:26), the Abraham-chiasm (11:27–22:24), the Jacob-chiasm (25:12–36:43), and the Joseph-chiasm (37:1–50:26). I will sometimes round off the units to chapters, using, for instance, 12–22 for the Abraham-chiasm. We will consider the center of the chiastic structure of Genesis in the final section of this chapter.

§3 THE CHIASTIC STRUCTURE OF THE SUBUNITS OF GENESIS

Each of the chiastic units will be briefly presented and discussed, and then relationships between them will be examined. The chiastic structures that immediately follow cover the whole of Genesis, and corresponding units are font-coded. After the presentation of the whole, each subunit will be discussed in turn.[15] Here is a key to the font-coding scheme:

Bold—Blessing (Gen 1:28)
ALL CAPS—Seed of the woman's line of descent
SMALL CAPS—Sin and Enmity (Gen 3:15)
Italics—Family Strife and Deliverance
Normal—Border and central statements

---

15. I have adapted the chiastic structures for Genesis 11:27–22:24, 25:12–36:43, and 37:1–50:26, from those found in Mathews, *Genesis 11:27–50:26*, 90, 377, 680.

We will first look at the chiastic structures in this section, making some comments on the font-coding along the way before considering it more fully in §4 below.

TABLE 11.1 The Chiastic Structure of Genesis

1:1–2:3, Creation
 2:4–4:26, Toledot of Heaven and Earth
  5:1–6:8, Toledot of Adam
  6:9–9:29, Toledot of Noah
  10:1–11:9, Toledot of the Sons of Noah
 11:10–26, TOLEDOT OF SHEM

   11:27–32, Genealogy of Terah
   12:1–9, Blessing of Abraham: Land, Seed, Blessing
   12:10–20, SISTER-FIB (Exodus Preview)
    13–14, Lot
     15 Eliezer, Faith, Covenant, Exodus
     16 Hagar, Ishmael
     17, Circumcision, Covenant with Isaac
    18–19, Lot
   20:1–18, SISTER-FIB 2
  21–22, BIRTH AND OFFERING OF ISAAC,
   BLESSING RESTATED
  22:20–24, Genealogy of Nahor

    23, Sarah's Death
    24, A Wife for Isaac
    25:1–11, Abraham's Death (see Isaac's death in 35:27–29)

  25:12–19, Ishmael and Isaac Toledots (25:12; 25:19)
   25:20–26:5, REBEKAH'S CHILDREN, PROMISE TO
    ISAAC
   26:6–35, Isaac Deceives Philistines and Has Strife
    27:1–28:9, Stolen Blessing and Flight to Paddan-aram
    28:10–22, Jacob's Dream at Bethel
     29:1–30, Laban Deceives Jacob
      29:31–30:24, Jacob's Seed Born
      30:25–43, Jacob's Flocks Born
     31, Jacob Deceives Laban
    32, Jacob Sees Angels and Wrestles with God
    33, Jacob Blesses Esau and Returns from Paddan-aram

> 34, SONS OF JACOB DECEIVE AND HAVE STRIFE WITH
> SHECHEM
> **35, God's Promise to Jacob, Rachel Dies Birthing Benjamin**
> 36:1–43, Esau Toledot (2x, 36:1; 36:9)

37:1–11, Joseph Dreams
   37:12–36, Jacob Mourns "Death" of Joseph
     38:1–30, JUDAH AND TAMAR
      39:1–23, JOSEPH SOLD TO EGYPT
       40–41, Joseph, Savior of Egypt
        42–43, Journeys of Brothers to Egypt
         44, Joseph Tests His Brothers
         45, Joseph Reveals Himself
        46:1–28, Journey of Family to Egypt
       46:28–47:12, Joseph, Savior of His Family
      47:13–31, EGYPT SELLS ITSELF TO JOSEPH
     48:1–49:27, Blessing of Joseph and Judah
   49:28–50:14, Joseph Mourns Death of Jacob
50:15–26, Joseph Provides

§3.1 Genesis 1:1–11:26

This proposal for the structure of Genesis 1:1–11:26 takes its cues from the use of the term *toledot*, rendered "generations" in the ESV, in Genesis 1–11, a term that will also prove significant for the structures of the units to follow:

1:1–2:3, Creation
   2:4–4:26, TOLEDOT OF HEAVEN AND EARTH
     5:1–6:8, Toledot of Adam
     6:9–9:29, Toledot of Noah
   10:1–11:9, TOLEDOT OF THE SONS OF NOAH
11:10–26, TOLEDOT OF SHEM

At the beginning God blesses the world with existence, and he blesses man in particular (Gen 1:28). At the end of this unit we see the line of descent from Shem. Concern for blessing and seed, then, brackets the first chiastic structure of Genesis. Within this we see the beginnings of sin with the fall in Genesis 3 and the murder of Abel in Genesis 4, matched by the enmity of the seed of the serpent, whose origins are outlined in Genesis 10, with their building project in 11:1–9. In the center of this chiastic structure we have the line of descent from Adam (5:1–6:8), which reaches back to the command to Adam to be fruitful and multiply in 1:28 and forward to the line of descent of Shem in 11:10–26. Also at the center we find the deliverance of Noah at the flood (6:9–9:29). The centerpoint of chiastic structures often links up with beginning and end, and the blessing of Noah in 9:1 recalls that of Adam in 1:28, while it is Noah's son Shem, also delivered on the ark, whose genealogy appears at the end of this unit. At the beginning of Genesis 6 the sinful intermarrying of the sons of God and daughters of men anticipates similar marital improprieties near the center of the chiastic structures through the rest of Genesis.

§3.2 Genesis 11:27–22:24

The chiastic structure of Genesis 11:27–22:24 is particularly clear. Opening with the genealogy of Terah in 11:27–32, it closes with the genealogy of Terah's son (Abraham's brother) Nahor in 22:20–24. Understanding the chiastic structure of the book keeps us from thinking Nahor's geneology is a random insertion. Far from that, it serves both as a key structural marker and to introduce characters who figure prominently in what follows.

> 11:27–32, Genealogy of Terah
> > 12:1–9, **Blessing of Abraham: Land, Seed, Blessing**
> > > 12:10–20, SISTER-FIB 1 (Exodus Preview)
> > > > 13–14, *Lot*
> > > > > 15 Eliezer, Faith, Covenant, Exodus
> > > > > 16 Hagar, Ishmael
> > > > > 17, Circumcision, Covenant with Isaac
> > > > 18–19, *Lot*
> > > 20:1–18, SISTER-FIB 2
> > 21–22, BIRTH AND OFFERING OF ISAAC, BLESSING RESTATED
> 22:20–24, Genealogy of Nahor

There are significant correspondences between, on the one hand, God calling Abraham to go from his country, his kindred, and his father's house to the land he will show him in Genesis 12:1, and on the other, God calling Abraham to take his son, his only son Isaac, whom he loves to one of the mountains of Moriah he will tell him in 22:1–2. These two great tests of faith bracket the main body of the Abraham narrative in Genesis, and the promise that God would make Abraham a great nation in Genesis 12:2 at long last begins to be realized with the birth of Isaac in 21:1–7.

Just as the blessing of Adam (Gen 1:28) marked the beginning of the first unit, with concern for the line of descent of the seed marking the end of it (11:10–26), so here too, God blesses Abraham in 12:1–3, and then concern for the seed manifests in 21–22, with the initial blessing being re-stated and significantly elaborated upon in 22:17–18.

Why are there two stories of Abraham telling the sister-fib about Sarah to protect himself, one in Genesis 12:10–20, another in 20:1–18? Because Moses is putting repeated events in parallel, using the chiastic structure of the literature to forge typological relationships.[16] These stories are intentionally parallel and part of the author's communicative strategy.

Similarly, in Genesis 13–14 and 18–19 we have two sections of material that deal with both Lot and Abraham. In the first, Lot and Abraham separate (Gen 13), and then Abraham rescues Lot (Gen 14). The second inverts the order, as Abraham intercedes for Lot and Sodom (Gen 18), and then Lot separates from Sodom before its destruction (Gen 19). The way that Abraham delivers and intercedes for his kinsman Lot recalls the way that Noah built an ark for the salvation of his family, which stood at a similar juncture in the book's earlier chiastic structure. Similarly, there will be interactions between Jacob and his kinsmen, Esau and Laban, in the next chiastic structure, and between Joseph and his brothers in similar position in the one after that. Moses intends his audience to think about these relationships in light of one another.

In the center of this section we have human sin wrapped in the grace of God: Abraham thinks Eleazar will be his heir in Genesis 15:2–3, but when God promises him descendants like the stars of heaven in 15:4–5, Abraham believes, is reckoned righteous, and receives covenantal revelation that prophesies the exodus in 15:7–20. Grace. The sin comes in Genesis 16, where just as Adam listened to the voice of his wife (3:17), Abraham listened to the voice of his wife and went in to Hagar. The doubling of Abraham's wives will be repeated at the same point of the literary structure of the Jacob narrative, but in God's mercy it is followed by God's gracious gift of the

---

16. Cf. the fascinating discussion of what Adam should have done in Morales, *Who Shall Ascend the Mountain of the Lord?*, 180–84.

covenant sign of circumcision and the promise that Sarah will conceive in Genesis 17.

§3.3 Genesis 23:1–25:11

The deaths of Sarah and Abraham result from sin's entrance into the world (Gen 3:19, 22; Rom 5:12), but their burial in the land attests to hope that goes beyond the grave. Similarly, Isaac's life shows that a dead corpse of a womb can be made to live, and the long story about Abraham's servant seeking and acquiring a wife for Isaac results in a marriage that will continue the line of descent of the seed of the woman.

> 23, Sarah's Death
>> 24, A Wife for Isaac
> 25:1–11, Abraham's Death (see Isaac's death in 35:27–29)

The problem of death and the promise of life are centered in the literary structure of the book of Genesis. The realization of the hope of life can be heard from the mouths of babes and infants, by which God establishes his strength, to still the enemy and the avenger (Ps 8:2). We will return to Genesis 24 in the final section of this chapter.

§3.4 Genesis 25:12–36:43

The chiastic structure that began at Genesis 11:27 started with the phrase, "Now these are the generations of Terah" (וְאֵלֶּה תּוֹלְדֹת תֶּרַח) then focused on his son Abraham. The one that begins at 25:12 likewise begins with the phrase, "These are the generations of Ishmael" (וְאֵלֶּה תֹּלְדֹת יִשְׁמָעֵאל), followed shortly by 25:19, "These are the generations of Isaac" (וְאֵלֶּה תּוֹלְדֹת יִצְחָק). Isaac's name is in the heading, but his son Jacob is on center stage. The double *toledot* ("generations") at the beginning of this unit (25:12, 19) is matched by the double *toledot* at the end, where we have "These are the generations of Esau" (וְאֵלֶּה תֹּלְדוֹת עֵשָׂו) twice, first at 36:1 and again at 36:9. The final unit of text, 37:1–50:26, likewise begins, "These are the generations of Jacob" (אֵלֶּה תֹּלְדוֹת יַעֲקֹב, Gen 37:2), then largely focuses on Joseph. As can be seen from these, and as holds true for those in Genesis 1–11, the narrative that follows the *toledot* tends to deal with those who descend from the named progenitor (the two Esau *toledots* at 36:1 and 9 being the exception to this pattern).

25:12–19, Ishmael and Isaac Toledots (25:12; 25:19)
  25:20–26:5, REBEKAH'S CHILDREN, PROMISE TO ISAAC
    26:6–35, ISAAC DECEIVES PHILISTINES AND HAS STRIFE
      27:1–28:9, Stolen Blessing and Flight to Paddan-aram
        28:10–22, Jacob's Dream at Bethel
          29:1–30, Laban Deceives Jacob
            29:31–30:24, Jacob's Children Born
            30:25–43, Jacob's Flocks Born
          31, Jacob Deceives Laban
        32, Jacob Sees Angels and Wrestles with God
      33, Jacob Blesses Esau and Returns from Paddan-aram
    34, SONS OF JACOB DECEIVE AND HAVE STRIFE WITH SHECHEM
  35, God's Promise to Jacob, Rachel Dies Birthing Benjamin
36:1–43, Esau Toledot (2x, 36:1; 36:9)

Within the outer *toledot* frames, we have again the focus on blessing and seed, with the births of Jacob and Esau and the revelation that Jacob was God's chosen in 25:20–26:5 matched by the reiteration of the promise to Abraham and Rachel's death giving birth to Benjamin in Genesis 35. With Genesis 36 given to Esau's generations, the end of the Jacob narrative is punctuated by the death of Isaac in 35:27–29, an account that closely corresponds to that of the death of Abraham in 25:8–10, which marked the end of the Isaac narrative and the shift into the Jacob story.

Abraham twice told the sister-fib (Gen 12:10–20; 20:1–18), and Isaac does the same and has strife with the Philistines in Genesis 26:6–35. The matching unit in Genesis 34 narrates the defiling of Dinah and the slaughter of Shechem.

Then begin a series of rings that deal largely with conflict: Jacob steals Esau's blessing and flees to Paddan-aram in 27:1–28:9, only to return from Paddan-aram and urge Esau to receive his blessing in Genesis 33. In Genesis 28:10–22 God reveals himself to Jacob at Bethel, with angels ascending and descending on a flight of steps, and in Genesis 32 Jacob sees angels and wrestles with God, having his named changed. In Genesis 29:1–30 Laban deceives Jacob, and in Genesis 31 Jacob deceives Laban. The central section here has Jacob being fruitful and multiplying in offspring (Gen 29:31–30:24) and livestock (30:25–43).

My attention was drawn to the parallels between the chiastic structures of Genesis by study of this unit, Genesis 25–36, in comparison with the previous, Genesis 12–22. The font-presentation of the lines (italics, bold, all caps, etc.) reflects the similarities in the units. As mentioned above, there are four wide-angle chiastic structures of the book of Genesis: 1–11, 12–22, 25–36, 37–50. In each case the outermost rings are in **bold** font (blessing) and ALL CAPS (seed). Moving inward, the next rings are SMALL CAPS (enmity/sin), and the ones inside those are in *italics* (family conflict/deliverance), with normal font at the center and on the edges.

Consider with me the parallels between the Abraham-chiasm (Gen 12–22) and the Jacob (Gen 25–36), beginning from the center of each. At the center of unit 2 we find Abraham's sin of faithless polygamy with Hagar in Genesis 16, surrounded by him being reckoned righteous by faith and receiving the covenant in Genesis 15 and 17. At the center of unit 3 we find Jacob likewise committing the sin of polygamy, and in spite of that God blesses him with abundant children and livestock.

From the centerpoints of the chiastic structures of units dealing with Abraham and Jacob, let us work toward Genesis 23–25 from each direction. Doing so, I have *italicized* Genesis 18–19 and 27:1–28:22. The Lord reveals himself to Abraham at the beginning of Genesis 18, Abraham intercedes for Sodom, and then the Lord destroys Sodom in Genesis 19. In Genesis 27, Jacob destroys his family by stealing the blessing, and then God reveals himself to him in Genesis 28. The sequence is inverted.

Continuing to work toward Genesis 23–25 from the centerpoint of the unit on each side, we find Abraham's second sister-fib in Genesis 20 and Isaac's commission of the same sin in Genesis 26, both in SMALL CAPS. After that we find the fulfillment of the promise of seed to Abraham in the birth of Isaac along with Abraham's final test, offering Isaac, and the reiteration of the blessing in Genesis 21–22, matched by the long awaited (twenty years!) birth of Jacob and Esau and the reiteration of the blessing of Abraham to Isaac in 25:20–26:5. The genealogy of Nahor in 22:20–24 is matched by the Ishmael and Isaac *toledots* in 25:12–19.

We also find similarities between the Abraham and Jacob chiasms if we start at the centerpoint of each and work away, toward the beginning of the book in Abraham's case, toward the book's end in Jacob's. Thus Abraham's triumph over the kings from the east in Genesis 14 corresponds to Jacob wrestling with God on his way home from the east in Genesis 32,[17] as the separation of Lot and Abraham in Genesis 13 corresponds to the reunion/separation of Jacob and Esau in Genesis 33.[18] When we recognize that Genesis 12:10–20 stands across from Genesis 34 in the book's literary structure, we see the thematic proximity of these two units to one another: God works a preview of the exodus in the liberation of Sarah in 12:10–20, and then he works a preview of the conquest in the putting of Shechem under the ban in chapter 34 (not denying for a second the sinfulness of what Simeon and Levi did). The promises made to Abraham in 12:1–9 work as a wide-angle latch with the same promises made to Jacob in Genesis 35:9–15 (cf. also 1:28; 17:5, 6).

The chiastic structures of the Abraham (Gen 11:27–22:24) and Jacob narratives (25:12–36:43) are inversions of one another.[19] Abraham was called from Haran in the east (11:31; 12:4) to the land of promise in Genesis 12. Jacob is sent from the land of promise to Haran in the east in chapter 28 (28:10). Whereas God tested Abraham in Genesis 22, Jacob tests God with his vow in 28:20–22. John Walton explains, "In contrast to God's placing conditions on Abraham (leave your country, etc.) so that the promises can be realized, Jacob puts conditions on God before God can become the 'beneficiary' of the promises Jacob offers. . . . Everything is backward here."[20] At the end of Jacob's journeys, however, he will come home. The Lord has touched his hip and put him out of joint (32:25). Dempster says of Jacob, "He wins the fight by losing—by being broken—and facing up to his identity. Consequently, he tells God who he is (Jacob the deceiver, the heel-grabber) and has his name changed to Israel (God's fighter)."[21] As Mathews notes, "Upon his return to Canaan, Jacob will traverse the same route as that of his grandfather Abraham (12:6–7; 33:18; 35:1)."[22]

---

17. Abraham has 318 men in Genesis 14:14. Esau has 400 men in 32:6.

18. Lot lifts up his eyes in 13:10, then Abraham lifts up his eyes in 13:14. Jacob lifts up his eyes in 33:1, then Esau lifts up his eyes in 33:5. Compare also the way the land could not bear both Lot and Abraham in 13:6, nor could it bear both Jacob and Esau in 36:6–7.

19. Watson (*Classical Hebrew Poetry*, 206) writes, "Chiasmus also expresses *reversal* of existing state. . . . chiasmus can express *antithesis* or contrast . . ."

20. John H. Walton, *The NIV Application Commentary Genesis* (Grand Rapids: Zondervan, 2001), 573–74.

21. Dempster, *Dominion and Dynasty*, 87.

22. Mathews, *Genesis 11:27–50:26*, 439.

§3.5 Genesis 37:1–50:26

The Joseph story begins with Joseph's dreams (37:1–11) and ends with the provision he makes for his family (50:15–26). From there the next step is Jacob mourning the apparent death of Joseph (37:12–36), matched near the end by Joseph mourning the actual death of Jacob (49:28–50:14). The ALL CAPS line dealing with the line of descent runs, surprisingly, through Judah and Tamar in Genesis 38, which in the chiastic structure stands across from the **bold** line dealing with blessing in Genesis 48–49, where Jacob blesses Joseph and his sons but especially Judah. The SMALL CAPS lines begin with Joseph sold to Egypt in Genesis 39 but then have Egypt selling itself to Joseph in Genesis 47. Joseph saves Egypt (Gen 40) and his brothers journey there (Gen 41), and then the family moves to Egypt (Gen 46) where Joseph also saves them (Gen 47). At the center of this chiastic structure Joseph tests his brothers (Gen 44) before revealing himself to them (Gen 45).

37:1–11, Joseph Dreams
    37:12–36, Jacob Mourns "Death" of Joseph
        38:1–30, JUDAH AND TAMAR
            39:1–23, JOSEPH SOLD TO EGYPT
                40–41, *Joseph, Savior of Egypt*
                    42–43, *Journeys of Brothers to Egypt*
                        44, Joseph Tests His Brothers
                        45, Joseph Reveals Himself
                    46:1–28, *Journey of Family to Egypt*
                46:28–47:12, *Joseph, Savior of His Family*
            47:13–31, EGYPT SELLS ITSELF TO JOSEPH
        48:1–49:27, Blessing of Joseph and Judah
    49:28–50:14, Joseph Mourns Death of Jacob
50:15–26, Joseph Provides

As noted briefly above, within the chiastic structures, matching themes are dealt with in consistently similar fashion.

If we were to lay each chiastic structure on top of another, we would find that the outer rings always deal with the blessing and the seed, within that are rings dealing with sin and enmity, followed by rings dealing with family conflict and/or deliverance, down to the central feature of the chiasm. We can depict the pattern as follows:

Blessing
  Sɪɴ/Eɴᴍɪᴛʏ
    Family Conflict and Deliverance
      Central Feature
    Family Conflict and Deliverance
  Sɪɴ/Eɴᴍɪᴛʏ
SEED

We will consider the impact the literary structure has on our understanding of the typological connections Moses forges with these themes in the next section.

§4 THEMES DERIVED FROM COMPARISON OF THE SUBUNITS

The claim of this chapter is that Moses intended his audience to discern typological patterns between the parallels he built into his narrative. This section explores the three themes seen above—blessing and seed, sin and enmity, and family conflict and deliverance—along with a fourth that combines the central element of each chiastic structure: faith, polygamy, deception, and revelation. By now the reader will not be surprised to find that I present them as a chiasm:

  §4.1 The Blessing and the Seed
    §4.2 Sin and Enmity
    §4.3 Family Conflict, Intercession, and Forgiveness
  §4.4 Faith, Polygamy, Deception, and Revelation

By creating these chiastic structures, Moses has built folds into the narrative, bringing the ends together, creating turning points in the middle, aligning intervening sections. Bending the narrative in this way draws characters and events together so that they can be associated with one another, compared and contrasted, and similar events are more easily synthesized for the learning of God's ways. Just as some characters are brought together, others are pushed farther away, so that subtle differences take on greater significance.

§4.1 The Blessing and the Seed

As noted above, the outer rings of the chiastic structures of Genesis, the seams of its units, communicate God's blessing (**bold**) on the chosen seed (ALL CAPS). In God's good pleasure, he makes man in his image and blesses him, commanding him to be fruitful and multiply (Gen 1:28). Even when the man sins, God promises that the seed of the woman will triumph (3:15), and the Creation-chiasm (Gen 1–11) centers and ends with concern for the line of descent (genealogies in Gen 5 and 11). God will bless the world by saving it through the seed of promise.

In the Abraham-chiasm, Genesis 11:27–22:24, genealogies bracket the blessing of Abraham at beginning (Gen 12:1–9) and end (22:17–18). The major concern of this unit is the fact that those through whom God has promised that the seed will come need to have their reproductive capacities resurrected from the dead. God does just that by blessing Abraham and Sarah with Isaac, and after his miraculous birth from death in Genesis 21, he is received back from death through the substitute offered in Genesis 22. Death further surrounds the finding of a wife for Isaac, as in Genesis 23 Sarah dies, then Abraham in Genesis 25, but not before sending his servant to find a wife for Isaac in Genesis 24.

Once again genealogies (Gen 25:12–19; 36:1–43) precede births and blessings in the third section, Genesis 25:12–36:43. This fold in the narrative puts Rebekah's barrenness (25:21) in the same narrative place as Sarah's (11:30), both following genealogical summaries at the beginning of a unit,[23] and Isaac and Rebekah's twenty year wait for God to bless them with children (25:20, 26) is much like the twenty-five year wait of Abraham and Sarah for Isaac (12:4; 21:5). Though Moses does not elaborate on these points, their position in the literary structure signals their significance. As the beginning of the unit deals with births (25:21–26), so it also deals with blessing: the younger is identified as the chosen (25:23), and God promises Isaac that he will establish the oath he swore to Abraham (26:3, cf. 26:1–5). The concern for blessing and seed at the end of the unit manifests when God confirms his promise to Jacob (35:9–15) and Rachel dies from the painful process (cf. 3:16) of giving birth to Benjamin (35:17–18).

The final section (Gen 37:1–50:26) opens by associating Joseph, the son of Israel/Jacob's old age (37:3), with Isaac, who was earlier called the son of

---

23. Genealogical summary in Gen 11:27–29, Sarah's barrenness in 11:30. Genealogical summary in Gen 25:12–19, Rebekah's barrenness in 25:21.

Abraham's old age (21:2, 7).[24] After Joseph is sold into slavery, the narrative turns to the account of Judah and Tamar in Genesis 38, because at the end of the book we will learn that though the blessing will be pronounced over the sons of Joseph (48:15–20), the seed of Judah will be blessed in even greater ways (49:8–12; cf. 1 Chr 5:1–2).

Moses uses chiastic structures in Genesis to align both the characters who receive the blessing and the miraculous and surprising ways that their line of descent continues. Sarah, Rebekah, and Rachel are all called barren, and only the steadfast love of the creating and redeeming God could bring Isaac to life from Sarah's dead womb, family harmony out of the hissing cauldron of spite in Jacob's household, and the seed of promise from Judah taking Tamar for a cult prostitute.

§4.2 Sin and Enmity

There is sin and enmity across the book of Genesis, but the book's typological and chiastic structures bring out significant distinctions between sin and enmity. My point is not that these are technical terms for different categories of transgression but that Moses shows his audience that though all sin,[25] the seed of the woman repent and find forgiveness and righteousness, while the seed of the serpent set themselves against the Lord and his anointed (cf. Ps 2:1–3). It is one thing to believe God's promises, endeavor to live in a way that pleases him, and yet stumble into sin because of ignorance, weakness, and waywardness (cf. Heb 5:2). It is another thing altogether to reject God's prohibitions and commandments and set oneself against his people.[26] All humans sin, and God put enmity between the seed of the woman and the seed of the serpent (Gen 3:15), but God's people seek to live at peace with all so far as it depends upon them (cf. Rom 12:18).

The next ring moving inward in the corresponding palistrophes of the narrative of Genesis deals with sin and enmity (statements in SMALL CAPS). In the Creation-chiasm the man and woman transgress in the garden (Gen 3:1–7), the enmity is introduced (3:15), and immediately manifests in the murder of Abel (4:8). We get hints at what we can expect from Lamech's boasting

---

24. The only other character so described in Genesis will be Benjamin in 44:20.

25. For discussion see James M. Hamilton Jr., "Original Sin in Biblical Theology," in *Adam, the Fall, and Original Sin: Theological, Biblical, and Scientific Perspectives*, ed. Hans Madueme and Michael Reeves (Grand Rapids: Baker, 2014), 189–208.

26. "Cursed be Canaan" (Gen 9:25). "Him who dishonors you I will curse" (12:3). "Cursed be everyone who curses you" (27:29).

(4:23–24), hints that are developed in the account of Nimrod's might and his founding of Babel and Shinar (10:8–11), with its presumptuous tower (11:1–9).

In the Abraham and Jacob-chiasms, sin and enmity appear in the brutality of the men Abraham and Isaac encounter. The callous inhumanity of these men becomes apparent only on the fourth of these rings, when Shechem seizes Dinah to lay with her (34:2). In the ensuing narrative, Shechem and his father seek to negotiate a marriage but never apologize or in any way indicate that they feel any remorse for the outrage (34:3–12). That such behavior was possible, that the patriarchs operated in cultures where such acts were tolerated, apparently prompted the "sister-fibs" they told in the first three rings: Abraham twice passed Sarah off as his sister (12:10–20; 20:1–18), and Isaac repeated the lie (26:6–11). The patriarchs sinned, and the narrative does not excuse their failure. But the enmity of the rapacious men of the culture (Gen 34) was the context in which they failed to protect their wives. By placing each of these episodes where he does, just inside the outer ring dealing with the blessing and the seed, Moses prompts his audience to connect the sister-fibs and the rape of Dinah that they might be read in light of one another.

Reflection on these rings in light of one another prompts the audience of Genesis to see the enmity between the seed of the woman and the seed of the serpent, the brutality of which the seed of the serpent are capable, and also the sinful cowardice of Abraham and Isaac in telling the lie. Their women really are in danger, as the violation of Dinah in Genesis 34 shows, but Moses teaches his audience that danger does not authorize sin. Later biblical narratives will present Boaz in the book of Ruth ensuring the safety of the women under his care apart from falsehoods about their identity (Ruth 2:8–9), and the proactive protection of Boaz will find fulfillment in the one who will stand between his people and those who threaten them with the words, "I told you that I am he. So if you seek me, let these men go" (John 18:8, ESV). Judah foreshadows the one to come from his line when he offers himself in Benjamin's place (Gen 43:8–9; 44:18–34, esp. 44:33).

In the Joseph-chiasm, though he has been sold into Egypt, Joseph there resists temptation (Gen 39:6–12), which initially only makes things worse for him, landing him in prison (39:13–20). Through his faithfulness and God's blessing, however (39:21–23), Joseph is eventually freed (41:14), exalted (41:38–46), and the whole situation is reversed: the one sold to Egypt has all Egypt sell itself to him, saying, "You have saved our lives" (47:25, cf. 47:13–31).

This no doubt anticipates the one who "emptied himself, by taking the form of a servant" (Phil 2:7, ESV), but through faithfully resisting temptation and completing his course of suffering unto death (2:8), was exalted and given "the name that is above every name" (2:9), that all might bow to him and confess him Lord (2:10–11; cf. Gen 42:6).

§4.3 Family Conflict, Intercession, and Forgiveness

Every time, in all four major chiastic units of Genesis (Gen 1–11; 12–22; 25–36; 37–50), it happens the same way: the outer ring dealing with the blessing and the seed has a ring just inside itself dealing with sin and enmity, and inside that is a ring that presents family conflict and deliverance. Every time. This cannot but be intentional.

The Creation-chiasm sees family conflict near its center in a way that will anticipate the central sections of the Abraham and Jacob narratives, with the perversion of marriage as the sons of God took daughters of men as wives (Gen 6:1–4). Abraham and Jacob will stray from God's design for marriage in another way, taking more than one wife. Moses positions these marital deviations in a way that they are aligned in the structure of his narrative, thereby critiquing each. In the Creation-chiasm, family deliverance focuses on the line of descent in Genesis 5 and the way Noah and his family are delivered on the ark.

In the corresponding rings of the Abraham-chiasm, family conflict initially results in a separation of Lot from Abraham in Genesis 13, followed by Abraham delivering Lot from captivity in Genesis 14. On the other side of this ring Abraham intercedes for Lot and Sodom in Genesis 18, and then God answers that prayer by delivering Lot from Sodom's destruction in Genesis 19. Tragically, after the flood Noah sinned by getting drunk, his nakedness was shamefully exposed, and he was shamed by his son Ham (Gen 9:20–29). Lot experienced a parallel sinful drunkenness, exposure, and shameful dishonor perpetrated by his daughters (19:30–38). The parallels between the aftermath of the flood and the aftermath of the destruction of Sodom, with both Noah and Lot getting drunk and being shamed by their children, strengthen the connections between these rings.

At this juncture of the Jacob-chiasm, Isaac's younger son blows up his family by stealing Esau's blessing with the help of his mother, resulting in a twenty-year separation (Gen 27–28). For her part in the debacle, after a last mention of Rebekah when Jacob is sent away (28:5), she is never mentioned again in the narrative until a reference to her being buried with Isaac comes near the end (49:31). As if to rub salt in the wound and draw attention to her omission from the narrative, the death of her nurse is noted (35:8), but there is no mention of Rebekah's death. On the other side of this ring we find Jacob's return to the land to insist that Esau receive his blessing (Gen 32–33, esp. 33:11).

The climactic instance of family conflict and deliverance in Genesis comes in the Joseph-chiasm, when as he is in the process of saving Egypt (Gen 40–41), his brothers come before him (42–43). On the other side of this ring the family journeys to Egypt (46:1–28) where Joseph intercedes for them and proves to be their savior (46:28–47:12).

The family conflicts that Moses aligns through the chiastic structures in Genesis include perversions and distortions of marriage, the dishonoring of fathers, conflict between brothers, deception, and all this brings about painful separations. Moses also aligns family deliverances through these chiastic structures, however, and these involve: a man who believes God's warnings of judgment and builds an ark for the salvation of his family; another who risks everything to engage in a dangerous rescue mission to deliver his kinsman from captivity, then later interceding for that kinsman's life, seeking mercy from the Holy One; an estranged brother having his agility crippled by God as he returns home to give back what he had stolen; a brother offering himself as a substitute for the beloved of his father; and a brother sold into slavery rising from the pit to forgive his repentant brothers. One would arise in whom all these things would be fulfilled, and he would assert of the Scriptures, "it is they that bear witness about me" (John 5:39), and "if you believed Moses, you would believe me; for he wrote of me" (5:46, ESV).

§4.4 Faith, Polygamy, Deception, and Revelation

The more desperate the condition, the more wonderful the coming of hope. The dirtier the sin, the more miraculous the cleansing and forgiveness. The more unworthy the offender, the deeper the praise for the saving mercy. There is sin in Genesis, but there is also salvation.

As mentioned above, the marital sin of Genesis 6:1–4, near the center of the Creation-chiasm, anticipates the marital sin near the center of the Abraham and Jacob-chiasms. Abraham took Hagar as a second wife (Gen 16), and Sarah's dissatisfaction with that recurred in the family discord and strife between Jacob and his two wives, the sisters Rachel and Leah (29:31–30:24).

But marital sin and polygamy are not the only things at the center of these chiastic structures. In Abraham's case he believed the Lord and was reckoned righteous thereby (15:6), and God gave him the revelation of the exodus and the covenant and circumcision (Gen 15, 17). In the Jacob-chiasm, the Lord made him fruitful and multiplied him—in seed and livestock—in spite of the sin and difficulty (29:31–30:43). All parents are sinners, but babies come into the world as fresh and full of promise as new morning mercy. Those babies may grow up, like Judah, to sell their own brothers into slavery (37:26–28) and use a prostitute (38:15–18), but God can reveal his righteousness (38:26) and bring about Christlike self-sacrifice (43:8–9; 44:33). The wronged brother, moreover, who was betrayed and sold, can ascend to the place of lordship, understand God's purposes (45:5, 8), call his brothers to draw near (45:4), calm their raging and anxiety (45:5), and forgive them with a kiss (45:15a), and with those who could not speak peacefully to him (37:4) he can commune in conversation (45:15b).[27]

For all the sin of these patriarchs, God remains faithful to the promises he made to Abraham. In the Joseph-chiasm we have the great resolution to all the fraternal conflict in the book of Genesis, as Judah steps forward to offer his life for that of Benjamin (Gen 44:18–34), and Joseph reveals himself to his brothers and forgives them (Gen 45:1–15). The self-sacrificial love of Judah (Gen 44) and the forgiveness extended by Joseph (Gen 45) stand at the center of the final chiastic structure of the book of Genesis.

Moses has linked the family deliverance at the end to the family deliverance at the beginning by means of the phrase, "to keep alive." The family deliverance at the center of the Creation-chiasm has the Lord telling Noah to bring the animals into the ark:

- "to keep them alive with you" (6:19, לְהַחֲיֹת);
- "to keep them alive" (6:20, לְהַחֲיוֹת);
- "to keep their offspring alive" (7:3, לְחַיּוֹת).

Joseph likewise tells his brothers why the Lord sent him to Egypt:

- "to keep alive for you many survivors" (45:7, וּלְהַחֲיוֹת);
- "that many people should be kept alive" (50:20, לְהַחֲיֹת).

---

27. I am thankful for the way Sam Emadi brought these features of the narrative to my attention.

The only other instance of an infinitive construct with a *lamed* prefix on the "to live" verb חָיָה in Genesis is at 19:19, where Lot says, "you have shown me great kindness in saving my life" (לְהַחֲיוֹת). This is one of the many links between the flood narrative and that of Sodom. Moses hereby signals that when God saves, he keeps survivors alive through the likes of Noah and Joseph. They typify an even greater Savior, who will bring about an even greater salvation.

§5 CHIASTIC AND TYPOLOGICAL STRUCTURES

Just prior to the narration of the death of the aged father (Gen 25:1–11), Moses positions the story of the sending of the servant to get a wife for Isaac at the central turning point in the narrative structure of Genesis. In the opening paragraphs of this book, we saw micro-level indicators that Moses instantiates a pattern beginning in Genesis 24. Here we consider macro-level indicators of the same. We begin with considerations of how Moses ties the Genesis narrative together in Genesis 24 and then move to the structure of the chapter itself.

We have seen how the story of Abraham spans a chiastic structure from Genesis 11:27–22:24. Near the beginning of Genesis 24, Moses quotes from the beginning of the Abraham-chiasm, before quoting from its end near the chapter's end. Moses references the blessing of Abraham in Genesis 12:1–3 in 24:1, before alluding to 12:1 and quoting 12:7 in 24:7 (italics in the ESV texts below are my emphasis).

Genesis 12	Genesis 24
12:1, Now the LORD said to Abram, "Go from your country and your kindred and your *father's house* to the *land* that I will show you.	24:7a, The LORD, the God of heaven, who took me from my *father's house* and from the *land* of my *kindred* . . .
12:2, And I will make of you a great nation, and *I will bless you* and make your name great, so that you will be a blessing.	24:1, Now Abraham was old, well advanced in years. And *the LORD had blessed Abraham in all things.*
12:7, Then the LORD appeared to Abram and said, "*To your offspring I will give this land.*" So he built there an altar to the LORD, who had appeared to him.	24:7b, and who spoke to me and swore to me, "*To your offspring I will give this land,*" he will send his angel before you, and you shall take a wife for my son from there.

Moses again references the blessing of Abraham near the midpoint of the chapter at Genesis 24:35, "The LORD has greatly blessed my master, and he has become great" (ESV, cf. esp. Gen 12:2). As he cites the beginning of the Abraham-chiasm at the beginning of Genesis 24, so he cites the end of the Abraham-chiasm at the end of Genesis 24, quoting Genesis 22:17 in 24:60, in the words spoken to Rebekah (ESV, italics my emphasis):

Genesis 22	Genesis 24
22:17–18, I will surely *bless* you, and I will surely *multiply your offspring* as the stars of heaven and as the sand that is on the seashore.	24:60, And they *blessed* Rebekah and said to her, "Our sister, *may you become thousands of ten thousands,*
And your *offspring shall possess the gate of his enemies*, and in your offspring shall all the nations of the earth be blessed, because you have obeyed my voice.	and may your *offspring possess the gate of those who hate him*!"

By quoting the beginning and end of the Abraham-chiasm at the beginning and end of the chapter, Moses uses Genesis 24 to close and open: he closes the Abraham story by tying the key promises to Isaac, signaling that the line of descent will continue through the marriage with Rebekah; and he opens the next unit which will detail how the blessing of Abraham is passed to the seed in that line of descent. The allusions and quotations of the blessings of Abraham are chiastically placed through Genesis 24:

Gen 24:1, Yahweh had blessed Abraham in everything.
  Gen 24:7, To your seed I will give this land.
  Gen 24:35, Yahweh has exceedingly blessed and made great Abraham.
Gen 24:60, May your seed possess the gate of his enemies.

As Genesis 24 looks back to the blessing of Abraham, it also looks forward to the Jacob and Joseph chiasms. There are striking similarities between the accounts of Abraham's servant meeting Rebekah and Jacob meeting Rachel. When the servant arrives at the well (Gen 24:11), he prays to the Lord (24:12–14), and we read in Genesis 24:15, "Before he had finished speaking, behold, Rebekah, who was born to Bethuel the son of Milcah, the wife of Nahor, Abraham's brother, came out with her water jar on her shoulder" (ESV). Similarly, when Jacob arrives at the well (29:2), he engages the shepherds in conversation (29:4–8), and we read in Genesis 29:9–10, "While he was still speaking with them, Rachel came with her father's sheep, for she was a shepherdess. Now as soon as Jacob saw Rachel the daughter of Laban his mother's brother . . ." (ESV).

Both accounts also tell of the beauty of Rebekah and Rachel (Gen 24:16; 29:17), and this feature also connects the stories of Isaac and Jacob with Abraham, who likewise had a beautiful wife (12:11).[28] Rebekah's response to the servant in Genesis 24 is paralleled by Rachel's response to Jacob in Genesis 29: both women run home; in both cases Laban (Rebekah's brother, Rachel's father) comes running out in response, to bring first the servant then Jacob to his home; and both narratives present Laban asking a question (translations in the table below follow the ESV).

Genesis 24	Genesis 29
24:28–31, Then the young woman ran and told her mother's household about these things.	29:12–15, and she ran and told her father.
[29]Rebekah had a brother whose name was Laban. Laban ran out toward the man, to the spring. [30]As soon as he saw the ring and the bracelets on his sister's arms, and heard the words of Rebekah his sister, "Thus the man spoke to me," he went to the man. And behold, he was standing by the camels at the spring.	[13]As soon as Laban heard the news about Jacob, his sister's son, he ran to meet him and embraced him and kissed him and brought him to his house. Jacob told Laban all these things, [14]and Laban said to him, "Surely you are my bone and my flesh!" And he stayed with him a month.

---

28. Compare also the twenty-five years Abraham and Sarah waited for Isaac (Gen 12:4; 21:5), the twenty years Isaac and Rebekah waited for Jacob and Esau (25:20, 26), the twenty years Jacob served Laban (31:38, 41), and the twenty-two years between Joseph being sold into slavery and his revelation of himself to his brothers (37:2; 41:46, 53–54; 45:6). Similarly, Jacob served Laban seven years for Leah, then another seven years for Rachel (29:18, 27), just as Joseph predicted seven years of plenty, followed by seven years of famine (41:26–30). Laban claims to have learned by divination (30:27), a claim Joseph makes part of his revelatory ruse (44:5, 15).

Genesis 24	Genesis 29
³¹He said, "Come in, O blessed of the Lᴏʀᴅ. Why do you stand outside? . . ."	¹⁵Then Laban said to Jacob, "Because you are my kinsman, should you therefore serve me for nothing? Tell me, what shall your wages be?"

These parallels arise from the structural centrality of the need for a wife, first for Isaac then for Jacob, to continue the line of descent of the seed of promise. That structural centrality also highlights the typological development, the repetitions at the level of historical correspondence suggesting the audience can expect more of the same.

The servant's mission in Genesis 24 also anticipates the way the Lord will "prosper" Joseph in everything he does (Gen 39:2, 3, 23). Four times the text speaks of Yahweh "prospering" the servant's way, and twice the servant speaks of Yahweh "leading" him in "the way." The verb "prosper" (צָלַח) appears in Genesis only in chapters 24 and 39 (24:21, 40, 42, 56; and 39:2, 3, 23), forging a strong connection between Abraham's servant and Joseph. The terms "prosper" and "way" also feature prominently in Psalm 1, and they are chiastically distributed through Genesis 24:

> Gen 24:21, . . . to know whether Yahweh had prospered his way or not.
> Gen 24:27, . . . Yahweh led me in the way . . .
> Gen 24:40, . . . Yahweh . . . will prosper your way
> Gen 24:42, . . . O Yahweh, if you are . . . prospering my way . . .
> Gen 24:48, . . . who led me in the way
> Gen 24:56, . . . Yahweh has prospered my way!

The servant sent to find a wife for Isaac in Genesis 24 prospers in the same way Joseph, a servant sent to prepare the way for Israel's descent into Egypt (Ps 105:17), will prosper in Egypt, first in Potiphar's house (Gen 39:2, 3) then in prison (39:23). This is the kind of prospering that meditating on the Scriptures will give to Joshua (Josh 1:8), and it is the kind of prospering spoken of in Psalm 1:3—prospering enjoyed by the blessed man who meditates on Torah day and night (1:2), leading the "congregation of the righteous" (1:5) in the "way" Yahweh knows (1:6).

The patterns seen in Genesis 24 will echo across the scrolls of the Scriptures until they find full resonance in Christ, the blessed man, of whom it can be truly said that everything he does "prospers," who never strayed from the "way" known to Yahweh, and who took up the role of the servant as the beloved son sent for a bride. The typological development through the Bible's literary structures draws our attention to the patterns and frames their beauty.

Within Genesis 24 itself, Moses presents a matching literary structure in which the servant takes the oath Abraham makes him swear, prays for God's help and receives it, and then responds in worship. Having experienced this sequence in the first half of the chapter, the servant then retells the same events in the same order in the second. This creates a repeated pattern within the chapter, a bi-paneled chiastic structure that is preceded by the blessing of Abraham in 24:1 and concluded with the blessing of Isaac, Rebekah, and their seed in 24:59–67.[29] The literary structure of Genesis 24 is depicted in Table 11.1, which is also font-coded as follows:

Italic text is used for the key summary of the unit.

Bold text represents the blessing of Abraham.

SMALL CAPS text denotes Yahweh leading the servant in the way of truth.

Bold Italic text marks key mentions of the servant of Abraham.

BOLD SMALL CAPS text designates the servant bowing in worship.

ITALIC ALL CAPS text marks Yahweh prospering the way.

ITALIC SMALL CAPS text denotes the gifts the servant gives Rebekah and his worship.

ALL CAPS text represents the seed of the woman who will conquer and reign.

Normal text is used for summary statements and those that speak of Yahweh, God of Abraham and his lovingkindness.

---

29. See the "tortoise shell" and "ring" diagrams in Douglas, *Thinking in Circles*, 9, 20, 23, 48, 110, 118. In his writings on the fiction of J. K. Rowling (and her pseudonym Robert Galbraith) at https://www.hogwartsprofessor.com, John Granger often refers to these structures as "turtle-backs." What is meant can be seen on Table 11.2, where as you go down the left side of the diagram you get that side of the turtle shell, the ring of which is completed as you make your way back up the right side.

TABLE 11.2 The Literary Structure of Genesis 24

24:1, Yahweh had blessed Abraham	
24:2–9, *The Oath:* No Canaanite Wife, Wife from Kindred **24:2, Servant of Abraham** **24:7, To Your Seed I Will Give This Land**	24:49, Will Rebekah's Family Do Lovingkindness and Truth 24:49–58, Take Her and Go as Yahweh Has Spoken **24:52, Bowed in Worship** *24:56, YAHWEH PROSPERED WAY*
24:12, Yahweh, God of my Lord Abraham 24:10–21, *The Prayer Offered and Answered* 24:21, YAHWEH PROSPER WAY	*24:42, YAHWEH PROSPER WAY* *24:42–48, The Prayer Offered and Answered* *24:47, Rebekah's Family, Ring and Bracelets, Worship* **24:48, Bowed and Worshiped,** led in the way of truth
24:22–32, Ring and Bracelets, Rebekah's Family, Worship **24:26, Bowed and Worshiped** 24:27, Yahweh, God of My Lord Abraham, Lovingkindness and truth, led in the way	**24:34, Servant of Abraham** **24:35, Yahweh Has Exceedingly Blessed and Made Great Abraham** 24:33–41, *The Oath Again:* No Canaanite Wife, Wife from Kindred
24:59–67, *Isaac and Rebekah and Their Seed* **24:59–61, Rebekah Blessed and Sent/Taken** 24:60, MAY YOUR SEED POSSESS THE GATE OF HIS ENEMIES 24:62–67, Isaac and Rebekah	

As noted above, Abraham's servant first pursues the mission he took an oath to undertake (Gen 24:1–33), then he recounts the same actions in the same order (24:34–49). This means that the statement discussed in the opening paragraphs of this book in Genesis 24:7b, "he will send his angel before you," which is echoed in Exodus 23:20 and Malachi 3:1, recurs within Genesis 24 at 24:40 when the servant retells the story: "But he said to me, 'The Lord, before whom I have walked, will send his angel with you and prosper your way . . .'"

The chiastic "turtle-back" (see nearby footnote) structure of Genesis 24 affords Moses the opportunity to create repetition within the chapter, generating significance. The micro-level indicator of the repeated line and event-sequence joins the macro-level literary structure to signal that Moses intended his audience to understand that the sending of the servant for a covenant partner in Genesis 24 typified the sending of Moses to Egypt for Israel.[30] Malachi understood this pattern, and he employed the same strategies to prophesy of the new covenant (Mal 3:1). Mark presents John the Baptist as the messenger sent to prepare the way before Jesus (Mark 1:2), where fulfillment is inaugurated. The consummation of the fulfillment is awaited, but God "made it known by sending his angel to his servant John, who bore witness to the word of God and to the testimony of Jesus Christ, even to all that he saw" (Rev 1:1b–2, ESV).[31]

The one to whom the Scriptures point, whose coming we await, is the true and better Adam, bridegroom and beloved. He is the great priest over the heavenly house of God, giving us the new and living way by which we draw near. Our prophet like Moses, by whom God accomplished the fulfillment of the exodus. The king of God's creation, he is the righteous sufferer, who himself bore our sins in his body on the tree. His praise will know no end.

---

30. Listeners to the BibleTalk podcast will recognize that here I concede the point urged upon me by my friend Sam Emadi. He's right! And I have been convinced.

31. LXX Mal 3:1, ἰδοὺ ἐγὼ ἐξαποστέλλω τὸν ἄγγελόν μου . . .
  Rev 1:1b, ἀποστείλας διὰ τοῦ ἀγγέλου αὐτοῦ τῷ δούλῳ αὐτοῦ Ἰωάννῃ . . .

BIBLIOGRAPHY

Abernethy, Andrew T., and Gregory Goswell. *God's Messiah in the Old Testament: Expectations of a Coming King*. Grand Rapids: Baker, 2020.

Ahearne-Kroll, Stephen. *The Psalms of Lament in Mark's Passion: Jesus' Davidic Suffering*. Society for New Testament Studies Monograph Series. New York: Cambridge University Press, 2007.

Allison, Dale C., Jr. *The New Moses: A Matthean Typology*. Minneapolis: Fortress, 1994.

Alter, Robert. *The Art of Biblical Narrative*. 2nd ed. New York: Basic, 2011.

Ansberry, Christopher B. *Be Wise, My Son, and Make My Heart Glad: An Exploration of the Courtly Nature of the Book of Proverbs*. Beihefte aur Zeitschrift für die alttestamentliche Wissenschaft. New York: De Gruyter, 2010.

Averbeck, R. E. "Tabernacle." Pages 807–27 in *Dictionary of the Old Testament: Pentateuch*. Edited by T. Desmond Alexander and David W. Baker, 807–27. Downers Grove, IL: InterVarsity, 2003.

Baker, David L. *Two Testaments, One Bible: The Theological Relationship Between the Old and New Testaments*. 3rd ed. Downers Grove, IL: InterVarsity, 2010.

Barber, Michael. *Singing in the Reign: The Psalms and the Liturgy of God's Kingdom*. Steubenville, OH: Emmaus Road, 2001.

Basil, Saint. *On the Holy Spirit*. Translated by David Anderson. Crestwood, N.Y: St Vladimir's Seminary Press, 1980.

Bass, Derek Drummond. "Hosea's Use of Scripture: An Analysis of His Hermeneutic." PhD diss., The Southern Baptist Theological Seminary, 2008.

Bates, Matthew W. *The Birth of the Trinity: Jesus, God, and Spirit in New Testament and Early Christian Interpretations of the Old Testament*. New York: Oxford University Press, 2015.

———. *The Hermeneutics of the Apostolic Proclamation: The Center of Paul's Method of Scriptural Interpretation*. Repr., Waco: Baylor University Press, 2019.

Bauckham, Richard. *The Climax of Prophecy: Studies on the Book of Revelation*. Edinburgh: T&T Clark, 1993.

————. *The Theology of the Book of Revelation*. New Testament Theology. New York: Cambridge University Press, 1993.

Bauer, Walter. *A Greek-English Lexicon of the New Testament and Other Early Christian Literature*. Edited by Frederick William Danker. Translated by W. F. Arndt and F. W. Gingrich. 3rd ed. Chicago: University Of Chicago Press, 2001.

Beale, G. K. "Did Jesus and His Followers Preach the Right Doctrine from the Wrong Texts? An Examination of the Presuppositions of Jesus' and the Apostles' Exegetical Method." Pages 387–404 in *The Right Doctrine from the Wrong Texts? Essays on the Use of the Old Testament in the New*. Edited by G. K. Beale. Grand Rapids: Baker, 1994.

————. "The Descent of the Eschatological Temple in the Form of the Spirit at Pentecost: Part 1: The Clearest Evidence." *Tyndale Bulletin* 56 (2005): 73–102.

————. *The Temple and the Church's Mission: A Biblical Theology of the Dwelling Place of God*. New Studies in Biblical Theology. Downers Grove, IL: InterVarsity, 2004.

Beckwith, Roger T. *The Old Testament Canon of the New Testament Church and Its Background in Early Judaism*. Grand Rapids: Eerdmans, 1985.

————. "The Unity and Diversity of God's Covenants." *Tyndale Bulletin* 38 (1987): 93–118.

Beetham, Christopher A. "From Creation to New Creation: The Biblical Epic of King, Human Vicegerency, and Kingdom." Pages 237–54 in *From Creation to New Creation: Essays in Honor of G. K. Beale*. Edited by Daniel M. Gurtner and Benjamin L. Gladd. Peabody: Hendrickson, 2013.

Bell, Richard H. *The Irrevocable Call of God: An Inquiry into Paul's Theology of Israel*. Wissenschaftliche Untersuchungen zum Neuen Testament 184. Tübingen: Mohr Siebeck, 2005.

Brouwer, Wayne. "Understanding Chiasm and Assessing Macro-Chiasm as a Tool of Biblical Interpretation." *Calvin Theological Journal* 53 (2018): 99–127.

Brown, William P. "The Pedagogy of Proverbs 10:1–31:9." Pages 150–82 in *Character and Scripture: Moral Formation, Community, and Biblical Interpretation*. Edited by William P. Brown. Grand Rapids: Eerdmans, 2002.

Brueggemann, Dale A. "The Evangelists and the Psalms." Pages 263–78 in *Interpreting the Psalms: Issues and Approaches*. Edited by David Firth and Philip S. Johnston. Downers Grove, IL: InterVarsity, 2005.

Burk, Denny. "Discerning Corinthian Slogans through Paul's Use of the Diatribe in 1 Corinthians 6:12–20." *Bulletin for Biblical Research* 18 (2008): 99–121.

Calvin, John. *Institutes of the Christian Religion*. Edited by John T. McNeill. Translated by Ford Lewis Battles. Philadelphia: Westminster John Knox, 1960.

Caragounis, Chrys. *The Son of Man: Vision and Interpretation*. Wissenschaftliche Untersuchungen zum Neuen Testament 38. Tübingen: Mohr Siebeck, 1986.

Carr, David M. *Writing on the Tablet of the Heart: Origins of Scripture and Literature*. New York: Oxford University Press, 2005.

Chapman, David W., and Eckhard J. Schnabel. *The Trial and Crucifixion of Jesus: Texts and Commentary.* Wissenschaftliche Untersuchungen zum Neuen Testament 344. Tübingen: Mohr Siebeck, 2015.

Chase, Mitchell L. *40 Questions About Typology and Allegory.* Grand Rapids: Kregel, 2020.

———. "The Genesis of Resurrection Hope: Exploring Its Early Presence and Deep Roots." *Journal of the Evangelical Theological Society* 57 (2014): 467–80.

Chester, Andrew. *Messiah and Exaltation: Jewish Messianic and Visionary Traditions and New Testament Christology.* Wissenschaftliche Untersuchungen zum Neuen Testament 207. Tübingen: Mohr Siebeck, 2007.

Cole, Robert L. *Psalms 1–2: Gateway to the Psalter.* Sheffield: Sheffield Phoenix, 2013.

Collins, Jack. "A Syntactical Note (Genesis 3:15): Is the Woman's Seed Singular or Plural?" *Tyndale Bulletin* 48 (1997): 139–48.

Collins, John J. *Daniel: A Commentary on the Book of Daniel.* Hermeneia. Minneapolis: Fortress, 1993.

Coloe, Mary L. *God Dwells with Us: Temple Symbolism in the Fourth Gospel.* Collegeville, MN: Glazier, 2001.

Crump, David. *Encountering Jesus, Encountering Scripture: Reading the Bible Critically in Faith.* Grand Rapids: Eerdmans, 2013.

Daniélou, Jean. *From Shadows to Reality: Studies in the Biblical Typology of the Fathers.* Translated by Wulstan Hibberd. London: Burns and Oates, 1960.

Daube, David. *The Exodus Pattern in the Bible.* London: Faber, 1983.

Davidson, Richard M. *Typology in Scripture: A Study of Hermeneutical Typos Structures.* Berrien Springs, MI: Andrews University Press, 1981.

Deenick, Karl. "Priest and King or Priest-King in 1 Samuel 2:35." *Westminster Theological Journal* 73 (2011): 325–39.

Dempster, Stephen G. *Dominion and Dynasty: A Biblical Theology of the Hebrew Bible.* New Studies in Biblical Theology 15. Downers Grove, IL: InterVarsity, 2003.

———. "The Servant of the Lord." Pages 128–78 in *Central Themes in Biblical Theology: Mapping Unity in Diversity.* Edited by Scott J Hafemann and Paul R House. Grand Rapids: Baker, 2007.

Douglas, Mary. *Thinking in Circles: An Essay on Ring Composition.* New Haven: Yale University Press, 2010.

Duguid, Iain M. *The Song of Songs: An Introduction and Commentary.* Tyndale Old Testament Commentaries. Downers Grove, IL: InterVarsity, 2015.

Eichrodt, Walther. "Is Typological Exegesis an Appropriate Method." Pages 224–45 in *Essays on Old Testament Interpretation.* Edited by Claus Westermann. Translated by James Barr. London: SCM, 1963.

Eller, Vernard. *The Language of Canaan and the Grammar of Feminism.* Grand Rapids: Eerdmans, 1982.

Ellis, E. Earle. Foreword to *Typos: The Typological Interpretation of the Old Testament in the New,* by Leonhard Goppelt. Translated by Donald H. Madvig. Grand Rapids: Eerdmans, 1982.

———. "Jesus' Use of the Old Testament and the Genesis of New Testament Theology." *Bulletin for Biblical Research* 3 (1993): 59–75.

———. *The Gospel of Luke.* New Century Bible Commentary. Grand Rapids: Eerdmans, 1981.

Emadi, Matthew. "You Are Priest Forever: Psalm 110 and the Melchizedekian Priesthood of Christ." *Southern Baptist Journal of Theology* 23 (2019): 57–84.

Emadi, Matthew Habib. "The Royal Priest: Psalm 110 in Biblical-Theological Perspective." PhD diss., The Southern Baptist Theological Seminary, 2015.

Emadi, Samuel Cyrus. "Covenant, Typology, and the Story of Joseph: A Literary-Canonical Examination of Genesis 37–50." PhD diss., The Southern Baptist Theological Seminary, 2016.

Fairbairn, Patrick. *Typology of Scripture.* 1845. Reprint, Grand Rapids, MI: Kregel, 1989.

Fisher, Milton C. "The Canon of the Old Testament." Pages 385–92 in vol. 1 of *The Expositor's Bible Commentary.* Edited by Frank E. Gaebelein. 12 vols. Grand Rapids: Zondervan, 1979.

Foer, Joshua. *Moonwalking with Einstein: The Art and Science of Remembering Everything.* New York: Penguin, 2011.

Foulkes, Francis. "The Acts of God: A Study of the Basis of Typology." Pages 342–71 in *The Right Doctrine from the Wrong Texts? Essays on the Use of the Old Testament in the New.* Edited by G. K. Beale. Grand Rapids: Baker, 1994.

Gage, Warren Austin. *The Gospel of Genesis: Studies in Protology and Eschatology.* Winona Lake, IN: Eisenbrauns, 1984.

Gane, Roy. *Cult and Character: Purification Offerings, Day of Atonement, and Theodicy.* Winona Lake, IN: Eisenbrauns, 2005.

Garrett, Duane A. *A Commentary on Exodus.* Kregel Exegetical Library. Grand Rapids: Kregel, 2014.

———. *Proverbs, Ecclesiastes, Song of Songs.* New American Commentary. Nashville: Broadman & Holman, 1993.

———. *The Problem of the Old Testament: Hermeneutical, Schematic, and Theological Approaches.* Downers Grove, IL: InterVarsity, 2020.

Garrett, Duane A., and Paul R. House. *Song of Songs, Lamentations.* Word Biblical Commentary. Nashville: Thomas Nelson, 2004.

Gentry, Peter J. "A Preliminary Evaluation and Critique of Prosopological Exegesis." *Southern Baptist Journal of Theology* 23, no. 2 (2019): 105–22.

———. "The Son of Man in Daniel 7: Individual or Corporate?" Pages 59–75 in *Acorns to Oaks: The Primacy and Practice of Biblical Theology.* Edited by Michael A. G. Haykin. Toronto: Joshua, 2003.

Gentry, Peter J., and Stephen J. Wellum. *Kingdom through Covenant: A Biblical-Theological Understanding of the Covenants.* Second Edition. Wheaton, IL: Crossway, 2018.

Gibson, Jonathan. *Covenant Continuity and Fidelity: A Study of Inner-Biblical Allusion and Exegesis in Malachi*. Library of Hebrew Bible/Old Testament Studies 625. Edinburgh: T&T Clark, 2019.

Gilbert, Stuart. *James Joyce's Ulysses*. New York: Vintage Books, 1959.

Girgis, Sherif, Robert George, and Ryan T. Anderson. "What Is Marriage?" *Harvard Journal of Law and Public Policy* 34 (2010): 245–87.

Goppelt, Leonhard. *Typos, the Typological Interpretation of the Old Testament in the New*. Grand Rapids: Eerdmans, 1982.

Grant, Jamie A. *The King As Exemplar: The Function of Deuteronomy's Kingship Law in the Shaping of the Book of Psalms*. Academia Biblica 17. Atlanta: Society of Biblical Literature, 2004.

Hahn, Scott W. *Kinship by Covenant: A Canonical Approach to the Fulfillment of God's Saving Promises*. New Haven: Yale University Press, 2009.

Hall, Stuart George, ed. *Melito of Sardis On Pascha and Fragments: Texts and Translations*. Oxford: Clarendon Press, 1979.

Hamilton, James M., Jr. "A Biblical Theology of Motherhood." *Journal of Discipleship and Family Ministry* 2, no. 2 (2012): 6–13.

———. "Canonical Biblical Theology." Pages 59–73 in *God's Glory Revealed in Christ: Essays in Honor of Tom Schreiner*. Edited by Denny Burk, James M. Hamilton Jr., and Brian J. Vickers. Nashville: Broadman & Holman, 2019.

———. "David's Biblical Theology and Typology in the Psalms: Authorial Intent and Patterns of the Seed of Promise." In *The Psalms: Exploring Theological Themes*. Edited by David M. Howard and Andrew J. Schmutzer. Bellingham, WA: Lexham, forthcoming.

———. *Ezra and Nehemiah*. Christ-Centered Exposition Commentary. Nashville: Broadman & Holman, 2014.

———. *God's Glory in Salvation through Judgment: A Biblical Theology*. Wheaton, IL: Crossway, 2010.

———. *God's Indwelling Presence: The Holy Spirit in the Old and New Testaments*. NAC Studies in Bible and Theology 1. Nashville: Broadman & Holman, 2006.

———. "John." Pages 19–308 in *ESV Expository Commentary: John–Acts*. Edited by Iain M. Duguid, James M. Hamilton Jr., and Jay Sklar. Wheaton, IL: Crossway, 2019.

———. "Original Sin in Biblical Theology." Pages 189–208 in *Adam, the Fall, and Original Sin: Theological, Biblical, and Scientific Perspectives*. Edited by Hans Madueme and Michael Reeves. Grand Rapids: Baker, 2014.

———. *Psalms*. 2 vols. Evangelical Biblical Theology Commentary. Bellingham, WA: Lexham, forthcoming.

———. *Revelation: The Spirit Speaks to the Churches*. Preaching the Word. Wheaton, IL: Crossway, 2012.

———. "Rushing Wind and Organ Music: Toward Luke's Theology of the Spirit in Acts." *Reformed Theological Review* 65, no. 1 (2006): 15–33.

———. *Song of Songs: A Biblical-Theological, Allegorical, Christological Interpretation*. Focus on the Bible. Fearn: Christian Focus, 2015.

———. "Suffering in Revelation: The Fulfillment of the Messianic Woes." *Southern Baptist Journal of Theology* 17, no. 4 (2014): 34–47.

———. "The Exodus Motif in Biblical Theology." Pages 77–91 in *The Law, The Prophets, and the Writings: Studies in Evangelical Old Testament Hermeneutics in Honor of Duane A. Garrett*. Edited by Andrew M. King, William R. Osborne, and Joshua M. Philpot. Nashville: Broadman & Holman, 2021.

———. "The Lord's Supper in Paul: An Identity-Forming Proclamation of the Gospel." Pages 68–102 in *The Lord's Supper: Remembering and Proclaiming Christ Until He Comes*. Edited by Thomas R. Schreiner and Matthew R. Crawford. Nashville: Broadman & Holman, 2010.

———. "The Messianic Music of the Song of Songs: A Non-Allegorical Interpretation." *Westminster Theological Journal* 68 (2006): 331–45.

———. "The One Who Does Them Shall Live by Them: Leviticus 18:5 in Galatians 3:12." *Gospel Witness* (August 2005): 10–14.

———. "The Virgin Will Conceive: Typological Fulfillment in Matthew 1:18–23." Pages 228–47 in *Built upon the Rock: Studies in the Gospel of Matthew*. Edited by John Nolland and Daniel Gurtner. Grand Rapids: Eerdmans, 2008.

———. "Typology in Hebrews: A Response to Buist Fanning." *Southern Baptist Journal of Theology* 24, no. 1 (2020): 125–36.

———. "Was Joseph a Type of the Messiah? Tracing the Typological Identification between Joseph, David, and Jesus." *Southern Baptist Journal of Theology* 12 (2008): 52–77.

———. *What Is Biblical Theology?* Wheaton, IL: Crossway, 2014.

———. *With the Clouds of Heaven: The Book of Daniel in Biblical Theology*. New Studies in Biblical Theology. Downers Grove, IL: InterVarsity, 2014.

———. *Work and Our Labor in the Lord*. Short Studies in Biblical Theology. Wheaton, IL: Crossway, 2017.

Haste, Matt. "A Type of the Marriage of Christ: John Gill on Marriage." *Puritan Reformed Journal* 6 (2014): 289–302.

Hays, Richard B. *Echoes of Scripture in the Gospels*. Waco, TX: Baylor University Press, 2018.

———. *The Conversion of the Imagination: Paul as Interpreter of Israel's Scripture*. Grand Rapids: Eerdmans, 2005.

Hensley, Adam D. *Covenant Relationships and the Editing of the Hebrew Psalter*. Library of Hebrew Bible/Old Testament Studies 666. New York: T&T Clark, 2018.

Hirsch, E. D. *Validity in Interpretation*. New Haven: Yale University Press, 1967.

Hoskins, Paul M. *Jesus as the Fulfillment of the Temple in the Gospel of John*. Paternoster Biblical Monographs. Waynesboro, GA: Paternoster, 2006.

Huey, F. B. *Jeremiah, Lamentations*. New American Commentary. Nashville: Broadman & Holman, 1993.

Hugenberger, Gordon P. *Marriage as a Covenant: Biblical Law and Ethics as Developed from Malachi*. Leiden: Brill, 1994.

"Institution, n." In *OED Online*. Oxford University Press. http://www.oed.com/view/Entry/97110.

Jamieson, R. B. "1 Corinthians 15.28 and the Grammar of Paul's Christology." *New Testament Studies* 66 (2020): 187–207.

———. "Hebrews 9.23: Cult Inauguration, Yom Kippur and the Cleansing of the Heavenly Tabernacle." *New Testament Studies* 62 (2016): 569–87.

———. *Jesus' Death and Heavenly Offering in Hebrews*. Society for New Testament Studies Monograph Series 172. New York: Cambridge University Press, 2019.

Johnson, S. Lewis. "A Response to Patrick Fairbairn and Biblical Hermeneutics as Related to the Quotations of the Old Testament in the New." Pages 791–99 in *Hermeneutics, Inerrancy, and the Bible: Papers from ICBI Summit II*. Edited by Earl D. Radmacher and Robert D. Preus. Grand Rapids: Zondervan, 1984.

Keller, Timothy. *Preaching: Communicating Faith in an Age of Skepticism*. New York: Viking, 2016.

Kerr, Alan R. *The Temple of Jesus' Body: The Temple Theme in the Gospel of John*. London: Sheffield Academic Press, 2002.

Kidner, Derek. *The Message of Jeremiah: Against Wind and Tide*. Leicester: InterVarsity, 1987.

Kiuchi, Nobuyoshi. *Leviticus*. Apollos Old Testament Commentary. Downers Grove, IL: InterVarsity, 2007.

Kynes, Will. *An Obituary for "Wisdom Literature": The Birth, Death, and Intertextual Reintegration of a Biblical Corpus*. Oxford: Oxford University Press, 2019.

Leithart, Peter J. *1 & 2 Kings*. Brazos Theological Commentary on the Bible. Grand Rapids: Brazos, 2006.

Levenson, Jon D. *Resurrection and the Restoration of Israel: The Ultimate Victory of the God of Life*. New Haven: Yale University Press, 2008.

Lindars, Barnabas. *New Testament Apologetic*. Philadelphia: Westminster, 1961.

Longenecker, Richard N. *Biblical Exegesis in the Apostolic Period*. 2nd ed. Grand Rapids: Eerdmans, 1999.

Lucas, Ernest C. *Daniel*. Apollos Old Testament Commentary. Downers Grove, IL: InterVarsity, 2002.

Marx, Karl, and Friedrich Engels. *The Communist Manifesto*. New York: Penguin, 2002.

Mathews, Kenneth A. *Genesis 1–11:26*. New American Commentary. Nashville: Broadman & Holman, 1996.

———. *Genesis 11:27–50:26: An Exegetical and Theological Exposition of Holy Scripture*. New American Commentary. Nashville: Broadman & Holman, 2005.

Millar, J. Gary. "1–2 Kings." Pages 491–898 in vol. 1 of *ESV Expository Commentary*. Edited by Iain M. Duguid, James M. Hamilton Jr., and Jay Sklar. Wheaton, IL: Crossway, 2019.

Mitchell, Christopher W. *The Song of Songs*. Concordia Commentary. Saint Louis: Concordia, 2003.

Mitchell, David C. *The Message of the Psalter: An Eschatological Programme in the Book of Psalms*. Journal for the Study of the Old Testament Supplement Series 252. Sheffield: Sheffield Academic Press, 1997.

Moberly, R. W. L. *The God of the Old Testament: Encountering the Divine in Christian Scripture*. Grand Rapids: Baker, 2020.

———. *The Theology of the Book of Genesis*. Old Testament Theology. New York: Cambridge University Press, 2009.

Montanari, Franco. *The Brill Dictionary of Ancient Greek*. Edited by Madeleine Goh and Chad Schroeder. Boston: Brill, 2015.

Moo, Douglas J. *The Old Testament in the Gospel Passion Narratives*. Sheffield: Almond Press, 1983.

Morales, L. Michael. *Exodus Old and New: A Biblical Theology of Redemption*. Essential Studies in Biblical Theology. Downers Grove, IL: InterVarsity, 2020.

———. *Who Shall Ascend the Mountain of the Lord? A Biblical Theology of the Book of Leviticus*. New Studies in Biblical Theology 37. Downers Grove, IL: InterVarsity, 2015.

Nabokov, Vladimir. *Lolita*. Edited by Alfred Appel Jr. Revised, Updated, Annotated Edition. New York: Vintage, 1991.

Ortlund, Raymond C. *God's Unfaithful Wife: A Biblical Theology of Spiritual Adultery*. New Studies in Biblical Theology 2. Downers Grove, IL: InterVarsity, 2003.

Oswalt, John N. *The Book of Isaiah, Chapters 40–66*. New International Commentary on the Old Testament. Grand Rapids: Eerdmans, 1998.

Ounsworth, Richard. *Joshua Typology in the New Testament*. Wissenschaftliche Untersuchungen zum Neuen Testament 2/328. Tübingen: Mohr Siebeck, 2012.

Pao, David W. *Acts and the Isaianic New Exodus*. Grand Rapids: Baker, 2002.

Petterson, Anthony R. "Zechariah." Pages 631–728 in *ESV Expository Commentary: Daniel–Malachi*. Edited by Iain M. Duguid, James M. Hamilton Jr., and Jay Sklar. Wheaton, IL: Crossway, 2018.

Philpot, Joshua M. "See the True and Better Adam: Typology and Human Origins." *Bulletin of Ecclesial Theology* 5, no. 2 (2018): 79–103.

———. "Was Joseph a Type of Daniel? Typological Correspondence in Genesis 37–50 and Daniel 1–6." *Journal of the Evangelical Theological Society* 61 (2018): 681–96.

Rad, Gerhard von. "Typological Interpretation of the Old Testament." Pages 17–39 in *Essays on Old Testament Interpretation*. Edited by Claus Westermann. Translated by John Bright. London: SCM, 1963.

Rendtorff, Rolf. *The Canonical Hebrew Bible: A Theology of the Old Testament*. Leiden: Deo, 2005.

Robar, Elizabeth. *The Verb and the Paragraph in Biblical Hebrew: A Cognitive-Linguistic Approach*. Studies in Semitic Languages and Linguistics. Boston: Brill, 2015.

Robertson, O. Palmer. *The Christ of the Prophets*. Phillipsburg: P & R, 2004.

Rose, Wolter. *Zemah and Zerubbabel: Messianic Expectations in the Early Postexilic*

Period. Library of Hebrew Bible/Old Testament Studies 304. Sheffield: Sheffield Academic Press, 2000.

Rowe, C. Kavin. *Early Narrative Christology: The Lord in the Gospel of Luke*. Grand Rapids: Baker, 2009.

Sailhamer, John H. "Genesis." Pages 1–284 in vol. 2 of *The Expositor's Bible Commentary*. Edited by Frank E. Gaebelein. 12 vols. Grand Rapids: Zondervan, 1990.

Schaper, Joachim. *Eschatology in the Greek Psalter*. Wissenschaftliche Untersuchungen zum Neuen Testament 2/76. Tübingen: J.C.B. Mohr Siebeck, 1995.

Schreiner, Thomas R. "Original Sin and Original Death: Romans 5:12–19." Pages 271–88 in *Adam, the Fall, and Original Sin: Theological, Biblical, and Scientific Perspectives*. Edited by Hans Madueme and Michael Reeves. Grand Rapids: Baker, 2014.

Sequeira, Aubrey, and Samuel C. Emadi. "Biblical-Theological Exegesis and the Nature of Typology." *Southern Baptist Journal of Theology* 21, no. 1 (2017): 11–34.

Sequeira, Aubrey Maria. "The Hermeneutics of Eschatological Fulfillment in Christ: Biblical-Theological Exegesis in the Epistle to the Hebrews." PhD diss., The Southern Baptist Theological Seminary, 2016.

Smith, Jay E. "The Roots of a Libertine Slogan in 1 Corinthians 6:18." *Journal of Theological Studies* 59 (2008): 63–95.

Steinmann, Andrew E. *Daniel*. Concordia Commentary. Saint Louis: Concordia, 2008.

———. *Proverbs*. Concordia Commentary. Saint Louis: Concordia, 2009.

Steinmetz, David C. "Uncovering a Second Narrative: Detective Fiction and the Construction of a Historical Method." Pages 54–65 in *The Art of Reading Scripture*. Edited by Ellen F. Davis and Richard B. Hays. Grand Rapids: Eerdmans, 2003.

Thompson, J. A. *The Book of Jeremiah*. Grand Rapids: Eerdmans, 1980.

Tigay, Jeffrey H. *The JPS Torah Commentary: Deuteronomy*. Philadelphia: Jewish Publication Society, 1996.

Tolkien, J. R. R. *The Return of the King*. Boston: Houghton Mifflin, 1965.

Vanhoozer, Kevin J. *Is There a Meaning in This Text? The Bible, the Reader, and the Morality of Literary Knowledge*. Grand Rapids: Zondervan, 1998.

Waltke, Bruce K. *An Old Testament Theology: An Exegetical, Canonical, and Thematic Approach*. Grand Rapids: Zondervan, 2007.

———. *The Book of Proverbs, Chapters 15–31*. New International Commentary on the Old Testament. Grand Rapids: Eerdmans, 2005.

Walton, John H. "Creation." Pages 155–68 in *Dictionary of the Old Testament: Pentateuch*. Edited by T. Desmond Alexander and David W. Baker. Downers Grove, IL: InterVarsity, 2003.

———. *Genesis*. NIV Application Commentary. Grand Rapids: Zondervan, 2001.

Watson, Wilfred G. E. *Classical Hebrew Poetry: A Guide to Its Techniques*. New York: T&T Clark, 2001.

Watts, Rikki E. *Isaiah's New Exodus in Mark*. Grand Rapids: Baker, 2000.

Welch, John W., and Daniel B. McKinlay, eds. *Chiasmus Bibliography*. Provo, UT: Research, 1999.

Wenham, Gordon J. "Sanctuary Symbolism in the Garden of Eden Story." Pages 399–404 in *I Studied Inscriptions from Before the Flood: Ancient Near Eastern, Literary, and Linguistic Approaches to Genesis 1–11*. Edited by Richard Hess and David Toshio Tsumara. Winona Lake, IN: Eisenbrauns, 1994.

———. *The Book of Leviticus*. New International Commentary on the Old Testament. Grand Rapids: Eerdmans, 1979.

Williams, Peter J. *Can We Trust the Gospels?* Wheaton, IL: Crossway, 2018.

Wilson, Victor M. *Divine Symmetries: The Art of Biblical Rhetoric*. Lanham, MD: University Press of America, 1997.

Yarbrough, Robert W. "Adam in the New Testament." Pages 33–52 in *Adam, the Fall, and Original Sin: Theological, Biblical, and Scientific Perspectives*. Edited by Hans Madueme and Michael Reeves. Grand Rapids: Baker, 2014.

Zakovitch, Yair. *"And You Shall Tell Your Son—": The Concept of the Exodus in the Bible*. Jerusalem: Magnes, 1991.

SCRIPTURE INDEX

EXODUS

SUBJECT INDEX[1]

---

1. The letter *t* after a page number indicates a table.

God's purpose for the institution of, 327
and spiritual infidelity, 307–10
typological understanding of
in Hosea, 318–21
in Isaiah, 311–16
in Jeremiah, 316–18
in the Song of Songs, 321–24
meaning of a text, the most important
criterion for determining the, 18
Melchizedek
meaning of the name, 68
the (king) priest, 68–70
typified priesthood of Jesus, 64
"memory palace," 334
micro-level indicators for determining
authorial intent. *See chapter 1,*
"Introduction to Promise-Shaped
Typology" (1–32)
Mosaic (or, Sinai) covenant, 21, 64, 71, 72,
78, 81, 91, 112, 232, 308, 265, 311,
312, 317–18, 320, 321, 324
Moses
Noah and (points of contract between),
111–15
as a prophet, 111, 115–17
points of contact between Elijah–Elisha
and Joshua–, 131–33
prophets like, 118–19, 137–40
rejected then exalted, 178–79
the Torah and the Leviticult, 298–99
"Most High," 58–60. *See also* God Most
High
mountain of God, 227, 228, 299, 234, 297.
See Horeb; *see also* Mount Sinai
Mount Sinai, 22, 114, 158, 172, 230, 234–35,
236, 263, 302, 319
Mount Zion, 141, 142, 172, 234–35

new Adam(s)
Abraham, Isaac, and Jacob as, 40–42,
45–51
Christ as, 56–62
David as, 54–56
Israel as, 51–54
Noah as, 36–40

new covenant, 37, 64, 78, 81, 82, 87, 114, 115,
187, 247, 271, 273, 277, 299, 303, 304,
306, 308, 311, 312, 314–18, 320, 321,
323, 324–25, 326, 327, 360
new creation, 29, 221, 233, 224, 225, 228,
229, 232, 237, 238, 246, 247, 249, 251,
252–53, 288
correspondences between Eden and the,
252–53
the cosmic temple of the, 252–53
new exodus, 21, 31, 121, 201, 218, 254, 256, 262,
271–72, 275, 280–83, 319, 320, 325
new Jerusalem, 31, 252–53, 283
Nicodemus (ruler of the Jews), 160–61, 218
Nimrod, 44, 350
Noah. *See also* Noahic covenant
new-Adam, 36–40
as a prophet, 94
Noahic covenant, 23, 39, 42, 70, 112, 114, 115
normative hermeneutic, 25–26

parable of the ten virgins, 326
parable of the wicked tenants, 107, 213, 215–17
parallelism, 332–33
Passover, 69, 254, 265, 267–70, 272, 273, 275,
276, 278, 280, 283, 302
Passover lamb, 273, 275, 276, 283
Paul, exodus typology in the writings of,
273–80
Peninnah (wife of Elkanah), 44
Pentecost, 248, 251, 302
Philip, apostle, 152, 217–18
"poison for food," 199
polygamy, 43, 44, 344, 347, 352–53
Potiphar's wife, 15
presence of God
the goal of the tabernacle/temple, 303
through the indwelling Holy Spirit today,
304
priesthood, Christ fulfills the, 291–97
priests. *See chapter 3, "Priests"* (63–91)
Aaron and the, 72–73
Adam the (king) priest, 64–68
Christ makes his people, 297
Israel the (king) priest nation, 70–72

AUTHOR INDEX